ECONOMICS

ECONOMICS

A GENERAL TEXTBOOK FOR STUDENTS

BY

FREDERIC BENHAM

SIR ERNEST CASSEL READER IN COMMERCE
IN THE UNIVERSITY OF LONDON

THIRD EDITION

LONDON
SIR ISAAC PITMAN & SONS, LTD.

First Edition	.	*May, 1938*
Reprinted	.	*Jan., 1939*
Second Edition	.	*1940*
Third Edition	.	*1943*
Reprinted	.	*1945*
Reprinted	.	*1946*
Reprinted	.	*1947*

SIR ISAAC PITMAN & SONS, LTD.
PITMAN HOUSE, PARKER STREET, KINGSWAY, LONDON, W.C.2
THE PITMAN PRESS, BATH
PITMAN HOUSE, LITTLE COLLINS STREET, MELBOURNE
UNITEERS BUILDING, RIVER VALLEY ROAD, SINGAPORE
27 BECKETTS BUILDINGS, PRESIDENT STREET, JOHANNESBURG

ASSOCIATED COMPANIES
PITMAN PUBLISHING CORPORATION
2 WEST 45TH STREET, NEW YORK
205 WEST MONROE STREET, CHICAGO
SIR ISAAC PITMAN & SONS (CANADA), LTD.
(INCORPORATING THE COMMERCIAL TEXT BOOK COMPANY)
PITMAN HOUSE, 381–383 CHURCH STREET, TORONTO

BOOK PRODUCTION WAR ECONOMY STANDARD

THE PAPER AND BINDING OF
THIS BOOK CONFORM TO THE
AUTHORIZED ECONOMY STANDARDS

MADE IN GREAT BRITAIN AT THE PITMAN PRESS, BATH
D7—(B.293)

PREFACE

This book is a fairly complete introduction to the science of Economics. It aims at giving a realistic account of how the economic system works to-day in a country such as Great Britain. It is written for beginners, although some topics are developed more fully than is usual in an elementary work. I hope it will prove useful as a textbook both for University students and for those preparing for the examinations of the Civil Service and of professional bodies.

The last few years have seen important changes both in economic doctrine and in economic practice. It seemed to me that there was a need for a new textbook which gave some account of those changes.

Among the developments in doctrine incorporated in this volume we may name: the greater stress laid on the notion of choice between alternatives, and of scales of preferences, the concept of "utility" as something absolute and measurable being discarded and "opportunity-cost" being emphasized rather than "real-cost"; improvements in the theory of Diminishing Returns and of the economies of large-scale production; the analysis of monopoly, or imperfect competition, in terms of marginal cost and marginal revenue; and the treatment of money as a liquid asset, the demand to hold money varying with "liquidity-preference" and with the rate of interest. Considerable concessions have been made to the views of Lord Keynes, but I can hardly be regarded as one of his followers. For the most part I have either avoided controversial questions or left them open, stating the various points of view.

Among the changes in economic practice which we discuss are: the changes in the London Money Market and in the policy of the Bank of England since Great Britain left gold in September, 1931; the consequences of the "cheap money" policy; the growth of Restriction Schemes; the creation of exchange equalization funds or, in some countries, of a complete system of exchange control; and the growth of Protection by duties and quotas.

I am very grateful to my colleagues, who have helped me in

many ways. They are largely responsible for any merits which this book may have, and but for them it might not have been written at all.

I shall be very glad to receive, especially from teachers, suggestions for further improvements to be made if there is another edition.

My thanks are due to Messrs. Vickers Ltd. for permission to include the chart on page 170.

FREDERIC BENHAM

LONDON SCHOOL OF ECONOMICS
April, 1938

PREFACE TO THIRD EDITION

THE present edition contains two new chapters: on "The Theory of Costs" and on "War Economics." The chapter on "Interest" has been completely re-written. Two diagrammatic notes have been added: at the end of Chapter III and at the end of Chapter XV. In order to keep the book a reasonable length, the chapter on "The State" (which dealt with Public Finance, usually regarded as a separate subject) and the section on "Idle Resources" (which, apart from one or two definitions, said little that could not, and cannot now, be found elsewhere in this volume) have been deleted.

The bulk of the book stands as it was written. There are some trivial changes such as "the war of 1914" in place of "the war" and a footnote or comma added or removed here and there. The last chapter is a discussion of the economics of war, with special reference to Great Britain; but it also serves the purpose of bringing the book more up-to-date on facts and figures.

I am very grateful to all who have given me suggestions for improving the book, and I shall welcome further help of this kind.

August, 1942

CONTENTS

CHAPTER IV

Price With a Fixed Demand

CHAPTER V

Changes in Demand

CHAPTER VI

Demand, Supply, and Price

Appendix. Indifference Curves

BOOK II
PRODUCTION

CHAPTER VII
The Volume of Production

CHAPTER VIII
Division of Labour

CHAPTER IX
Combinations of Factors

CHAPTER X
Capital

CHAPTER XI

Production Under a Dictator

BOOK III

THE WORKING OF THE PRICE-SYSTEM UNDER CAPITALISM

CHAPTER XII

The Controlling Power of Demand

CHAPTER XIII

The Problems of the Firm

CHAPTER XIV

The Mobility of Factors of Production

CHAPTER XV

Monopoly

CHAPTER XVI

The Theory of Costs

CHAPTER XVII

Wages

CHAPTER XVIII

Interest

CHAPTER XIX

Rent

CHAPTER XX

Economic Progress

BOOK IV
MONEY AND BANKING

CHAPTER XXI
The Nature and Functions of Money

CHAPTER XXII
Banks

CHAPTER XXIII
Money Markets and Central Banks

CHAPTER XXIV
The Value of Money

BOOK V
INTERNATIONAL TRADE

CHAPTER XXV
The Theory of International Trade

CHAPTER XXVI
Balances of Payments

CHAPTER XXVII
Free Exchange Rates

CHAPTER XXVIII
The Gold Standard

CHAPTER XXIX

Exchange Control

CHAPTER XXX

Import Duties and Quotas

WAR

CHAPTER XXXI

War Economics

BOOK I
DEMAND

ECONOMICS

CHAPTER I

GENERAL SURVEY

1. ACTIVITY AND WANTS

THE world is at work. The farm labourer is in the fields, tending the cattle or sowing the seed or gathering the harvest. The factory worker is controlling the machines, feeding them with the raw materials which they transform into manufactured goods. The miner is extracting mineral deposits from beneath the surface of the earth. The clerk is recording transactions in the office, the doctor is advising patients in his consulting room, the teacher is instructing pupils in the school. Transport workers are moving persons and goods from one place to another, by land or sea or air. By telegraph and telephone, by cable and wireless, orders and instructions are transmitted with amazing speed. The wheels of economic activity are whirling round.

Our task is to discuss this activity: to show how it comes about and what are its results. But we shall not describe it in any detail, for such a description would occupy far too much space. A book with chapters headed: "On a Norfolk Farm," "Down a Yorkshire Coal Mine," "Round the Ford Works at Dagenham," "A Visit to Lloyd's," and so on, would make interesting reading, but it would have to be very long to give anything like a complete picture of the multifarious activities of the economic world. Moreover, while such a description would provide a most useful background of knowledge for the student of economic problems, it would throw little light upon those problems, for description can never take the place of analysis. A student who had mastered such a book, and who had studied numerous photographs or, better, cinematograph films, which supplemented and illustrated the text, would have a wide and valuable knowledge of technical processes, and of how people earn their living. But he would know little more than when he started as to why different goods have different prices, why some workers earn more than others, why an industry is prosperous at one time and depressed at another; in short, he would have learnt little about how the economic system works. And that is precisely the subject of the present volume.

Let us begin by asking why all this activity takes place. Every wage-earner, for example, knows well enough why he goes to work. He may like his job, or he may not; in any event, he goes to work in order to earn wages. But he does not want the money which his employer pays him for its own sake; he wants it for what it will buy. He wants it in order to satisfy, as far as possible, his wants for what we shall call consumers' goods—that is, for food, clothing, house-room, and all the other things the consumption of which constitutes his standard of living. If he had no such wants, or if his wants could be satisfied without any effort on his part, he would not go to work. He works that he may eat or, more generally, that he may consume.

This is equally true of everybody who contributes towards economic activity, whether by his personal exertion or by investing his money or permitting others to use his property. It may be that a man will choose a job that he prefers rather than one which is better paid; it may be that a business man will sometimes sell cheaply, from motives of charity, to a poor customer. But the vast majority of people engage in economic activity mainly in order to get a money income, and they want the money to purchase consumers' goods. We may remark, in passing, that this by no means implies that most people are selfish or sordid or base. A person's character will show itself in the way he disposes of his income. He may spend most of it upon his wife or children or other dependants; he may give largely to charity. But he wants a money income to provide himself and his family with consumers' goods; it is the wants which consumers' goods satisfy that give the main stimulus to economic activity.

If we turn from the motives of an individual to the functions performed by different kinds of economic activity, we find that the whole productive apparatus is directed towards producing consumers' goods. Only a small part of the work of the world consists of giving the final touches to consumers' goods and delivering them to the final consumer. Behind the shopkeeper who sells, let us say, a cotton shirt there stretches a vast army of workers, all of whom, aided by natural resources and buildings and machinery and means of transport, have played their part in making possible the presence of the shirt in the shop. There are the workers on the cotton plantation, in the ginning works, in the spinning mill, in the weaving shed, and in the works which bleaches or prints or dyes the cloth, and in the factory which makes the shirt. There are the transport workers—lorry-drivers, railwaymen, and seamen. There are the bankers and merchants concerned, and their clerks. And even so, the catalogue is far from complete. The miners who hewed the coal to make the coke to feed the blast furnace which made the pig-iron which made the steel which made the spindles contributed only a very tiny part indeed towards the shirt. But it was a necessary part, and the ultimate object (from the standpoint of the community) of their labour was achieved only by the consumption of the shirts which it helped to produce.

It is easy to see that the whole economic apparatus, under capitalism, depends upon sales and, ultimately, upon sales to the final consumers. An operative in, say, a spinning mill works in order to get wages. Why does his employer pay him wages? Because he hopes that his receipts from the sale of the yarn will exceed his various expenses, including the wages which he pays, and will thus yield him an income for himself. And why do other firms buy his yarn? Clearly for the same reason: they hope to sell the cloth at a price which will give them a profit. But, in general, yarn and cloth are not wanted for their own sakes; they are intermediate products in a chain of processes which culminates and has its purpose in the consumption of cotton clothing. One intermediary buys from another in the hope that, after transforming the commodity into a form more suitable for satisfying wants, he in turn will be able to sell it at a profit. The chain may be very long, but always at the end of it stands the final consumer who buys the consumers' good.

We conclude, therefore, that the rationale of economic activity is to satisfy human wants by producing consumers' goods.

2. ECONOMIC DECISIONS AS CHOICES

People are constantly deciding how they will use their time and energy and property and how they will spend their money.

Millions of such decisions are made every day. It is these decisions which determine the nature and extent of economic activity.

Every one of these decisions is a choice between alternatives, if we may use this word in the sense of "different courses of action," for the "alternatives" between which a choice must be made are often very numerous. The "cost" of a thing, in the last resort, is the thing which was most nearly chosen instead: the alternative which was forgone. Thus a woman may decide to go on a holiday instead of buying a fur coat: the "cost" of the holiday, in this sense, is the fur coat which she would otherwise have bought. A man may decide to work overtime: the "cost" of the things he buys with the extra money is the leisure which he has forgone. A farmer may decide to grow barley rather than oats: the "cost" of the barley is the oats which would otherwise have been produced. Economists use the term "opportunity-cost" (or, less frequently, "displacement-cost") to denote "cost" in this sense. The concept of opportunity-cost is of great importance in economic analysis.[1]

We may divide economic decisions into private decisions and business decisions. There are four important kinds of private decisions. (1) A man must decide how he will divide his time between remunerative work and leisure. (2) He must decide how much of his income he will spend, upon present consumption, and how much he will save, in order to provide for the future. (3) He must decide in what form he will hold his assets: how he will distribute the total value of his assets among different kinds of assets. (4) He must decide how he will distribute his expenditure among different consumers' goods.

Clearly these decisions are all connected with one another. The size of his income will vary with the amount of work he does, and if he decides to save more the total value of his assets will be greater, and the sums available for current expenditure will be less, than they would otherwise have been. A fifth kind of decision is sometimes important: the decision to choose one job rather than another. In so far as a worker prefers one job to another, and is prepared to forgo, up to a point, a higher wage in order to take the job he prefers, this kind of decision also should be classed as "private."

[1] See Robbins, "Remarks on Certain Aspects of the Theory of Costs": *Economic Journal*, 1934.

Later we shall discuss these decisions at some length. For the moment we shall confine ourselves to some general remarks about them. To begin with, we have called them "private" because they all depend upon the tastes of the persons concerned. Different people have different tastes. One man is glad to work longer hours in order to get more pay, while another prefers his leisure; one man is thrifty and another is a spendthrift; one loves spinach and another hates it. There is no accounting for tastes. Unless we know the tastes of a person, it is impossible to predict what he will do when constrained to make the kind of choice under discussion.

We may point out at once that all these choices relate to the apportionment of some fixed total among different "uses." Twenty-four hours a day, a given money income, a fixed total value of assets, a definite sum available for expenditure, has to be distributed, and the more of it is devoted to one use the less of it is available for other uses. As time goes on, the size of the total available may change (except for the twenty-four hours a day). The man may get a bigger income, or may decide to save more, or the value of his assets may rise, or conversely. He may then divide the total among different uses in different proportions, even if his tastes remain the same. But at the moment when he makes his decision, the total is fixed. If there were no such limitations, if everybody could have everything he wanted without any effort, there would be no need to make choices, involving the sacrifice of alternatives forgone, and there would be no economic problems. Economic problems arise precisely because people are compelled to choose.

The word "decision" suggests a deliberate choice made after carefully considering, and rejecting, possible alternative courses. Many economic decisions are made in this way; most people have to watch their shillings, if not their pennies, and cannot afford to be careless. But some decisions are made impulsively, on the spur of the moment, and others would perhaps not be called decisions in ordinary speech, for they are the result of habits formed in the past: people may just go on doing what they have done before, until something happens to make them consciously ask themselves whether they would not prefer to do something different. Nevertheless all such acts of choosing, whether deliberate or impulsive or the result of habit, can be treated as "decisions," for we are trying to explain how the economic system works and are therefore interested in the results of these acts of choosing, and the results are the same however much or little deliberation took place before they were made.

We turn now to "business" decisions. These are made by the person or committee controlling the policy of a firm. We shall use the term "entrepreneur" to stand for such a person or committee. The entrepreneur must decide what his firm shall produce, how large its output shall be, what methods of production shall be used, and where its various establishments shall be located. Later we shall discuss such decisions at length. For the moment we may merely note that, provided we make the reasonable assumption that the entrepreneur wishes to get as big an income as possible for himself (supposing him to have already made his "private" decision as to how much time he will devote to his business rather than to his leisure), these decisions are not questions of taste. On the contrary, if we know the different alternatives which confront an entrepreneur, we can often predict exactly which course he will adopt, for often one course will clearly give him a bigger income for himself than any other. The main reason why we cannot always predict what he will do is that he may sometimes give considerable weight to his belief that various prices will change in one way rather than another, and we cannot say *a priori* whether he will take an optimistic or a pessimistic view.

The great problem for a community, regarded as an economic organization, is what to produce. Its members want consumers' goods, but it is quite impossible to provide everybody with as many consumers' goods, that is with as high a standard of living, as he would like. If all people were like Jains—members of an Indian sect who try to subdue and extinguish their physical desires—it might be done. If consumers' goods descended frequently and in abundance from the heavens, it might be done. As things are, it cannot be done. There are not enough consumers' goods to satisfy wants at all fully—only the fortunate few are rich enough to have practically as high a standard of living as they wish. Why are there not enough consumers' goods? All goods, except gifts of Nature, are produced. In order to produce them we need such things as land and labour and machinery. Economists call such things means of production or factors of production. Consumers' goods are scarce, relatively to the desire for them, because means of production are scarce. Man's energy is limited, and to multiply the people would also multiply the need; and there is not an unlimited amount of good land and other natural resources or of plant and equipment. Hence total output is limited.

But a community must somehow decide how its available means of production shall be used. For many of them are capable of alternative uses. Thus much land can grow any one of several crops, or can be used for pasture for different kinds of animals, or can serve as a golf course or a park or a building site. Much labour can be used for any one of a number of different tasks, and many buildings and machines can serve any one of several purposes. It is clear that if more land is used for growing wheat less is available for other uses, if more labour is used in making armaments less is available for other industries, and so on. Thus a community in deciding how means of production shall be used is deciding what assortment of goods shall be produced out of the infinite number of alternative assortments which could be produced from the means of production available. That is, it is deciding which wants shall be satisfied at the expense of leaving others unsatisfied.

3. SOCIAL INSTITUTIONS

The main purpose of this book is to show how a modern community such as Great Britain or the United States organizes itself in order to solve the problem of how to use its means of production. We shall discuss the working of the price-mechanisms, the influence of banking policy, the extent to which a trade union can raise the wages of its members, the foundations and results of monopoly power, and allied topics. But we shall pause here, at the outset, to consider very briefly how the problem might be solved.

One possibility is central planning. One person or committee could act as an economic dictator, surveying all the resources, human and material, of the community, and deciding how they should be used and what should be done with their products. Soviet Russia attempts something of this kind.

The magnitude of such a task is enormous. Analytically, the task can be stated in a brief phrase: how to use the resources available. But in order to carry it out, the dictator must make a vast multitude of decisions, and to carry it out at all well he must somehow obtain and digest a very large amount of information. He must decide how each worker and each piece of land is to be employed. He must decide where each works is to be located and what methods of production it must use. He must decide what plants are to get the various materials and equipment which are produced, how many houses are to be built, and where, and a host of similar questions. Clearly no single person or committee could do all this unaided. In practice, the business of suggesting decisions on whole groups of problems would be delegated to various subordinate committees, who in turn would rely largely on the advice of local sub-committees. The planning organization as a whole, including all those engaged in obtaining information, would absorb a considerable proportion of the personnel and other resources of the community: this, as far as it goes, is a point against such a system. Further, it would be very difficult for the dictator (or central planning committee) to co-ordinate successfully the suggestions of the various subordinate committees. For example, each industry might demand so many workers, or so much coal, and there might not be nearly enough workers or coal to give every industry all it requested. In the last resort, that is to say, the dictator could not split up his economic problems and delegate the solution of one set of problems to one body and of another to another body. He himself would be compelled to make the final decisions. Only a superman could avoid making many mistakes; that is to say, taking many decisions which he afterwards regretted or found to be impracticable. Consumers, of course, would have to take what they were given instead of ordering what they wanted. They would consume what the dictator chose them to consume.

The opposite extreme to complete central planning is a system of *laisser-faire*, in which everybody does what he likes with himself and his possessions. In so far as a community has a State or similar authority, which enforces certain rules of conduct, it does not practise complete *laisser-faire*. The practical question is how far the State goes in restricting individual freedom of action. Every State "intervenes" or "interferes" to some extent, but some States go much further than others.

Nearly all States try to prevent their subjects from killing or injuring one another and from forcibly taking one another's possessions, and try to see that contracts are carried out. This brings us to the institution of Property. If anybody could have anything which he was powerful enough to seize, output would be very limited. A man would hesitate to sow for somebody else to reap; he would be reluctant to construct a building which would probably be taken from him when it was completed. At present, people are averse from adding to their tangible possessions in a country where the confiscation of possessions (following a revolution, for example) seems likely in the near future. The institution of Property gives persons and other bodies the right, subject to limitations imposed by the State, to keep and use land, buildings, and other resources recognized as "belonging" to them, and to consume or exchange their products.

It is generally agreed that the institution of Property is desirable. Nobody prefers "the law of the jungle." Nor does anybody want to deprive a person of the exclusive right to the use of a purely personal possession such as his tooth-brush. The controversial question is whether means of production, such as land and railways and factories, should be owned by the State or by private persons.

Private property, in contrast to central planning, means decentralization of the task of obtaining information and making decisions. It means also that what is produced depends on the valuations of consumers and not on those of the dictator. A man who owns a piece of land presumably tries "to get the most out of it." If he is going to consume its products himself, he will grow, out of all the various possible assortments, that assortment which he prefers. If he is producing for exchange—which means, under a price-system, for sale—he will produce that assortment for which he expects to get most in exchange—in money terms, he will try to make his receipts exceed his costs by the greatest possible margin. This means that he will be guided by the valuations of consumers: out of the various alternatives open to him, he will choose that which he thinks consumers will prefer, because it is that which will give him the greatest return for himself. Similarly with methods of production. He will try to use those methods which produce any given output in the cheapest possible way. It will be in his own interest to give consumers what they want and to produce it as efficiently as possible. The tasks of estimating the probable future demand for different products, of finding out the potentialities of his land, of discovering the cheapest methods of production, are not performed by any planning authority, but by the owner himself. We shall show later that it is in the interest of the community for a given output to be produced as cheaply as possible. For the prices of the various means of production tend to reflect the value which they can produce in other fields. Efficiency in production means economizing scarce means of production by not using one collection of means of production to produce a given output when a cheaper collection would give the same result.

The real contrast to central planning, therefore, is a system of private property, with the State defending the rights of property-owners. But clearly the State must also limit these rights to some extent in the interests of other members of the community. A man who set his house on fire might endanger the houses of his neighbours. It seems reasonable that the owner of land needed for a railway or road should be compelled by the State to sell it for that purpose at a price based on what it could earn in other uses. But if, on the whole, people are free to do what they please with themselves and their property, the social system is known as capitalism. We discuss it more fully in a later chapter. Here we wish only to point out that under capitalism the nature and extent of economic activity depend upon the countless decisions, both "private" and "business," taken by individuals each acting as he thinks best. They are guided in their decisions by prices and by their expectations of how prices will change. Their decisions in turn affect prices and help to make them what they are. Economics is very largely a study of how prices are formed and of the functions which they fulfil.

Not all economic activity, however, is guided by the price-mechanism and undertaken for gain. The Family is still a most important institution. Parents maintain and bring up their children from motives of affection and the mother often makes decisions on behalf of the household as a whole.

The world as a whole has been termed The Great Society. Improvements in transport and communication have brought different regions much more closely into touch with one another. Events in one part of the world often have considerable repercussions in other parts. The main way in which people in one country virtually co-operate with people in others is through foreign trade. It would be clear to an observer looking down on the world, that somehow the people in one country (or district) agree with people elsewhere to send them various commodities in return for others. Nevertheless the existence of national Governments means that the system of social organization differs between countries. Although, even before the war, the British Government in many ways limited freedom of enterprise and the rights of property-owners, Great Britain was much nearer than Germany or Italy to *laisser-faire*. In this book we shall have mainly in mind the system prevailing in Great Britain and other democratic countries before the war.

Our task will be to describe and analyse, rather than to praise or condemn. But it may be well to mention here, albeit very briefly, the main objections usually raised against the institution of Private Property as it exists in practice.

In the first place, it gives rise to a considerable inequality of incomes. Private property, in a country such as Great Britain, is very unevenly distributed among persons. The few have a great deal, the many very little. Hence the fortunate few get considerable incomes from ownership, and can live very comfortably, if they choose, without doing any work, while the bulk of the population get little or nothing as interest, profits, or rents. The right of inheritance and bequest helps to perpetuate this inequality. Moreover, as we shall explain in the chapter on Wages, the children of well-to-do parents have a considerable advantage over the children of poor parents in qualifying for and obtaining well-paid posts and in setting up in business on their own account. Inequality of income implies inequality of opportunity and this implies a waste of potential talent which remains undeveloped.

In the second place, the concentration of a large amount of property under the control of one person or group may lead to monopolistic action. The owner may make a bigger profit for himself by withholding some of it from use, instead of employing it all to help satisfy the wants of consumers. We discuss this at some length in the chapter on Monopoly.

In the third place, a small minority of persons may exert a predominant influence in some fields of economic activity. We do not attach much weight to the complaint that workers must take orders from foremen and managers. This seems inevitable if production is to be at all efficient. It exists in Soviet Russia as much as elsewhere. It also seems reasonable and desirable that those who take the risks of a business should control its policy. The workers in a particular firm will not accept lower wages because that one firm is doing badly, but the shareholders must accept lower dividends: it is they who take the risks. Yet in practice the policy of large groups of companies may be controlled by two or three men, holding quite a small proportion of the total capital, who by means of devices such as the creation of holding companies[1] have obtained the deciding voice. A further point is that a few such men may exert an altogether disproportionate influence on the policy of the Government. For example, they may obtain "protection" against imports which compete with the goods which they sell, although this may be against the interests of consumers.

A modern State does something to diminish the results of inequality and, if it wished, it could do more. The rich are taxed heavily and a good deal is spent on social services such as public health, education, and the relief of poverty. Most States make some attempt to prevent or control monopoly, and here again they could do more. They could also, by appropriate company legislation and in other ways, prevent a small minority from exerting an undue influence. On the other hand, even in Great Britain and other democratic countries, the State itself creates or fosters various kinds of monopolies and seems sometimes to be swayed too much by pressure from particular groups.

We must warn the reader that this book does not discuss whether capitalism is better or worse than some other system, such as communism, or what types of economic and social reform are desirable. These are difficult questions on which different people hold widely different opinions. In my view, reasoned and informed judgments on them require a considerable study of economics and of political science. A discussion of them therefore seems out of place in an elementary work such as this.

[1] Described on pages 168–171.

4. PRICES AND THE PRICE-SYSTEM

Economic activity is largely regulated, under capitalism, by the mechanism of the price-system. Changes in prices act as indicators both to producers and to consumers. If consumers buy more of a particular product its price tends to rise and this makes it profitable for producers to increase their output of it. If a particular commodity becomes more difficult to produce, or if there is less of it than before (owing, for example, to a bad harvest), its price tends to rise, warning consumers that its relative scarcity has increased and inducing some of them, if not all, to economize more than before in their consumption of it. Thus consumers make their wishes known to producers, and are themselves induced to act in accordance with changes in relative scarcity, without any central planning organization, through the price-system.

This volume, like every book on economic theory, will be largely occupied with explaining how the price-system works and how the relations between different prices are determined. It may be useful, in this introductory chapter, to make a few remarks on the notion of "price" and on the way in which all prices are interdependent and together form a "system."

The price of anything is the sum of money paid—not merely asked or offered but actually paid—in exchange for it. We should perhaps explain the term "value," for the price of anything may be defined as its value in terms of money.

Value, as used in modern economic writings, means always value in exchange. It is inevitably relative, since the value of one thing must always be expressed in terms of another; there can be no such thing as "intrinsic" value in the modern economic sense of the term. The value of *X* in terms of *Y* is the amount of *Y* which can be obtained in exchange for *X*. If 1 lb. of tea exchanges for 4 lb. of sugar, the value of 1 lb. of tea in terms of pounds of sugar is four, or, to say the same thing in other words, the value of 1 lb. of sugar in terms of pounds of tea is a quarter. The value is the ratio or rate at which tea and sugar exchange against one another.

In fact, values are nearly always expressed in money, and are then termed prices. Absolute prices are affected, as we shall see later, by changes in the supply of money or in the demand for money. There can be a general rise or fall of prices; all prices may rise, or all prices may fall. But, by definition, there can be no general rise or fall in values. If the price of everything doubles, this means that the value of money has halved. But changes in relative prices are much more significant than changes in absolute prices. For example, a worker's standard of living depends both upon his money wage and upon the prices of the things which he buys. If his money wage doubles and the prices of the things which he buys all more than double, his standard of living will fall. In the same way, a firm's profits depend both upon its money receipts and its money costs. A rise in the selling prices of its products tends to raise its profits, but if at the same time the prices of the materials and other factors of production which it must buy increase still more, its profits may fall.

We shall speak of prices rather than of values. But, until we come to the theory of money, we shall be concerned mainly with relative rather than absolute prices: with the problem of why some prices are higher than others and of why prices change relatively to one another.

The reader will doubtless have noticed that we are using "price," in conformity with our definition, in a much wider sense than the popular one. A wage, or salary, is a price, for it is paid in exchange for a certain amount of labour. If workers are paid by results, as when a miner is paid a "piece-rate" of, say, 3s. for every ton of coal that he hews, the unit of labour service is the "piece": in this case, a ton of coal hewn. If they are paid by time, the unit is usually an hour's work or a week's work or, for some highly paid workers, a month's work or a year's work. The "rent" of a piece of land, or of a building or part of a building, or of a cinematograph film, is the price paid for the use of it for a stated period of time. Interest is the price paid, per unit of time, for the loan of money. The rate of interest is usually expressed as the percentage per annum of the interest to the sum lent. Rates of foreign exchange between different currencies are also prices: for example, the price of £1 sterling is so many French francs.

A study of prices throws considerable light upon incomes. The money income of a person may be provisionally defined as the amount of money which he gets for himself—that is, after paying his business expenses—during a period of time such as a week or a year. Thus every price which is paid forms part of the gross income of the recipient, but his net income is the excess of his total receipts over his business expenses, which themselves consist of prices.

The payments made by an entrepreneur for labour services or for the loan of money or for the use of property constitute net income to the recipients, if they incur no business expenses in supplying these services. Thus the price paid to a wage-earner for a week's work may represent his income from work for that week, and the rent paid to a landlord for the use of his land for a year may represent his income for that year. Clearly such prices have a double aspect. They represent income to the recipients but they represent costs to the entrepreneur—for example, the employer or the farmer—who pays them.

Incomes paid under contract, like wages and interest and rents, can be treated as prices. But a price is usually expressed as so much per unit. The rate of interest, to repeat, is expressed as an annual percentage on the amount lent. Thus the income received by a person from the loan of money depends both on the rate of interest and on the amount of money he lends. In the same way, the weekly wage of a worker paid by results depends both on the piece-rate and on the amount of work he does. We discuss wages and interest and rent fairly fully in later chapters. But it should be remembered that in so far as Economics attempts to explain why incomes are unequal it must take account of the fact that ability and property are unequally distributed among persons. A study of prices does not tell the whole story.

"Profits," in the rather loose sense of the incomes of entrepreneurs (including persons such as barristers and hawkers working on their own account and also those who hold ordinary shares and therefore get a proportion of the profits of a company), depend upon prices, in that they are the excess of receipts over costs, but they are not in themselves prices, since nobody pays them.

Other incomes which are not prices are those received as private or collective gifts, such as a father's allowance to his son or an old-age pension given by the State.

At this stage we can perhaps give some examples of how different prices are related. If beef were to become more plentiful and therefore cheaper, this would probably exert a downward influence on the prices of substitutes for beef, such as mutton. If house accommodation were to become more plentiful and therefore cheaper, this would probably stimulate the demand for furniture and might well raise its price. During recent decades the decline in the number of horses in Western countries has considerably reduced the output of oats. In so far as land previously used for growing oats could be used instead for other crops, such as wheat and barley, this has tended to increase the output of such crops and has therefore exerted a downward influence upon their price. The development of machinery has greatly increased output, thereby raising the general standard of living, but the substitution of machinery for labour may reduce the wages of the particular labour displaced: thus the introduction of power-looms reduced the earnings of hand-loom weavers.

The concept of opportunity-cost throws some light upon relative prices. Let us borrow a simple example from Adam Smith. Suppose that in a primitive hunting community a day's labour will enable a man to kill either two beaver or three deer. Then two beaver will exchange for three deer. If they exchanged for less than three deer, nobody would hunt beaver, for by capturing three deer he could obtain more beaver (in exchange for the deer) than by catching the beaver himself. The consequent shortage of beaver would then raise their price until two beaver were again worth three deer. Similarly, if two beaver exchanged for more than three deer, men would hunt beaver instead of deer, until the ratio of two to three was again restored in the market. This assumes that all men are equally skilful hunters both of beaver and of deer, and have no preference for one occupation rather than the other, and that a day's labour will always produce either two beaver or three deer. The rate of exchange between beaver and deer must then be the same as the opportunity-cost ratio, namely two to three; changes in the relative demand for beaver and deer cannot affect their relative prices, but only the relative quantities of each that are produced.

This concept is equally valid for a modern community, but it is more difficult to apply because factors of production are combined in different ways in different industries. In general, however, we can say that the value of anything produced by a factor, or a group of factors, will tend to be equal to the value of anything else which a similar factor, or group of factors, is producing. This assumes that factors of production can readily move from one industry to another, and will do so if they can thereby produce something of greater value, thus earning more for themselves.

There is a close connection between the price of a durable good and the price of the services which it yields. The price of the good is "derived" from the price of its services and tends to equal the expected value of its future services, "capitalized" at the current rate of interest. Thus £100 face value 2½ per cent Consols is simply the right to £2 10s. a year for ever. If the current rate of interest is 5 per cent, anybody can obtain £2 10s. a year for ever by investing £50; hence the market price of 2½ per cent Consols will be only £50. Again, suppose that a house is expected to yield £100 a year net, after meeting expenses such as the cost of repairs. If the current rate of interest is 5 per cent, the house will tend to be worth £2000, since an outlay of £2000 will produce an income of £100 a year; if the current rate of interest is 4 per cent, the house will tend to be worth £2500, and so on. If investors can obtain a higher yield from Consols or houses than from other investments they will tend to buy Consols or houses, and this will raise their market price until the yield on them is no higher than on other investments, and, conversely, if the yield from them is lower than from other investments, the demand for them will fall, thus reducing their price and thereby increasing the percentage yield on money newly invested in them. Thus the value of a fixed-interest security or of a durable good tends to equal the expected net annual value of its future services multiplied by 100 and divided by the current rate of interest. All this means is that the present value of a definite future income will vary with the current rate of interest.

CHAPTER II
MARKETS

1. THE WORLD MARKET AND LOCAL MARKETS

A MARKET is commonly thought of as a place where commodities are bought and sold. Thus fruit and vegetables are sold wholesale at Covent Garden Market and meat is sold wholesale at Smithfield Market. But there are markets for things other than commodities, in the usual sense. There are real estate markets, foreign exchange markets, labour markets, short-term capital markets, and so on; there may be a market for anything which has a price. And there may be no particular place to which dealings are confined. Buyers and sellers may be scattered over the whole world and instead of actually meeting together in a market-place they may deal with one another by telephone, telegram, cable, or letter. Even if dealings are restricted to a particular place, the dealers may consist wholly or in part of brokers or agents acting on instructions from clients far away. Thus agents buy meat at Smithfield on behalf of retail butchers all over England, and brokers on the London Stock Exchange buy and sell securities on instructions from clients all over the world. We must therefore define a market as any area over which buyers and sellers are in such close touch with one another, either directly or through dealers, that the prices obtainable in one part of the market affect the prices paid in other parts.

Modern means of communication are so rapid that a buyer can discover what price a seller is asking, and can accept it if he wishes, although he may be thousands of miles away. Thus the market for anything is, potentially, the whole world. But in fact many things have, normally, only a local or national market.

This may be because nearly the whole demand is concentrated in one locality. Few people who are not Scottish care to tackle the curious concoction known as haggis; the market for pelota rackets is practically confined to the Basque country; the blue tunic, with red and yellow trimmings, worn by the Lapps is rarely sold to others. But of course such goods may be supplied by firms in other parts of the world, to be sold in the district where they are demanded.

These special local demands, however, are of quite minor importance. The main reason why many things have not a world market is that they are costly or difficult to transport.

The lower the value per ton of a good, the greater is the percentage addition made to its price by a fixed charge per ton-mile for transport. Thus, if coal is £2 a ton and tin £200 a ton at the place of production, a given transport charge forms a percentage of the price of coal a hundred times greater than of the price of tin. Hence transport costs may restrict the market for goods with a low value per ton, even if, as is often the case, they are carried at relatively low rates. It may be cheaper to produce, say, coal or iron ore at *A* than at *B*, but the cost of transporting it from *A* to *B* may outweigh the difference in production costs, so that it is produced for local consumption at *B*, and *B* does not normally form part of the market for the output of *A*. For example, coal is produced much more cheaply in the United States than in Europe, but, owing to the cost of transporting coal by rail from the inland mines to the Atlantic seaboard of the United States, American coal seldom finds its way to Europe.

Sea transport, however, is very much cheaper than land transport. Hence commodities of this type produced near a port can often be sent profitably quite long distances by sea. Thus Swedish iron ore comes by sea from Narvik to the Ruhr, and British coal is exported to Canada and South America.

The markets for real estate are local. Soil has been transported from French vineyards to California, and historic mansions have been demolished in Europe to be re-erected in the United States, but as a rule land and buildings are not transported.

Some goods, like new bread and fresh cream and strawberries, must be consumed very soon after they have been produced, and this restricts their sale to local markets. Other goods do not travel well. Thus many local wines which cannot stand transport can be bought in the district more cheaply than similar wines which have a wider market. The development of refrigeration, and of other devices which enable foodstuffs to be preserved and transported, has greatly widened the market for such things as meat and fish and some kinds of fruit. But such devices often transform the articles, from the standpoint of consumers, into a different commodity. Condensed milk is not the same as fresh milk, and chilled meat or frozen butter has not the same taste as fresh.

Many workers are reluctant to move to a different country, or even to a different part of their own country, to get a higher wage. This should not be exaggerated. Before the war of 1914, over a million persons a year emigrated overseas from Europe. Following it, there were considerable movements of population within Great Britain away from the depressed areas towards the more prosperous South. Employers may take the initiative. Thus girl textile workers have been engaged in Yorkshire to work in Australia, and during the inter-war years French employers engaged groups of Poles and Italians to work in the coal-mines and steel-works of France. Nevertheless labour markets are mainly local, or at any rate national.

Transport services by rail or tram are obviously local in that passengers or goods must travel between points on the fixed track. A firm may charter, for example, a Greek ship rather than an English ship, if it is cheaper, but low railway rates in Belgium are no help to a firm which wishes to send goods across Canada. In the same way, such things as gas, water, and electricity, supplied by means of pipes or wires, cannot be sold to places not connected with the system of pipes or wires.

A country or district may impose import duties upon certain goods coming from elsewhere. If the duties are not prohibitive —that is, if some taxed goods nevertheless come in—the country or district still forms part of the world market for these goods. The duty may make the price in the "protected" area much higher than the price in the exporting districts, but if this outside price falls, greater quantities of the goods will cross the tariff barriers, thus reducing the price inside them, and conversely if the outside price rises. But if the import of a good is restricted by quota to some stated quantity, its price in the restricting area is divorced from its world price and the restricting area forms a separate market. During recent years many quota restrictions have been enforced, particularly by countries in Western Europe. The number of immigrants may also be restricted by quota, as in the United States, and some countries may forbid the export of capital.

It should be remembered, however, that even if the goods cannot move to the purchasers, the purchasers may be able to move to the goods. Thus if housing or electricity is cheap in one district people will tend to move to that district rather than elsewhere, and employers may build new works in one place rather than another because the local labour is cheaper.

2. WHAT IS A COMMODITY?

In ordinary speech we apply the term commodity to what is often a whole class of commodities. There are many different varieties of wheat, wool, cotton, bread, potatoes, cigarettes, and indeed of almost any "commodity" one can think of. One variety of a producers' good may serve a somewhat different purpose from another; and some consumers may prefer one variety of a consumers' good to another because of some real or imagined difference in quality. It may be that all or some of the different varieties are very close substitutes for one another, and that many purchasers do not mind which of them they take. More often, however, some purchasers have a strong preference for one variety rather than another, and this may lead to considerable divergence between their prices. Each variety is really a separate commodity for which there is a distinct demand.

An interesting illustration is afforded by the relative prices of British and Danish bacon during recent years. From 1930 to 1932 the price of first quality British bacon was over a third higher than the price of first quality Danish bacon. Most of the bacon sold in Great Britain was Danish, 6 or 7 million cwt. being imported every year. Then the import of Danish bacon was restricted. In 1936 about 3½ million cwt. of both British and Danish bacon were sold in Great Britain; as compared with 1930 the British supply had doubled and the Danish supply had halved. The price of Danish bacon was higher than the price of British. The restriction of Danish supplies brought to light the fact, previously unsuspected, that many purchasers had a preference for Danish bacon rather than British. The moral of this is that we must not assume that the relative prices of different varieties of a "commodity" will always bear the same relation to one another. Two units do not really belong to the same commodity unless they are perfect substitutes: that is, unless every potential purchaser would be quite indifferent as to which of the two he received for his money.

A manufacturer may differentiate a particular product from similar products made by rival firms by attaching to it a "trade-mark" which the law forbids others to use. Many varieties of consumers' goods—motor cars, toilet requisites, patent medicines, foodstuffs, and so on—are "branded" in this way. As a rule, the maker of a branded article advertises it in order to create a demand for his brand rather than for rival brands. Other varieties of the commodity, whether branded or not, may be very similar to his product, but since he alone can use that particular trade-mark he has a monopoly of his product.

The same physical thing is logically a different commodity when it is in a different place. For example, a steel tube at Corby is a different commodity from the same steel tube at Capetown, and sells for a different price. The difference in price arises from costs of transport, including such items as insurance charges and importers' profits, and from import duties.

In the same way, the same thing is logically a different commodity at one time from what it is at another, and may command a different price. The transport of goods over time forms a part of economic activity just as much as their transport over space. Many middlemen, including shopkeepers, carry stocks in order to supply their customers' requirements promptly, and this is a service for which customers are willing to pay: it saves them from the inconvenience of carrying considerable stocks themselves. Two or three centuries ago the grain supply of a region came mainly from the annual local harvest. If nobody had deliberately stored grain to sell it again later, it would have been plentiful and cheap soon after the harvest, but would have become considerably scarcer and dearer in the months just before the next harvest. Speculators rendered a useful service by buying grain soon after the harvest, thus making it less cheap at that time, stocking it, and selling it later, thus making its price less dear towards the close of the harvest year. They made a profit for themselves, for which they rendered a service to consumers by reducing the fluctuations in prices and consumption over the year. Since then the great improvement in transport facilities has rendered this type of service less important for most commodities. Nowadays hardly a month passes in which wheat is not harvested in some quarter of the globe, ready to be sent wherever it is demanded, so that the danger of famine or serious shortage in any area is slight. Consumers can similarly obtain most commodities at any time from the current output of some region or other, provided that they can afford to pay for them, and world stocks of most commodities are small, as a rule, compared with the annual output. Nevertheless, middlemen still render a useful service by holding some stocks to cover the period before the next shipments arrive and to provide a safeguard against an unexpected temporary shortage. Moreover, the bulk of the world output of some goods still takes place at one particular season of the year. A leading example is cotton. The bulk of the world's cotton (at least until recently, since the American Government restricted its output) is grown in the United States and is picked in the late summer and early autumn. Hence the bulk of the crop must be "carried" by somebody, if spinners and others are to have a steady supply over the year. The tendency, therefore, is for the price of cotton to rise steadily from one October to the next, the rise being sufficient to make it profitable to hold stocks of cotton. But of course the price may rise in fact more or less than this, or may fall, owing to changes in the demand for cotton, or in the expected size of next year's crop, as the year goes on.

3. PERFECT AND IMPERFECT MARKETS

A market is said to be perfect when all the potential sellers and buyers are promptly aware of the prices at which transactions take place and of all the offers made by other sellers and buyers, and when any buyer can purchase from any seller, and conversely. Under such conditions the price of a commodity will tend to be the same (after allowing for costs of transport, including import duties) all over the market. If one seller is prepared to accept less than others, orders will stream towards him until he is sold out or raises his price to that asked by his competitors or (exceptionally, when he holds a large proportion of the total stocks) until rival sellers are constrained to reduce their prices to the level of his. Conversely, if a seller asks more than his rivals for the same commodity he will find no purchasers, for although some buyers will be prepared, if necessary, to pay more than the price ruling at the moment, they will not deal with one seller if they can get the same commodity more cheaply from others.

This assumes that the thing dealt in is a "commodity" in the strict sense of the term, different units of it being perfect substitutes for one another. Of course, one variety of a so-called commodity may sell for more than another. This does not mean that the market is imperfect: the different varieties are really different commodities. They may conceivably be physically the same, but if a distinctive label or trade-mark, coupled with an advertising campaign, leads some buyers to prefer one branded article to another they are in effect different commodities.

Some goods, such as wheat, are physically capable of being divided into "grades" in such a way that all the units in a given grade are practically homogeneous, so that each grade is a commodity in a strict sense. The grading is usually performed by some body representing the sellers. Careful grading is in the interests of the sellers, as well as of the buyers, for the market is thereby widened. A buyer can confidently purchase goods which he has not seen on the basis of the grade (or other standard description) given to them by the marketing organization, knowing exactly what he will get. Grading also makes possible sales for future delivery even if the goods have not been seen by the buyer, or are not yet in existence, and permits dealings in options.

Some goods, however, cannot be graded or described with sufficient accuracy to be purchased without being seen and examined. Thus buyers of raw wool, or their representatives, want to inspect each lot of wool before making an offer for it, and buyers of tea taste samples before bidding; wool-buying and tea-tasting are skilled occupations. Such goods are usually sold in lots by auction. At a later stage in their life history it may be possible to grade them. Wool tops can be graded, and tea can be blended so that one package sold to retail consumers is indistinguishable from another bearing the same brand.

A market is imperfect when some buyers or sellers, or both, are not aware of the offers being made by others. Thus the market for second-hand books is imperfect. It is still possible, occasionally, for a customer to buy a book from one bookseller and re-sell it at a profit to another. In general, retail markets are somewhat imperfect. For example, some shops may constantly sell suitcases for one or two shillings more than other shops in the same town are charging for similar cases.

The development of communications during recent decades has tended to make markets less imperfect. Dealers in commodities, securities, capital, and foreign exchange cannot afford to pay more, or to accept less, than they need. The prices paid in one centre rapidly become known in other centres. A wheat dealer who has chartered a ship to carry wheat, which he has bought, from an exporting country can instruct the captain of the ship by wireless to go to a different port if he learns that prices in that port are temporarily higher than elsewhere. A firm holding a balance of money in New York can transfer it to London if a relative rise of short-term interest rates in London makes it profitable to do so. International securities owned by persons all over the world may be offered for sale in a particular stock exchange if they temporarily command a higher price there than elsewhere. Telegraph and telephone, cable and wireless, enable price-differences between different centres to be smoothed out very rapidly.

On the other hand, the growth of Government intervention during recent years has worked in the opposite direction. Higher tariffs have increased price-differences between countries. Quantitative restrictions on the import of goods, the immigration of labour, and the export of capital have tended to separate national markets from one another. Moreover, the number of branded articles has tended to increase; this splits up the market for a "commodity" by "differentiating" different varieties which come to be regarded by consumers as different commodities.

If buyers and sellers are not in close touch with one another, it is often possible for middlemen to make a profit, and render the market less imperfect, by acting as intermediaries. They may themselves hold stocks, which they buy as cheaply as possible, thus tending to equalize the prices received by different sellers, while competition between themselves tends to equalize the prices paid by different buyers: such a middleman must make his existence known to buyers in order to do business and a buyer can compare the prices asked by two or three middlemen before purchasing. Some middlemen do not themselves hold stocks but collect and give information, putting sellers and buyers into touch with one another and charging a commission on completed deals. Real estate agents and private labour exchanges (for instance, for domestic servants or teachers) are examples. In the same way, trade papers make a profit by disseminating information; for example, the prices realized at book auctions are published every week or month, thus making the type of bargain mentioned above less common than it would otherwise be. In general, middlemen clearly perform a useful function, for it is always possible for sellers to try to deal with buyers directly, or conversely, if they think it more profitable.

Monopoly and the possibility of charging different prices for very similar things are discussed in a later chapter.[1]

4. TYPES OF TRANSACTIONS

The various things for which prices are paid may be divided into the eight groups of (1) consumers' goods, (2) producers' goods, (3) labour services, (4) real estate, (5) loans of money, (6) paper titles, (7) rights, and (8) other currencies.

(1) Consumer's Goods

A consumers' good is desired for its own sake; it directly satisfies a want. Under this heading we may include services such as those rendered by doctors and houses and cinemas and means of transport, in so far as they directly satisfy the wants of consumers.

Although the main object of economic activity is to produce consumers' goods, the value of sales to consumers forms only a small part of the total value of all transactions. In Great Britain during recent years it has seldom exceeded £4000 million a year, the value of retail sales by shops and public-houses forming rather more than half of this total, whereas the total value of all transactions has probably reached at least £50,000 million a year. This is due partly to the large volume of transactions in stocks and shares and other paper titles and partly to the fact that materials and other goods often change hands a number of times before being sold, in their finished form, to the final consumer.

Retail markets, as we have already mentioned, are somewhat imperfect. Some people do not think it worth their while to take the time and trouble required to discover where an article can be bought slightly more cheaply, or whether a shopkeeper can

[1] It should be noted that goods produced under conditions of imperfect competition (or monopoly) may have a perfect market.

be induced to make some reduction on the price which he quotes. Others buy at a particular shop because it is close at hand and therefore convenient, or because they can obtain credit there, or because they like the service or amenities which they get there, or because they trust that particular shop to supply them with goods of good quality. Branded articles are nearly always sold at fixed prices and appeal to people who do not like to spend time in bargaining or comparing qualities. Shops selling mainly homogeneous articles at fixed prices, such as different brands of cigarettes and tobacco, tend to be distributed over space in the same way as the population. They cater to the convenience of the consumers. Shops which cater for bargain hunters, on the other hand, tend to be grouped together—like the second-hand book shops in Charing Cross Road and the fruit and vegetable stalls found in clusters in big cities—so that buyers can readily compare prices and qualities.

A careful purchaser, who is prepared to spend time in bargain hunting and bargaining and to postpone or anticipate some wants in order to take advantage of sales, can doubtless obtain appreciably more for a given money outlay than a careless one. But it should be remembered that this difference is not all net gain; against it must be set the time and effort and inconvenience, and possibly the extra fares, which it entails.

(2) Producers' Goods

A producers' good is wanted not for its own sake but for the sake of the contribution it makes towards the output of consumers' goods. It thus satisfies wants only indirectly; in the last resort, the demand for such goods is "derived" from the demand for the consumers' goods which they help to produce. Under this heading we may include the services, as well as the goods, which firms buy from other firms to enable them to carry on their activities. Thus they may pay for being supplied with water or gas or electricity or telephone service; they may pay for having their goods transported from one place to another; they may pay to have their property insured against loss or damage; and they may pay for various kinds of financial and banking services.

Many goods—for example, raw materials such as crude rubber and spelter and iron ore and intermediate products such as steel bars and cotton yarn and wool tops—are nearly always producers' goods, since they seldom directly satisfy wants. Other goods, however, may be used either as consumers' goods or as producers' goods. Thus coal burnt in the domestic hearth falls under (1), while coal burnt in a factory falls under (2): and the services rendered by a railway in carrying passengers to their holidays fall under (1) but its services in carrying freight or commercial travellers fall under (2). This fact, however, does not make our classification useless; economic analysis is concerned with the functions of goods, with the part which they play in the economic system, rather than with their origin or their intrinsic qualities.

There is little imperfection in most markets for producers' goods. It is part of the business of a retailer to know something of the qualities of the goods which he stocks and to compare carefully the offers made to him by sellers. He will doubtless be visited by commercial travellers, representing manufacturers or wholesalers, and he himself may visit wholesalers to see their samples or consult the relevant trade journals to see what advertisers are offering.

A good example of a market in the popular sense of the term is Smithfield Market. The market-place is owned by the Corporation of London, which rents stalls to sellers on a weekly tenancy. The sellers are mainly meat-importing companies, who have either bought the cattle and sheep outright from farmers overseas or have agreed to slaughter, process, transport, and sell the stock for them in return for a commission. The sellers compete with one another; there is no combine or price-ring among them. The buyers are mainly representatives of chains of butchers' shops, or of restaurants and hotels or of butchers throughout the country. Both sellers and buyers are experts, and buyers examine the meat on the spot. There is consequently very little variation in the prices paid for similar lots on the same day.

The sellers and buyers of almost any producers' goods can readily get in touch with one another and compare prices quoted and offered by different firms. Most large cities have special "markets" for particular commodities, or for groups of them, where sellers and buyers, or their agents, can meet and deal. Thus London has its Metal Exchange, Rubber Exchange, Coal Exchange, Iron and Steel Exchange, Baltic Exchange, Corn Exchange, Wool Exchange, and others. Some of the dealings are in services. Thus Lloyd's is a market for every kind of insurance business. A shipowner or merchant, wishing to insure his cargo, can go there—or employ a marine insurance broker to go there on his behalf—and inquire at what rates the various underwriters are prepared to undertake the business. Again, the chartering of ships (in addition to large transactions in grain and other commodities such as soya beans and oil seeds and timber) is conducted on the Baltic. To revert to commodities, the actual bales of wool to be offered for sale by auction in the afternoon are available for inspection by buyers in the morning, and purchases in the London Corn Exchange (but not in the Baltic) are made on the basis of samples displayed there, but in most of the London Exchanges the goods are not displayed and are bought from their description in terms of recognized grades and qualities. Buyers can resort to arbitration if the goods do not conform to specification or come up to sample.

(3) Labour Services

In so far as these are rendered, as by domestic servants, directly to consumers, and paid for by consumers, they fall under (1). But most workers are engaged by an employer who wants their services not for his own consumption but for the contribution they make towards the output of whatever he is selling. Thus the demand for most labour services is "derived," in the last resort, from the demand for consumers' goods. An apparent exception, to be considered later, is the demand of Governments for such workers as teachers and policemen, whose products are not sold.

In some countries minimum wages for each of a number of occupations are fixed from time to time by the Government or by Courts or Boards set up by the Government for that purpose. In Australia minimum wages for most workers are fixed in this way. In Great Britain, 48 Trade Boards, covering over 1,100,000 workers, have been set up under the Acts of 1909 and 1918 to fix minimum wages for various low-paid occupations. In addition, the wages of agricultural workers are regulated by a Board and local Wages Committees: in England and Wales under the Act of 1924 and in Scotland under the Act of 1937.

Although the membership of British trade unions is at present below 5 million, rates of wages for most occupations and grades are fixed by negotiation between the relevant trade union and the relevant association of employers. Usually variations of wages between districts are permitted and the agreement covers other matters, such as hours of work, in addition to wages. The agreement usually stipulates that if either side wishes to change it a certain period of notice must first be given. Some agreements, such as that covering the wages of coal-miners, stipulate that wages shall vary in a prescribed manner with the profits of the industry; others, covering some 180,000 workers, mainly in iron and steel, that they shall vary with the prices of the products; and others, covering about 1¼ million workers, that they shall vary with movements in the Cost of Living Index of the Ministry of Labour. Some important groups of workers, such as domestic servants and clerks and typists, have not a strong trade union and a worker in such an occupation usually settles his wage by individual bargaining with his employer.

The British Government has set up a network of Employment Exchanges, intended to bring together employers seeking labour and workers seeking jobs. There are also many private employment agencies, especially for domestic servants, teachers, waiters, and members of the theatrical profession, and a number of posts are offered by advertisement in the press.

(4) Real Estate

One piece of land, or house, is different, at least in situation, from every other. Thus dealings on the basis of specification or samples are practically ruled out. Buyers wish to see the actual property, as a rule, before purchasing.

For this reason most of the business is in the hands of specialized agents who bring buyers and sellers together in return for a commission from the latter when a transaction is concluded. There are also advertisements, inserted by sellers or their agents, in the general press and in special journals. Although the goods sold are not homogeneous, the market in real estate is not very imperfect, for as a rule sellers try to get as high a price as possible, and buyers spend some time and trouble in discovering what alternatives are available, before a transaction is concluded.

(5) Loans of Money

We shall discuss different kinds of loans in our chapter on interest. Firms can usually obtain loans for fairly short periods from their banks. A very well-known borrower, such as the British Government, can appeal directly to the general public. A foreign Government, or large mining or industrial concern, which wished to raise a fairly large long-term loan in London would probably employ an issue house as its agent. The issue house—which we shall discuss later in its role of accepting house—will advise the borrower what terms to offer and will sponsor the loan, getting a commission (which may run into five figures) for its special knowledge and the use of its reputation. An established firm which wishes to raise additional capital can often get it by advertising in the financial press or by circularizing its shareholders. It is more difficult to raise capital for a new concern, unknown to the general public. The task may be undertaken by a company promoter, skilled in the ways of the City, who usually buys up the patent or the business and forms a company, re-selling the shares (at a profit) to the public, by advertising the prospectus or circularizing possible clients. During recent years the practice of raising new capital by "Stock Exchange introductions" has grown considerably in London: stockbrokers recommend new shares as good investments to their clients.

Money seeking investment is termed "free capital." The rate obtainable on free capital varies with the risk of default and the period for which the loan is made. The rate which a borrower of good standing would have to pay to obtain a particular kind of long-term loan is often indicated by the current price, and therefore the percentage yield, of similar fixed-interest securities on the Stock Exchange. Lenders have the alternative of purchasing existing securities (whether they yield a fixed or a variable return) or subscribing to "new issues."

(6) Paper Titles

These fall into two broad classes: those yielding a fixed income and those yielding a fluctuating return. Bills of exchange and Treasury bills, which we discuss later, represent short-term loans and logically fall within the former class. So do mortgages, which give lenders a claim on real estate if the borrower fails to meet his obligations. Loans raised by Governments and similar bodies, and debentures issued by companies, also yield "fixed interest": that is to say, the borrower undertakes to pay a fixed money income at regular intervals to the lenders. Ordinary stock and shares, issued by companies, yield "dividends" which fluctuate with the profits of the company. There are also hybrids, such as participating preference shares whose holders receive a fixed income plus something extra when profits are good. The main British market for stocks and shares—often called "securities"—is the London Stock Exchange.

(7) Rights

Payments are made for various rights. Thus one firm may make a periodical payment to another for permission to use a process of which the latter has a legal monopoly granted "by patent," and when a business changes hands the purchaser may pay the former owner a lump sum for his "goodwill": that is, for the right of trading as his recognized successor. Again, a man may purchase an "option" giving him the right to buy something, if he wishes, on or before some specified future date at the price stated in the "option."

(8) Other Currencies

Different countries have different currencies. Thus French francs, for example, can be purchased with English money. Usually the purchaser does not buy actual French coins or notes, but a balance in a bank in France which enables him to pay a debt expressed in francs. The price at which one currency can be bought with another is called "the rate of exchange" between them.

The London market in foreign exchange consists of the foreign departments of the banks, independent dealers, who often act as agents for foreign banks, and foreign exchange brokers, who deal solely on commission, bringing sellers and buyers into touch with one another, and not at all on their own account. The banks act mainly on behalf of their customers.

The market is practically perfect. Nearly all the business is carried on by telephone. Dealers and brokers often have private wires to their most important clients. A broker with a client wishing, say, to sell a certain number of dollars, will telephone various possible buyers until he finds one who will pay a rate which his client will accept. Telephone calls to Paris and other continental centres go on all day, and a good deal of business is carried out under instructions received by cable from New York and other distant centres. We may add that telephone bells do not ring in a foreign exchange office—if they did, the task of the operators would not be enviable. Two little glass discs are fixed in the switchboard under each of the names of the firms with which the dealer is in frequent communication. A red light or green light indicates that the connection has been made.

We have seen that the rationale of an economic system is to produce consumers' goods, and that the demand for other goods and services is, logically, "derived" from the demand for consumers' goods. The remaining chapters of Book I consider, at some length, the demand for consumers' goods, taking the supply of them more or less for granted. The influences affecting supply are discussed in Books II and III.

CHAPTER III
DEMAND

1. THE MEANING OF DEMAND

THE demand for anything, at a given price, is the amount of it which will be bought per unit of time at that price. Demand means always demand *at a price* ; the term has no significance unless a price is stated or implied. The bare statement that so many thousand motor cars a year or so many million tons of coal a year are demanded in Great Britain may be intended to mean that for some years the prices of motor cars and coal have been fairly steady and that every year the volume of sales in Great Britain has been very near the figure named. But such a statement, taken literally, does not make sense. For the volume of sales—that is, the demand—would be different if the prices were different. There is no doubt that if the prices of motor cars could be reduced enough twice as many would be sold and that if their prices went high enough their sales would be halved. The amount bought of anything will vary, and may vary considerably, with its price; in other words, the demand at one price is different from the demand at another price.

Clearly, demand must mean demand per unit of time: per year or per month or per week or per day. For purposes of illustration we shall take the week as the unit, since most workers are paid by the week and most housewives, therefore, plan their expenditure upon a weekly basis.

Demand, it will be noted, is not the same as desire or need. Doubtless many people who cannot afford a motor car would like one, and doubtless many children need more milk than they get, but unless desire or need is backed up by ability and willingness to pay it does not affect the volume of sales. The demand for a thing at a given price is the amount of it which would in fact be bought at that price.

2. DEMAND SCHEDULES AND DEMAND CURVES

A full account of the demand, or perhaps we can say the state of demand or the conditions of demand, for any good in a given market at a given time should state what the (weekly) volume of sales would be at each of a series of prices. Such an account, taking the form of a tabular statement, is known as a demand schedule.

The demand for a thing depends upon many influences. Thus the demand for a consumers' good depends upon the numbers of the consuming population, their money incomes, their tastes, and the prices of competing goods, as well as upon the price of the good itself. A demand schedule is drawn up on the assumption that all these other influences remain unchanged. It thus attempts to isolate the influence exerted by the price of the good upon the amount of it sold: to show the amount sold as a "function" of the price of the good.

We give below, by way of illustration, a portion of an imaginary demand schedule. We may suppose it to relate to the weekly demand for butter, sold retail, in Great Britain. In fact there are different varieties and grades of butter, as of most so-called "commodities," selling at different prices, but we shall suppose that the butter, or grade of butter, to which our figures refer is homogeneous. We shall also suppose that the market is perfect and that transport costs may be ignored. We give only a part of the demand schedule, partly because a complete schedule, showing the amount which would be bought at every possible price from zero up to the price at which sales fell to nil, would be far too long to reproduce, and partly because a price is unlikely to change very much in the near future if the other influences governing demand remain the same, so that as a rule only that part of the demand schedule in the neighbourhood of the ruling price is of practical significance.

At a price of

d.					
15	per lb.	10	million lb.	per week	would be demanded
14	”	13	”	”	”
13	”	14	”	”	”
12	”	17	”	”	”
11	”	20	”	”	”
10	”	21	”	”	”
9	”	22	”	”	”

The total consumers' outlay per week on butter—that is, the weekly amount of money spent by purchasers and received by sellers in exchange for butter—can readily be found by multiplying the price per unit by the number of units which would be bought at that price. Thus our schedule shows that the weekly consumers' outlay at a price of 15d. per lb. would be 150 million pence; at 14d. per lb. it would be 182 million pence; at 13d. per lb. it would be 182 million pence; at 12d. per lb. it would be 204 million pence; at 11d. per lb. it would be 220 million pence; at 10d. per lb. it would be 210 million pence; and at 9d. per lb. it would be 198 million pence.

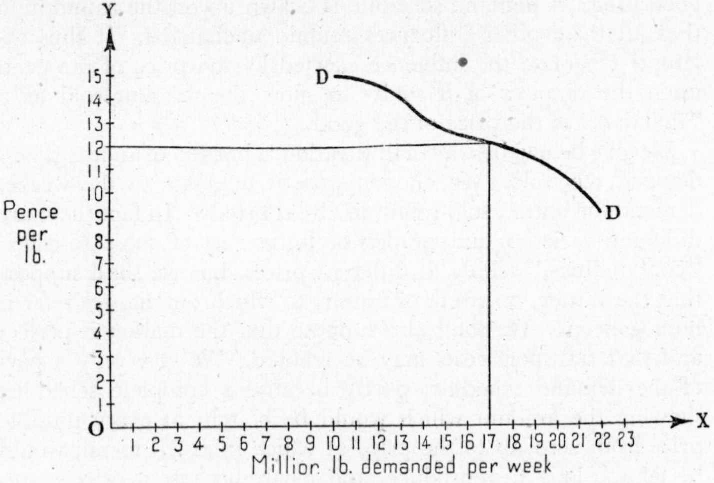

FIG. 1

The total amount of money which would be spent per week at any price appears as a rectangular area; thus the rectangle shown represents 12 × 17 million pence = 204 million pence (per week).

Our demand schedule consists of seven statements. Each of these statements can be represented by a point in a system of rectangular co-ordinates. It is usual to measure amounts demanded (per week) along the horizontal axis *OX* and the price per unit up the vertical axis *OY*. A point which is at a height of 12(d.) above *O* on our vertical scale and is 17 (million lb. per week) to the right of *O* on our horizontal scale means that at a price of 12d. per lb. 17 million lb. a week would be demanded. We can reasonably assume continuity. For example, we can assume that if 21 million lb. a week would be demanded at 10d. a lb. and 22 million at 9d. a lb., then some intermediate amount, greater than 21 million but less than 22 million, would be demanded at 9½d. a lb., and so on. On this assumption of continuity we can join together the various points to form (a portion of) a "demand curve."

3. THE DIFFICULTY OF ESTIMATING ACTUAL DEMAND SCHEDULES

It is easy to make up an imaginary demand schedule as we have just done for purposes of illustration. But it is by no means easy to make a good estimate of what the demand schedule for a particular good or service actually is.

At any given time a particular commodity has a certain price, and at that price a certain number of units are bought every day or every week. The problem is to discover how many units would be bought if the price were different. This problem cannot be solved merely by collecting statistics of what has happened in the past. It may be, for example, that three years ago the price of the commodity was 10 per cent higher than at present and the volume of sales was 30 per cent less than at present. It does not follow, however, that if the price were raised now by 10 per cent the volume of sales would be reduced by 30 per cent. For the other influences governing the demand for this commodity are probably different, and may be very different, to-day from what they were three years ago. For instance, during periods of prosperity both the prices and the sales of many commodities are greater than during times of depression. But at any given moment, whether times are good or bad, a rise in price will usually diminish the volume of sales. Statistics of prices and sales in the past can often throw some light upon the present state of demand, but they should be used with great caution, and full allowance should be made for differences in such factors as the size of the consuming population, their money incomes, their tastes, the state of trade, and the prices of other commodities, at different times. The best estimate of the state of demand can often be made by somebody in close touch with actual or potential purchasers who is aware of the alternatives open to them and can therefore make a good guess as to how they would respond to a given increase or reduction in price.

It is often in the interest of certain business men, Governments, and others to make a good guess at the prevailing state of demand for some particular commodity. Every seller who is in a monopolistic position, in that he can fix his own prices, is confronted with this problem. Whether the monopolist, in this sense, is an association of producers controlling the supply of a commodity such as tin or tea, or the manufacturer of a branded article, or merely the proprietor of a local cinema, he must be able to form a good estimate of the state of demand in order to know which price will give him the greatest profits. A Chancellor of the Exchequer, in search of revenue, should form some estimate of the state of demand for a commodity on which he is intending to impose a new tax or to increase the existing one. For the yield of the tax will vary with the volume of sales, and the rise in price due to the tax may reduce the volume of sales. Some years ago a British Chancellor of the Exchequer increased the rate of tax on sparkling wines. This led to an increase in their price, and their sales fell off so much that the revenue yielded was less than it had been formerly, when the rate of tax was lower. In the next Budget the tax on them was reduced to its former level. Again, the makers of, say, agricultural machinery sold mainly to wheat-farmers will find it to their advantage to make an estimate of the state of demand for wheat. For instance, an unusually large harvest may reduce the price of wheat so much that the total amount of money received by wheat-farmers is considerably less than usual, causing their orders for machinery to fall off.

Our task, however, is not to estimate the actual demand schedule, at the moment of writing, for any particular commodity, but to give a general account of how prices are formed. For that purpose we need a clear idea of the nature of a demand schedule. Each statement made in the demand schedule, and represented by a point on the demand curve, refers to a different hypothesis. If the price of butter were 13d. a lb., 14 million lb. a week would be bought. If, alternatively, the price were 11d. a lb., 20 million lb. a week would be bought, and so on. In fact, of course, there can be only one price at any one time. The actual price is, let us say, 12d. a lb. and 17 million lb. a week are bought. The demand schedule shows the state of demand, or the conditions of demand, at the moment. If the price were reduced to 11d. a lb., sales would expand to 20 million lb. a week. But this would not be a change in the state of demand. On the contrary, sales would expand to exactly 20 million lb. a week, no more and no less, only if the state of demand remained exactly the same. The demand schedule states how much would be bought at any given price. If the actual price changes, and the amount bought therefore changes also, as indicated in the demand schedule, the expansion or reduction in the volume of sales is due not to any change in the conditions of demand, which by hypothesis have remained the same, but to the change in the price actually ruling in the market.

A demand schedule, to repeat, shows how much would be bought per unit of time at any given price, provided that the other influences governing demand remain unchanged. If these other influences change, the old demand schedule ceases to be valid and must be replaced by a new one which gives a true picture of the state of demand which now exists in the market.

4. WHY MOST DEMAND CURVES SLOPE DOWNWARD

Most demand curves slope downward to the right throughout their length, although the slope may be much steeper in some parts than in others. This means that, unless something happens to change the state of demand, more will be bought at any given price than at any higher price; any rise in price will reduce the volume of sales, and any fall in price will expand the volume of sales, to a greater or less extent. We must now try to explain why this is so.

The total weekly sale of a consumers' good such as butter is composed of numerous sales of different amounts to different consumers. If the other influences governing the demand for butter remained the same, some consumers would buy more butter if its price per pound were lower and some would buy less butter if its price per pound were higher. We can illustrate this by showing how each of six consumers, A, B, C, D, E, F, might respond to changes in price.

Price per lb. d.	Amount per week bought by A	B	C	D (lb.)	E	F	Total lb.
15	2	Nil	¼	3	¾	1	7
14	2	Nil	¼	3¼	1	1½	8
13	2	½	¼	3½	1¼	1½	9
12	2	½	¼	3½	1¼	1¾	9¼
11	2	½	½	4	1¼	2	10¼
10	2	1	½	4½	1¼	2	11¼
9	2	1	¾	4¾	2	2	12½

At a lower price, some customers (like A) might buy no more than before, but some who bought none before (like B at a price of 14d. or over) would buy a little and others would increase the amount they purchased. In order to explain why total sales would be greater at a lower price we must consider the behaviour of an individual consumer, and the reasons for it.

We assume that our consumer has a fixed weekly sum of money to spend. (If money incomes changed, the state of demand would change.) He, or more probably she, must somehow decide in what way to spend this weekly sum. The more money he spends on butter the less is available for other goods. Hence his expenditure on butter can be said to reflect his *scale of preferences* as between butter and other goods.

If we knew a person's scale of preferences as between different consumers' goods, we could predict exactly how he would distribute a given weekly expenditure among different goods, provided that we knew the price of each good. His scale of preferences is the quantitative expression of his tastes.

The reader probably feels that the assumption that every consumer has a definite scale of preferences is not realistic. Let us consider some possible objections which may be urged against it.

It may be said that a consumer's purchases will vary with all kinds of circumstances, such as the climate or his state of health or the extent to which different goods are advertised. This is true. But we are regarding such a change as a change in his "tastes." If the tastes of consumers change, the old demand schedule no longer applies. We are considering why a given demand schedule takes the form that it does.

It may be said that even if a man's tastes remain unchanged he will not order a dinner exactly similar to the one he had yesterday. All this means is that we must consider a period sufficiently long to enable him to satisfy his desire for variety in such matters as diet.

It may be said that part of his weekly expenditure will already be "earmarked" owing to decisions he has made in the past. For example, he may have contracted to pay a certain weekly sum as the rent of his house. But he is free to spend the rest of his money as he pleases, and if, owing to changes in other prices, he wishes to move into a more expensive or a less expensive house, the matter can often be arranged: at the worst, he must wait until his lease expires.

It may be said that some persons buy on behalf of others. Thus housewives buy food for their families, parents buy clothes and other goods for their children, and people may buy some goods to give them as presents to others. But this does not in the least affect our argument. In order to explain the formation of prices we do not need to delve into the motives of purchasers. We need know only how they will distribute their expenditure when confronted with any given set of prices.

It may be said that few persons are aware of more than a portion of their scale of preferences. It is improbable, for example, that many housewives have reflected upon how much butter they would buy per week if its price fell to 1d. a lb. or rose to 5s. a lb., for there is no need to consider possibilities unlikely to arise. For that very reason we have used only a part of a demand schedule for purposes of illustration. But we must point out that our assumption is that a purchaser acts *as if* he had a definite scale of preferences. It is just conceivable that a person might not be consciously aware of his tastes. Nevertheless, if he behaved consistently we could construct the relevant part of his scale of preferences by observing his actions.

The above objections to our assumption, therefore, carry little or no weight. If it could be proved that most people act irrationally, in that they spend carelessly and impulsively, following no kind of plan or scheme, whether conscious or unconscious, this would be a valid objection to our assumption. But in fact most people do not behave like this. They cannot afford to do so. Their money incomes are so limited, relatively to their desires, that they are constrained to weigh alternatives and to think before they spend in order "to make the money go as far as possible."

Let us therefore consider a typical "rational" consumer, planning his expenditure. Suppose that he, or she, is careful enough to think about the pennies as well as the shillings. Given the prices ruling in the market, his problem is to distribute his expenditure among different goods in such a way as "to get the most out of it" from the standpoint of his own scale of preferences. He will try to purchase that assortment of goods which he most prefers, out of all the possible assortments which he could buy with the same money. If he succeeds, he will have arranged his expenditure in such a way that he would not willingly have spent a penny more on one good and a penny less on another.

Another way of expressing this is to say that he tries to get as much utility as possible from his weekly expenditure. The word "utility" has no moral significance. It may be that he would obtain more nourishment from his expenditure on food if he bought more of some foodstuffs and less of others; it may be that he would be more healthy if he spent more on food or exercise and less on clothes or amusements; it may be that he would be more efficient if he spent less on alcohol. But in order to understand the world as it is, we must study how people in fact behave and not how we think they ought to behave. To say that one assortment of goods gives him more utility than another means nothing more nor less than that he prefers the former assortment to the latter.[1]

We must now introduce the important conception of the margin. If our consumer succeeds in distributing the limited amount of money which he has to spend in the way he most prefers, the marginal utility to him of a pennyworth of any good which he buys will equal the marginal utility to him of a pennyworth of any other good that he buys. If we take a penny as our unit, and he spends 1s. a week on butter, the marginal utility to him of a pennyworth of butter is the addition made to his total utility by consuming 12 pennyworth of butter a week instead of 11 pennyworth. We can say, speaking loosely, that it is the extra utility yielded by the last penny per week which he spends on butter: this statement is a little loose in that any pennyworth of butter is indistinguishable from any other pennyworth. If he could get more utility by spending a penny less a week on butter (which could of course be done by purchasing butter at slightly less frequent intervals) and a penny more on, say, tea, he has not solved his problem correctly, and, realizing this, he will tend to spend more on tea and less on butter. If he does maximize his utility, he will not wish to transfer a penny per

[1] Of course a man's decisions as to what he buys depend on his estimates of what the relative utilities of different goods will be to him. He may anticipate wrongly. For example, he may buy a theatre ticket and be disappointed with the play. But such a divergence between expected utility and utility obtained is unlikely with goods which he habitually buys.

week from any one good to any other. For him, that is, the marginal utility of all the goods that he buys (taking a pennyworth as the unit) will be equal.

Now we must consider the so-called "Law" of Diminishing Marginal Utility. This is a generalization arrived at by introspection and by observing how people behave. It states that if a consumer, with given tastes, increases his (weekly) consumption of one commodity only, the marginal utility to him of that commodity will fall relatively to the marginal utility of other commodities. And this will be still more marked if, in order to increase his consumption of that commodity, he reduces his consumption of other commodities, for this will make their marginal utility to him rise relatively to that of the commodity in question. We state the Law in this lengthy way to avoid implying that absolute utility can be measured. The utility yielded by one good is always relative to the utilities yielded by other goods. A consumer can and does compare utilities—that is, the utilities of different goods to himself—although there is no way of measuring absolute utility.

In so far as most persons' scales of preferences do conform to this Law, we have an explanation of why most demand curves slope downward. A given consumer, let us say, has equated the marginal utility of butter with that of the other goods that he buys. As things are, he will not buy more butter per week, for in order to do so he would have to spend less on something else, and he values the something else which he would have to give up more highly than the extra butter which he would acquire. But if the price of butter falls, the situation is altered. He can now get more butter for each penny than before. He will therefore increase the amount of butter that he buys, thus reducing its marginal utility to him, until the marginal utility to him of the new enlarged "pennyworth" of butter is the same as that of a pennyworth of anything else. Thus a fall in the price of a commodity will usually cause more of it to be sold. Whether the total consumers' outlay on the commodity will be greater or less than before is another matter.

This concept of marginal utility, together with the concept of opportunity-cost, explains why the relative values of different goods are what they are. The preferences of each consumer determine how much of each good he will buy with any given constellation of prices. He will distribute his expenditure in such a way that the marginal utility to him of a pennyworth of one good is equal to that of a pennyworth of any other good that he buys. At the same time, the price of each good will be just low enough to sell the whole amount coming forward for sale week by week or year by year. And the amount of any good coming forward for sale depends on the means of production available and their alternative uses. If any means, or factor, of production can produce something more valuable by moving into another line it will tend to do so. Thus an increase in the amount of one good coming forward for sale will lower its relative marginal utility, assuming that all of it is sold, and will therefore lower its value relatively to other goods. And a change in tastes away from one good will similarly lower its relative marginal utility and therefore its relative value, if the supply remains the same.

It must be remembered that marginal, and not total, utility varies with relative prices. Suppose, for example, that a consumer spends 1s. per week upon bread and 1s. per week upon periodicals. This does not mean that the total utility which he derives from the periodicals is equal to the total utility which he derives from the bread. If he had to choose, he might prefer, say, half the bread to all the periodicals. But the last penny which he spends on periodicals yields him as much extra utility as the last penny which he spends on bread; if it were not so, he would spend more on bread and less on periodicals until each yielded him the same marginal utility. This concept of the margin helps to explain what has sometimes been called "the paradox of value." Bread, for example, is said to be more "useful" than jewellery: why, then, is it so much cheaper? We must look at the margin. A purchaser of jewellery may be spending so much already on food, dress, and other things, that he—or she—would rather spend, say, £10 a year on jewellery than use some of that £10 to buy *additional* food, dress, and so on. If he had to decide between going completely without food and going completely without jewellery, he would doubtless choose the latter. But this is not the kind of choice which in fact presents itself. People have to choose between a little more of this and a little less of that or a little more of that and a little less of this. They tend to equate marginal, and not total, utilities.

The unit of a commodity, in this connection, must always be the amount which can be bought for a given unit of money, such as a penny. To say that a consumer equalizes the marginal utility to him of bread and of milk does not mean that the last loaf of bread per week yields him the same additional utility as the last pint of milk per week. A loaf and a pint are arbitrary physical units. To make a comparison, we must measure in terms of the limited "resource" to be distributed among different uses; in this case the limited resource is money, the different uses are different goods, and the appropriate unit is the pennyworth.

The prices ruling on the market are the same for all consumers. Each consumer adjusts his purchases according to his own scale of preferences. The differences in the tastes of different consumers show themselves, therefore, not in the payment of different prices per unit but in the purchase of different amounts.

5. EXCEPTIONAL DEMAND CURVES

Some demand curves slope upward, indicating that more units would be bought at a higher price per unit, over part of their length. Of course, no demand curve slopes upward all the way —this would mean that the amount of money spent on the good would be greater, approaching infinity, if its price were higher.

Sometimes people become more anxious to buy a commodity when its price has risen because they think its price will rise still further. This applies particularly to securities of the type dealt in on the Stock Exchange. But such a phenomenon is best regarded as a change in the state of demand due to the change in people's expectations and not as a stable state of demand represented by an upward-sloping demand curve.

Some wealthy consumers may buy some goods, such as certain precious stones, mainly because they have a high price, thus enabling their possessors to display their wealth. Such consumers may buy more of such goods at a higher price per unit. But as a rule the market demand curve for such goods, representing the combined demand of all consumers, will slope downward.

It may occasionally happen, however, that owing to the ignorance of consumers the volume of sales will be greater if the price charged is higher. Thus it is said that a certain book of photographs was published just before the war of 1914 at

10s. 6d. and sold very few copies. After the war, it was re-issued at a price of £3 3s. and sold very well. Presumably consumers thought that a book of this kind which costs £3 3s. must be worth having. But such cases are infrequent.

The most important cases of exceptional demand curves are provided by commodities such as bread and potatoes. Over a certain range of prices it is quite likely that more bread or potatoes would be bought at a higher price.

Bread satisfies hunger and provides energy more cheaply, containing more calories per pennyworth, than almost any type of foodstuff commonly consumed in the Western world. Suppose that, following a rise in its cost of production, the price of bread were to rise. If the prices of other goods remained the same, and money incomes remained the same, consumers would be worse off than before: their real incomes would have fallen. A consumer would find that the weekly sum of money which he usually allotted to foodstuffs, rather than to rent or other things, would buy less than before owing to the rise in the price of bread. If he bought as much of everything else as before, therefore spending only the same amount of money as before on bread, he would be getting a smaller quantity of bread than before, and if he were very poor he and his family might really go hungry, getting too little food to satisfy their bare physical needs. Confronted with this situation, a very poor consumer might well readjust the distribution of his expenditure, cutting down on some other things, including more appetizing but less nourishing foodstuffs, in order not merely to maintain but actually to increase the quantity of bread he bought per week. That this might actually happen is suggested by the fact that a poor family often spends less on bread when its money income increases, prices remaining the same. Thus the demand curve for two or three commodities such as bread may slope upward for part of its length.

6. ELASTICITY OF DEMAND

An important economic concept is that of elasticity of demand. This concept relates to the effect of a small change in price upon the amount demanded.

The total amount of money which would be spent upon a commodity at a given price may be termed the total outlay upon the commodity at that price. If two prices, close to one another, would induce consumers as a whole to make the same total outlay, the elasticity of demand between those two prices is said to be equal to unity. Thus our illustrative demand schedule has an elasticity equal to unity between 14d. and 13d., the total outlay remaining constant at 182 million pence.

If the total outlay is greater at the lower price, the elasticity of demand is greater than unity between the two prices. This is so between 13d. and 12d., the total outlay being 182 million pence at 13d. and 204 million pence at 12d.

If the total outlay is greater at the higher price, elasticity of demand is less than unity between the two prices. This is so between 11d. and 10d., the total outlay being 220 million pence at 11d. and 210 million pence at 10d.

Thus elasticity of demand may be different, and usually is different, in different parts of a demand schedule. The demand for any commodity will have an elasticity less than unity beyond a certain point, since consumers will not be prepared to spend more than a certain proportion of their incomes upon any one commodity, owing to the pressure of other wants; but of course the total outlay upon many commodities is in fact well below such a maximum.

Fig. 1 shows the relation between the price per unit and the quantity bought. Another way of representing the same data is to show the relation between the total outlay and the amount bought. This is done, for our illustrative demand schedule, in Fig. 2. Here the price per unit is not shown directly. It can be obtained by dividing the total outlay by the number of units demanded. For example, if OM units are bought, the total outlay will be OR (pence) and the price (per lb.) will be $\frac{OR}{OM}$ (pence). Clearly such a diagram enables us to see at a glance whether the elasticity of demand at any point is greater or less than unity. If the curve is rising (from left to right), it is greater than unity; if the curve is falling, it is less than unity; if the curve is horizontal, it is equal to unity.

Given the numbers and incomes and tastes of consumers, the elasticity of demand for a commodity in the neighbourhood of a particular price depends upon the possibilities (as conceived by consumers) of substituting it for other commodities, and conversely. Thus the demand for beef may be very elastic over a certain range because a small fall in its price may lead to a considerable substitution of beef for other meat. The demand for orchids or diamonds may be very inelastic over a certain range if buyers do not regard other jewels or flowers as close substitutes.

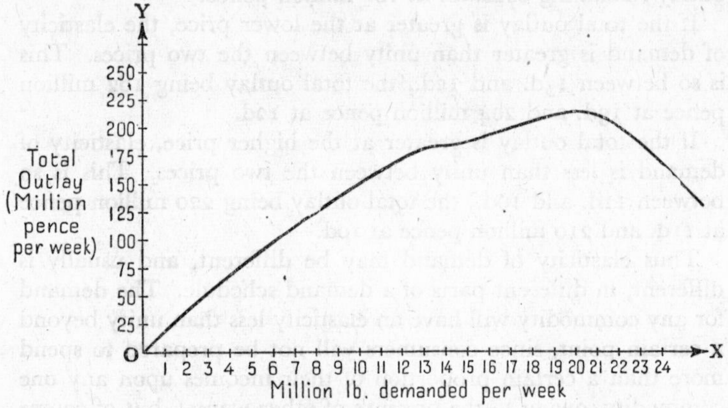

FIG. 2

This shows that the notion that the demand for luxuries is elastic and that for necessaries inelastic is not valid.

A further point is that many commodities are capable of a variety of uses. Thus the demand for coal is the sum of the demands of blast furnaces, railways, ships, gas-works, electricity-works, factories, homes, and so on. A fall in the price of such a commodity may cause a large expansion in the amount demanded for some particular use. To revert to butter, over a certain range a fall in its price might considerably expand the demand for butter for cooking purposes. This, however, would take place at the expense of such fats as lard and margarine: cases of this kind form no exception to our generalization that elasticity of demand depends upon the possibilities of substitution.

NOTE

The elasticity of demand at any price can be measured by the percentage increase in the amount demanded which would result from a fall of 1 per cent in that price; or, more generally, by the percentage increase in the amount demanded divided by the (small) percentage fall in the price.[1] For example, if a fall of 1 per cent in price expands sales from 1000 to 1020, or from 2000 to 2040, per unit of time, the elasticity of demand at that price is 2; if a fall of 2 per cent in price expands sales from 1000 to 1010, the elasticity of demand at that price is ½; if a fall of ½ per cent in price expands sales from 50 to 55, the elasticity of demand at that price is 20.

The result obtained by applying this method may be different from that obtained by noting the change in total consumers' outlay. Suppose that a fall in price of 10 per cent (from 100 to 90) causes sales to expand by 10 per cent (from 100 to 110). Elasticity of demand, measured by the above method, is exactly 1. But total outlay has fallen (from 100 × 100 = 10,000 to 90 × 110 = 9900). The divergence arises because the notion relates strictly to elasticity *at a point* and not over a finite range of price.[2]

In order to show[3] how the elasticity of a demand curve at a point P can be measured, let us take another point P', on the same demand curve, just below P, and join the two points by a straight line which cuts the Y axis in t and the X axis in T.

At a price of MP the amount demanded is OM.

At a price of $M'P'$ the amount demanded is OM'.

Call PR, the fall in price, p.

Call RP' the increase in sales, q.

The elasticity of demand is the proportionate increase in the amount demanded, $\frac{q}{OM}$, divided by the proportionate fall in price, $\frac{p}{PM}$.

$$\frac{q}{OM} \div \frac{p}{PM} = \frac{q}{OM} \times \frac{PM}{p} = \frac{q}{p} \times \frac{PM}{OM}.$$

The little triangle PRP' is similar to the large triangle PMT.

Hence $\frac{q}{p} = \frac{MT}{PM}$. Hence $\frac{q}{p} \times \frac{PM}{OM} = \frac{MT}{PM} \times \frac{PM}{OM} = \frac{MT}{OM}$.

[1] We owe this concept to Marshall (*Principles of Economics*, p. 102).

[2] On this whole subject see "The Diagrammatical Representation of Elasticity of Demand," by A. P. Lerner, in *The Review of Economic Studies*, Vol. I, No. 1. He shows how this divergence can be avoided by an appropriate measure of "arc elasticity" (over a finite range of price).

[3] Adapting the proof given by Marshall in his Mathematical Appendix.

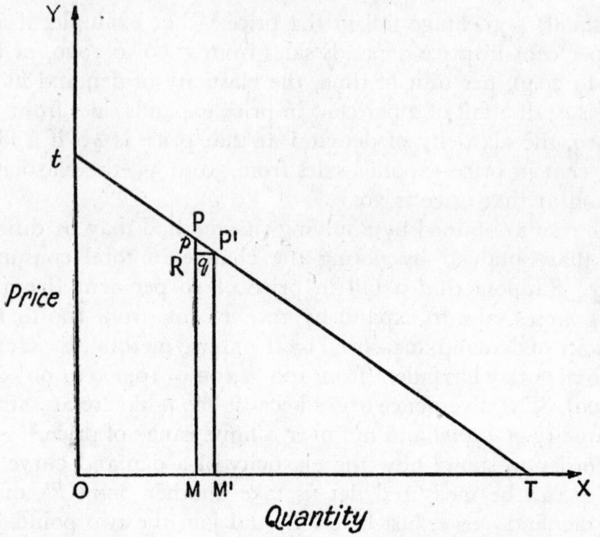

FIG. 3

When the distance between P and P' is diminished indefinitely, the two points coincide and Tt becomes the tangent to the demand curve at P.

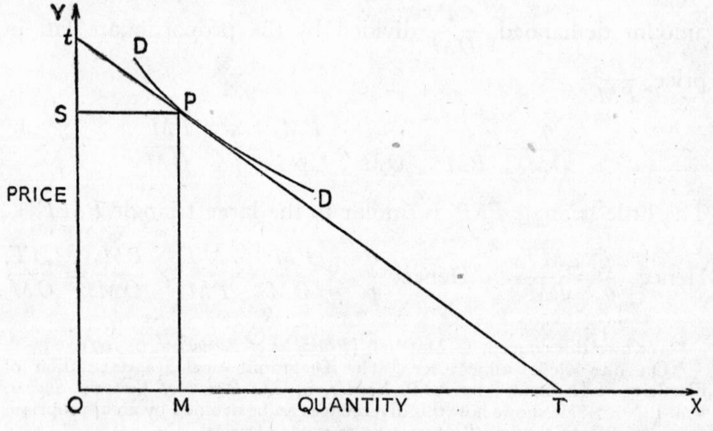

FIG. 4

The elasticity of demand at $P = \frac{MT}{OM}$ which is the same as $\frac{OS}{St}$ or $\frac{TP}{Pt}$.

Thus any straight-line demand curve tT, cutting the Y axis in t and the X axis in T, will vary in elasticity (however steep or

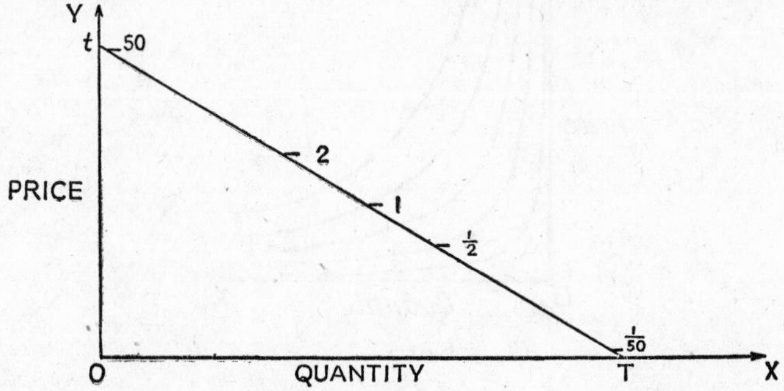

FIG. 5

gentle its slope) from infinity at t down to zero at T. One-third of the way down its elasticity will be 2; half-way down it will be 1; two-thirds of the way down it will be $\frac{1}{2}$; and so on.

Parallel demand curves will have different elasticities at the same price; for example—

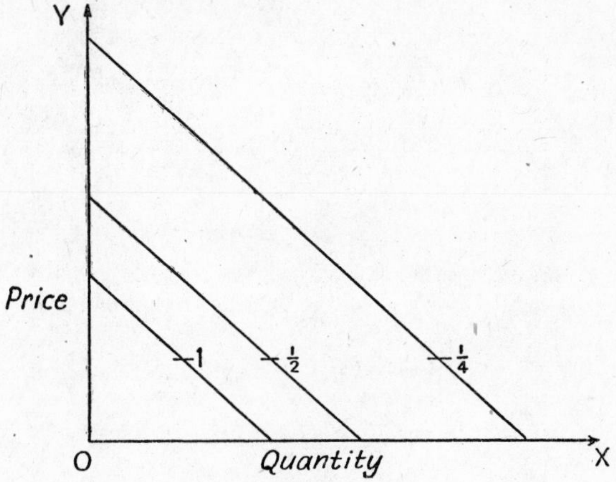

FIG. 6

If the elasticity of demand is equal to unity at any price, so that total consumers' outlay is always the same, the demand curve will be a rectangular hyperbola, such as any of the curves below.

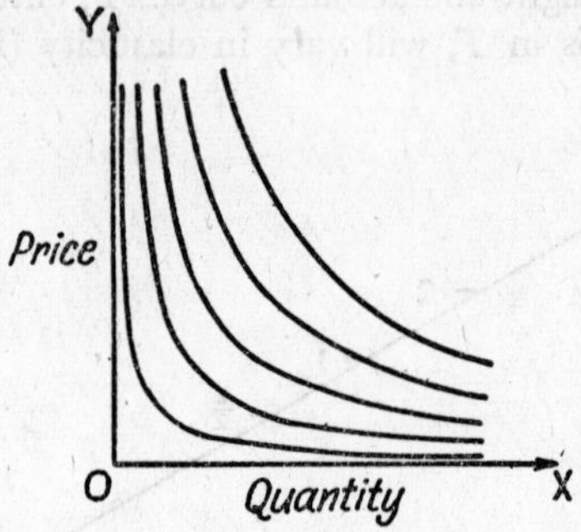

FIG. 7

CHAPTER IV
PRICE WITH A FIXED DEMAND

1. INTRODUCTION

We shall now consider how the price of anything is determined if the state of demand for it remains unchanged week after week. Since we are taking the demand as fixed and given, the price will depend on the supply: that is, on the amount of it for sale.

In ordinary speech the term "supply" may have any of several different meanings. It may mean the total stock in existence. The term is often used in this sense when the total stock cannot be increased, or can be increased by only a small percentage during the next year or two. Thus the "supply" of Cézanne pictures may mean all the pictures ever painted by Cézanne and still known to be in existence, and the world "supply" of gold may mean the total amount of gold in existence, since the annual output from the mines and rivers forms only a small percentage of that total. Again, the "supply" of anything which is currently produced may mean the normal output per unit of time. Thus it may be said that the world's supply of wheat is approximately so many million bushels a year. The term is more likely to be used in this sense if normally stocks are small, as are stocks of wheat, compared with the annual output. But "supply" may also mean the amount offered for sale per unit of time. This is the meaning which is of most use in economic analysis, and which therefore we shall adopt.

Supply in this sense means supply at a price, for more may be offered for sale at one price than at another. The state of supply, or conditions of supply, can be represented by a supply schedule, which can be shown graphically as a supply curve. We must discuss Production and the Theory of Costs before we can understand the influences which determine the quantity of any particular commodity which will be produced and offered for sale at each of a series of prices. For the present we shall take it for granted that as a rule at any given time (or so long as the other influences affecting supply remain unchanged) more would be supplied at any given price than at any lower price: that as a rule the supply curve slopes upward. The elasticity of supply is measured by the percentage increase in the amount supplied divided by the (small) percentage increase in the price. An illustrative supply schedule for butter is shown on page 58 and the corresponding supply curve is shown in Fig. 9.

2. PRICE WITH A FIXED (WEEKLY) SUPPLY

Let us suppose that a fixed amount of some commodity is produced and offered for sale every week. If the state of demand for it remains unchanged, there is no doubt what its price will be. At first there may be some small fluctuations in the price, but as the same conditions go on repeating themselves week after week the price will settle down at whatever level is just low enough to enable the whole amount to be sold each week.

Suppose, for example, that the commodity is butter and that the conditions of demand for it are those which we gave in our illustrative demand schedule. If the amount of butter coming forward for sale each week is 17 million lb., its price will be 1s. per lb. At a higher price than 1s., some butter would remain unsold each week. This would lead to a growing accumulation of unsold stocks, and, before long, sellers anxious to get rid of their stocks would reduce their prices. Nobody would have anything to gain by holding stocks unless the weekly amount of butter produced was expected to fall or the demand for it to increase; at first some sellers might think that one of these things would happen, but after a time they would realize that they had been mistaken. At a lower price than 1s., more than 17 million lb. a week would be demanded. Some would-be purchasers—prepared to pay, if necessary, more than 1s. per lb.—would be unable to buy. At first this might lead to queues of would-be purchasers lining up in front of the shops (as in Great Britain early in 1918 and in Germany during the post-war German inflation) in order to buy before the shop was sold out, but sellers would soon realize the situation and would raise their prices. The only price at which all the butter would be sold, and at which everybody could buy as much as he were prepared to pay for, would be 1s. per lb. This would be the "equilibrium" price, for it would equate the amount demanded and the amount offered for sale by restricting the (weekly) demand to the (weekly) supply available.

If the amount coming forward for sale each week were only 13 million lb., the price would settle down at 1s. 2d. per lb., for this price would be just high enough to restrict the amount demanded each week to 13 million lb.

When the weekly amount coming forward for sale is always

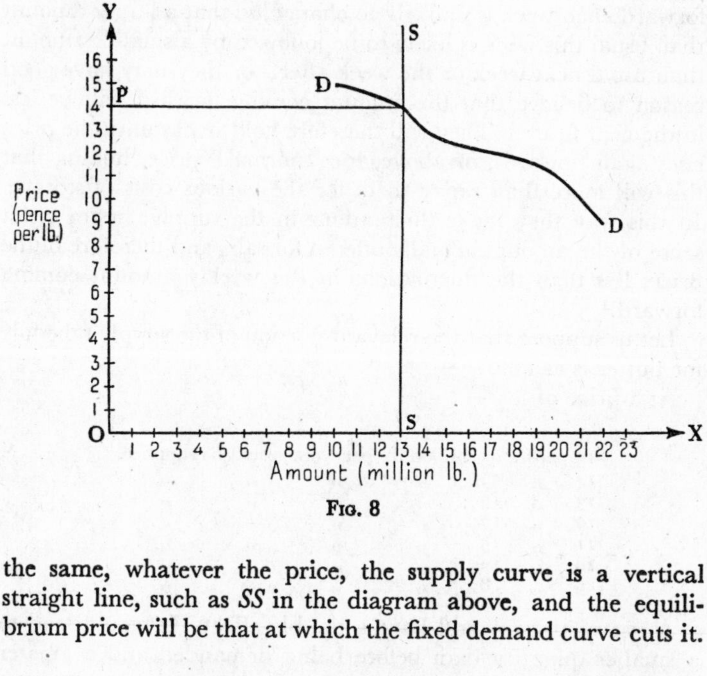

FIG. 8

the same, whatever the price, the supply curve is a vertical straight line, such as *SS* in the diagram above, and the equilibrium price will be that at which the fixed demand curve cuts it.

3. PRICE WITH A VARIABLE (WEEKLY) SUPPLY

Let us now suppose that the amount coming forward for sale is not the same every week. If nothing happens, such as a change in production costs, to cause a permanent change in the conditions of supply, variations in the weekly amount coming forward can be due only to temporary influences, such as changes in the weather. The question then arises whether the commodity can be stored without deteriorating. If, like strawberries, it cannot be kept more than a day or two without going bad, such chance variations in the amount coming forward will exercise their full effect upon the price. But if it can conveniently be stored, an increase in the amount coming forward will not reduce the price so much. After the price has been forced down some distance by the increased supplies, some sellers will think it more profitable to store their goods than to sell them at the relatively low price prevailing. They will know that the average amount coming forward each week is unlikely to change, so that a larger amount than usual this week is likely to be followed by a smaller amount than usual next week or the week after; or they may have good reason to believe that the amount coming forward will be less in the near future. They will therefore hold stocks until the price rises again towards, or above, the "normal" price, hoping that this will more than repay them for the various costs of storage. In this way they make fluctuations in the supply, in the strict sense of the amount actually offered for sale, and therefore in the price, less than the fluctuations in the weekly amount coming forward.[1]

Let us suppose that the relevant portion of the supply schedule for butter is as follows—

At a price of

d.							
15	per lb.	25	million lb.	per week	would	be supplied.
14	„	22	„	„	„	„
13	„	19	„	„	„	„
12	„	17	„	„	„	„
11	„	15	„	„	„	„
10	„	12	„	„	„	„
9	„	8	„	„	„	„

A rise in price would have a double effect. It would lead to a smaller quantity than before being demanded and a greater

[1] An illustration of this is afforded by the Meat Board of New Zealand, or indeed of any important overseas meat-exporting country. Shipments of meat from New Zealand may arrive in London at irregular intervals. It was thought that, in the past, the price of imported meat on Smithfield Market was unduly depressed when new shipments arrived and were offered for sale. The meat producers, partly for this reason, formed a Board to sell their meat for them. The Board owns premises near Smithfield, equipped with refrigerating apparatus, in which meat can be stored. When the Board thinks that the prevailing prices are too low, owing to a temporary increase of supplies, it withholds meat from sale in the hope that prices will subsequently become higher.

quantity than before being produced and offered for sale. Conversely, a fall in price would both expand the amount demanded and reduce the amount supplied. Nevertheless, if the conditions of supply and the conditions of demand both remained unchanged, the price would still settle down at 1s. per lb. For this is the equilibrium price at which the amount demanded equals the amount offered for sale week by week. It

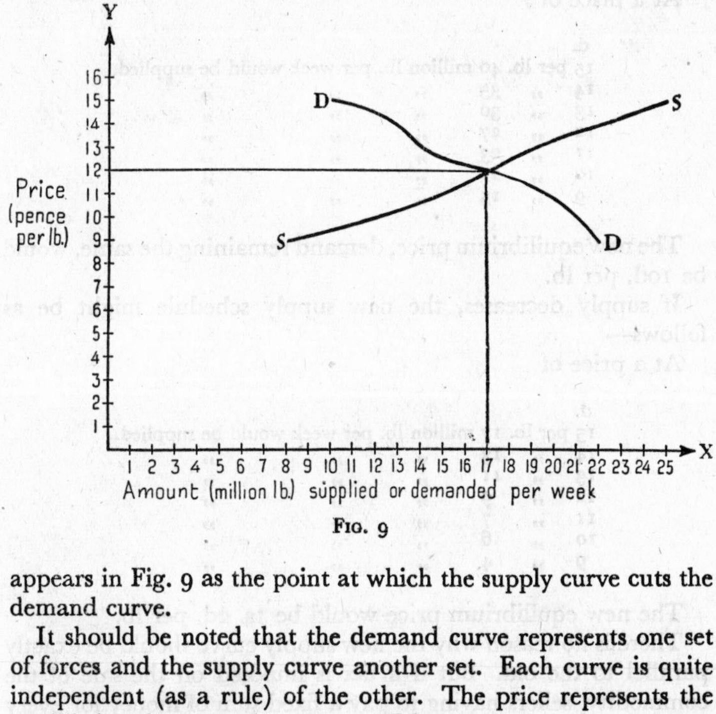

FIG. 9

appears in Fig. 9 as the point at which the supply curve cuts the demand curve.

It should be noted that the demand curve represents one set of forces and the supply curve another set. Each curve is quite independent (as a rule) of the other. The price represents the equilibrium between the two sets of forces.

If there is a change in the forces governing supply, the old supply schedule will no longer represent the prevailing conditions of supply, and must be replaced by one which does. Demand remaining the same, the new supply curve will probably cut the demand curve at a different point from the old one. That is to say, a change in the conditions of supply will probably lead to a change in the equilibrium price.

If, under the new conditions of supply, more will be offered for sale at any given price than before, this is termed "an increase of supply," and the equilibrium price will be lower than before. Conversely, if less will be offered for sale at any given price than before, this is termed "a decrease of supply" and the equilibrium price will be higher than before. For example, if supply increases, the new supply schedule might be as follows—

At a price of

d.					
15	per lb.	40	million lb.	per week	would be supplied.
14	"	35	"	"	"
13	"	30	"	"	"
12	"	27	"	"	"
11	"	23	"	"	"
10	"	21	"	"	"
9	"	15	"	"	"

The new equilibrium price, demand remaining the same, would be 10d. per lb.

If supply decreases, the new supply schedule might be as follows—

At a price of

d.					
15	per lb.	17	million lb.	per week	would be supplied.
14	"	13	"	"	"
13	"	11	"	"	"
12	"	9	"	"	"
11	"	7	"	"	"
10	"	6	"	"	"
9	"	4	"	"	"

The new equilibrium price would be 1s. 2d. per lb.

There is no reason why the new supply curve should be exactly parallel to the old. But if a tax is imposed on the sale of the commodity, sellers having to pay a fixed sum of money for every unit they sell, this can be represented by a "new" supply curve parallel to the old. The "new" curve is simply the old one shifted to the left. Thus if sellers of butter had to pay 1d. per lb. tax, the amount which would now be supplied at a market price of 1s. 2d. per lb. would be only 19 million lb. a week, for this is the amount which would be supplied at a net price of 1s. 1d. a lb. and the market price of 1s. 2d. represents a net price to the sellers of only 1s. 1d., since they must pay 1d. of it to the Government as tax. Similarly, the amount now supplied at 1s. 1d. would be 17 million lb., for this is the amount which would be offered for sale at 1s. net per lb.; and so on. If the demand curve slopes downward, the market price will not rise above its old level by the full amount of the tax. How much it will rise depends on the elasticities of supply and demand. If demand is very elastic, the demand curve being nearly horizontal

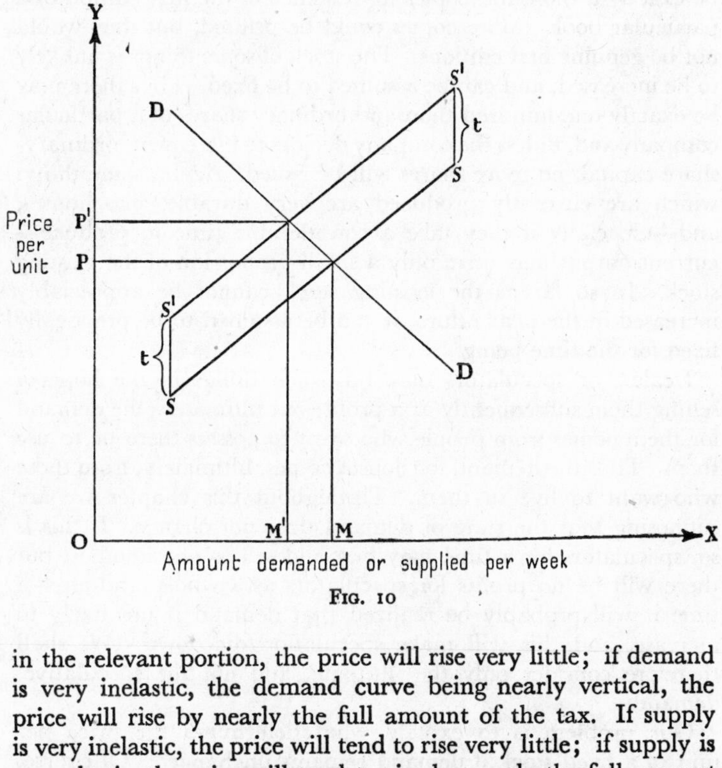

FIG. 10

in the relevant portion, the price will rise very little; if demand is very inelastic, the demand curve being nearly vertical, the price will rise by nearly the full amount of the tax. If supply is very inelastic, the price will tend to rise very little; if supply is very elastic, the price will tend to rise by nearly the full amount of the tax.

The diagram above shows how a decrease of supply, the old supply curve being *SS* and the new one *S′S′*, raises the price from *OP* to *OP′*, reducing the amount demanded and supplied from *OM* to *OM′*. It will be noted that if the change in supply is due to the imposition of a tax *t* on each unit sold, the new price *OP′* will not exceed the old price *OP* by the full amount of the tax. For convenience we have shown both the curves as straight lines.

4. PRICE WITH A FIXED STOCK

The stock of some things cannot be increased. Thus there may be exactly a thousand copies in existence of the first edition of a particular book. More copies could be printed, but they would not be genuine first editions. The stock of some things is unlikely to be increased, and can be assumed to be fixed. Thus there may be exactly one hundred thousand ordinary shares of a particular company and, unless the company decides to increase its ordinary-share capital, no more shares will be issued. Again, some things which are currently produced are very durable, like houses, and—especially if they take a considerable time to produce—current output may form only a small proportion of the existing stock. In so far as the existing stock cannot be appreciably increased in the near future, it can be assumed to be practically fixed for the time being.

Dealers or speculators may buy such things in the hope of selling them subsequently at a profit, but ultimately the demand for them comes from people who want to possess them or to use them. Thus the demand for houses comes, ultimately, from those who want to live in them. Throughout this chapter we are supposing that the state of demand does not change. If this is so, speculators for a time may buy and sell to one another, but there will be no profits for speculators as a whole, and after a time it will probably be realized that demand is not likely to increase, and this will make speculation die down. We shall therefore consider only the ultimate, and not the speculative, demand.

Our problem is to explain what determines the price per unit of a fixed stock if demand remains unchanged. Of course, if the different units are not homogeneous, they may have different prices. One house may sell or rent for less than another which is larger or more attractive or better situated; the two "houses" are really different commodities. But if different houses are fairly close substitutes, so that their prices tend to rise and fall together, our explanation will apply to what may be termed "the general level" of house prices. We shall take as our illustration the thousand copies of the first edition of a particular book, assuming that any copy is indistinguishable from any other and that the market is practically perfect.

Under these conditions there will be only one price for a copy of this first edition. But after a time no transactions will take place. Everybody who would be prepared to sell at that price will already have sold; everybody who would be prepared to buy at that price will already have bought; and, by hypothesis, the state of demand remains unchanged. The "price" would thus be the price which any possessor of a copy could get if he chose to sell it.

Every owner of a copy is a potential seller, but there is a price below which he will not sell. This price may be called his "reserve" price. If his reserve price were £100, and his copy were put up to auction and the highest bid made was £99 he himself would bid £99 10s. rather than part with his copy. Of course, different owners have different reserve prices, and if a man owns several copies he might be prepared to sell one copy more cheaply than a second, and so on.

Now let us go back to the time when transactions in copies were taking place, before the price settled down. Each owner of a copy at that time had his reserve price. Assuming that he would have been prepared to sell at his reserve price, we could construct a supply schedule from these reserve prices. Suppose that the highest reserve price is that of A, say £200; that the next highest is that of B, say £190; that the next highest is that of C, who wants at least £185; and so on. Suppose that the lowest price is that of Z, who wants only £50; the next lowest is that of Y, who wants only £55; and so on. The supply schedule would show that at a price of £50 one copy (that of Z) would be offered for sale, at a price of £55 two copies (those of Z and Y), and so on, concluding by stating that at £185 998 copies, at £190 999 copies, and at £200 the whole thousand copies, would be offered for sale.

Against this supply schedule we could set a demand schedule made up of the demands of all those who did not possess copies or who wish to buy additional copies. The equilibrium price could be shown on a diagram as the point at which the supply curve cuts the demand curve.

Another way of discovering the equilibrium price would be to lump together the reserve prices of the various owners and the demand prices of the would-be purchasers to form a combined demand schedule. For the reserve price of a potential seller (or, more strictly, a fraction below it) can be regarded as the price at which he "demands" his own copy.

Suppose, for example, that the would-be buyer with the highest demand price is A′, who would give £200, the next highest

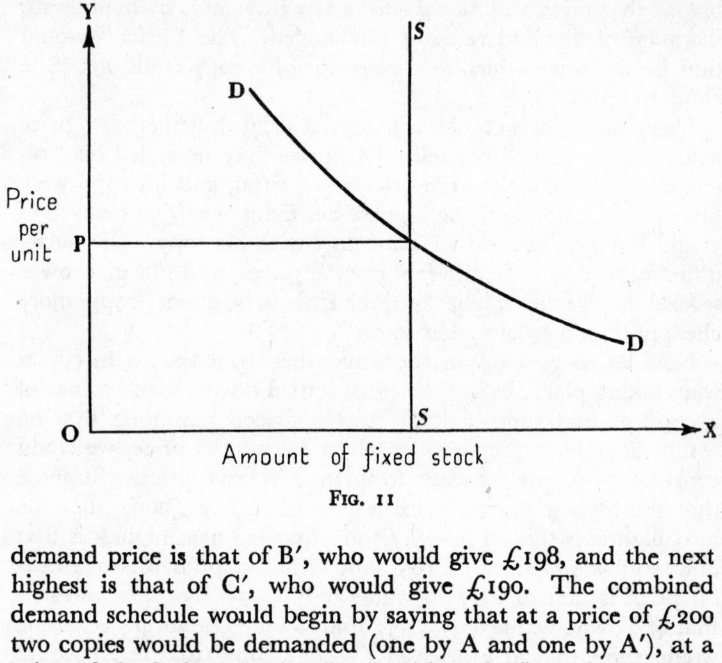

FIG. 11

demand price is that of B′, who would give £198, and the next highest is that of C′, who would give £190. The combined demand schedule would begin by saying that at a price of £200 two copies would be demanded (one by A and one by A′), at a price of £198 three copies (by A, A′, and B′), and at a price £190 five copies (by A, A′, B′, C′ and B). But there is no reason why any of these should pay such a high price, for there are plenty of sellers willing to sell for less. If the market is perfect, the price will settle down at the level just low enough to enable all the thousand copies to find permanent homes. This is shown in the above diagram. The vertical line *SS* represents the fixed stock of a thousand copies. The curve *DD* represents the combined demand schedule. The price, *OP*, will be that at which *DD* cuts *SS*. It is obvious that if the fixed stock was smaller, the equilibrium price would be higher, and that if the fixed stock was greater, the equilibrium price would be lower. Given the state of demand, the price will depend on the size of the fixed stock—diagrammatically, that is, on the distance from *O* of the vertical line *SS*.

CHAPTER V
CHANGES IN DEMAND

1. INCREASES AND DECREASES OF DEMAND

We have seen that although the state of demand for a good may remain unchanged, a fall in its price, due to an increase of supply, will probably cause the volume of sales to expand. This is sometimes termed an "extension" of demand, the term "increase" of demand being reserved for a change in the state of demand, more being bought at any given price than would have been bought before at that price. In the same way the term "contraction" of demand is employed to denote that sales fall off not because of a change in the state of demand but because of an increase in the price, and the term "decrease" of demand is reserved for a change in the state of demand, less being bought at any given price than would have been bought before at that price.

An increase or decrease of demand, in this sense, means that the conditions of demand have changed. The old demand schedule no longer gives a true picture of the state of demand and must be replaced by one which does. Instead of a movement along the existing curve—an extension or contraction—the old curve is replaced by a new one. Thus, if an increase occurred in the demand for butter, the old demand schedule, given on page 37, might be replaced by the following one—

At a price of

d.						
15	per lb.	20	million lb.	per week	would be	demanded.
14	,,	22	,,	,,	,,	,,
13	,,	25	,,	,,	,,	,,
12	,,	28	,,	,,	,,	,,
11	,,	30	,,	,,	,,	,,
10	,,	31	,,	,,	,,	,,
9	,,	32	,,	,,	,,	,,

An increase in the demand for anything would tend to raise its price; if the conditions of supply remain the same, it will raise its price. Thus if the supply schedule for butter remains as shown on page 58, the new equilibrium price, after the market had adjusted itself to the above increase in demand, would be 1s. 2d. per lb., for this is the price at which the amount coming forward for sale each week, namely 22 million lb., would equal the amount bought. In the following diagram an increase in demand is represented by a shift of the demand curve from *DD* to *D'D'*, raising the price from *OP* to *OP'*, and increasing the quantity sold from *OM* to *OM'*. A decrease in demand will of course have the opposite effect.

This chapter discusses the main influences affecting demand; it points out the main types of change likely to lead to an increase

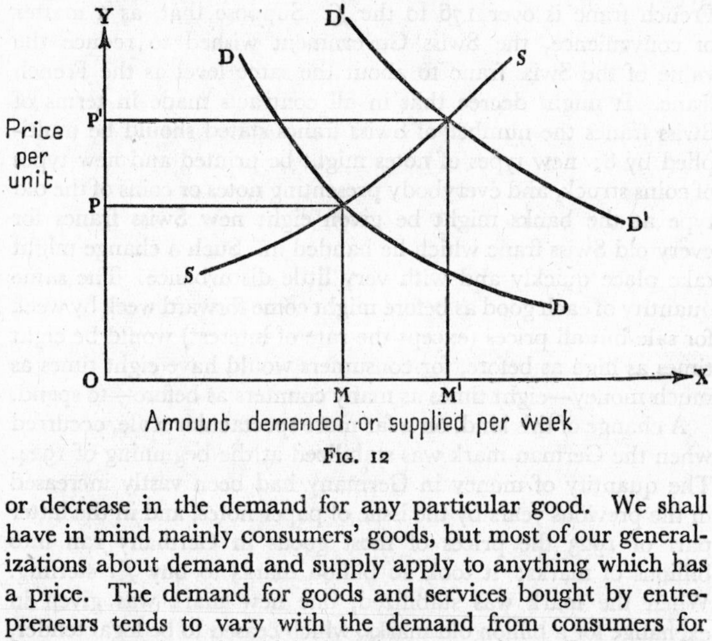

FIG. 12

or decrease in the demand for any particular good. We shall have in mind mainly consumers' goods, but most of our generalizations about demand and supply apply to anything which has a price. The demand for goods and services bought by entrepreneurs tends to vary with the demand from consumers for the consumers' goods which they help to produce. For example, a decrease in the demand for cotton clothing tends to be reflected in a decrease in the demand for raw cotton.

2. CHANGES IN THE AMOUNT OF MONEY

A change in the amount of money would usually lead to various other changes. It is unlikely that the relative prices of different goods would remain the same; and it is unlikely that the general level of prices would rise or fall in exactly the same proportion as that by which the amount of money had been increased or diminished. But we must defer our discussion of monetary changes to a much later chapter. For the present we shall regard money simply as a counter which facilitates the exchange of goods, and we shall merely compare two equilibrium situations which differ from one another only in the quantity of money available, without attempting to discuss the transition from the one situation to the other.

Let us assume that the Swiss franc is 20¾ to the £ and the French franc is over 176 to the £. Suppose that, as a matter of convenience, the Swiss Government wished to reduce the value of the Swiss franc to about the same level as the French franc. It might decree that in all contracts made in terms of Swiss francs the number of Swiss francs stated should be multiplied by 8; new types of notes might be printed and new types of coins struck, and everybody presenting notes or coins of the old type at the banks might be given eight new Swiss francs for every old Swiss franc which he handed in. Such a change might take place quickly and with very little disturbance. The same quantity of each good as before might come forward week by week for sale but all prices (except the rate of interest) would be eight times as high as before, for consumers would have eight times as much money—eight times as many counters as before—to spend.

A change of this kind, on a far more spectacular scale, occurred when the German mark was stabilized at the beginning of 1924. The quantity of money in Germany had been vastly increased in the previous years by the issue of paper notes, and in the latter part of 1923 the prices of most goods in Germany ran into billions of marks; it took 20 billion marks to buy £1 sterling. When the mark was stabilized, one new mark was given in exchange for a billion old marks, which ceased to be legal tender, and prices fell to about one-billionth of their previous level.

Some years ago, the prices of most things in France were about seven times their pre-last-war level. This was mainly because there was about seven times as much money in France as there was before the last war. But this increase in the quantity of francs took place over a number of years, and was not a change of the type supposed above, made overnight with a stroke of the pen. Hence it was accompanied by other changes which we cannot here discuss.

It is money which is offered in exchange for goods, and hence an increase in money incomes and in the money values of assets is likely to lead to an increase in the demand for goods and thereby to raise their prices. If we can imagine two societies which are similar in all respects except that the quantity of money is twice as great in one as in the other, all money incomes and prices would be twice as high in the former as in the latter.

3. CHANGES IN REAL INCOME

The "real" income of a person consists of goods and services which he can buy with his money income. During a period of depression an increase in the amount of money may sometimes promote recovery and increase real incomes by leading to the employment of men and resources previously idle. But this will by no means always happen, even in a depression; it is unfortunately impossible to increase real income whenever desired by simply printing more paper notes. The main way in which the real income of a community increases is by the progress of technique. Inventions and discoveries improve the state of technical knowledge, and their application to industry and trade enables more to be produced than before with the same amount of labour and other resources.

Increases in technical knowledge change the conditions of supply. For example, the last twenty years or so have witnessed continuous improvements in the technique of manufacturing motor cars. New and improved models have been put on the market, and costs of production have tended downward. The supply schedule for motor cars has been changing; at any stated price more cars of a given type would be produced and offered for sale to-day than some years ago. It may be thought, therefore, that changes in real income due to technical progress should be discussed under the heading of changes in supply and have no place in the present chapter, which deals with changes in demand. But this is not so. Many changes affect both the conditions of supply and the conditions of demand, and the progress of technique is a conspicuous case in point.

Let us suppose that the real income of a typical consumer increases by about 10 per cent, and that his tastes remain unchanged. It is most unlikely that he will distribute his expenditure over different goods in the same proportions as before.

It is most unlikely, that is to say, that he will buy just 10 per cent more, in amount, of every good which he bought previously. It is probable that he will increase his purchases of some goods by more than 10 per cent and of others by less than 10 per cent. He may diminish the quantity of some goods which he buys, or may even cease to buy them at all; and he may now purchase goods which previously he did not buy at all. His scale of preferences, we suppose, remains the same, but a change in his real income alters some, or all, of his demand schedules for different goods.

In fact, a change, such as the progress of technique, which leads to a general increase in real incomes is likely to change the supply schedules for different goods. But for the moment let us suppose, in order to concentrate upon the part played by demand, that there has been a general and uniform progress in technique, accompanied by an increase in the quantity of money sufficient to raise the money incomes of consumers and to leave supply schedules unchanged. We can then obtain a fairly good notion of how demand will change by observing how the expenditures of families at one level of income differ from those of families at another level. People certainly differ in their individual tastes, but they are sufficiently alike to warrant the deduction that if a whole group of families had their incomes raised to a higher level they would spend them in much the same way as families already at that level do in fact spend theirs.

Thus it seems fairly certain that if people's incomes increased, the proportion of their incomes which they spent on food would diminish and the proportion which they spent on bread would considerably diminish. For example, the inquiry conducted by the Ministry of Labour into working-class budgets in the United Kingdom in 1904 gave the following results—

Range of Weekly Income	Average Income	Average Expenditure on		Percentage of Income Spent on	
		Food	Bread	Food	Bread
s.	s.	s.	s.		
Under 25	21·4	14·4	3·0	67	14·3
25 to 29	27·0	17·8	3·3	66	12·3
30 to 34	31·9	20·8	3·3	65	10·3
35 to 39	36·5	22·3	3·4	61	9·2
40 and over	52·0	29·7	4·3	57	8·3

Much the same applies to rent. Thus the New Survey of London Life and Labour found that in East London the percentage of family income spent on rent fell from 21·4 per cent out of an average weekly income of 43s. to 6·1 per cent out of an average weekly income of 230s. A rise in the incomes of "middle-class" families often leads to a greater increase in their expenditure on such items as furniture, education, travel, and amusements than in their expenditure on food, clothing, and housing.

We should beware of drawing too precise conclusions from the many inquiries which have been made into family expenditures. For example, it does not seem true that the proportion spent on rent falls steadily as income increases. Over a certain range of incomes (for example, 100s. a week to 150s. a week in East London) an increase in income may lead to little, if any, increase in the amount of money spent on rent. People may keep the same house or flat or rooms as before. Beyond that range, the desire for social distinction may cause an increasing proportion of additional income to be spent on rent. The net result may be a continuous fall in the percentage spent on rent as income increases, but the rate of fall will not be regular. Again, the fall in the *per capita* expenditure on meat which has been going on for a number of years in the United States may be due partly to the general upward trend of real income and partly to a growing change in tastes away from meat and towards fruit and vegetables.

It seems fairly certain, however, that when a person's income rises he will tend to substitute what may be termed "superior" goods for cheaper but inferior goods which satisfied the same kind of need. Thus he may substitute butter for margarine, fresh milk for powdered or condensed milk, and hats for caps. He may actually spend less money on these inferior goods than before; indeed, he may cease to buy them at all. He will tend to increase his expenditure on the more appetizing kinds of foodstuffs, such as fruit and vegetables and dairy produce and meat, more than on such things as bread and potatoes. If the rise in his income is sufficient, he may buy goods which he could not previously afford at all. Thus he may purchase a motor car (which will mean that in the future he will be a consumer of petrol and may spend less than before on journeys by rail or tram or bus) or a refrigerator or a wireless set. This will not necessarily indicate a change in his tastes; it will happen simply because he can now satisfy his wants more fully.

Thus a rise in real incomes will tend to increase the demand for goods previously regarded as luxuries or semi-luxuries more than for goods of an "inferior" type. The percentage increase in a person's demand for a good due to a 1 per cent increase in his real income, or, more generally, the percentage increase in the amount demanded divided by the percentage increase in his income, is sometimes called his "income-elasticity of demand" for that good.

4. CHANGES IN POPULATION

Other things remaining the same, the total demand for any good will obviously vary with the size of the consuming population. But other things are not likely to remain the same.

If the population of a country increases owing to immigration, the immigrants will probably have somewhat different tastes from the others. Thus the demand for foods particularly desired by the immigrants—such as certain foodstuffs to which they are accustomed—will increase more than the demand for other things.

Apart from migration, the population of a country changes through births and deaths. A country whose population is increasing rapidly will have a high proportion of children and a low proportion of old people; a country whose population is declining or tending to decline will have the opposite. Most Western countries are now in the latter position. Thus in Great Britain in 1937 about 23 persons out of every 100 were under 15 and some 13 were over 60. In 1967 probably only about 10 persons out of every 100 will be under 15, whereas about 23 will be over 60. Clearly a change of this kind will increase the demand for things wanted mainly by elderly people, such as invalid port and artificial teeth and bath chairs, and will decrease the demand for things wanted mainly by children, such as perambulators and toys and bread.

An increase in the number of persons of marriageable age (which may come about without any change in the total size of the population) will lead to an increased demand for housing and furniture.

5. CHANGES IN THE DISTRIBUTION OF WEALTH

A person's power to demand depends on the size of his income and of his assets, in so far as he is prepared to sell assets, or to borrow against them, in order to spend the proceeds. A man who spends £2000 a year exerts ten times the "pull" on the market of one who spends only £200 a year, for one man's pound is as good as another's. Hence, if some people become more wealthy and others less wealthy than before, the demand for various goods and services is likely to change. For it is unlikely that the former will distribute their additional expenditure in exactly the same way as the latter used to distribute the expenditure which now they can no longer make. The demand for goods on which the former increase their expenditure is likely to rise and the demand for goods on which the latter cut down their expenditure is likely to fall.

Suppose that, by taxing the rich and subsidizing the poor, a society makes the distribution of wealth among its members much less uneven than it was. The demand for things bought mainly by the very rich, such as luxurious cars and mink coats and pearls, will fall. So will the demand for things bought mainly by the very poor, such as cotton stockings and horse-meat. On the other hand, the demand for things which the poor used to regard as semi-luxuries will increase.

6. CHANGES IN THE STATE OF TRADE

Fewer men and resources are unemployed, output is greater, total money income is greater, and the demand for nearly everything is greater, as a rule, during a period of good trade than during a period of depression. If prosperity is expected to continue and possibly to increase, the demand for producers' goods is likely to increase more than the demand for consumers' goods. Entrepreneurs will anticipate good or rising profits, and will therefore increase their orders for plant and equipment and for raw materials and intermediate products.

The opposite will happen if trade is bad and is expected to remain bad or to become worse. The demand for producers' goods will fall off more than the demand for consumers' goods. Consumers, being on the whole poorer than before, will tend to reduce their expenditure on durable consumers' goods such as furniture and household appliances.

7. CHANGES IN OTHER PRICES

The state of demand for a particular good may change because the prices of other goods have changed. If two goods are fairly close substitutes, a fall in the price of one is likely to decrease the demand for the other, and conversely. For example, if an increase in the amount of mutton coming forward for sale causes its price to fall, a number of housewives and others may buy mutton rather than beef and the demand for beef may decrease. On the other hand, if two goods are jointly demanded, being used together in more or less constant proportions, a fall in the price of one is likely to increase the demand for the other. For example, a fall in the price of motor cars will tend to expand their sales, thus leading to an increase in the demand for petrol.

These generalizations apply also to goods and services bought by producers. Thus a rise in the wages of a particular kind of labour may induce the employers concerned to replace some of that labour by machinery, so that the demand for such machinery may increase.

8. CHANGES IN TASTES

The tastes of consumers may change for all kinds of reasons. We shall not attempt to explain the vagaries of fashion, which decrees at one time that women's hair shall be short, thus decreasing the demand for hair-pins, and at another time that women's dresses shall be longer, thus increasing the demand for dress materials. Before the war of 1914, the preparation of ostrich and other feathers for women's hats was a flourishing industry in Paris; after the war feathers were out of fashion. In England, straw hats were worn at one time by most men in the summer: where are they now?

It is almost as difficult to explain changes of tastes in matters of diet. There seems little doubt that during recent years the British demand for beef and veal has fallen relatively to the demand for mutton and lamb and for bacon and pork. Is this because fewer families want big joints nowadays? It seems to be due mainly to a general change in tastes about which nothing can be said.

For convenience it is usual to include changes in demand arising from external circumstances such as changes in the weather under the general heading of "changes in tastes," for they do spring from a change in scales of preferences, although we know well enough what has brought about this change. Thus an increased demand for umbrellas may be due to a wet summer and an increased demand for refrigerators and cold drinks to a hot one. Progress in medicine and allied science may lead to changes in demand. People may spend more time sun-bathing, and increase their expenditure on sun-tan oil; they may buy more of certain foods because it becomes known that they contain vitamins.

Advertising and propaganda may lead to changes in tastes. People may drink more milk or eat more fruit or "buy British" because they are constantly urged to do so; and the demand for patent medicines and other branded articles is almost entirely the result of advertisement.

CHAPTER VI

DEMAND, SUPPLY, AND PRICE

1. CHANGES IN SUPPLY

For the moment we can give only a brief preliminary account of the influences affecting supply.

The cost of production of a commodity is composed of the prices of the various factors, including raw materials and intermediate products, used in producing it. A rise in the prices of some of these factors will increase costs and thereby change the conditions of supply. The supply curve will shift to the left: at any given price less will be produced and offered for sale than before. For example, during 1936 and 1937 the rise in the prices of timber, steel, and other materials changed the conditions of supply of such goods as houses, ships, and motor cars in this way. Of course a fall in factor prices will have the opposite effect.

Taxation imposed on output or sales, or on the possession or use of factors of production, will have the same tendency. An example of this has already been given.

An improvement in technique, which enables any given quantity of a commodity to be produced or marketed at a lower cost than before, will have the opposite effect.

The conditions of supply may be altered by such things as changes in the weather, fires, floods, dust-storms, and earthquakes, although such changes are often only temporary. Suitable weather conditions may lead to a large wheat harvest and thereby increase the supply of wheat; the destruction of steelworks by fire or by bombs will decrease the supply of steel.

The effect upon price of changes in supply, supposing demand to remain the same, was discussed in Chapter IV.

2. CHANGES IN BOTH SUPPLY AND DEMAND

Many changes will affect both the conditions of supply and the conditions of demand. We have seen that an increase in the amount of money which brings about a rise in money incomes will increase demand, but clearly it will also affect costs. The money which a wage-earner receives for his work is income from his standpoint but from the standpoint of his employer it is a cost. Improvements in technique tend to increase the supply of the goods in question, and we have seen that, by increasing real incomes, they lead also to changes in demand. If a particular kind of labour obtains higher wages, this will tend to raise the costs of whatever it helps to produce, and at the same time will increase the power to demand of the workers concerned. Indeed, it can be urged that any change will have repercussions throughout the economic system. But often these repercussions are so slight that they can safely be neglected.

Again, it often happens that over a certain period something occurs to change the conditions of supply of a commodity and something else occurs to change the conditions of demand for it. For example, an improvement in the technique of manufacturing motor cars may coincide with an increase in the demand for motor cars due, for instance, to a rise in real incomes or a change in the distribution of wealth.

If an increase in supply is accompanied by a decrease in demand, the price of the good will fall, and if a decrease in supply is accompanied by an increase in demand, the price of the good will rise. But if an increase in supply is accompanied by an increase in demand, or a decrease in supply by a decrease in demand, we know that output and sales will tend to expand in the former case and to contract in the latter, but we cannot say *a priori* what will happen to the price.

After the period of transition is over, and both producers and consumers have adjusted themselves to the new conditions, both the supply curve and the demand curve will be different from what they were before. The new equilibrium price will be represented by the point at which the two new curves cut one another.

It is because different changes often take place simultaneously that economists make so much use of the word "tends" and of the phrase "other things being equal" or "other things remaining the same." A large cotton crop will tend to reduce the price of cotton. But other things may not remain the same. For some reason the demand for cotton may happen to increase so much that the price of cotton actually rises. Nevertheless the big crop does tend to keep down the price. If the crop had been smaller, the same increase in demand would have brought about a still greater rise in the price.

3. SHORT-RUN AND LONG-RUN EFFECTS

It often takes some time for the effects of a change to work themselves out fully. If no further changes take place, a new equilibrium will eventually be reached, but the period of transition may last for months or even for years.

Suppose that there is a permanent increase in the demand for some commodity: the demand curve shifts to the right and stays there. If the existing stock of that commodity cannot be increased, as in our previous illustration of a first edition, its price will rise but there will be no direct effects upon productive activity. But if the commodity is currently produced, the tendency will be to produce more of it. For if the amount of it coming forward week by week for sale remains the same, its price will rise. It will thus become more profitable than before to produce it. Existing firms will tend to expand their output and new firms will tend to enter the industry.

It may be that a given increase in demand can readily be met by existing firms without any increase in their plant or equipment. The firms may have been working below capacity. This implies that they could increase their output somewhat and thereby reduce their average costs per unit, for some costs, such as the salaries of the manager and the office staff or the rent paid for the land or buildings, will increase little, if at all. We may point out that this in turn implies that such firms are in a "monopolistic" position in that they realize that an expansion of their output, given the demand, would reduce its price per unit. For if a firm thinks that it can market a larger output without affecting the price, and knows that it can reduce its costs per unit by working to full capacity, it will do so. The fact remains that some firms which were working below capacity can readily expand their output somewhat in response to an increase in demand. Possibly they may be glad to do so without raising the price: the supply curve in the neighbourhood of the existing price may be horizontal.

Again, most firms make several different products. If the demand for one product increases and the demand for another decreases, it may be possible to produce more of the former and less of the latter at the same cost and with the same plant and equipment and labour force. Thus consumers may demand more of one kind of cloth and less of another. If both kinds are made with the same looms, it may be quite easy for manufacturers to supply more of the former and less of the latter without any change in prices.

Moreover, changes in demand are often anticipated by producers, who take steps to alter their output without waiting for the stimulus of an actual change in price.

But adjustments cannot always be made so easily or so rapidly. A big increase in the demand for a manufactured good, leading to a substantial expansion in its output, may call for an increase in "capacity." New plant and equipment may be required; more raw materials may be needed; more workers may have to be trained in the relevant tasks. In the same way a big increase in the demand for a mineral may lead to the opening of new mines or the sinking of new shafts, and a big increase in the demand for an agricultural product may lead to the transference of land from other uses. Thus some time may elapse before output attains its new equilibrium level, and in the interval there may be a considerable rise in the price of the commodity.

An extreme illustration is provided by rubber. Trees do not begin to yield latex (the milky substance which is converted into rubber) until five to seven years after they have been planted. A big increase in the demand for rubber may therefore lead to a very large rise in its price, and its price may remain very high for several years, until the new trees planted in response to the increased demand begin to yield. For the time being, more rubber can be made available by drawing upon existing stocks and by "tapping" existing trees more frequently. But after a time stocks will become exhausted and increased tapping will diminish the yield; these are temporary expedients which cannot cope with a permanent increase in demand. Again, the high price of rubber will make it more profitable to "regenerate" old rubber. Thus during the period of transition the amount of rubber coming forward will be greater than before and its price will be much higher than before, and may vary somewhat from week to week with changes in supply. The new equilibrium will be reached, if no further changes take place, only after a number of years, with the output of rubber considerably greater than before and its price somewhat higher than before, but not as high as during the period of transition.

Clearly no single supply curve will suffice to depict conditions during a period of transition, for the state of supply will constantly alter as new plants come into operation, new mines are opened, and so on. Hence a supply curve, and therefore of course the supply schedule which it represents, is best regarded as showing how much would be supplied at any given price *after sufficient time has elapsed for the necessary adjustments to be made.*

4. DOWNWARD-SLOPING SUPPLY CURVES

We have assumed that the supply curve of a currently produced good will usually slope upward: that is to say, that a higher price would be required to call forth a greater output. An increase in the demand for it would cause more of it to be produced. But after sufficient time had elapsed for a new equilibrium to be reached would its price inevitably be higher than before?

It may be that an increased demand for a commodity coincides with improvements in the technique of producing it. The latter may lead to a fall in its price, but this leaves open the question of whether the fall in its price would have been greater or less if demand had not increased. In order to isolate the effects of a permanent increase in demand, let us consider what would happen if the state of technical knowledge were to remain the same.

More factors of production will be needed by the industry concerned. For example, it will need more raw materials or intermediate products and more labour qualified to perform the tasks required. It may be that more factors can be obtained for the same price as before, but as a rule a somewhat higher price will be required to call forth increased supplies or—what comes to the same thing—less suitable workers and materials will be employed at the price which used to be paid for more suitable ones. Thus costs will tend to increase. Is there any counteracting influence tending to reduce costs?

There is a common impression that such a counteracting influence exists in the economies of large-scale production. It is believed that a permanent increase in the demand for a manufactured good will lead ultimately to a fall in its price because, after the period of transition is over, it will be produced on a larger scale and therefore, it is thought, more cheaply.

This is sometimes true, but it is important to realize when and why it is true. There is no magic in the mere fact that more is being produced than before. We have seen that average costs will tend to fall if fuller use is made of plants previously worked below capacity. But why should they fall if the existing capacity is increased? Suppose that existing firms and plants are duplicated or that, let us say, a cotton-spinning firm expands, acquiring new buildings and managers and spindles and workers. There is no obvious reason why costs should fall. It is often urged that a country with a relatively small population, such as Australia, cannot produce many commodities as cheaply as, say, the United States or Great Britain, because she has a smaller home market and must therefore produce them on a smaller scale. This is true of some commodities, but not of most. It will usually be found that the small country has quite a number of factories producing the commodity in question. Its typical factory may be just as large as the typical factory in a big country. If not, it would usually be possible, by grouping the workers into fewer and larger factories, to make it so. How, then, would costs be reduced if the population were twice or ten times as large? If producing on a larger scale means merely having a thousand factories instead of a hundred, to produce ten times the former output, it is difficult to see in what the economies consist.

The fact is that costs will fall, as a rule, only if a larger output is produced by different and cheaper methods. Then the question at once arises why these methods, which by hypothesis were known before, were not used before. The answer must be that they demand large and expensive machines and other apparatus which are worth installing only if the demand is sufficiently large to enable them to be fairly fully utilized. To take a simplified example, an output of 1000 units per week may be produced by the old methods at a cost of £1000 per week, and an output of 5000 units per week could be produced, with the aid of a certain machine, at a cost of £2500 per week. If the conditions of demand had been such that 1000 units would sell for more than £1 each and 5000 units for less than 10s. each, it may not have been profitable to install the machine, for its capacity may be over 5000 units a week and its cost may not vary much with the extent to which it is utilized. If, now, demand increases, so that 5000 units a week sell for more than 10s. each, it becomes profitable to install the machine.

In the above example the conditions of demand relate to the market as a whole. Suppose that the market is Australia or, if the costs of transporting the commodity are sufficiently high to localize the market, the district around Sydney. If this market would previously have taken over 5000 units a week at a price above 10s., any firm would have found it profitable to install such a machine and undersell its rivals without waiting for an increase in demand. The commodities which a country is at a disadvantage in producing merely because its home market is small and it is distant from foreign consuming centres are commodities requiring large and expensive plant which is not worth while installing unless it can be utilized more fully than the conditions of demand in that country permit. Examples are motor cars, large ships, and certain types of machines.

An industry may expand without changing its methods of production, but the fact that its demand for certain goods has increased may enable these goods to be produced by different and cheaper methods and therefore supplied to it at a lower price than before. For example, the expansion of a textile industry may conceivably lead to a reduction in the price of textile machinery. But favourable repercussions of this kind are not very common.

Hence our conclusion is that, if the state of technical knowledge remains the same, an increase in the demand for a good or service will lead ultimately to a reduction in its price only if it makes profitable the utilization of machinery, and so on, not worth using before. Moreover, its price will fall only if the economies produced in this way more than counteract the tendency for costs to increase owing to the increased demand for the factors used by that industry. This will happen only in the minority of cases.[1] As a rule, the supply curve slopes upward. But in this

[1] It must be remembered that we are taking the state of technical knowledge as given. As time goes on, improvements in technical knowledge tend to reduce costs in many industries, but that is another matter. Any particular industry would probably have to pay somewhat more for some of its materials or labour if it expanded substantially, and not many of them would be able more than to counteract this by adopting methods of production already known but at present not worth while because demand is too small.

minority of cases we must say—if we are justified in applying to them the concept of a long-period supply curve—that the supply curve slopes downward for part of its length. But it may well be conceded that the supply curve is not a very suitable instrument to employ in dealing with problems of this kind.

5. JOINT SUPPLY

Two or more different goods are often produced together. Thus wool and mutton are joint products of sheep, and beef and hides are joint products of oxen. The less valuable product of a process is often termed a by-product. Thus the main product of a coke-oven is metallurgical coke; the coke-oven gas which is also produced is regarded as a by-product. On the other hand, the main product of a gas-works is gas and the gas-coke which is also produced is regarded as a by-product. Many chemical and other processes yield a whole range of by-products, although further separate treatment is often needed to turn a by-product into a form suitable for use or sale. All the by-products, taken together, may be more valuable than the main product. For example, the combined value of the by-products of the Chicago stockyards is said to be greater than the value of the meat.

This phenomenon of joint supply does not call for any substantial modifications of our reasoning. For it is usually possible to change the proportions in which the different goods are produced, although this sometimes involves changing the type of apparatus used, or of animal bred, and so on, and may therefore take some time. On the assumption that the entrepreneur will make as big an income as possible for himself, we can predict what he will do when confronted with given changes in prices. He will change the proportions in which the various products are produced if by so doing he increases his receipts more than his costs, or reduces his costs more than his receipts. For example, before the development of cold storage sheep were bred in New Zealand mainly for their wool. When it became possible to export mutton, the price of New Zealand mutton rose relatively to the price of wool, and cross-bred sheep, yielding more mutton but less wool, and wool of a poorer quality, were largely substituted for merinos.

But what if the proportions cannot be varied? Mr. Henderson, in his stimulating book *Supply and Demand*, asserts that it has not been found possible to vary the proportions in which cotton lint —that is, raw cotton—and cotton-seed are yielded by the cotton plant. About 2 lb. of cotton-seed will be produced for every 1 lb. of cotton lint. This means that the "unit" produced by the cotton-grower must be regarded as 1 lb. of lint plus 2 lb. of seed. But the demand for cotton lint is quite separate from the demand for cotton-seed. Each has its own uses and its own demand schedule. Thus, if an increased demand for cotton causes additional cotton to be produced, it will inevitably cause twice as much extra cotton-seed to be produced, and, if the state of demand for cotton-seed remains the same, its price will fall. But the "price" which a grower takes into account when considering whether to expand or to contract his output is the combined price which he gets for 1 lb. of cotton lint plus 2 lb. of cotton-seed. It is very seldom, however, that proportions cannot be varied.

6. THE LAWS OF SUPPLY AND DEMAND

A change in price does not come about by itself. It is the result of a change in conditions which alters the supply schedule or the demand schedule or both. If the change affects only the demand, the normal sequence will be an increase in demand leading to a rise in price which induces an extension of supply or, in the opposite case, a decrease in demand leading to a fall in price which induces a contraction of supply. Conversely, if the change affects only the supply the normal sequence will be an increase in supply leading to a fall in price which induces an extension of demand or, in the opposite case, a decrease in supply leading to a rise in price which induces a contraction of demand.

The distinction between increases and decreases, on the one hand, and extensions and contractions, on the other hand, is a useful aid to clear thinking. People sometimes speak as if a price could never permanently change. They say, for example, "an invention may reduce costs, increase supply, and lower price for the time being. But demand will increase, owing to the lower price, and this will send the price back to its original level." This of course is quite wrong. The demand curve remains the same; demand does *not* "increase" but is "extended," more being bought simply because the price is lower. There is, however, a new supply curve, which is lower than the original one, and hence the new equilibrium price will be below the original price.

We give below four "laws" of supply and demand. But it should be remembered that these laws, like all economic laws, are only generalizations about tendencies. We have pointed out that some demand curves may slope upward and some supply curves downward for part of their length and we shall see later that it is possible that less labour, or fewer savings, may be supplied at a higher price. There are often exceptions to law (3): many producers can and do increase their output of a particular good, when the demand for it increases, without a rise in its price.

(1) Price tends to equate the amount which sellers are prepared to offer for sale and the amount which buyers wish to buy.

(2) Usually a larger quantity of a commodity will be demanded at a lower price than at a higher price; and a larger quantity will be offered for sale at a higher price than at a lower price.

(3) An increase in demand tends to raise the price and to extend the supply; a decrease in demand tends to lower the price and to contract the supply.

(4) An increase in supply tends to lower the price and to extend the demand; a decrease in supply tends to raise the price and to contract the demand.

APPENDIX TO BOOK I

INDIFFERENCE CURVES

1. THE NATURE OF INDIFFERENCE CURVES

If there are only two goods between which a consumer can choose, his scale of preferences can be represented on a two-dimensional diagram by a series of indifference curves.

Let us suppose that a number of soldiers are stationed in an out-of-the-way place and that each receives a fixed weekly ration of, say, 10 tots of rum and 50 cigarettes. Each soldier is free to "swap" rum for cigarettes, or cigarettes for rum, with his comrades, but these are the only two goods which enter into the circle of exchange. If the tastes of the various soldiers are not exactly the same, and some have a stronger preference than others for cigarettes as against rum, a market will be established among the soldiers in which rum will be exchanged against cigarettes.

Let us consider the tastes of a soldier whom we will call A. He may like both rum and cigarettes. He would welcome an increased ration of either or both. Nevertheless he has a scale of preferences upon which he will act when he swaps rum for cigarettes, or cigarettes for rum, with his fellows. And it is possible to state his scale of preferences in exact quantitative terms and to represent it on a diagram.

He gets, like the others, 10 tots of rum and 50 cigarettes per week. Suppose we ask him how many extra cigarettes he would require, each week, to induce him to give up one of his tots of rum. Upon reflection, he might decide that he would do this for five extra cigarettes but not for 3, while if he were offered 4 extra cigarettes he would be undecided. This means that to him the combination of 10 tots of rum plus 50 cigarettes is equivalent to the combination of 9 tots of rum plus 54 cigarettes. He is indifferent as between these two combinations. He does not prefer one of them to the other. In the same way there are many combinations of rum and cigarettes which he will regard as equivalent to these two. For example, he may require a shade more than 10 extra cigarettes in order to give up 2 tots of rum. We thus get another combination—8 tots of rum and 60 cigarettes—which the soldier himself values neither more nor less highly than either of the other two. We can set out some of these combinations in a little table.

13	tots of rum	and	44	cigarettes
12	"	"	45	"
11	"	"	47	"
10	"	"	50	"
9	"	"	54	"
8	"	"	60	"
7	"	"	70	"

Such a table represents a part of his "scale of preferences" between rum and cigarettes. We do not inquire into the reasons for his preferences; we accept them as data.

We can show each of the combinations in this table as a point on a diagram, measuring, say, cigarettes along the horizontal axis *OX* and rum up the vertical axis *OY*. If we join these points (thus assuming continuity), we obtain a portion of what is called an "indifference curve." This is shown in Fig. 13.

The indifference curve slopes downward to the right. This is because an increase in one good not accompanied by a decrease in the other good would give the individual a combination which he preferred to the previous one.

The indifference curve is "convex to the origin." This reflects the fact that the more rum the soldier gives up in exchange for cigarettes, the greater will be the number of additional cigarettes required to induce him to give up yet another tot of rum, and conversely. A scale of preferences usually follows this rule, which is commonly known as the Law of Diminishing Marginal Utility. The marginal utility of one good falls, relatively to that of another, for any given individual, when his supplies of the former good increase while his supplies of the latter remain the same or, as in our example, diminish.

So far we have considered only one indifference curve of soldier A: that containing the combination 10 tots of rum plus 50 cigarettes. If the soldier is sufficiently aware of his own tastes to give correct answers to a number of further questions, we can learn a great deal more about his scale of preferences. For example, we can begin with the combination of 11 tots of rum and 55 cigarettes. It is certain that he prefers this combination to 10 tots of rum plus 50 cigarettes. Suppose that he possessed the former combination. He might be able to say, upon reflection, how many additional cigarettes he would require to compensate him for giving up one of his 11 tots of rum, how many for giving up 2 tots, and so on. In this way we could obtain another indifference curve. This new curve would lie farther from the point *O* on our diagram than the first curve. Every point on this new curve would represent a combination of rum and cigarettes which the soldier himself valued neither more nor less highly than the combination of 11 tots of rum plus 55 cigarettes, which is represented by a point lying on this new curve. But we know that he prefers 11 tots of rum and 55 cigarettes to 10 tots of rum and 50 cigarettes. Therefore he prefers any combination lying on the new curve to any combination lying on the old one.

In this way we could get a large number of indifference curves and *the resulting "indifference map" would record our soldier's scale of preferences as between rum and cigarettes.* The indifference curves are thus a kind of photograph of the soldier's tastes. Or they may be likened to contour lines. Each curve represents, so to speak, a greater height than the curve to its left or below it. The object of the individual will be to reach the greatest height possible for him under the limitations of his fixed income and of the rate of exchange between the two goods in the market. He will try, that is, to reach the position he most prefers out of all the positions open to him.

Suppose, for example, that the rate of exchange established in the market is one tot of rum against 10 cigarettes. Soldier A would clearly gain by exchanging 2 tots of his rum against cigarettes. This would give him 8 tots of rum and 70 cigarettes. But, by hypothesis, he would just as soon have 8 tots of rum and 60 cigarettes as the 10 tots of rum and 50 cigarettes with which he begins. Eight tots of rum and 70 cigarettes, therefore, represents a preferred position to him. He is on *another* indifference curve, one which he prefers to the one on which he started.

The "map" of his indifference curves enables us to read off exactly what he would do at any given rate of exchange. Suppose the rate established in the market is one tot of rum against 10 cigarettes. Then if a soldier, with a ration of 10 tots of rum and 50 cigarettes, exchanged all his cigarettes for rum he would have

15 tots of rum, and if he exchanged all his rum for cigarettes he would have 150 cigarettes. This is represented on the diagram by the straight line *AB*, joining the point on the vertical axis which represents 15 tots of rum to the point on the horizontal axis which represents 150 cigarettes. The initial ration of 10

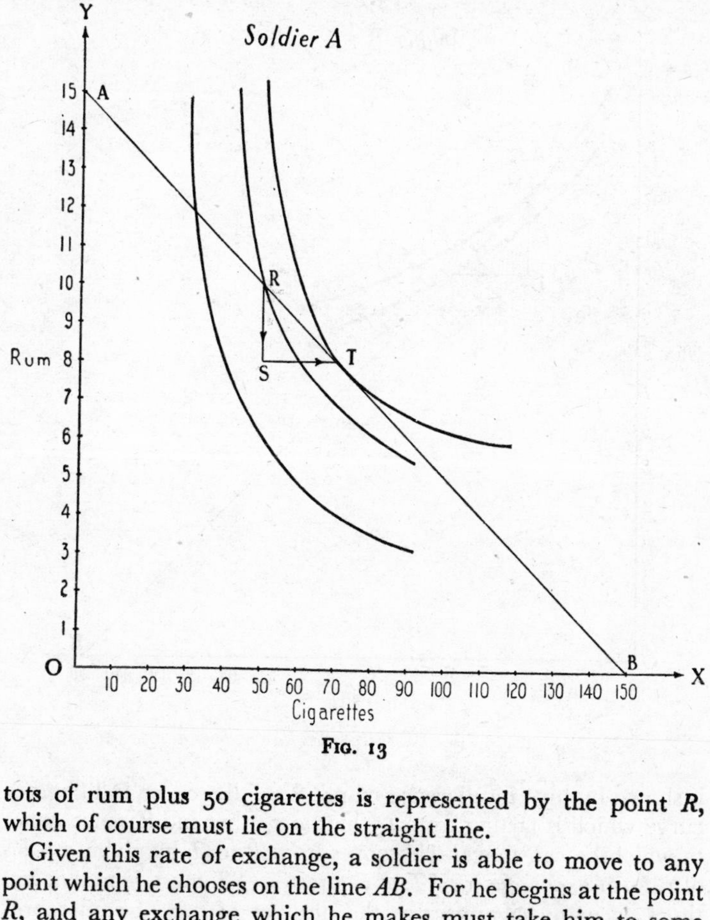

FIG. 13

tots of rum plus 50 cigarettes is represented by the point *R*, which of course must lie on the straight line.

Given this rate of exchange, a soldier is able to move to any point which he chooses on the line *AB*. For he begins at the point *R*, and any exchange which he makes must take him to some other point on *AB*. What will he do? We know that if he can move from one indifference curve to another which lies farther from *O* he will do so, because he will prefer any combination on the latter curve to any combination on the former. Therefore he must move to that point on the line *AB* at which *AB* is tangential to one of his indifference curves. In Fig. 13, soldier A will move from the point *R* to the point *T*. *T* represents the position which he most prefers out of all those open to him: this

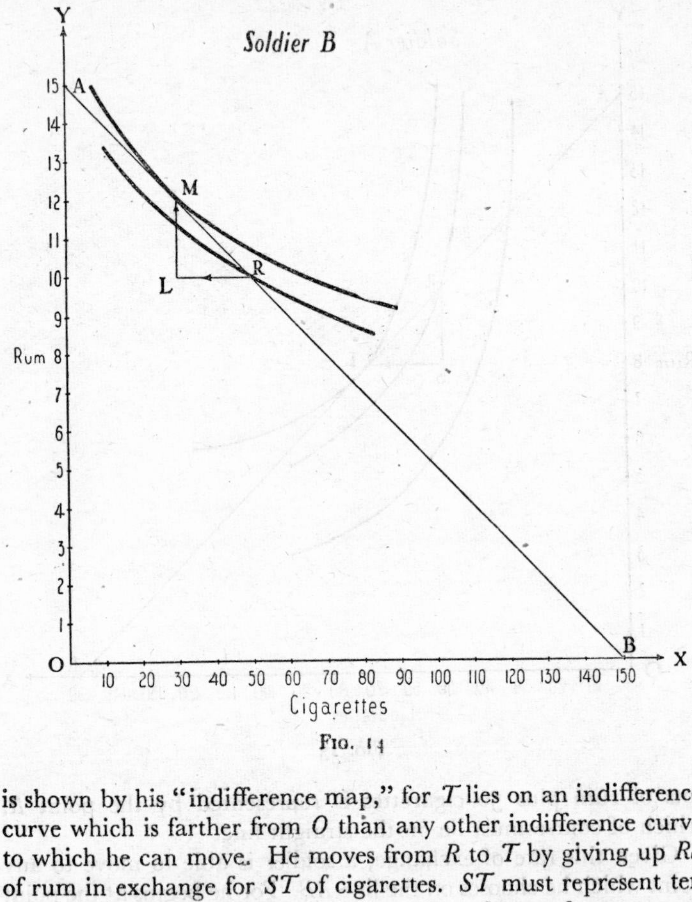

FIG. 14

is shown by his "indifference map," for *T* lies on an indifference curve which is farther from *O* than any other indifference curve to which he can move. He moves from *R* to *T* by giving up *RS* of rum in exchange for *ST* of cigarettes. *ST* must represent ten times as many cigarettes as the number of tots of rum represented by *RS*, since the triangles *AOB* and *RST* are similar.

Let us now briefly consider the preferences of another soldier, whom we may call B, who has a stronger preference than A for rum as against cigarettes. The relevant portion of his indifference curve, containing the combination 10 tots of rum plus 50 cigarettes, may be as follows—

13	tots of rum	and	15	cigarettes
12	"	"	23	"
11	"	"	33	"
10	"	"	50	"
9	"	"	70	"
8	"	"	100	"
7	"	"	150	"

At a rate of exchange of one tot of rum against 10 cigarettes, this soldier would clearly gain by exchanging 20 cigarettes against rum. This would give him 12 tots of rum and 30 cigarettes. But by hypothesis he would just as soon have 12 tots of rum and 23 cigarettes as the 10 tots and 50 cigarettes with which he begins. Twelve tots of rum and 30 cigarettes, therefore, represent a preferred position to him. He is on *another* indifference curve, one which he prefers to the one on which he started.

The scale of preferences of soldier B is shown in Fig. 14. He will move from the point *R* to the point *M*, giving up *RL* cigarettes in exchange for *LM* rum.

It will be noted that two soldiers can both gain by exchanging with one another. The contention that exchange is "barren," because the value obtained is only equal to the value given up, is quite false. Both parties gain, each moving to a position which he prefers, because their tastes—their scales of preferences—are different. And clearly two people could gain by exchanging, even if their tastes were the same, if in the first place one possessed a different assortment of goods from the other.

2. EXCHANGE WITH ONLY TWO GOODS

If our soldiers constitute a perfect competitive market, in the sense that each is aware of all the bargains that are struck and of all the offers which each of his comrades makes, there will be only one rate of exchange between rum and cigarettes. This can be proved by showing that two rates are impossible. Suppose that soldier A were exchanging rum for cigarettes with soldier B at a rate of 1 tot of rum for 15 cigarettes and that soldier C were exchanging rum for cigarettes with soldier D at a rate of 1 tot of rum for 5 cigarettes. Clearly it would pay B and C to get together at some intermediate rate—say, at a rate of 1 tot of rum against 10 cigarettes. In this way B would get 50 per cent more rum for his cigarettes and C would give only half as much rum as before for any given number of cigarettes. Since the market is perfect, every soldier knows what is going on and therefore two different rates cannot exist.

It may take some time to find the equilibrium rate, but if each soldier's tastes remain the same, the same kind of situation keeps repeating itself week after week and before long a rate of exchange will be found which will be permanent. It will be the "equilibrium" rate, because at that rate every soldier who wants to swap rum for cigarettes can swap as much as he wishes and every soldier who wants to swap cigarettes for rum can swap as much as he wishes.

In practice, the equilibrium rate would be found by trial and error. But if we knew the scale of preferences of each soldier, and the quantity of rum and cigarettes received each week by each soldier, we could easily discover what it would be. For we should know what each soldier would want to do at any given price and we should find that at one price alone the amount of rum which would be offered (by soldiers wanting cigarettes in exchange) would be the same as the amount of rum demanded (by soldiers offering cigarettes in exchange).

For example, if the "price" of a tot of rum were 20 cigarettes, some soldiers would wish to give up rum, obtaining cigarettes in exchange. We could add together the amounts of rum which each of these soldiers would wish to give up. This would give us the total "supply" of rum which would be offered in exchange at this price. (Looking at the matter from the other side, this number of tots multiplied by 20 would be the number of cigarettes demanded at this "price.") Some soldiers, on the other hand, would wish to give up cigarettes in exchange for rum. The total amount of rum which these soldiers, taken together, would wish to acquire at this price would give us the demand for rum (and therefore the supply of cigarettes) at this price. The price at which the amount of rum supplied would be the same as the amount demanded (implying, of course, that the amount of cigarettes demanded would be the same as the amount supplied) would be the equilibrium price.

Suppose we found that the equilibrium price would be 10

cigarettes for 1 tot of rum. No other price could be maintained for any length of time. If for a time the price ruling were, say, 9 cigarettes per tot, more cigarettes would be offered against rum than would be accepted. Some soldiers anxious to exchange cigarettes for rum would be unable to do so. Some of these soldiers would rather give 10 cigarettes or even 11 or 12 or more cigarettes for a tot of rum than restrict themselves to the 10 tots in their ration. They would therefore offer a higher "price." They would offer more than 9 cigarettes per tot of rum in order to make sure of getting some extra rum. This would drive up the market "price" until it settled at a level at which everyone who wanted to exchange would be able to exchange as much as he wished—at a level, that is, at which supply would equal demand.

3. CHANGES IN DATA

Once the equilibrium rate of exchange between rum and cigarettes has been established, it will continue indefinitely unless some change takes place in the data. Let us consider in what ways the data may change and how each type of change may cause the rate of exchange to alter.

(1) The ration may be increased or decreased, without changing the proportion of rum and cigarettes. For example, each soldier may be given 20 tots of rum and 100 cigarettes, or 5 tots of rum and 25 cigarettes, or 11 tots of rum and 55 cigarettes. It may be thought that a change of this kind would leave the rate of exchange unaltered. But this is very unlikely. For although the tastes of each soldier remain the same as before, it is unlikely that he will be prepared to give up exactly the same number of cigarettes to get an additional amount of rum, or conversely, now that the size of his ration is altered. Suppose that the ration is doubled. It may happen, for example, that each soldier would now be prepared to give up more cigarettes than before in order to have an additional tot of rum. A soldier who would not previously have given up more than, say, 12 cigarettes (thus reducing his cigarettes to 38) in order to get an additional tot (thus increasing his tots to 11) may now be prepared to give up, say, 15 cigarettes (thus reducing his cigarettes to 85) in order to get an additional tot (thus increasing his tots to 21); a soldier who would not previously have given up more than,

say, 3 cigarettes to get an additional tot may now be prepared to give up, say, 5; and so on. Under such conditions, rum would still be exchanged against cigarettes, since different soldiers would continue to have different scales of preferences, just as before, but in the new equilibrium the value of a tot of rum in terms of cigarettes would be higher than in the old.

(2) The proportion of rum to cigarettes in the weekly ration may be changed. Suppose, for example, that the ration becomes 10 tots of rum and 60 cigarettes. This will cause the value of cigarettes in terms of rum to fall. For every soldier will now be prepared to give more cigarettes than before to get additional rum; or, to put it the other way round, will require more cigarettes than before to compensate him for the loss of a given amount of rum. Hence the supply of rum offered in exchange for cigarettes, at the old rate, will now be insufficient to meet the demand, and competition among soldiers anxious to exchange cigarettes against rum will drive up its price. But if the quantity of both rum and cigarettes comprised in the ration is increased or decreased, and at the same time the proportion of rum to cigarettes is changed, we cannot be certain *a priori* how the rate of exchange will be affected. The change in the proportion will tend to increase the value of the good whose proportion has fallen. The change in the size of the ration may reinforce this tendency, but, on the other hand, it may weaken it or even outweigh it.

(3) The distribution of the total weekly amount of rum and cigarettes among the soldiers may be changed. Instead of each soldier receiving the same ration as every other, some may be given larger rations than others. This would clearly give more weight than before to the tastes of those who now receive increased rations. If, for example, most of them have a stronger preference for cigarettes, as against rum, than the rest of the soldiers, this will tend to raise the value of cigarettes in terms of rum.

(4) The personnel of the soldiers might change: for example, one regiment might be replaced by another. This would give us a new set of "indifference maps" and it would be merely a coincidence if this did not cause an alteration in the rate of exchange.

(5) There might be a general change in tastes, in favour of either rum or cigarettes. For example, all the soldiers might be

more or less influenced by propaganda against alcohol, and this of course would lower the value of rum in terms of cigarettes.

Whatever change, or combination of changes, took place in the data, we could always determine the new equilibrium rate of exchange if we knew the ration received by each soldier and the scale of preferences of each soldier. It might, of course, take some time for the soldiers themselves to discover it. If the data were changing frequently, an equilibrium might never be attained. Nevertheless, at any moment the rate of exchange in the market would be tending towards the rate which would maintain equilibrium under the prevailing conditions.

4. EXPENDITURE CURVES AND DEMAND CURVES

A set of indifference curves, representing the scale of preferences of a given individual between two goods, will of course remain valid provided that his tastes do not change. His income may change, or the rate of exchange between the two goods may alter, without causing any change in the indifference curves, for these portray his personal scale of preferences, and nothing else.

If we have a diagram showing the indifference curves of an individual, it is easy to show how he would respond to changes in his income. For this purpose it is convenient to suppose that he receives his income entirely in one commodity and then exchanges some units of that commodity against some units of the other. In Fig. 15 units of commodity A are measured up the vertical axis OY and units of commodity B are measured along the horizontal axis OX. Our individual periodically receives an income of OA units of commodity A. The market rate of exchange between A and B is represented by the slope of the line AB. The combination of A and B which he most prefers out of all those open to him is represented by the point Q. He will therefore exchange AR of A against RQ of B, consuming OR of A and OS ($= RQ$) of B. If his income increases to OA_1, the combination he most prefers out of all those open to him is represented by Q_1, and so on. (The rate of exchange between A and B by hypothesis remains the same, so that A_1B_1 is parallel to AB.) If we join together the various Q's we obtain (part of) what may be termed his "expenditure curve." This shows how he would divide any given income between the two goods A and B, provided that his scale of preferences (represented by the indifference curves) and the market rate of exchange between A and B (represented by the slope of the line *AB*) remained unchanged.

Similarly we can show how he would divide a given income *OA* between A and B at each of a series of prices. A rise in the price of B, in terms of A, is shown by a steeper slope of *AB*. Since his income is fixed in terms of A, at *OA*, a rise in the price of B

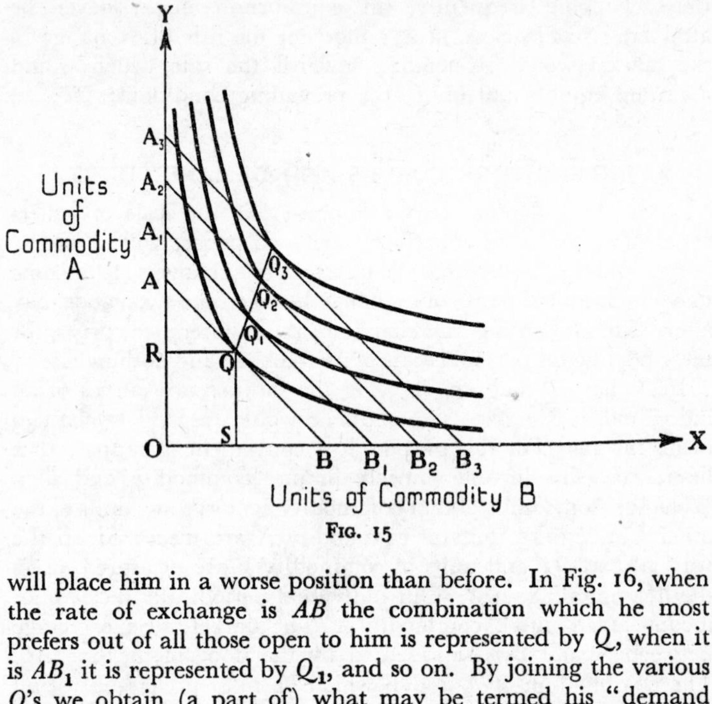

FIG. 15

will place him in a worse position than before. In Fig. 16, when the rate of exchange is *AB* the combination which he most prefers out of all those open to him is represented by *Q*, when it is AB_1 it is represented by Q_1, and so on. By joining the various *Q*'s we obtain (a part of) what may be termed his "demand curve." This shows how he would distribute his fixed income of *OA* between A and B at each of a series of prices.

Indifference curves can be used to portray a person's scale of preferences between any two alternatives, provided there are only two. Thus they can portray his scale of preferences as between income and leisure, showing how he would divide his twenty-four hours each day between leisure and remunerated work at any given rate of pay per hour. Again, they can be used to show his scale of preferences between present and future consumption, between liquid assets and income-yielding assets, and so on. For any scale of preferences relates to the disposal of some given total among different uses. When there are only two uses, it can be depicted by a series of indifference curves on a two-dimensional diagram. Often there are more than two uses —for example, there are usually more than two goods available

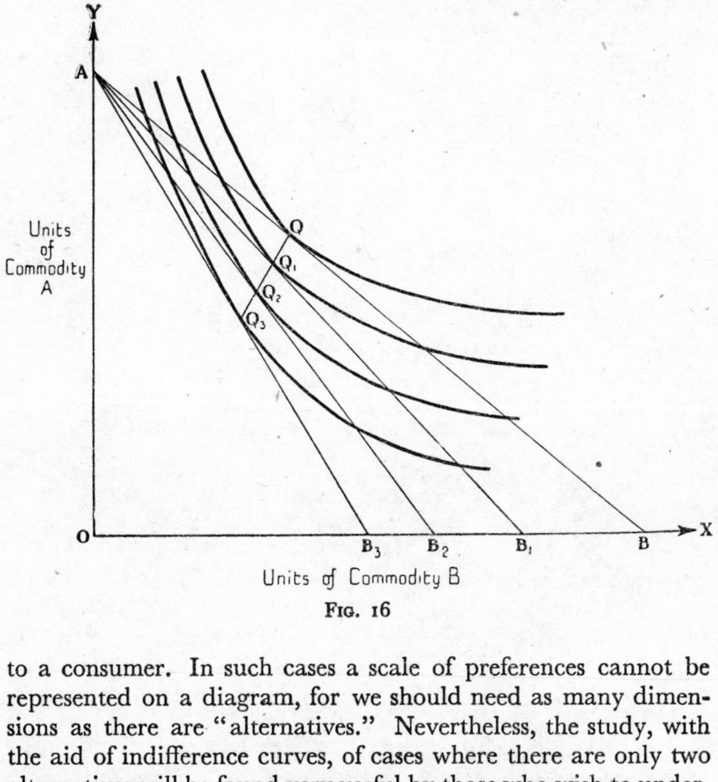

FIG. 16

to a consumer. In such cases a scale of preferences cannot be represented on a diagram, for we should need as many dimensions as there are "alternatives." Nevertheless, the study, with the aid of indifference curves, of cases where there are only two alternatives will be found very useful by those who wish to understand the Theory of Choice and its implications. It is useful, but it is not absolutely essential, and as it may be found difficult we have relegated it to an Appendix.[1]

[1] For a fuller account, see Hicks, J. R., and Allen, R. G. D.: "A Reconsideration of the Theory of Value" in *Economica*, N.S., Vol. I.

BOOK II
PRODUCTION

CHAPTER VII

THE VOLUME OF PRODUCTION

1. THE NATURE AND SIGNIFICANCE OF PRODUCTION

HITHERTO we have more or less taken it for granted that certain quantities of the various consumers' goods come forward, week by week, for sale. We must now consider the forces which determine what these quantities are. This, of course, is a large question, and most of the present volume will be concerned with one or another aspect of it. This chapter merely gives a preliminary survey of the ground to be covered.

All goods, except gifts of Nature, come into existence by being produced. We are embarking upon a study of production. Let us pause, at the threshold, to point out the great significance for social welfare of the volume of production per head of population: of the quantity and quality of the goods and services produced.

Many warm-hearted persons study economics because they hope it will throw light upon the causes of poverty and will thereby show how poverty can be abolished. It is this, said the great economist Marshall, which lends to the science its highest interest. Many think that the main goal of economic policy should be to improve the condition of the people, that is, to raise the general standard of living. But the standard of living of a person is the goods and services which he consumes. To say that a family is poor is to say that it lacks sufficient food, clothing, housing, and other consumers' goods. Poverty is, indeed, a relative term. To-day the family of a British workman, drawing unemployment relief, is fed and clothed and housed on a scale enjoyed only by a small minority in Eastern countries to-day or in the Great Britain of a hundred years ago. Nevertheless it is a scale which, judged by modern standards, is woefully inadequate. Recent investigations have shown that about half the families in Great Britain cannot afford the minimum diet required to give them reasonable protection from disease. Many children are physically under-developed, simply because their parents cannot afford to feed them properly. And if we ask why there is not more food, better housing, and in general a more adequate supply of consumers' goods available, the answer must be that the volume of production is not big enough. Manna no longer falls from Heaven. Consumers' goods must be produced. In a modern community something is done, and doubtless more could be done, to relieve poverty by sharing the available goods and services more evenly: by taxing the rich for the benefit of the poor. But social reformers have not a great deal to hope from redistribution of this kind. The rich are so relatively few in numbers that even a completely equal distribution of wealth which had no adverse repercussions upon the volume of production would do comparatively little to raise the standard of living of the masses. We cannot escape the fact that consumption is limited by the amount produced. In the short run, current output can be supplemented from stocks, and men and materials can be diverted from the production of buildings, machinery, and other capital goods towards the production of consumers' goods. But such devices can raise the standard of living only for a short time. It is necessary to maintain working capital, such as stocks of materials and other goods, and fixed capital, such as machinery, in order to keep up the output of consumers' goods. The volume of production, given the population, determines the standard of living.

It is true that the people of one country may be helped by charity or by loans from people in other countries. They may thus receive goods from abroad for which, at the moment, they pay nothing. But international charity rarely reaches very large dimensions, and loans are supposed to be repaid—if they are not, the country finds it difficult to borrow abroad in the future. For the most part, the consumers' goods which a country receives from abroad are paid for, in effect, by goods which it produces and exports in exchange. The more it produces, the more it has available, week by week, to consume within its borders or to exchange against imports. We shall postpone a study of international trade until Book V. Until then we shall write, for the most part, as if the community we are considering is a "closed" one, having no economic relations with any other. This will simplify the exposition, and the necessary qualifications will be added later. But clearly even for a country with a good deal of international trade our broad conclusion holds good. The main determinant of its general standard of living is the quantity and quality of the goods and services which it produces per week, month, or year; briefly, its volume of production. The great reason why, for example, the general standard of living is so much higher in the United States than in, say, China is that the volume of production per head of population is so much greater in the United States.

We hope that enough has been said to show that the volume of production is of very great significance for social welfare. But perhaps we should comment on the notion, which some people seem to hold, that the productive capacity of the world is so great that it would be an easy matter, if only production were organized by technicians or if only the banking and credit system were changed, to produce more than enough for everybody. Let us translate this claim into figures. Suppose that enough were produced to give every man, woman, and child as much as £5 a week will buy at the present time. This could hardly be called luxury. Yet, in order to achieve it, output in Great Britain, even if shared equally among the population, would have to be trebled, and in most countries it would have to be considerably more than trebled. It may be doubted whether those who hold this notion realize the magnitude of the claim which they are making. Frankly, it is so fantastic that it is difficult to see upon what evidence, however slender, it is based.

It is true that sometimes goods are deliberately destroyed, the most striking modern example being the 2 million tons of coffee destroyed in Brazil during 1931–4. But apart from war, only a tiny fraction of the total world output of all goods is destroyed. It is also true that men and resources are unemployed or worked on short time or below capacity. This is indeed a serious problem whose importance we do not wish to minimize. At the bottom of a slump the percentage of unemployment in an industrial country may for a time rise above 20 or even above 30. But, taking the world as a whole, and good years together with bad, continuous full employment would add perhaps 5, and at the outside 10, per cent to the total output.[1] This would be a great

[1] This estimate may strike some readers as low. They should remember that unemployment is mainly an industrial rather than an agricultural phenomenon. Total world unemployment, at the bottom of the Great Depression, was some

gain, but it would go only a small part of the way towards the ideal alleged to be capable of immediate realization.

It is more probable that those who believe in this claim have been impressed by the rapid expansion of certain industries, such as the motor-car industry, during recent years, and believe that what is possible for one industry is possible for all. Would that this were true! Then indeed the economic problem would disappear. But unfortunately output in one industry can expand only by drawing labour and materials and other resources away from other industries. If we want more motor cars or more armaments we must go short of other things. Doubtless, many works are not equipped in the most up-to-date way, but to "modernize" an industry requires capital, and that means less capital for other industries. Doubtless, methods of production could be improved, and will be improved as the march of technical progress continues, but experience shows that, taking agriculture and other branches of production together and not looking only at two or three industries where the application of "mass-production" methods has proved possible, a rate of expansion of 4 or 5 per cent a year per head is the utmost for which we can hope. And at the present moment, with technical knowledge as it is, producers are conducting their operations, spurred by the desire for profits and the fear of bankruptcy, to the best of their ability. Without the aid of a magic wand to produce new resources from nowhere and to endow men with much greater intelligence and skill and strength than they possess at present, it is quite inconceivable that the vast expansion of output claimed to be practicable could possibly take place. The economic problem, the problem of making the best use of productive resources because goods are scarce relatively to human wants, will not disappear in our lifetimes nor in those of our children or grandchildren.

Another confused notion is that a great deal of labour, such as the work done by clerks and servants and actors, is

---

30 million, whereas the occupied population of the world approached 1000 million. Even for an industrial country, 10 per cent is a very high estimate. Twenty per cent unemployment was practically unknown before 1930. Before the war of 1914 10 per cent was rare, and the average was somewhere near 5. Moreover, "unemployment" of plant and other resources is usually less than unemployment of labour, and unemployed workers and other factors are, on the whole, less efficient than those remaining in employment.

"unproductive," because it is not directly concerned with the production of goods. But what is production? Man cannot create matter. He cannot bring goods into existence out of nothing. The farmer arranges seeds in the soil in such a way that they draw sustenance from the earth and from the air and grow into plants. The shoemaker converts a piece of leather into a pair of shoes. The milkman brings milk from the dairy to the home. The shopkeeper holds a stock of goods from which his customers may select as and when they wish. Production consists in changing the form of matter or moving goods from one place to another or holding stocks of goods over time.

From the standpoint of the individual, his work is productive if it procures him an income. The question whether a particular kind of work is productive from the standpoint of the community is really a question for social philosophers. Granted that the final object of production is to satisfy the wants of consumers for consumers' goods,[1] all economic activity is productive in so far as it enables these wants to be satisfied more fully. For example, various activities are required in order to transform coal embedded in the earth into a domestic fire. The activities of the miners who hew the coal, of those engaged in transporting it, of the merchants who organize the distribution of the coal to the numerous consumers who demand it, and of the domestic servants who prepare the fires, are all "productive." It is sometimes urged that there are too many "middlemen" in one line or another. But it is always open to producers to sell directly to consumers if they wish. If they find it pays them better to sell to middlemen, the presumption is that the latter are useful links in the chain. It could doubtless be urged that activities which prove subsequently to have been misguided and useless, such as the work preparatory to constructing a canal which is never completed, are "unproductive," but of course this is a conclusion which can be drawn only after the event. Some may contend that, for example, the drink trade diminishes efficiency and is therefore "unproductive," but it cannot be denied that it satisfies consumers' wants. However, we must leave this and

[1] The producers themselves may derive a certain satisfaction from their activity. We shall refer to this in connection with Wages and with Unemployment; for the present we can leave it on one side without invalidating the discussion.

kindred questions to be discussed by social philosophers and others.

2. THE MEASUREMENT OF THE VOLUME OF PRODUCTION

The volume of production of a community is its output of goods and services per unit of time. The unit of time usually chosen for purposes of measurement is the year. This is a convenient unit, as the output of many goods and services varies with the seasons. In particular, a number of important crops are harvested, in any given country, once a year, so that a country may produce much more during the harvest months than during other months and, incidentally, if its exports consist largely of such crops they will be greater during the months following the harvest than during the other months, although the extent of this difference depends on how far stocks are held in the importing rather than in the producing countries.

It is only the output of consumers' goods and services which directly affects the standard of living[1] but, as we have seen, producers' goods of all kinds, from buildings and machinery to raw materials and semi-finished products, are required to bring about the output of finished consumers' goods. The work done, for example, in preparing the ground for the seed or in making a road is just as much "production" as the work done in adding the final touches to nearly-finished consumers' goods. Production in this broad sense goes on fairly regularly throughout the year; it is only the rate at which final products emerge from the productive process which varies from one season to another. We must therefore include goods and services of all kinds in the volume of production.

It is clearly necessary to avoid double-counting. Materials pass through various stages before they finally emerge embodied in finished goods. Thus wheat is embodied in flour and flour is embodied in bread. If all the wheat and all the flour and all the bread were included, the flour would be counted twice over and the wheat three times over. As a rule, therefore, in computing the volume of production the output of any establishment is

[1] We are thinking of a closed community. An open community may export producers' goods, receiving in exchange imports of consumers' goods for current consumption. Thus Great Britain exports, among other things, coal and machinery, and imports mainly foodstuffs.

taken "net," the value of the materials used (including, for example, the fodder consumed by cattle on farms and the heat, light, and power used by factories) being deducted from the value of the output in order to obtain the net value added by the establishment to the materials used.

Again, depreciation presents a problem. Part of the total output of a country consists of repairs, renewals, and replacements. If these were not made, the "capital" of the country—its material assets—would be less at the end of the year than at the beginning, and this would tend to reduce the volume of production in the future. It is usual, therefore, to measure the net volume of production after deducting "depreciation": to say, for example, that 10 per cent of the output is required to maintain capital intact. But it is very difficult to say exactly by how much the total capital of a country has in fact increased or diminished over a year, or exactly what percentage of the volume of production would be required to maintain capital intact.

Many thousands of different kinds of goods and services are produced. How is it possible to add them together to form a statistical total which can be used to compare the volume of production of one year with that of another year? The only possible way is to add together their money values, avoiding double-counting. But prices in one year will differ from prices in another. The *value* of output may be greater in the year when prices are high although its *volume* may be less. Various devices can be used to try to eliminate the effects of price changes in order to get a comparison of volume. Thus the output of any year can be valued at the prices ruling in some year taken as the "base" year. For example, if 1930 is chosen as the base year, and the price of a bushel of wheat in 1930 was 5s., every bushel of wheat produced in subsequent years will be valued, for this purpose, at 5s., whatever its actual price may be, and similarly with all other goods and services. In this way the output of every year is valued at the prices ruling in 1930. Suppose that the actual value of production in 1930 was £4000 million and in 1937 £5000 million, but that if everything produced in 1937 was valued at its price in 1930 the output of 1937 would come to only £4400 million. It would then be said that the volume of production in 1937 was 10 per cent greater than in 1930, although its actual value was 25 per cent greater.

But no such device can fully overcome the difficulty. The problem is in fact insoluble. What we are really trying to measure is the extent to which the output of one year will satisfy wants more fully than the output of another year. As time goes on, changes take place in the numbers and composition of the population, in their tastes, in the distribution of wealth, and in the kinds of goods and services produced. Exactly the same output might give much more satisfaction in 1930 than in 1935, for in the latter year people might want more keenly than before goods of which relatively few were produced in 1930, and less keenly than before goods of which relatively many were produced in 1930, whilst the incomes of those people whose demand for the former goods was greatest might have increased relatively to the incomes of others. No method of calculation can allow for such changes. But even if such changes are relatively unimportant, the composition of the output will change as time goes on. Let us take an extreme example. Suppose that in 1930 the value of the bacon produced and of the eggs produced was the same. In 1935, owing to swine fever on the one hand and a wave of fertility among the hens on the other hand, only half as much bacon was produced as in 1930, but 50 per cent more eggs. Is it reasonable to say that the wants for bacon and for eggs were together satisfied as fully in 1935 as in 1930? Yet their combined value, measured at 1930 prices, was the same in both years. Further, new goods, and new types and qualities of goods, come into use as time goes on. One has only to look at an early cinematograph film to see the many changes that have taken place in our clothes, furniture, motor cars, and so on. The more the composition of the output differs between two years, the more difficult it is to make a comparison. This means, in practice, that comparisons between years which are far apart have less significance than between years which are fairly close together, although even the latter can never be more than rough approximations.

But although accurate measurement is not possible, no reasonable person can doubt that the volume of production per head in Great Britain to-day is much greater than it was a hundred years ago or than it is in, say, India at the present time. And the difficulty of measuring it does not make it any the less important. We now turn, therefore, to the question of what determines the volume of production in a country with a given population.

3. INFLUENCES AFFECTING PRODUCTION

Among the forces which determine the volume of production of a community, its social organization and institutions play a large part. In Book III we shall give a general account of how production is organized under capitalism, which is the system prevailing in all modern democratic countries. But there are also other influences affecting production which operate under any form of social organization. The present book confines itself to a discussion of these influences.

They can be grouped under three broad heads. In the first place, there are influences beyond the control of man. Production may be diminished by earthquakes or floods or dust-storms; suitable weather conditions lead to good harvests and unsuitable ones to poor harvests.

In the second place, production is profoundly influenced by the technical knowledge of the community. Economic progress in the past has been due mainly to inventions and discoveries which increased man's control over Nature. However society may be organized, the man who discovers how to make two blades of grass grow where only one blade grew before is a benefactor—always assuming that the community wants grass and does not object to the new methods (as the inhabitants of Erewhon objected to machinery).

In the third place, production depends upon the means of production, or "factors of production," available, and the manner in which they are utilized. Consumers' goods are scarce, relatively to human wants, because the means of producing them are scarce. We cannot all have, for example, as much milk as we want. Milk is scarce because cows are scarce and cows are scarce because land and labour, to provide them with food, are scarce. We could double or treble the output of milk, but only at the cost of diminishing the output of other goods, by diverting land and labour away from the production of other goods and into the dairying industry. The amounts and kinds of consumers' goods which can be produced are limited, given the state of technical knowledge, by the means of production available.

We must point out, however, that an increase in the supply of labour due not to more work being done per man (or to the acquisition of robots) but to an increase in the population, might not raise the general standard of living. It would almost certainly increase total output, but it would increase also the number of persons among whom the output was shared and the percentage increase in population might exceed the percentage increase in output.

4. FACTORS OF PRODUCTION

We shall have a good deal to say, in the pages which follow, about factors of production. Hence it seems desirable to point out at once some of the difficulties and ambiguities of this concept.

Anything which contributes towards output is a factor of production. Coal is a product from the standpoint of the owner of the coal-mine, but in so far as it is used as a producers' good, as in the boiler-room of a factory, it is a factor of production. The finished products of one firm are factors of production in so far as they are used as materials by another. In short, any ingredient which "goes into" the productive process at any stage is a factor of production.

Some factors, however, cannot be appropriated by man, cannot be bought and sold, and are therefore usually left on one side in economic discussions. Sunshine is an obvious example. If one acre enjoys more favourable climatic conditions than another, it will produce more and, under a price-system, will be worth more, as agricultural land, than the other. The difference in sunshine affects the productivity of the land, but only the land, and not the sunshine, is commonly regarded as a factor of production. It is really the services rendered by a factor which contribute towards output, and not the factor itself. This may seem a hair-splitting distinction, but failure to note it may cause much confusion. An employer wants labour services, man-hours of work performed, and not men as such. Under slavery, men are bought and sold, but the price given reflects the estimated net capitalized value of their future services: it is the services, and not the men as such, which contribute to production. A given number of men may perform more or less work per year. They may work more or fewer hours, or with greater or less intensity. Hence the expression "the supply of labour" is ambiguous. It may mean the number of workers, or the number of man-hours of services rendered, or the actual amount of work performed. Similarly, for example, the machinery in a factory can be worked for eight hours a day only or, under a two-shift or three-shift system, for sixteen or twenty-four hours.

Further, a given amount of factor-services may make a greater or smaller contribution to output. The same land may produce more in one year than another simply because the climate is better. A man may exert just the same effort in broadcasting whether he is heard by a thousand or by a million listeners. A business man may exert just the same effort in reaching decisions whether they relate to pounds or to hundreds of pounds. Capital goods such as roads or bridges can also be utilized more or less fully.

We must of course bear these facts in mind, but at the same time it seems desirable to distinguish between the factors themselves and their product. The actual factors of production are the men, the land, and producers' goods of all kinds.

It is customary to group all factors of production under the three broad heads of Land, Labour, and Capital. There is not very much significance in this classification. It implies that every kind of worker, whether he be a captain of industry or a famous surgeon or a navvy, must be lumped together under Labour. It implies that land can readily be distinguished from capital, although it would puzzle a railway company or a dock company to make the distinction. And it groups together the most diverse factors, from shops to lorries and lubricating oil, under Capital.

The distinction between land and capital is often said to reside in the fact that land is a gift of Nature while capital is produced by man. Land and labour are said to be original means of production and capital is said to consist of produced means of production. But the productivity of land and labour (as also of capital goods themselves) can be increased by the investment of capital. Land can be improved by clearing it, draining it, fertilizing it, and so on. Much land, in old countries, is largely man-made and it is impossible, and unnecessary, to distinguish the original land from the subsequent improvements. In the same way workers can be made more productive by investing capital in training them. Deposits of minerals, however, can be depleted but cannot be increased. For example, the great iron-field of Lorraine will be exhausted, if ore continues to be taken from it at the rate of recent years, in about seventy years.

This threefold division into Land, Labour, and Capital is quite inadequate for some purposes. For example, if all land is lumped together and the acre is taken as the unit, we are constantly faced with the difficulty that one acre may differ very greatly in productivity from another, since an acre is merely a measure of area. We cannot therefore make any definite statements as to what happens when an additional acre is employed in the production of, say, wheat, for this additional acre may be very different from the acres already employed. In the same way one kind of labour may be very different from another, and there are numerous kinds of equipment, materials, and other goods.

The best solution seems to be to sub-divide Land and Labour and Capital, grouping together all similar acres or workers or goods, and considering each group as a separate "factor of production." Each unit of any given factor will thus be a practically perfect substitute for any other unit of that same factor. This gives us a very large number of "factors," but it is the only method of classification which makes economic analysis possible.

But we must explain one point. It will be remembered that most means of production are not completely specific, but on the contrary are capable of certain alternative uses. Suppose that Mr. Owen Jones gives up coal-mining and becomes a competent builders' labourer. Are we to say that the supply of factors of production remains the same, because Mr. Owen Jones is still Mr. Owen Jones, or are we to say that the supply of one factor, namely coal-miners, has diminished and that the supply of another factor, namely builders' labourers, has increased? We shall take the latter view. It must be remembered, however, that some investment of capital (in training workers, fencing land, and so on) may be necessary to convert one type of factor (such as wheat-land) into another (such as sheep-land).

5. THE PLAN TO BE FOLLOWED

We shall divide our study of the influences affecting production into two parts. Certain influences which are of a general and technical nature, in that they always operate whatever the system of social organization may be, are discussed in the present Book. We show how output is increased by division of labour, or specialization, and by the use of more "capitalistic" methods of production, and how changes in the proportions of the factors used affect the volume of output of any given product and the "marginal product" attributable to a given factor in that line of production. We conclude with a brief sketch of the economic problems which would confront an all-powerful dictator, and of how he might solve them. The second part of our discussion will be found mainly in Book III. There we try to show how the problems of what to produce, and by what methods, are solved, and how the technical facts discussed in the present book are taken into account, under capitalism.

But we have to proceed by stages. The monetary and banking system has a great influence on production, but we must postpone a full account of it until Book IV. Again, a discussion of the influence exerted by international trade and migration and investment is postponed to Book V. Moreover, the problem of unemployment is closely connected with monetary policy and the trade cycle, so that the discussion of it in Chapter XVII is incomplete. For the present, we are assuming a closed community in which the monetary system works smoothly and there is full employment.

It will be appreciated that a discussion of the causes of natural phenomena such as earthquakes and of events such as wars and inventions, which may exert a great influence upon production, falls outside the scope of the science of economics. But economics can and does throw light on their effects upon output and prices. We shall assume, for the most part, that the supplies of the various factors, and the state of technical knowledge, are given, as indeed, at any moment, they are. But we shall also try to show how changes in the supplies of factors (such as those due to earthquakes and wars) and in technical knowledge and in tastes affect the size and composition of the output, the methods of production used, and the prices of factors and goods. Our remarks upon these topics will be found mainly in the following Book.

CHAPTER VIII

DIVISION OF LABOUR

ADAM SMITH begins his *Inquiry into the Nature and Causes of the Wealth of Nations* with a discussion of the division of labour. He says—

The greatest improvement in the productive powers of labour, and the greater part of the skill, dexterity, and judgment with which it is anywhere directed, or applied, seem to have been the effects of the division of labour. [He takes an example from the trade of pin-making.] A workman not educated to this business (which the division of labour has rendered a distinct trade), nor acquainted with the use of the machinery employed in it (to the invention of which the same division of labour has probably given occasion), could scarce, perhaps, with his utmost industry, make one pin in a day, and certainly could not make twenty. But in the way in which this business is now carried on, not only the whole work is a peculiar trade, but it is divided into a number of branches, of which the greater part are likewise peculiar trades. One man draws out the wire, another straights it, a third cuts it, a fourth points it, a fifth grinds it at the top for receiving the head; to make the head requires two or three distinct operations; to put it on is a peculiar business, to whiten the pins is another; it is even a trade by itself to put them into the paper; and the important business of making a pin is, in this manner, divided into about eighteen distinct operations, which, in some manufactories, are all performed by distinct hands, though in others the same man will sometimes perform two or three of them. I have seen a small factory of this kind where ten men only were employed, and where some of them consequently performed two or three distinct operations. But though they were very poor, and therefore but indifferently accommodated with the necessary machinery, they could, when they exerted themselves, make among them about twelve pounds of pins in a day. There are in a pound upwards of four thousand pins of a middling size. Those ten persons, therefore, could make among them upwards of forty-eight thousand pins in a day. Each person, therefore, making a tenth part of forty-eight thousand pins, might be considered as making four thousand eight hundred pins in a day. But if they had all wrought separately and independently, and without any of them having been educated to this peculiar business, they certainly could not each of them have made twenty, perhaps not one pin in a day; that is, certainly not the two hundred and fortieth, perhaps not the four thousand eight hundredth part of what they are at present capable of performing, in consequence of a proper division and combination of their different operations.

Under division of labour one man alone may "make" a commodity, such as a pair of shoes or a chair, exchanging units of this commodity for other goods which he wants. Even so, he would probably not produce his own raw materials or tools. In a modern community it is the exception for one person alone to make a commodity.

In a factory or on a railway or ship or any other productive unit the workers are usually divided into groups, each performing a different task, as in the above illustration of pin-making. Scores or hundreds of different "occupations" may be found inside the same works. And nearly all goods require the co-operation of a number of different industries to transform the raw materials into the finished product. For example, the transformation of raw cotton into handkerchiefs (in the hands, or pockets, of the consumers) requires the co-operation of the "industries" of cotton-growing, cotton-ginning, cotton-spinning, cotton-weaving, bleaching and finishing, and of the relevant branches of wholesaling and retailing, to say nothing of transportation, building, the manufacture of textile machinery, warehousing, advertising, and so on. This implies that the labour involved is specialized into many different occupations, each performing one or more specialized tasks.

Even in primitive communities there is some division of labour, but a modern economy carries it to far greater lengths. The modern economic world is based upon division of labour. Without it, each household would have to produce for itself everything which it consumed. Only a fraction of the present population could exist and that fraction only at a very low standard of living.

We should beware, however, of attributing all the increase in productivity per head which has taken place during recent generations to the development of division of labour. Part of it has been due to the continuous increase of technical knowledge (although this itself has been greatly facilitated by division of labour, which permits men to specialize in different branches of research). Part of it, again, has been due to the growth of capital, although this too has been facilitated by the increased output made possible by division of labour. In many cases, to create new occupations by splitting up production into more processes requires more capital, in such forms as specialized machines and equipment. Thus division of labour and technical progress and the growth of capital combine together to increase output.

Division of labour could equally well be termed specialization. For it involves the specialization of means of production to particular uses—the creation of numerous "factors of production" in our sense of the term. It involves the specialization of land and capital, as well as of labour.

Let us consider first the specialization of labour. To take a simple example, suppose that two men both make exactly the same kind of simple wooden toy and sell their toys in the streets. Suppose the first man can make 20 toys in two hours but takes six hours to sell them, while the second man takes six hours to make 20 toys but only two hours to sell them. If the two men join forces, the first—specializing on making—can make 80 in eight hours and the second—specializing on selling—can sell these 80 in eight hours. Their combined output is doubled by division of labour.

There is equally an advantage in specialization if one man can do everything better than another but his superiority is more marked in one line than in others. Suppose that in a week A can make either 10 shoes or 10 handbags and actually makes 5 of each, while B can make either 8 shoes or 4 handbags and actually makes 4 shoes and 2 handbags. By joining forces and specializing, A on handbags and B on shoes, their joint weekly output is increased from 9 shoes and 7 handbags to 8 shoes and 10 handbags—an increase, supposing shoes and handbags to be of equal value, of 12½ per cent. Although this is a very simplified example, the principle it illustrates is of great importance. We discuss it at some length in Chapter XXV under the title of "Comparative Costs," but it applies to all factors (in so far as they can specialize) and to internal just as much as to international trade.

The special aptitudes of different persons for different tasks may be either innate or acquired. Division of labour enables differences in natural aptitudes to be utilized. It also enables persons to acquire an aptitude for a particular task by learning it and practising it. We thus get a wide range of occupations. This specialization, of course, implies a subsequent exchange of products. It would not be possible if each person had to produce all that he consumed.

In the same way different areas of land are specialized to different tasks. Some land may be naturally suitable for certain products, owing to its mineral resources or its climate and soil. Other land may be made suitable, for example by irrigation. Most specialized land is a blend of natural and acquired advantages. We may again illustrate by a simple example how specialization may increase production. Suppose there are two areas: one specially suited for wheat and the other for tea. If each is self-supporting, the first produces, say, 1000 units of wheat and 200 of tea; the second, say, 1000 of tea and 200 of wheat. If the first produces only wheat, it can produce, say, 2000 units and if the second produces only tea it can produce, say, 2000 units of tea. Thus instead of having only 1200 wheat and 1200 tea produced between them, by specialization they can have 2000 of each—*from the same means of production.* The first area can then exchange some of its wheat against tea from the second area.

Specialization of equipment, as we know it to-day, is made possible by division of labour. If each man did everything for himself, he would have to provide all the tools he required. Specialization economizes tools, since only the specialist in each line need have a set of his special tools. But it also does much more. It enables elaborate machinery to be used which it would not be worth while for one man to use for himself alone, even if he could construct it. Division of labour makes large-scale production possible.

Thus specialization gives men products they could not otherwise get. Without it, a man incapable of, say, playing a musical instrument would never hear music (unless he overheard his neighbour, who could play). A man living where tropical products could not be grown would have to go without them. People in a region without coal or oil or water-power could never utilize these sources of power. And men who could do some specialized things would be no better off. A saxophone player may enjoy his vocation if he can obtain the necessaries and comforts of life by playing a saxophone for a few hours a day—but if he could provide himself with nothing but moans from his saxophone he would perish miserably. There was once an African tribe whose area produced only bananas and the food value of bananas is so low that these unfortunate people had to munch bananas all day long. Specialization also provides men with products which they *could* produce for themselves but which they can get in greater quantities or with less effort by specializing on something else and exchanging: as in our wheat and tea example.

It is important to realize that division of labour is limited by the extent of the market. A doctor whose practice was confined to a small village would not be able to specialize upon one particular branch of his art. Indeed he might have to supplement his earnings as a doctor by doing some other kind of work. Again, an island eminently suitable for growing bananas but unable to export would probably be used largely for growing other things which the inhabitants desired in addition to bananas.

But the most striking illustration of this principle is the use of specialized and elaborate equipment. A large shoe factory, with elaborate machinery, can produce many more shoes than could be produced by the same amount of labour and capital divided among scores of tiny workshops. But if its sales were restricted to a small area, the machinery would lie idle for most of the time and the people of that small area could probably have satisfied their wants more fully by putting less capital into simpler shoe machinery and using the rest of their capital for other purposes.

Some products can be produced more cheaply in one place than another, but this advantage may be outweighed by the cost of transporting them. Clearly, inventions which reduce transport costs extend the scope of division of labour by widening the market.

Under division of labour it is not true that every factor is used for the purpose to which it is best suited. Most factors are not completely specific. They are capable of doing any of several things. Thus a man might be the best bricklayer in the community and only the tenth best architect. If architects were much scarcer, relatively to the demand for them, than bricklayers, the wants of consumers might be satisfied more fully if he devoted himself exclusively to architecture. Similarly, some of the best wheat-land in the world might also be fairly suitable for growing grapes. If there was a greater relative scarcity of vineyards than of wheat-land, the wants of consumers might be satisfied more fully if it were used for growing grapes.

The introduction of demand, and consumers, into this

discussion does not imply that our generalizations are restricted to a community organized on a basis of production for profit. For example, under a complete dictatorship, the dictator would be the consumer, in the sense of the person who exercised demand. However the community were organized, the wants of those in a position to make their choice effective could be satisfied much more fully, from a given supply of means of production, by taking full advantage of division of labour.

CHAPTER IX

COMBINATIONS OF FACTORS

1. FIXED AND VARIABLE PROPORTIONS

FEW economic tasks can be performed by one factor alone. Nearly every form of economic activity requires the services of two or more different factors of production, acting in combination. Labour as well as land is required to grow wheat and machinery as well as labour is required to make pins. Hence the illustrations which we gave in the previous chapter—of men making toys and of land growing wheat or tea—were not very realistic. The number of toys which a given man can make per hour is not fixed: it will be greater if he has good tools than if he has poor ones. The amount of wheat which a given piece of land will yield per year is not fixed: it will be greater (up to a point) if more labour and agricultural machinery are employed in conjunction with the land. This in no way affects the validity of our conclusions about division of labour, but it does raise the very important issue of what determines the methods of production in different industries, in the sense of the proportions in which the different factors are combined in each industry.

It may be that, in order to perform a certain task, different factors of production must be combined together in fixed proportions. Some plants seem to be planned to employ a fixed number of workers, and it appears obvious that taxicabs and taxi-drivers must be combined in the proportion of one to one.

But this is by no means the general rule. On the contrary, the general rule is that the proportions between the different factors can be varied. For example, a farmer as a rule can either acquire more land or buy more agricultural machinery or engage more labour, and a manufacturer as a rule can either substitute machinery for labour or do the opposite.

Even when the proportions appear to be fixed they can often, in fact, be changed, although this sometimes involves a change in the nature of the product. For example, in a large works more or fewer men can usually be employed in supervising; and a manufacturer may sometimes find it profitable, in the long run, to employ more men testing his products in order to avoid delivering imperfect specimens to his customers. Even in the case of taxicabs, the proportions are not absolutely fixed. Taxicabs in New York are larger and more luxurious than in London—that is to say, there is more capital per taxi-driver—while it is said by an eminent authority[1] that in Japan there are frequently two men at a time engaged in the task of operating a taxicab.

Even when the proportions really are more or less fixed, they are usually fixed only in the short run. This is due mainly to the fact that capital goods wear out or are scrapped, and need not be replaced by exactly similar capital goods. For example, if capital became more abundant relatively to labour, a blast furnace of the type requiring about twelve men to work it could be replaced by one of a more elaborate type, with devices for automatic charging, requiring only about four men to work it. In the same way ring-frame spindles, operated by relatively unskilled women, could replace mule-spindles, operated by relatively skilled men, although this would probably mean that a coarser type of yarn was produced.[2]

We shall therefore proceed upon the assumption that the proportions of the factors combined together to perform a given task *can* be varied. This raises the question of the effect upon output of changes in the proportions of the different factors employed. This question has usually been discussed in connection with the celebrated Law of Diminishing Returns.

2. THE LAW OF DIMINISHING RETURNS

The English classical economists considered this Law in relation to agriculture. They said that if population increased more agricultural produce would be demanded. But the total amount of land, they said, was fixed. Therefore as more men were employed in agriculture the average amount produced per

[1] *Japan*, by H. G. Moulton, page 398.

[2] The conditions under which capital goods, although not worn out, would be scrapped and replaced by others of a different type are discussed on pages 132–133.

man would tend to fall.[1] For example, if twice as many men were employed on the land, the total amount of produce would be less than double. This tendency, they said, might be counteracted for a time by the progress of knowledge, but it is always present. This view led them strongly to advocate a reduction in the birth rate, in order to raise the standard of living.

Actually the amount produced per man from the land has tended to increase rather than to diminish throughout the whole of recorded history; and this upward trend has been greatly accentuated during the last hundred years or so. This has been due to all kinds of inventions and discoveries, such as the discovery of the principle of rotation of crops, inventions of agricultural machinery, improved methods of fertilizing the soil, and discoveries of new varieties of crops which are more prolific or are better able to resist various diseases or various types of unfavourable climate. One consequence of this has been that, although the standard of living, so far as food is concerned, has risen greatly in most countries, the proportion of persons engaged in agriculture has steadily fallen. When one man's labour on the land produced food for little more than one family, the bulk of the population had to be rural and engaged in agriculture. Now that one man's labour on the land produces enough for three families (even at the present higher standard of living) two-thirds of the population can be, and are, set free for non-agricultural production, and can live in towns.

The progress of knowledge has thus proved to be a stronger force than the tendency to diminishing returns. But this tendency is always present. The Law of Diminishing Returns states how output would vary if the proportions of the factors were altered *at a given moment* and this rules out any changes in knowledge. It shows the alternatives which present themselves at any

[1] They said that this would happen for two reasons. In the first place, returns per man from the better land would diminish as it was worked more intensively. In the second place, worse land would be brought into cultivation. But their measurement of land in non-homogeneous acres does not affect the argument. For the worse land would be brought into cultivation only because returns per man from the better land diminished sufficiently to make the worse land worth cultivating: after a point, additional labour could produce as much upon the worse land as upon the better land. Hence the problem arises only because returns to labour diminish upon the given area of "better land" already cultivated.

moment, and, as we shall see, it applies to all branches of production and not only to agriculture.

Let us suppose, to begin with, that in any branch of production doubling *all* the factors would exactly double the total product, increasing *all* the factors by 10 per cent would increase the total product by exactly 10 per cent, and so on. In reality this may not be so. An increase in the scale of production may make it worth while to use specialized machinery or to make greater use of division of labour among the workers. We shall consider this question later. At present we leave it on one side, since our immediate problem concerns changes in the *proportions* of the different factors.

In order to simplify, we shall consider only two factors, land and labour—each of uniform quality—engaged in the production of, let us say, wheat. We can suppose, if we wish, that each worker is equipped with a given set of tools. We give an imaginary arithmetical illustration of how the output of wheat would vary, per square mile, with changes in the number of men employed per square mile. It is important to bear in mind that the number of men per square mile can be, for example, doubled either by doubling the total number of men, the amount of land remaining the same, or by halving the total amount of land, the number of men remaining the same, or by some increase in the number of men coupled with an appropriate decrease in the amount of land.

The table on p. 124 shows three stages. The first stage includes all combinations with fewer than eight men per square mile. Seven men per square mile gives the highest average product per man. As the number of men per square mile is increased from one to seven the average product per man is increased. The reason for this is that a square mile is too large an area for fewer than seven men to tackle: they waste some of their effort in trying to work it all. (Any reader who objects to these figures is at liberty to substitute a hundred, or a thousand, square miles for one square mile—but it cannot be doubted that *some* area of land will be too large for six men to cope with.) Hence, however small might be the number of men engaged in wheat-growing, and however large might be the amount of land available, they would not (if they realized the facts) attempt to work more than one square mile per seven men. Suppose, for example, that in a new colony 70 men were engaged in wheat-growing and had an almost unlimited amount of free land at their disposal. The greatest amount of wheat they could produce would be 12,000 units and they could produce this only by concentrating upon 10 square miles of land, leaving the rest of the land alone. If they tried to work, say, 70 square miles at a time they would produce only 7000 units of wheat. Hence this first stage, provided men know what they are doing, will never be found in practice.

PRODUCT OF LABOUR (IN UNITS OF WHEAT) PER SQUARE MILE OF LAND

Number of Men (per Square Mile)	Total Product (per Square Mile)	Average Product	Marginal Product
1	100	100	100
2	250	125	150
3	450	150	200
4	646	161·5	196
5	837	167·4	191
6	1022	170·3	185
7	1200	171·4	178
8	1370	171·2	170
9	1531	170·1	161
10	1682	168·2	151
11	1822	165·6	140
12	1950	162·5	128
13	2065	158·8	115
14	2166	154·7	101
15	2252	150·1	86
16	2322	145·1	70
17	2375	139·7	53
18	2410	133·8	35
19	2426	127·6	16
20	2422	121·1	− 4
21	2397	114·1	− 25

The second stage includes all combinations from eight to nineteen men per square mile. Up to this point the output per square mile continues to increase, although the output per man is diminishing.

The third stage includes all combinations containing more than nineteen men per square mile. If more than nineteen men per square mile are employed on a given area of land, the total output from that area could be increased by reducing the number of men to nineteen per square mile. The maximum output from a given area of land is 2426 units of wheat per square mile, and, in order to obtain this, nineteen men, and not more, are required. The reason for this is that when there are more than nineteen (and again if the reader does not like these figures he may substitute nineteen hundred or nineteen thousand) the men impede one another: too many cooks spoil the broth. Hence the third stage would never be found in practice, for it contains too large a proportion of labour. The only stage found in practice would be the second.

In this second stage it is clear from the table that as the proportion of labour to land increases, the average product per man diminishes. And as the proportion of land to labour increases, the average product per square mile diminishes. To see this from the table, we must read it upwards. As the number of men per square mile diminishes (that is, as the proportion of land to labour increases) from nineteen to seven, the output per square mile diminishes. (As some readers tend to think of one factor as fixed in amount, we shall illustrate this particular case by supposing the number of men to be fixed at 18. If they work one square mile, the table shows that their total output will be 2410 units. If they work $1\frac{1}{2}$ square miles what will their total output be? They will then be 12 to the square mile, so that their total output will be 150 per cent ($\frac{18}{12}$) of 1950 units, namely 2925 units. If they work 2 square miles they will be 9 to the square mile, so their total output will be twice 1531, namely 3062. Hence—

18 men produce
on 1 square mile 2410 units = 2410 per square mile,
on $1\frac{1}{2}$ square miles 2925 units = 1950 per square mile,
on 2 square miles 3062 units = 1531 per square mile.

As the amount of land per 18 men increases, the average product per square mile diminishes. It will now, perhaps, be clear that this can be seen directly from the table.)

Hence we conclude that (apart from indivisibilities, which will be explained and discussed later) in practice every factor will be combined with other factors in such a proportion that if it alone were increased its average product would diminish. We should expect to find, that is, that every factor yields diminishing average returns. There is nothing peculiar about land or agriculture: this rule applies to every factor and to every industry. And, indeed, this is exactly what our common sense would lead us to expect. If any one factor alone were increased by, say, 10 per cent, the quantity of the other factors remaining the same, we should expect the total product to increase by less than 10 per cent. If this were not so, then all the food in the world could be produced from one small plot of land, since the

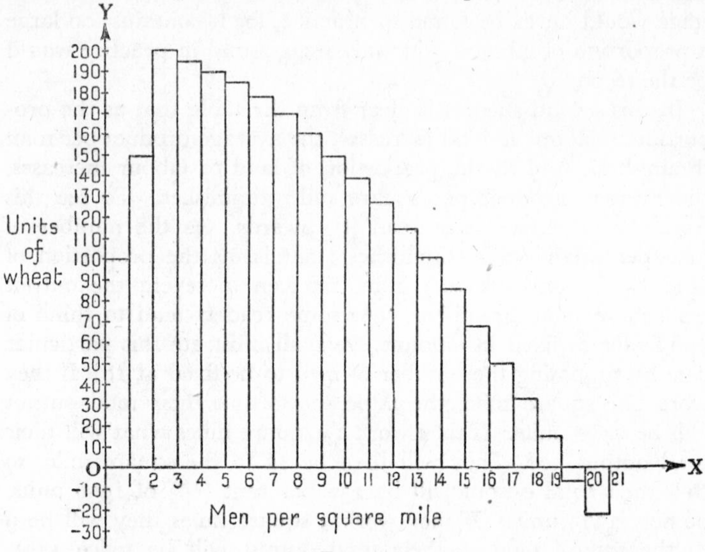

FIG. 17

output from that plot could be doubled indefinitely by doubling the men and other factors employed upon it.

We turn now to the *marginal* product of a factor. This is the addition to the total product due to the addition of one more unit of the factor. The last column of our table shows the marginal product of labour per square mile. Increase the number of men per square mile from, say, seven to eight and the marginal product of labour (per square mile) falls from 178 units to 170 units. This figure of 170 is obtained by subtracting 1200—the output per square mile when there are seven men per square mile—from 1370—the output per square mile when there are eight men per square mile. It would be misleading to say that the extra 170 units are "due to the eighth man" since, by definition, the eighth man is no more and no less efficient than any of the others. The 170 units are the marginal product of labour per square mile when eight men are employed per square mile. The marginal product of labour, per square mile, is shown in Fig. 17. Reading from left to right, the first rectangle or pillar represents the product when there is one man (namely 100 units), the second rectangle represents the amount added (namely 150

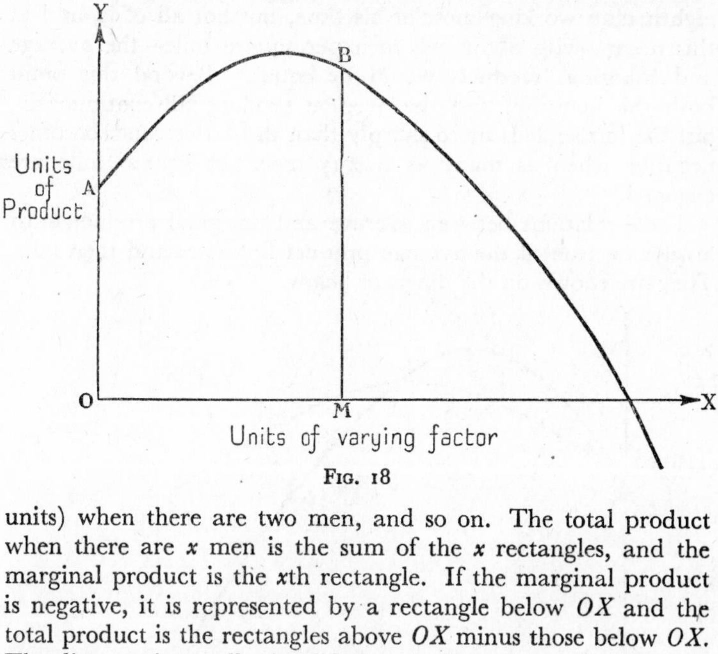

FIG. 18

units) when there are two men, and so on. The total product when there are x men is the sum of the x rectangles, and the marginal product is the xth rectangle. If the marginal product is negative, it is represented by a rectangle below OX and the total product is the rectangles above OX minus those below OX. The diagram is usually simplified, as in Fig. 18, by showing only the smoothed curve. The total product of OM men is the area $OABM$; their marginal product is BM.

It will be noted that, in our table, the marginal product of labour at first rises more sharply, as we suppose the number of men per square mile to increase, than the average product of labour. The marginal product of two men (per square mile) is 150 units and of three men 200 units as against an average product of 125 and 150 units. The marginal product of labour begins to fall (when more than three men per square mile are engaged) while the average product continues to rise until it reaches a maximum (when seven men per square mile are engaged). At this point the marginal product and the average product are equal. (They are not exactly equal—178 as against 171·4—in our table because we do not show "fractions of a man" per square mile. The true maximum average product is a little higher than 171·4 and would be reached when the number of men engaged per square mile was seven plus an eighth man working most of his time, but not all of it, and at this point—with about 7·8 men per square mile—the average and marginal products would be equal.) Beyond this point both the marginal and the average product fall continuously, but the former falls more sharply than the latter, and becomes negative when as many as twenty men per square mile are engaged.

These relations between average and marginal product must always be true[1] if the average product first rises and then falls. They are shown on the diagram below.

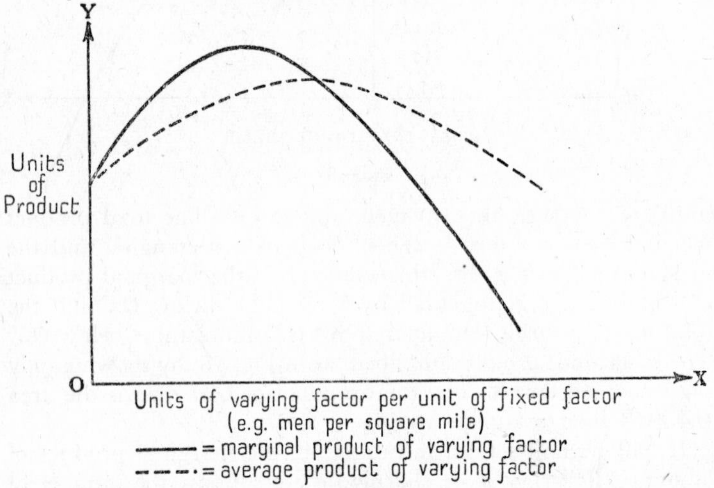

FIG. 19

We may now state the Law of Diminishing Returns. *As the proportion of one factor in a combination of factors is increased, after a point, the marginal and average product of that factor will diminish.*

[1] It is difficult to "explain" this. As long as the marginal product is above the average product, the latter must be rising, and as long as the marginal product is below the average product, the latter must be falling. When the two are equal, the average product is neither rising nor falling: i.e. it is at a maximum. Some readers may be able to convince themselves by working out

This assumes that the state of technical knowledge is given and that there are no "economies of scale."

3. THE ALLOCATION OF FACTORS AMONG INDUSTRIES

At any moment a community possesses definite quantities of the various means of production.[1] We must now give a preliminary answer to the question of what determines how these means of production are allocated among different industries. It is this allocation, of course, which determines what assortment of goods and services is produced.

In answering this question we must bear in mind that most branches of production require the co-operation of several different factors, and that most factors of production are capable of rendering service in any one of several industries.

The reader may be tempted to conclude from the hypothetical figures of our table that the "best" proportion of labour to land in wheat-growing would be seven men per square mile, since this is the proportion which maximizes the average product per man. But this would be true only if wheat-land were so abundant that the community could use as much as it wished *without thereby diminishing the production of anything else*. And this is not likely. Much wheat-land is capable of producing other things—oats, barley, sheep, grapes, and so on—and, as a rule, to allot sufficient land to wheat-growing to maximize the average product per worker in wheat-growing would inevitably mean reducing considerably the output of alternative products. The community

---

illustrations in terms of cricket scores. Or we can think of men being arranged in a row. If the first man is 5 ft. tall, the second 5 ft. 2 in., the third 5 ft. 6 in., and the fourth 6 ft., these increases in the "marginal height" will make the "average height" increase, but it will remain below the "marginal height." Thus the average height of these four men will be only 5 ft. 5 in. Now suppose that subsequent men are progressively shorter—say the fifth man is 5 ft. 11¾ in., the sixth 5 ft. 11¼ in., and so on. Clearly for some time the average height in the row will continue to increase. When the average height reaches a maximum, it is neither increasing nor decreasing—for a moment the curve representing it is neither rising nor falling, and must therefore be horizontal. The last addition neither raises nor lowers the previous average, hence it must equal it. Thus if the average height of our men first rises and then falls, and if at the point when it ceases to rise the next man does not make it begin to fall, his height must equal the average height of the men in the row.

[1] For the present we can neglect the fact that given men can do more or less work.

must somehow distribute its land among different industries in such a way that it would not prefer to have more land in one industry and correspondingly less in another. *This result is achieved when the community places the same value upon the marginal product of land (the addition to the total product resulting from the addition of one more unit of land) in every industry in which land is used.* This means that, on the figures given in our table, *less* than one square mile of land will be employed in conjunction with every seven men in wheat-growing. For if one square mile were employed with every seven men, the marginal product of land in wheat-growing would be zero—the last increment of land (given the number of men) would have added practically nothing to the total output of wheat and further additions of land would actually diminish it. The labour force, being fewer than seven to a square mile, would be trying to work more land than it could properly manage and would get a bigger product by leaving some land unused[1]. But (unless land is so abundant that, under competition and a pricing-system, its price is zero) the marginal product of this land in other industries will be positive and may be quite considerable. Hence sufficient land cannot be spared for wheat-growing to maximize the average output of wheat per man. Land is scarce and must be economized.

The same point can be illustrated, perhaps more clearly, if we consider labour. Granted that land is scarce, it might seem that the "best" proportion of labour to land in wheat-growing would be between nineteen and twenty men per square mile, since this is the proportion which maximizes the output of wheat per square mile. But this proportion would mean that the marginal product of labour in wheat-growing was zero. The last increment of men (given the amount of land) would have added practically nothing to the total output of wheat, and further additions of men would actually diminish it. If nineteen to twenty men per square mile were employed in wheat-growing, the transference of some of these men to other industries would undoubtedly increase the total output of those other industries. *The equilibrium situation is that in which the community places the same*

[1] For example, our table shows that if 8000 men tried to work 2000 square miles their total product would be only 1,292,000 units (for they would be 4 to the square mile). If they left half this land unused their total product would be 1,370,000 units (for they would be 8 to the square mile).

value upon the marginal product of (homogeneous) labour in every industry. Let us illustrate by a simple example. Suppose that 100 square miles have been allotted to wheat-growing and that 1000 men are employed in conjunction with this land. The transference of 100 of these men to other industries would diminish the output of wheat by 15,100 units. Is there anything which these 100 men can produce elsewhere which the community values so highly that it is prepared to reduce its output of wheat from 168,200 units to 153,100 units in order to obtain it? If so, the tendency will be to transfer these men. If not, the question arises, of whether enough men are employed in wheat-growing. An additional 100 men would increase the total output of wheat from 168,200 to 182,200 units. But it would reduce the output of the other industries from which the men were transferred. Is there anything which 100 men are producing in other industries which the community would be willing to forgo in order to obtain this increase in the output of wheat? If so, the tendency will be to transfer men to wheat-growing. In the same way we can ask whether the community would prefer to transfer some of the 100 square miles from wheat-growing to other uses, or conversely. When the answer to all these questions is No, equilibrium has been attained, in the sense that there will be no incentive (unless some change occurs in the data) for any factor to move out of one line and into another. *The value of the marginal product of a factor will be the same in every line in which it is employed.*

For the sake of simplicity we have spoken as if there were only two factors, land and labour, each of uniform quality and each capable of a number of alternative uses. Actually, there are many different factors—many different kinds of land and labour and capital goods—and some factors can be used for only one or two purposes. Nevertheless the conclusions of this section are valid: they do apply to the real world. We shall return to them when we study the working of the price-system under capitalism.

4. UNUSED FACTORS

The contention that "a community should use *all* its resources" sounds plausible, but probably few would agree with it if they realized its implications. Since very few economic tasks can be performed by one factor alone, and since a community usually has a large number of factors—different grades of land, and so on—people can often satisfy their wants more fully by leaving some factors of production completely unused. Suppose, for example, that a community has two coal deposits, one of thick seams near the surface and the other of thin seams, deep down and difficult to work. If it concentrates entirely on the better deposit, 1000 men will suffice to produce a million tons a year; if it concentrates entirely on the worse deposit, it will take 5000 men to produce a million tons a year; and if it gets half a million tons a year from each, 3000 men (500 + 2500) will be required. If the community wants around a million tons of coal a year, clearly it would be sheer waste to work the worse deposit: by concentrating only on the better deposit fewer men will be required to produce a given amount of coal. It will pay to work the worse deposit only when the better deposit has been worked to such an extent that the transference of labour from it to the other one would yield more coal. All this of course is on the assumption that the community desires only to satisfy its wants for consumers' goods as fully as possible from the factors of production available. If it regards the employment of large numbers of men in coal-mining as an end desirable in itself, this reasoning does not apply.

We may perhaps mention some other applications of this same principle. The community may attain its ends more fully by not attempting to cultivate relatively barren or badly situated land. A greater product may be obtained by concentrating entirely on the better land.

The principle applies also to material equipment. Suppose, for example, that a new type of machine is invented which will perform a certain task more efficiently than the type of machine at present in use for that purpose. The community may attain its ends more fully by applying the invention at once and scrapping all the old-type machines, even if many of them are practically new. Whether this will be so depends on two things.

(1) Suppose that a machine of the new type (if it were produced) and a machine of the old type (which has already been produced) would each last for ten years. Can the community satisfy its wants more fully over these ten years by using the less efficient machine, which is already in existence, or by employing co-operating factors, such as labour, to produce a machine of the

new type and to operate it? If the latter, then the community would gain by producing the new machine and scrapping the existing one.

(2) But this is not all. The community has a limited supply of savings. Some of these savings would be absorbed in producing machines of the new type. A still greater gain might be possible by using its limited savings in other ways and by continuing to work the existing machines. But if this is not so, then clearly the best course is to scrap all existing machines of the old type.

This point is not fully realized by those who deplore what they call "the loss of capital" due to inventions and who wish to restrict, for example, the competition of road transport in order to preserve the capital value of the railways.

A final example of our principle may be drawn from public works to relieve unemployment. It is sometimes urged that any such relief works must increase production since the unemployed will produce something instead of nothing. This may not be true. In order to produce something—say, roads—the unemployed must be combined with other factors such as engineers, supervisors, equipment, and materials. These co-operating factors, including the labour and capital employed in making the equipment and producing the materials, must be drawn from other uses. As a consequence of this reshuffle, the total assortment of goods and services produced *may* satisfy the wants of the community less fully than the assortment which would have been produced in the absence of relief works. But again we must point out that this is not necessarily conclusive. The community may prefer to maintain the morale and working habits of the unemployed even at this cost. Further, some economists argue that under certain conditions such relief works may lead to a general revival of economic activity. For such reasons we sometimes find relief schemes in operation—for example, some of those in America under the "New Deal"—although it would be considerably cheaper for the Government to pay the unemployed weekly sums of money without demanding any work from them in return.

5. THE ECONOMIES OF LARGE-SCALE PRODUCTION

Hitherto we have assumed that doubling all the factors engaged in an industry would exactly double the total output of that industry, increasing every factor by 10 per cent would increase the total output by exactly 10 per cent, and so on. This may not be true. The expansion of an industry may make possible what are known as "economies of scale."

The reason for this is that a different method of production may be adopted. We are not supposing any increase in technical knowledge. But if the scale of an industry is increased, it may be possible to take greater advantage of specialization. Men may specialize more upon particular tasks, and machinery may be used which previously was not worth while. Take, for example, printing. When the numbers of men and the amount of capital employed are small, hand printing-presses may be used, although the people concerned know quite well how to construct and operate a linotype machine. Multiply the men and the capital engaged by ten, and one or more linotype machines may be used and some men may specialize as compositors, others as proof-readers, and so on. The total output of the printing industry may increase more than tenfold and the marginal product of every factor may be greater than it was before.

The careful reader will note again the ambiguity of the term "factor." We can say either that the amount of the factor "capital" has increased tenfold or that one type of capital good —linotype machines—has replaced another type—hand printing-presses. But there is no dispute about the facts, and as the former method of stating them is customary in this connection, we shall follow it.

We may remark that "small-scale" methods of production may be used in an industry although its total output is fairly large and although large-scale methods would seem more efficient. The reason is that the product may be fairly costly to transport, and the consumers may be in a number of centres scattered over a wide area, so that the gain from producing in a large-scale plant would be outweighed by the cost of distributing the products. An expansion of the industry may make it worth while to use large-scale methods in each of a number of centres.

We have supposed all the factors engaged in an industry to increase by the same percentage. The same broad result may follow if some factors increase more than others, so that the proportions of the various factors alter. For example, a large increase in the capital employed in an industry may cause the adoption of methods of using it which were previously known but not worth while, because the proportion of capital available was too small. Thus it might become worth while to construct a waterworks and to lay pipes for the conveyance of water instead of carrying it in buckets.

A large increase in the scale of an "industry" may result in a separation of processes and occupations. For instance, instead of one man making a carpet some firms may do the spinning, others the weaving, others the dyeing, and so on, and many new occupations may be created in connection with the various kinds of specialized machinery used.

During the last few generations, we have had a great and continuous improvement in the technique of nearly every branch of economic activity, coupled with an increase in population and a still greater increase in capital. The "returns" to practically every factor in every industry have increased—*over time.* But at present we are ruling out, for purposes of analysis, increases in technical knowledge. How, then, can economies of scale arise? If all the methods, machinery, and so on, are known, why are they not used when the output of the industry is relatively small?

The reason is that some factors are *indivisible* and are not worth using unless the demand for their products is large enough to keep them sufficiently employed. Thus a considerable increase in the demand for a commodity or a service may make possible the use of indivisible factors which were previously not worth while installing.

This concept of indivisibility needs some explanation.

Many things must be a certain minimum size in order to perform the required tasks. Why has not every city an underground railway? Tiny carriages, lifts, and so on, might serve for Lilliputians but not for us. The size of human beings imposes a certain minimum, and the potential volume of traffic is large enough to warrant an underground railway only in the very largest cities. A tiny conveyer-system might serve for toy motor cars, but to produce cars of the usual size it must be on a certain minimum scale and is worth installing only if the demand for cars is sufficient to enable it to be fairly fully utilized. In the same way there is an absolute minimum to the size of a linotype machine, a blast furnace, and a host of other capital goods.

Such things would not be worth installing if they had to remain idle most of the time owing to the limited demand for their products.

Some factors are more efficient, up to a point, the bigger they are. Consider, for example, a ship. The carrying capacity of a ship increases roughly with the cube of its dimensions, in the same way that a 2 × 2 × 2 box holds eight times as much as a 1 × 1 × 1 box. But, up to a point, the resistance of a ship in the water increases roughly as the square of its dimensions. Hence, within limits, bigger ships need less equipment and fuel and crew per unit of carrying-space. And the same general principle applies to steam-engines, electric-power plant, water-works, flour-mills, and very many other types of plant and equipment.

A man also is indivisible. A night watchman may be able quite well to watch a certain building but he cannot simultaneously watch a building half its size at one end of the town and another building half its size at the other end of the town. One doctor is not a tenth as good as ten doctors each of whom has specialized in a different branch of medicine.

Thus the use of an indivisible factor, being an aspect of specialization or division of labour, is limited by the extent of the market. An increase in the extent of the market, whether it comes about by a growth of population or by cheaper transport or by an increased preference for the commodity or service in question, may make it possible to take advantage of economies of scale, although, of course, the scope for such economies is different in different industries. And these economies always involve the use of indivisible factors of production.

6. CONSTANT AND INCREASING RETURNS

We have seen why economies of scale may be possible. But, *given* the scale of production in an industry, how can a small increase in the amount of one factor, in that industry, raise its marginal product? Or how can an increase of, say, 10 per cent in one factor alone raise the total output of the industry by 10 per cent or more, showing constant or increasing average returns to that factor?

The answer is again to be found in the concept of indivisibility.

Indivisibility may be present in the product. Suppose that the task consists of moving some heavy object, like a steel bar or a grand piano. Two or three men may scarcely be able to move it at all. Ten men, for example, may be able by their combined efforts to do three or four times as much work of this kind as five men. Hence doubling the men over this range—from five to ten—would more than double the product. Over this range there would be increasing returns to labour.

But the most important indivisibilities are those of specialized factors. It may be worth while to employ some indivisible factor although the demand is not sufficient for it to be used to capacity. For example, it may be worth while to use a ship of, say, 2000 tons on a certain route although it is known that its total cargo-space will seldom be filled. It may be worth while to set up plant for producing electricity sufficient to meet a peak demand although for most of the time the demand may be considerably smaller. In a shop it may be worth while to employ a staff of assistants large enough to cope fairly well with the rush hours, although they may be idle for part of the time.

In these circumstances there may be constant or even increasing returns to the other factors. For example, if the crew of a ship is increased by 10 per cent, the ship may be able to carry 10 per cent or more than 10 per cent additional passengers or cargo, because previously it was working below capacity. The average and marginal product of the labour working the ship would remain constant or increase. Again, an increase in the number of receiving sets might make possible a corresponding increase in the number of listeners without involving any change in the programmes of the transmitting stations. Only the sets would increase and they would yield constant average returns: an increase of 10 per cent in the number of sets would increase the amount of "listening-in" by 10 per cent because the "indivisible" programmes would be more fully utilized.

Obviously the phenomena discussed in this chapter would be present in any community, however organized. We shall see later how they affect costs under a price-system.

CHAPTER X

CAPITAL

1. THE DEFINITION OF CAPITAL

It is often urged, and rightly, that a precise definition of terms is essential to clear thinking. But this does not mean that one definition of a term must be right and all others wrong. Often any one of several possible definitions, provided that it is clear and unambiguous, will serve as well as another for the purpose in hand: the choice between them is little more than a matter of taste. This is so with the term Capital. It has been defined by economists in a number of different ways, but any one of several (if not all) of these ways will serve equally well to help in explaining how an economic system works, and this is the main task of Economics.

It is generally agreed that capital is a *stock* or *fund* existing at a given moment, as opposed to income, which is a *flow* over time: so much per week or per year. The capital of an individual, in a society based on private property, may include paper titles such as stocks and shares which give him the right to a fixed money income or to a certain proportion of the profits made by a company. From the standpoint of a (closed) community, however, capital consists of material assets or goods. Some writers speak of "human capital," but it is usual, in the absence of slavery, to exclude human beings.

This stock of goods, at any moment, which constitutes the capital of the community, at that moment, certainly includes produced means of production, such as factories and machinery and railways, together with raw materials and other "intermediate products" in course of being transformed into finished commodities. It is generally agreed that it should include stocks of consumers' goods held by "producers" and traders, both shopkeepers and others, since a process of production is not completed until the commodity is in the hands of the final consumer. But it is a matter of opinion whether it should include land, or consumers' goods in the hands of consumers, or both.

The argument for excluding land is that it consists of gifts of

Nature whose supply cannot be increased by man. If land is defined in this way, the argument is valid. True, it is function and not origin which matters when we consider the extent to which man is aided in production by his environment: a canal may be just as useful as a river. But it is desirable to distinguish between capital, which can be increased by man, and gifts of Nature, which cannot. The difficulty is, however, that much land—in the usual sense of the term—is man-made. A community can save and invest by improving its land as well as by increasing its stock of other goods. And it is almost impossible in practice to distinguish between original gifts of Nature and improvements made by man; otherwise we could include the latter, but not the former, in capital. Perhaps the best solution is to admit that logically we should include land in our concept of capital but to urge that it is such an important category of capital that it is convenient to follow the usual practice of treating it separately.

The argument for excluding consumers' goods in the hands of consumers from capital is presumably that the process of production, as far as they are concerned, is completed. But this is not true. In the last analysis, consumers' goods are wanted for the flow of services which they yield. For example, coal yields a flow of warmth as it is consumed in a fire, houses yield a flow of shelter, and food yields a flow of nutrition. Thus a house may yield services to its owner, who lives in it, for many years; and the same applies, over a shorter period, to other fairly durable consumers' goods such as furniture and radios and motor cars. Stocks of food, clothing, and so on, are held, like stocks in factories or shops, to avoid the trouble of making very frequent purchases of small amounts and as a reserve against possible contingencies. It seems unnecessary to follow the practice of those economists who declare that a man's motor car, for instance, is to be regarded as capital when he is using it for business but not when he is using it for pleasure. It might be urged that there will be no further financial transactions concerning consumers' goods in the hands of consumers. But that is not so: for example, a consumer may decide to let a furnished room in his house or to hire out his private yacht. Hence I agree with those economists who include consumers' goods in the hands of consumers in capital. They are sometimes called "consumers' capital."

We therefore define capital as the stock of goods of all kinds, including land, existing at a given moment. But for most purposes we shall treat land separately.

2. THE ACCUMULATION OF CAPITAL

We are not concerned at present with the distinction between "capitalist" communities, like those of Great Britain and the United States, and "non-capitalist" communities, like that of Soviet Russia. This distinction rests upon the ownership and control of the capital. But it is clear that any community will have some capital, whoever may own or control it. Our present purpose is to show how capital may be increased, and how such an increase may enable the community to satisfy its wants more fully in the future, by augmenting the future output of consumers' goods and services.

This is fairly clear if we think of "consumers' capital." If a community produces more houses and furniture and other fairly durable consumers' goods, then after a time it will have a bigger stock of these goods and they will continue to contribute directly to the satisfaction of wants until they are worn out. The greater the stock of houses at any moment the greater will be the output of "shelter" in the future.

The same applies to "producers' capital," the only difference being that such goods contribute indirectly, and not directly, to the satisfaction of wants. To take a simple example, the use of boats may enable men to catch more fish. The contribution of the boats is an indirect one. Consumers want fish and not boats, but the boats enable their desire for fish to be satisfied more fully.

Granted the technical fact that the use of boats increases the productivity of men engaged in fishing, the question arises of how a community—wanting fish and knowing that it could get more fish if it had boats—could acquire boats. We use boats purely as an illustration: our answer applies equally to the accumulation of any other kind of capital, including consumers' capital and improvements to land.

A community could acquire boats simply by working longer hours, devoting the extra time to boat-building. This would involve a sacrifice of their leisure. If they did not wish to give up, for the time being, some of their leisure, only three broad courses would be open to them.

The first course would be to store some of the food, clothing, and other consumers' goods which they produce. Suppose that after eleven months they had stored enough to provide them with supplies for a further month. During that month they could all set to work to produce boats instead of consumers' goods.

The second course would be for them all to devote part of each working day to the production of boats. If, for example, they worked twelve hours a day and devoted one of these twelve hours to building boats, they would have as many boats at the end of a year as under the first plan.

The third course would be to arrange for some of their number, say one-twelfth, to work only at boat-building, the others supplying them from day to day with consumers' goods. This plan is the one which corresponds to actual practice. It has the advantage of enabling some men to specialize in the art of boat-building, and it avoids the necessity of keeping large stores of food.

Under any of these courses, the community, for the time being, would produce and consume fewer consumers' goods than before. Labour, and other factors of production, which might have been employed in the direct production of consumers' goods would be employed instead in producing boats. This labour has, as its ultimate object, an increase in the output of fish. It does not achieve this object until a considerable time has elapsed. In the first place, it takes time to build a boat. In the second place, the boat lasts for some time. Thus the fruits of the labour employed in building a boat are the increased supplies of fish obtained, owing to the use of the boat, during the life of the boat. The average length of time between the "input" of this labour and its final "output" may thus be considerable. Clearly the part played by capital derives its importance from the fact that production takes time. If consumers' goods were all produced instantaneously, without any preliminary work in producing instruments of production, raw materials, and so on, and if no consumption goods were durable, like houses, there would be no possibility of increasing output by adopting methods of production which involve the use of more capital.

In the last resort, all capital may be regarded as the product of labour and land. We include land because at any rate the raw materials—the wood, in the case of a boat—probably require land for their production. Tools, themselves capital, may be used to produce capital goods but the tools themselves are the product of labour and land. But to increase the amount of capital—in the sense of the stock of goods in existence—requires what is usually called "waiting." It involves a renunciation, for the time being, of consumption. Some people consume less than they could in order that capital may be produced.

The incentive to "wait," in this sense, is that output can be increased by the use of more "capitalistic" or "roundabout" methods of production: that is, of methods involving the use of more capital. Of course, not all roundabout methods are more productive than direct methods, but people choose only those which are. If, for example, the boats built by our imaginary community were to take a year to build and were to last for five years, a considerably greater output of fish might be obtained over those six years by constructing and using the boats than by using *the same factors of production* to catch fish without the aid of boats.

3. MAINTAINING CAPITAL INTACT

Suppose that the boats of our hypothetical community have a life of five years, after which they are of no use. If our community, having obtained the boats, made no provision for replacing them, at the end of five years they would be back where they began, boatless, and would have to begin the cycle all over again if they still thought that the extra fish were worth the requisite amount of "waiting." But if they wished to maintain a constant output of fish, they would make provision, during these five years, for replacing the boats by new ones immediately they had worn out. Instead of using all their available labour, and other factors, during those five years, to produce consumers' goods, they would employ some in boat-building, so that they would always have the same number of boats in good condition, old ones being replaced by new ones immediately they wore out. This is termed "maintaining capital intact."

This concept, however, presents difficulties if applied to a period over which there are changes in tastes or technique or external conditions. Suppose that all the members of our community changed their scales of preferences in favour of meat as against fish. In order to maintain their capital intact they would have to divert some factors from the task of replacing boats to the task of increasing the equipment required to produce meat. Suppose, again, that an improvement in knowledge or in external conditions—say, the discovery of new fishing-grounds or an immigration of fish—enabled more fish to be caught per man. Capital could be maintained intact by maintaining a smaller number of boats, yielding the same output of fish as before. In general, capital is maintained intact if—given the co-operating factors—the output of consumers' goods which it helps to produce in any period is regarded by consumers as yielding them equivalent satisfaction to that yielded by the output of any other period.

4. CAPITAL CONSUMPTION

Suppose that our community suddenly decided—because, for example, it believed that the end of the world was at hand—to cease bothering about the future. It could considerably raise its standard of living by diverting labour and other factors from making repairs and renewals and replacements of existing capital towards more direct methods of producing consumers' goods. Of course, this higher standard of living could not be maintained for long. Worn-out plant and equipment would not be replaced, buildings would not be kept in good repair, stocks of goods held in reserve would diminish, and the growing shortage of capital would reduce the output of consumers' goods. The community would be constrained to return to more and more primitive methods of production, and, if it persisted in consuming its capital, it would be reduced in the end to an extremely low standard of living. But in the short run it could increase its output of consumers' goods, and therefore its standard of living, by employing more of its factors on the direct production of consumers' goods (with the aid of existing capital, as long as it lasted) instead of maintaining or increasing its capital. This process is known as "capital consumption." During a war a country may be constrained to consume some of its capital by diverting factors from such occupations as erecting and repairing buildings to the more urgent task of trying to win the war.

5. CONCLUSIONS

The conclusions which we have obtained from our study of these imaginary simple cases apply to the modern world of reality. Most consumers' goods are produced, in a modern community, by highly capitalistic methods. For example, cotton goods are in part the final product of the labour employed in growing the cotton, in part they are the final product of the labour employed in mining the coal to smelt the iron which made the spindles, and so on. The great bulk of all the goods existing at any moment are not consumers' goods but producers' goods. By far the greater part of the productive activity which is going on at any moment will not come to final fruition for months or even years.

We need add only a few remarks to bring our example of the boats into harmony with reality. In the first place, there are many different consumers' goods. A community must somehow choose to what extent it wishes to increase the output of some consumers' goods more than of others. The application of more capitalistic methods to the production of, say, fish, need not involve a corresponding increase in the output of fish, since factors previously employed in producing fish can be set free for other tasks: fewer factors, employed in a more capitalistic way, can produce the same output of fish as before.

In the second place, the state of technical knowledge usually permits a choice between a whole range of methods in producing any given commodity. One method is more capitalistic and more productive than another, a third is still more capitalistic and still more productive, and so on. For example, boats may be made more or less durable, or may be equipped with motors. The community must somehow choose to what extent it is worth "waiting" in order to obtain a still greater output in the future.

In the third place, capital goods do not usually remain in perfect technical condition and then suddenly collapse, like the wonderful "one-hoss shay." Part of the activity involved in maintaining capital intact consists of making repairs.

In the fourth place, productive enterprises all need to carry stocks of goods, which may include stocks of their own final products as well as of raw materials, fuel, intermediate goods, and so on. These stocks are a necessary element in the productive process. They must be carried mainly because of unforeseen contingencies. For example, a manufacturer may receive an unexpected "rush" order, and therefore carries stocks of his finished product. He may not be able to secure all the raw materials he wants every day, and therefore carries a stock of them. These stocks form part of his capital.

Finally, we should remember that there are other methods of making provision for the future, apart from increasing the stock of capital. Factors of production can be used to increase the productive capacities of human beings, by educating and training them or by improving their health and physique. Further, factors of production can be devoted to promoting the progress of technical knowledge, for example, by means of research. These two methods are alternatives to increasing capital, and they, too, involve "waiting."

CHAPTER XI

PRODUCTION UNDER A DICTATOR

1. INTRODUCTION

Any community, however organized, must somehow decide what to produce. It cannot fully satisfy all its economic wants. It must decide to what extent it will satisfy some of its wants at the cost of leaving other wants unsatisfied. This means that it must decide how it will distribute its limited stock of factors of production among different "industries."

It will be instructive to consider how this problem would be solved by a dictator. We may suppose that all his subjects obey him gladly, performing whatever tasks he sets them to the best of their abilities, so that he need not set aside factors of production for the purpose of maintaining his authority, and we may further suppose that he is able to survey the economy as a whole and, somehow surmounting the serious difficulties mentioned in Chapter I, to weigh different possible alternatives against one another. He may choose whatever courses seem to him to be in the best interests of his people, but in any event he alone makes the final decisions. It is his scale of preferences, whatever may be the motives which shape it, which is the ultimate arbiter.

2. ONE SCARCE FACTOR

Suppose that there is only one scarce factor of production: homogeneous labour. All other means of production are so abundant that there is no need to economize them. Let us call them "land." Then, in every industry, whatever amount of labour may be employed will be combined with that amount of land which maximizes its product. Given the number of men in any industry, average output per man will be as high as possible. Of course, this does not mean that the proportions of labour and land will be the same in all industries. The amount of land per man which will maximize the output per man will probably be different in each industry. If our arithmetical example on page

124 of Chapter IX represented the situation in wheat-growing, the proportions would be 1 square mile of land to each seven men, since either a greater or a smaller proportion of land would give a smaller output per man.

But our dictator would have to decide how to distribute his labour force among the different industries. He would distribute it in such a way that he would not value the additional product obtainable by moving a man from any one industry to any other more highly than the amount of the product of the former industry which he would thereby forgo. That is to say, his equilibrium distribution of labour would be such that, according to his valuation, the marginal product of labour in every industry would be equal.

3. TWO SCARCE FACTORS

Next suppose that there are two scarce factors: homogeneous labour and homogeneous land. Since they are both scarce, he will combine them in such a way that both all the land and all the labour are employed (assuming that their proportions, in each industry, can be varied). In no industry will labour have enough land, assisting it, to maximize average output per man. For if it had, additional land in that industry would diminish the total output of that industry: the marginal productivity of land in that industry would be zero. But land is scarce, so that if other industries had additional land they would considerably increase their output. Hence sufficient land cannot be spared for any one industry to maximize average output per man. This means that in all industries the proportion of labour to land will be greater than the proportion which maximizes average output per man, so that the marginal productivity of labour in all industries must be diminishing. Exactly the same reasoning applies if we transpose the words labour and land. There is not enough labour available to maximize output per acre, so that the marginal productivity of land in all industries must be diminishing.

The equilibrium distribution of labour and land among industries will be such that, according to the valuation of the dictator, the marginal product of labour in any industry is equal to the marginal product of labour in every other industry, and the marginal product of land in any industry is equal to the marginal product of land in every other industry. For under these conditions the dictator will have nothing to gain by any further transfer of either labour or land between industries.

It must be emphasized that the valuations of the dictator will determine his decision. Suppose, to take a simple example, that he has 1000 men producing 20,000 bushels of wheat and another 1000 men producing 20,000 bushels of barley. It may be that the transfer of 100 men from the wheat industry to the barley industry would diminish the output of wheat by only 1000 bushels, or 5 per cent, and would increase the output of barley by 2000 bushels, or 10 per cent. But the dictator, knowing this, may not make the transfer. He may very well prefer 20,000 bushels of wheat and 20,000 bushels of barley to 19,000 bushels of wheat and 22,000 bushels of barley. His aim is not to maximize the number of bushels, or tons, of total product, nor to transfer factors whenever the percentage addition to one product exceeds the percentage thereby forgone of another product. His aim is simply to obtain that assortment of goods, out of the multitudinous possible assortments, which he most prefers.

4. MANY SCARCE FACTORS

In reality there are many scarce factors—many different kinds of labour and of land and of produced means of production—but the above analysis applies. A dictator would employ all units of all scarce factors and would distribute them so that the marginal product of any factor was the same, according to his valuation, in all industries in which it was employed.

The dictator would take account of indivisibilities. He might know, for example, that doubling the factors engaged in the motor-car industry would quadruple its output by permitting the introduction of a conveyer system and increased division of labour among the men. Nevertheless he might decide to leave the motor-car industry as it was, preferring the present product of the factors which would have to be transferred to three times the present output of motor cars. Again, he might know that the output of certain commodities—for example, houses or dresses—could be greatly increased, without employing more factors, by "standardization." For if only two or three types were produced, it might be worth while to introduce certain "indivisible" means of production or to utilize existing "indivisible" factors more fully. Nevertheless he might prefer the existing diversity to a larger output of standardized goods.

5. SPECIFIC FACTORS

Let us now suppose that certain factors are specific. Some land, for example, is suitable only for forests. How will this affect the problem? There are four possibilities.

(1) If there is so much of this forest-land that not enough other factors can be spared to utilize it all, it will be a free good. Enough of this land will be combined with, say, labour to maximize the average output per man in this industry and its marginal productivity, therefore, will be zero.

(2) If other, non-specific, land is equally suitable for forests, and the dictator's relative desire for forests is so great that he employs other land, in addition to the specific forest-land, for this purpose, the marginal productivity of the forest-land will be the same as that of other land. Under these conditions its specificity will have no effect.

(3) The dictator may utilize all the specific forest-land, but no other land, for growing forests. If the forest-land were capable of other uses, he would transfer some of it to the other industries. Under these conditions the marginal productivity of forest-land, while it may be positive, will be less than the marginal productivity of other land. For it will be used in a greater proportion (relatively to labour) than if it were non-specific.

(4) It may be that no other land can grow forests and that, if it could, the dictator would employ some of it, in addition to the specific forest-land, for that purpose. Then the forest-land will be combined in a smaller proportion with labour than if the other land were able to grow forests, so that its marginal productivity will be higher than that of other land. But the marginal productivity of labour, as valued by the dictator, will be the same on forest-land as on other land. If, by transferring some workers from one kind of land to another, he could get extra products which he preferred to those he would have to give up, he would do so.

6. JOINT SUPPLY

We have assumed that each industry produces only one product. In reality most industries produce a number of different products. This, however, makes no essential difference to the foregoing conclusions.

It may be that an industry cannot avoid producing two or more products in practically fixed proportions. For example, in cotton-growing a pound of raw cotton may be inevitably accompanied by about two pounds of cotton-seed. But this merely means that the dictator must balance the possibility of using factors of production to produce an extra quantity of cotton plus double that quantity of cotton-seed against the possibility of using them to produce such and such a quantity of some other commodity.

As a rule, however, it is possible to vary the proportion in which two or more commodities are jointly produced. For example, sheep can be bred to yield either more wool or more mutton, and types of coal can be selected for coking which yield either more coke or more gas. Thus our dictator can survey the possible assortments of different goods available from given factors and plan production to obtain that assortment which he most prefers.

7. PROVISION FOR THE FUTURE

Our dictator will have to decide, in distributing his factors of production among different industries, to what extent and in what ways he will sacrifice a potential output of consumers' goods in the immediate future for the sake of a greater output in the more distant future. Let us consider, in general terms, the chief ways in which he could thus make the productive activity of the community more "capitalistic" or "roundabout."

(1) There would certainly be plenty of scope, given the state of technical knowledge, for increasing future output by using factors of production to increase the stock of capital—for example, by constructing such things as machinery and buildings to be used in the various industries. Thus the dictator may know, or may be informed by his technical experts, that the output of certain agricultural products could be considerably increased by the use of more fertilizer, that the output of pig-iron could be considerably

increased by constructing larger and more "up-to-date" blast furnaces, that the volume of traffic handled by the railways could be considerably increased by electrifying the railways, and similarly for practically every branch of production.

(2) He may know that to set aside factors of production for different kinds of research would very probably yield increased knowledge which, when applied to production, would considerably increase output.

(3) He may know that he could increase future output by using factors of production to improve, in various ways, the productive capacities of the working population. We have assumed that every worker performs his task to the best of his ability. But his ability might well be increased by training and instruction. To assume a given state of technical knowledge is by no means to assume that every worker is equipped with sufficient relevant knowledge to do his job to the best of his physical and mental capacity. For example, the efficiency of farmers might be increased if they were carefully instructed how to apply the results of research work performed upon experimental farms.

This general heading covers the provision of education and training to the children who will later become workers. It covers also the maintenance and improvement of the physical capacities of present and future workers by setting aside factors of production to prevent sickness and accident and to maintain workers in health and physical efficiency. This may well involve keeping them adequately supplied with "necessaries for efficiency" such as food. A certain minimum of consumers' goods per worker is necessary to maintain life: larger amounts, above this minimum, may indirectly contribute towards future output by increasing the physical capacities of the workers.

(4) The dictator may know that he can convert certain factors into others. For example, certain forest-land may be turned into land capable of growing crops at the cost of present expenditure in clearing it. Again, certain coal-miners may be converted into, say, builders' labourers at the cost of present expenditure in training them for this new occupation.

It will be observed that, in order to obtain "greater efficiency" in production, our dictator must make some sacrifice of present output of consumers' goods. He must use his factors of production in a more "roundabout" way, diverting some of them from the production of consumers' goods to such uses as the production of additional machinery, the promotion of research, the diffusion of existing knowledge, and the service of preventive medicine. But it is certain that he will not utilize all the possibilities open to him of increasing future output in these ways. Probably it would be possible for him to use all his available factors of production in ways, such as constructing new roads and railways and power-plant and buildings, which would yield a greatly increased output in the future—provided that workers remained alive to produce it. But, as we have seen, a certain output of consumers' goods would be necessary to maintain his labour force alive, and greater outputs would yield fruit, up to a point, by increasing the productive efficiency of the workers. Further, our dictator might not regard his workers merely as instruments to be supplied with more or fewer consumers' goods as engines are supplied with more or less fuel. He might choose to sacrifice the present to the future only to a certain extent, even if his subjects thereby enjoyed a standard of living well above that sufficient to supply them with "necessaries for efficiency."

Our dictator, then, will consider all the different ways in which the future output of consumers' goods could be increased by setting aside factors of production to perform tasks which would yield fruit only in the future. Taking account of the probable future yields of different forms of "investment," he will decide to what extent, and in what ways, he will make production more "capitalistic." The technical experts whose schemes have been rejected will doubtless complain that their industries are "inefficient" and badly need more up-to-date equipment. But "efficiency" is a vague and question-begging term. Not all wants can be fully satisfied, and not all potential investment opportunities can be utilized, for factors of production are limited in amount. The economic problem is one of choosing between possible alternatives. Under our present assumptions, the choice is exercised by the dictator. His technical advisers have performed their task when they have informed him of the available possibilities. Such terms as "efficient" have no meaning when applied to his decisions, for he alone knows his own scale of preferences.

We must now consider how these problems are decided in a modern capitalist economy.

BOOK III

THE WORKING OF THE PRICE-SYSTEM UNDER CAPITALISM

CHAPTER XII

THE CONTROLLING POWER OF DEMAND

1. THE DISTINGUISHING FEATURES OF CAPITALISM

WE have seen how a dictator would solve the problem of what to produce: of how to use the available factors of production. We must now consider how this problem is solved in a modern capitalist community. We shall consider also the connected question of what forces determine the relative remuneration of the different factors. This question hardly arises under a complete dictatorship, since everybody gets what the dictator chooses to give him.

The economic system of Great Britain, the United States, France, and indeed all democratic countries, is capitalism. The working of the system varies between these countries, especially as to the amount of control exerted by the State, but the generalizations which follow are substantially true of all of them.

A capitalist economy is the antithesis of an economic dictatorship. There is no central planning of production as a whole. The State operates certain industries, such as the Post Office, imposes various restrictions upon the use of property, exercises some regulation over working conditions, and prevents or restricts the production and sale of certain commodities. Subject to the limitations imposed by the State, everybody is more or less free to do what he likes. The economic activities of the community are determined by the apparently unco-ordinated decisions of a multitude of different persons, since each owner of a factor of production (including workers, who—in the absence of slavery—own their own labour) is free to use it as he pleases, and to dispose of its earnings as he wishes.

This freedom may be expressed by saying that the three distinguishing features of capitalism are: (1) Private Property, (2) Freedom of Enterprise, and (3) Freedom of Choice by Consumers.

The institution of Private Property means that the owner of any kind of property may use it, or may hire it to somebody else, provided he complies with the law of the State, as he pleases.

Thus if a man owns some land he may turn it into a private park, or build upon it, or use it for growing, say, wheat, or lease it to somebody else or leave it idle. His choice is restricted, of course, to the realm of what is possible. His land may be too small in area to make a full-size golf course and it may not receive enough sunshine to produce bananas. But within this realm he is free to do whatever he pleases with the land—and to keep or exchange whatever it yields him. The land is his private property.

The institution of Freedom of Enterprise means that a man is free, provided he complies with the law of the State, to engage in whatever economic activity he pleases. He may start any kind of business he wishes. If he is already running a business, he may close down for as long as he thinks fit. Or he may engage in whatever occupation, and work for whatever employer, he pleases; and he may transfer to another job or may remain idle just as he wishes. Of course his range of choice is limited. He may not be able to command sufficient capital to set up in business for himself (except, perhaps, in such activities as hawking). He may not have the capacities necessary to obtain employment in some lines and he may lack the training required to find employment in others. But, within the range open to him, his choice is free.

The institution of Freedom of Choice by Consumers means that people are free, provided they comply with the law of the State, to dispose of their money as they please. A man can buy whatever commodities he thinks fit. If he wishes, he can hoard some of his money. If he wishes, he can save some of it, investing it in whatever way he pleases. Here again, of course, there are limits to what is possible. Many people receive too little, as payment for their labour or for the use of their property, to enable them either to enjoy a very high standard of living or to save any considerable amount. But within these limits, and subject to the limitations made and enforced by the State, they are free to do what they will.

We must now answer our question. What are the forces which determine how the available factors of production are used?

2. THE SOVEREIGNTY OF THE CONSUMER

The answer is that under capitalism the consumer is king. The final purpose of all productive activity is to produce consumers' goods. The owner of any factor of production will use it—subject to minor qualifications to be mentioned shortly—for whatever purpose seems likely to yield him the greatest money return. But the money returns, the earnings of factors of production, come in the last resort from the money paid by consumers for the goods which these factors help to produce. Hence it is the preferences of consumers, as shown by the ways in which they spend their money, which determine what shall be produced.

This would be quite clear if all goods were produced to order. The directions of economic activity would then be determined by the orders given by consumers. Retailers would pass on these orders to wholesalers, wholesalers to manufacturers, manufacturers to producers of intermediate products, and so on. In fact most goods are produced *in anticipation* of consumers' demands. Entrepreneurs pay many factors of production *before* their products are sold. But this does not alter the fundamental truth of the above statement. Entrepreneurs act upon their anticipations of consumers' demand. If their anticipations are correct, they themselves obtain a larger money return than if they are wrong. If they turn out to be wrong, entrepreneurs change their plans, to bring them into line with the wishes of consumers. Production is controlled by demand or rather, for the most part, by anticipated demand. Under a dictatorship it is the valuations of the dictator which determine, within the limits of what is technically possible, how factors of production are used. Under capitalism the controlling force is the valuations of consumers, as shown by the ways in which they spend their money.

Of course there are limitations upon the power of consumers to determine what shall be produced. In the first place, there are the limitations imposed by what is physically possible, given the amount of factors available and the state of technical knowledge. Many different assortments of goods can be produced, but there is always an upper limit beyond which, in order to have more of one good, consumers must have less of other goods. This limitation appears, to an individual consumer, in the form of the prices which rule in the market. The amount of money which he has to spend, or to save, is limited: hence, at given prices, only a certain range of possibilities is open to him. He must choose what he will have and what he will forgo. And the combined choice of all consumers controls the directions taken by productive activity in the future. In the second place, there are the limitations imposed by the State. The sale of some goods, such as certain drugs, may be prohibited; the sale of others, such as alcoholic drink, may be restricted; the production of others, such as tobacco, may be taxed, raising their prices. Moreover, the State may take some of the consumers' money and spend it upon public purposes. Nevertheless we can assume that in a democratic community the State acts more or less in accordance with the wishes of most of the citizens, so that this limitation upon the sovereignty of the consumer is more apparent than real. In the third place, there is the existence of monopoly in all its forms. We shall discuss this later. It is true that if there is an increase in the demand for a monopolized commodity it will usually pay the monopolist to respond to the wishes of the consumers by increasing his output. Nevertheless, at any moment, consumers do not get the assortment of goods which they most prefer. Monopolists use their monopoly power to prevent more factors of production from entering their field, although such factors could produce a greater value within it than they are producing outside it—although, that is to say, consumers would prefer to forgo some things at present produced in order to have more of the monopolized products. And we must remember that monopoly may be present not only in the production of consumers' goods but also in the production of intermediate products, and, in the form of powerful professional associations and trade unions, in the production of certain kinds of labour services.

It is sometimes asserted that advertising and salesmanship impose a further limitation upon the sovereignty of consumers who do not really exercise free choice but are cajoled or hypnotized into buying what advertisements and salesmen tell them to buy. There is not much force in this contention. Many non-advertised goods meet with a wide sale, and usually if one brand of a commodity is widely advertised, so are rival brands, and the consumer must decide between them. In any case, a monarch may be advised and cajoled, as to some of his activities, even by his slaves, but he remains a monarch none the less. Another argument, namely that consumers are constrained to purchase standardized commodities in many lines, has even less weight. There are sometimes considerable economies (associated with the use of indivisible equipment) to be gained by producing large quantities of standardized goods, and such goods can therefore be sold more cheaply. But any consumer is free to decide between buying a mass-produced good at a lower price and a different type (which, if necessary, he can order) at a higher price.

The question of whether the sovereignty of the consumer is desirable falls outside the scope of economic science. Some urge that consumers, on the whole, tend to buy ugly things rather than beautiful ones, show a poor taste in literature, music, and the other arts, and—if left to themselves—would purchase harmful drugs and adulterated foodstuffs or would go without adequate nourishment in order to buy drink or silk stockings or go to cinemas. They contend that it would be better to give consumers what is good for them rather than what they want. Others reply that they prefer not to leave questions of taste to the dictatorship of the Government and that if people are not free to make mistakes they are unlikely to achieve anything worth while. Again, it must be remembered that the pull exerted on the market by a man with £2000 a year is ten times as great as the pull of a man with £200 a year. Production is governed not by the "needs" of consumers but by their "effective demand": by the sums of money actually expended, or expected to be expended. Hence it is often urged that a reduction in the inequality of incomes is desirable. But these are matters of opinion. Our present task is to show how capitalism works, not to discuss its merits or defects.

3. ILLUSTRATIONS

We shall now give a few simple illustrations of how the productive activities of a community may change in accordance with the wishes of consumers. The reader is warned that these illustrations ignore certain defects in the actual working of the economic system in modern capitalist countries. In particular, they ignore monopoly and they assume that the monetary mechanism works smoothly. But we must proceed by stages. We are now giving a broad and somewhat idealized picture of capitalism. Later we shall consider at some length how the picture is modified by the existence of monopoly and by fluctuations in investment which lead to trade depressions.

Let us begin with a change in the tastes of consumers. They have, let us say, a greater desire for wheat (or its products) relatively to barley (or its products) than before. If the amounts of wheat and of barley coming forward for sale remain the same, the price of wheat will rise and the price of barley will fall. This will cause more wheat and less barley than before to be produced. Suppose that, in the old equilibrium, the price of wheat was the same as the price of barley. Then all land which could produce more wheat than barley was producing wheat, and conversely. Suppose that, following the change in the scales of preferences of some consumers in favour of wheat as against barley, a new equilibrium is reached in which the price of wheat is 10 per cent above the price of barley. Then all land which can produce (plus co-operating factors) either a certain quantity of barley or more than ten-elevenths that quantity of wheat will be under wheat. The price-mechanism will have induced owners of land capable of producing more barley than wheat, but less than 10 per cent more, to transfer it from barley to wheat in accordance with the change in the preferences of consumers.

This is a simple example, for we have supposed that given land (and labour and equipment) can produce either wheat or barley. In practice, a change in demand may lead to a whole series of responses by the productive mechanism. Some land may be abandoned; some equipment may be scrapped; some workers may move to a different part of the country; there may be a considerable "reshuffle" of factors among industries. But factors will move into another line only if their owners expect them to earn more there—only, that is, if it appears that consumers would value their contribution to production in the new line more highly than they value their present contribution.

Let us suppose now that an increase in technical knowledge (not requiring more "waiting") makes it possible to produce more of a commodity than before from a given amount of factors. Consumers would wish the new method to be adopted. They could then have a greater quantity of that commodity, without forgoing anything else; or, alternatively, some factors could be diverted from that industry to increase the output of other goods, without thereby diminishing the output of the commodity in question. Under the stimulus of the price-mechanism, the new method *will* be adopted, since those producers who adopt it will increase their own incomes. The benefit is passed on to consumers because, under competition, the output of the commodity will increase and its price will therefore fall.

Let us now consider an increased desire by consumers to save—to forgo present consumption in order to have more to consume in the future. By saving more, they spend less on consumers' goods. In order to increase their future incomes, they invest what they save. The fall in demand for consumers' goods induces some factors of production to move out of the industries producing them. At the same time, the increase in investment leads to a greater demand for factors in industries producing raw materials, constructional goods, machinery, and so on. Hence the structure of production becomes more "capitalistic," in accordance with the wishes of consumers.

Finally, let us consider what determines the channels into which free capital—that is, money seeking investment—will flow. There are always many possible ways of increasing the output of this, that, or the other commodity by making methods of production more capitalistic. Investors, however, will aim at as large a money return as possible from their capital. They will take account, therefore, not only of the technical possibilities of increasing physical output but also of the probable future selling prices of the various alternative products whose supply they could increase. They will be guided, that is, by their anticipations of future demand—of the valuations of consumers.

We hope it is now clear that, although no single consumer may be able to change existing prices, it is the sum-total of consumers' actions which controls the directions taken by the whole mechanism of production. It is true that we have not considered the difficulties which may stand in the way of a rapid adaptation to a change in the preferences of consumers or in the state of technical knowledge. We deal with these matters in Chapter XIV. Our present aim has been to establish the fact that under capitalism the final arbiter is the consumer.

4. THE SOURCE OF CONSUMERS' INCOMES

We have seen that, under capitalism, the consumers are supreme. But who are these consumers, and whence do they obtain the money incomes which enable them, through the price-mechanism, to control the directions taken by productive activity? The consumers are none other than the owners of factors of production, and their incomes—apart from private or collective gifts, such as parents' allowances to their children or State pensions—are simply the earnings of the factors which they own: the remuneration received for their labour or for the use of their property.

This complicates any study of periods of transition. Suppose, for example, that there is an increased demand for agricultural products. The earnings of agricultural land will increase and the owners of such land will thereby be enabled to exert a greater influence than before, in their capacity of consumers, upon the price-mechanism. It would be incorrect, therefore, to assume that the income of every consumer is fixed and given. Nearly every kind of economic change will tend to alter the relative earnings of different factors of production and hence the relative incomes of different consumers.

Nevertheless our dictum of the sovereignty of the consumer remains valid. And it is equally true that so long as consumers place a higher value upon the services rendered by certain factors in one line than in another there will be a tendency for such factors to move from the latter line to the former.

CHAPTER XIII

THE PROBLEMS OF THE FIRM

1. THE ROLE OF THE ENTREPRENEUR

We have seen that nearly all commodities are produced by a number of different factors working in combination. This means that some persons must perform the task of combining different factors together, by hiring other factors to co-operate with those factors which they themselves possess. Economists usually call these persons "entrepreneurs." There is no really suitable English word for them: "enterpriser" sounds too dashing and "undertaker" a little sinister.

We shall use the term "entrepreneur" to mean the person or group of persons controlling the policy of a firm. The firm is a collection of factors—land, buildings, plant and equipment, workers, materials, and so on—controlled by an entrepreneur. These definitions are not quite as circular as they sound. A firm is a separate planning unit and it is the entrepreneur who does the planning.

The next section discusses the main ways in which firms may be legally organized. We there point out that those who are apparently the entrepreneurs sometimes do not in fact control the policy of their firms. The holders of ordinary shares in a public company have the legal right to appoint and dismiss directors and thereby to control the policy of the company. In fact the policy may be controlled by one or two directors, or by an active minority of the shareholders, or by a holding company having a majority of the shares. The remainder of the chapter, however, leaves this complication out of account.

It will be remembered that under capitalism, in contrast to a system of central planning, the tasks of obtaining information and making decisions are, for the most part, decentralized. They are performed largely by entrepreneurs. Each entrepreneur acts independently in his own interests. If he is beginning his career as an entrepreneur, he enters whatever industry offers him, in his view, the best prospects. If he decides to build, say, a new factory he chooses whatever location seems the most profitable. He produces whatever commodities he thinks will pay him best and employs those methods of production which seem to him the most profitable. As time goes on, some industries expand and others contract (or if all expand some expand more than others and if all contract some contract more than others), the location of industry changes, some improvements in technical knowledge are put into practice, to a greater or smaller extent, and others are not, more or less use is made of labour-saving devices, and so on. All such changes are mainly due to the multitudinous decisions of entrepreneurs. The way in which a community solves its problems of what to produce, and how to produce, and where to produce, depends mainly upon the policies adopted by its various firms.

It is the entrepreneur who bears most of the risks of industry. Since it takes time to produce goods and to sell them, he usually contracts to make fixed payments to the factors which he hires—to pay fixed rates of wages to his various workers, a fixed rent to his landlord, a fixed sum periodically as interest on the money he borrows, and so on—without being quite certain of the amount of money he will get from the sale of their products. Hence the gain from an unforeseen rise in selling prices, or the loss from an unforeseen fall, accrues mainly to entrepreneurs: "profits" fluctuate more over time than other forms of income.

Economic conditions are constantly changing. The demand for some goods rises while the demand for others falls. Some factors become scarcer and therefore dearer relatively to others. Changes in technical knowledge are constantly taking place. The extent to which an entrepreneur is successful depends on how far he is correct in realizing what changes have taken place, are taking place, and will take place, and how they affect, or will affect, his firm. His judgment of the situation and his forecast of future trends will lead him, as a rule, to do whatever seems most likely to maximize his own income. But under perfect competition the policy which best serves his own interests is also the policy which conforms most closely to the wishes of consumers. It pays him best to give consumers what they want. It pays him to divert factors from elsewhere if their marginal products will be more valuable when they are employed by him. The prices of the various factors represent the valuations placed by consumers on their marginal products in their present uses, so that if it pays him to employ factors now employed elsewhere (and if necessary to offer them some inducement to move) it follows that consumers prefer what these factors will produce under him to what they are producing now. Moreover, it pays him to produce any given output as cheaply as possible, and this means that he employs those factors (provided that under his control they render services at least as valuable as they would render elsewhere) which can best be spared from other uses. Thus the price-mechanism tends to harmonize the desire of entrepreneurs for profits and the desire of consumers to satisfy their wants as fully as possible from the factors of production available.

In fact this harmony of interests is by no means complete. It is disturbed by imperfect competition, or monopoly. We discuss this at length in Chapter XV. It is disturbed in so far as some forms of activity cause costs to other people or confer benefits on other people which do not enter into the costs or receipts of those engaged in these activities and therefore do not affect their decisions: for example, the 75,000 tons of soot which fall on London in the course of a year impose costs—higher laundry bills, discomfort, and so forth—on many people, but these costs are not charged against those who produce the smoke. It is also disturbed in so far as directors act for their own gain against the interests of their shareholders, or Governments act in the interests of a particular group and not in those of the community as a whole, or firms deceive consumers by misleading advertisements or deceive investors by misleading accounts of their financial position and prospects. It will be remembered, moreover, that it is a harmony based on the existing distribution of wealth and income among persons. And even when the harmony of interests between entrepreneurs and consumers is complete, how fully these interests are achieved depends largely on the ability and flair of the entrepreneurs. We do not argue for one moment that capitalism, as it actually exists, even approaches perfection. Any system of social organization, however, would in practice have its drawbacks. People will make mistakes, and some of them will be corrupt or unjust or intolerant, under any form of society. It is not our purpose to discuss whether some other system would be better than capitalism or to what extent and in what manner the working of capitalism could be improved. Our purpose is to show what many people fail to understand: that the price-system really is a system and that, in so far as it is permitted to work freely, it does guide economic activity into those channels which consumers most prefer. It is with this purpose in mind that we shall consider the problems which confront the entrepreneur and the manner in which he solves them.

2. FORMS OF ENTREPRENEURIAL ORGANIZATION

It is possible for the owner of any kind of factor to act as entrepreneur. Thus a landowner may borrow money with which he hires workers and buys machinery, fodder, fertilizer, seed, and so on, to employ in conjunction with his land; or a group of workers may form an association and run a factory with the aid of borrowed money. But it is often difficult for persons with few material assets of their own to borrow, and hence it is mainly owners of capital who undertake the tasks of entrepreneurship. They may leave all except the very broadest question of general policy to a hired manager, but even so the final responsibility is theirs, since they have to bear any losses, and have the power to dismiss the manager and appoint another in his place. At this stage a brief account of the main forms of entrepreneurial organization may be useful.

Individual Proprietorship was the dominant form in the period of small-scale industry and even to-day the majority of firms *in number* (but not in importance) are "one-man concerns" controlled by a single entrepreneur. This form of organization is still predominant in agriculture, which in most countries is the most important single branch of productive activity, and in retail trade.

Partnership is the relation which subsists between persons carrying on a business in common. The powers, rights, and duties of each partner are defined in the Partnership Agreement; if this is silent on any point, the Partnership Act of 1890 applies. All of the partners usually contribute to the capital although sometimes a partner contributes only ability, but, in any event, every partner is liable to the extent of all his possessions for the debts of the firm. In view of this serious responsibility the Partnership Act requires the consent of all the partners to certain important matters such as changing the nature of the business, or admitting a new partner, but in ordinary everyday matters of business a majority of partners will bind the others. This form of entrepreneurial organization is well suited to the business of solicitors, accountants, estate agents, doctors, and the like, and is very prominent in these professions.

The Limited Partnerships Act of 1907 makes possible a variation of the partnership. It provides for **limited partnerships** with one or more "general partners" liable for all debts and obligations of the firm, and one or more *limited partners* who contribute a stated sum and are liable for no more than this provided they do not take part in the general management of the business. However, little advantage has been taken of this Act owing to the superior advantages of registering under the Companies Act as a **private limited company.**

The private company is one of the most important forms of entrepreneurial organization; it gives the members the advantage of limited liability and only two persons are needed to form it. It has advantages over the public company; for instance, it need not file an annual balance sheet with the Registrar of Joint Stock Companies and there are no restrictions on commencing business. However, a private company must by its Articles of Association (*a*) restrict the right to transfer its shares, (*b*) limit the number of its members to fifty (with certain exceptions), (*c*) prohibit any invitation to the public to subscribe for shares or debentures.

This is obviously a form of organization well suited to the medium-sized commercial and industrial organization which does not require finance from the public; moreover, it is an extremely useful method of trying out speculative ventures which a small group of people are prepared to back financially up to a defined limit, namely the capital subscribed. Many of these companies on reaching a certain stage of success are "floated off," that is to say, they are converted into **public companies**, the public being invited to put up money for expansion.

The device of limited liability was introduced in Great Britain in 1855 and permitted savers to invest in shares without becoming liable for the debts of the company beyond the extent of the nominal amount of the investment. This is clearly an important method of financing those industrial and transport businesses which require immediate heavy investment because there are considerable economies of large-scale production. If such companies ask the public for funds then they cannot comply with the legal provisions relating to private companies and must be registered as public companies. Incidentally the minimum number of members which a public company may have is seven, but there is no maximum number. Thus a company may have a nominal and issued capital of £1,000,000 divided into 1,000,000 ordinary shares of £1 each spread among perhaps a thousand members, who are joint entrepreneurs. The shareholders share the profits periodically among themselves in the form of "dividends," in proportion to their holdings of shares. In practice it would obviously be impossible for the shareholders all to take part in the management of the concern, so this function is delegated to a Board of Directors. The Board is nominally responsible to all the shareholders, but in point of fact the directors control the policy of the company effectively if they and their friends own a majority of the shares. Small shareholders usually play quite a passive part.

In order to attract capital as cheaply as possible, there are various market devices offering prospective shareholders a choice of terms. For example, cumulative preference shares guarantee the holders a fixed rate of dividend and if profits are not sufficient to pay the dividend in any year then it is to be made up out of the profits of future years. There are many other classes of shares, the element of risk being different in each class.

A company may borrow from the public by issuing debentures, which carry a fixed rate of interest and are usually secured by a charge on the company's assets, enabling the debenture-holders to seize the assets if their interest is not paid. The debenture-holders are not entrepreneurs but merely lenders, for they are entitled to their interest whether profits are made or not.

A useful device for centralizing the control of two or more companies without destroying their separate legal identities or any "goodwill" attached to their names is that of the holding company. Many large and important groups of establishments —for example, Vickers and Imperial Chemical Industries in this country and General Motors in the United States—are wholly or mainly controlled by a holding company. Some discussion of this device, therefore, seems appropriate.

The term "holding company" was originally used to describe

a company formed with the express object of acquiring a controlling interest, by buying a majority of the shares, in two or more operating concerns, but more recently it has come to include companies which, besides having a controlling interest in others, themselves carry on a business. The concerns which are controlled are known as subsidiaries. The table on page 170 shows the subsidiaries of Vickers Ltd., an important British holding company.

Suppose that a group of firms could achieve certain economies by combining together to pursue a common selling policy, to share the services of a staff of technical experts, to "pool" their various patents, and so on. One course open to them would be to sink their separate identities and amalgamate. But amalgamations are often difficult and expensive to arrange. Another course would be for them to form a cartel. But a cartel, as we explain in Chapter XV, is often a short-lived affair. Each firm retains its own identity and keeps a jealous eye on its own interests, so that as a rule only short-period agreements as to price and output are possible. The holding company is a looser form than an amalgamation; it can achieve economies hardly open to a cartel and is on a more permanent and unified basis; and it is simple and relatively cheap to arrange, for it requires nothing beyond a transfer of shares.

It is possible, under this device, for a few persons to control much more capital than they possess. Suppose, to take a simple hypothetical example, that such a group possesses just over £1 million in the form of shares which give it the control of company A, with a share capital of £2 million. Company A—the holding company—buys a majority of the shares in company B, which has a capital of £4 million, half in shares and half in debentures. (The debenture-holders, of course, exercise no control.) Company B buys a majority of the shares in company C, which has a capital of £8 million, half in shares and half in debentures; company C buys a majority of the shares in company D, which has a capital of £16 million, and so on. When this happens, the interests of the minority shareholders, not members of the controlling group, in the subsidiary companies may be endangered. Subsidiary companies are often allowed very considerable freedom of action. But the whole group of companies is essentially one firm, whose policy is dictated by the controlling group.

VICKERS LIMITED

GROUP OF COMPANIES

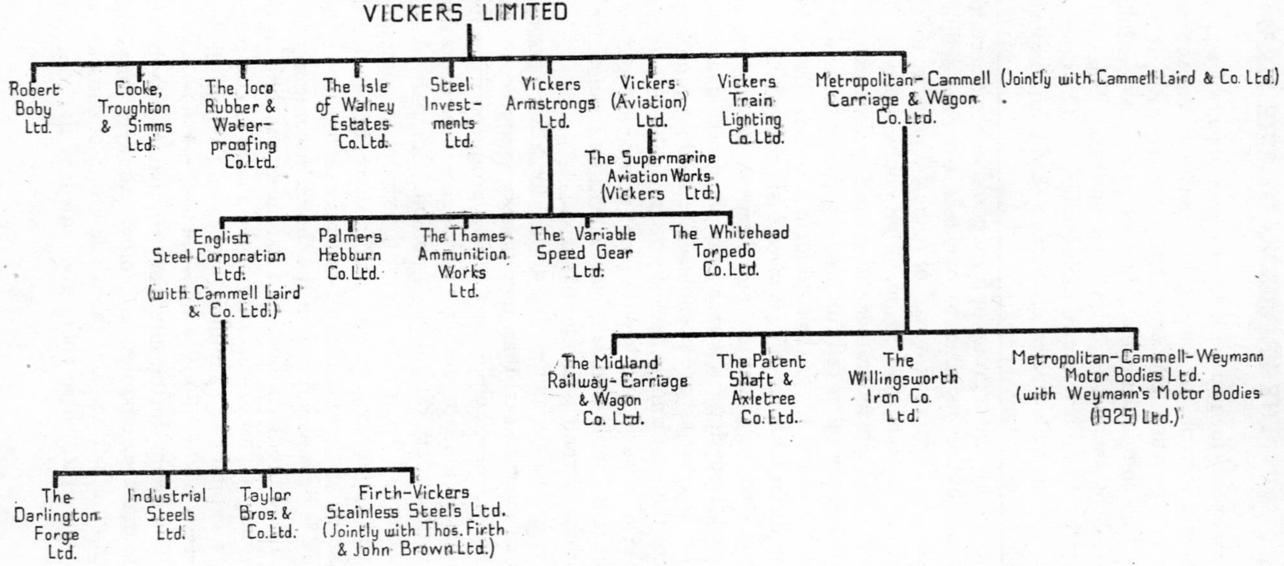
VICKERS LIMITED
Robert Boby Ltd.
Cooke, Troughton & Simms Ltd.
The Ioco Rubber & Water-proofing Co.Ltd.
The Isle of Walney Estates Co.Ltd.
Steel Invest-ments Ltd.
Vickers Armstrongs Ltd.
Vickers (Aviation) Ltd.
The Supermarine Aviation Works (Vickers Ltd.)
Vickers Train Lighting Co.Ltd.
Metropolitan-Cammell Carriage & Wagon Co.Ltd. (Jointly with Cammell Laird & Co. Ltd.)
English Steel Corporation Ltd. (with Cammell Laird & Co. Ltd.)
Palmers Hebburn Co.Ltd.
The Thames Ammunition Works Ltd.
The Variable Speed Gear Ltd.
The Whitehead Torpedo Co.Ltd.
The Midland Railway-Carriage & Wagon Co. Ltd.
The Patent Shaft & Axletree Co.Ltd.
The Willingsworth Iron Co. Ltd.
Metropolitan-Cammell-Weymann Motor Bodies Ltd. (with Weymann's Motor Bodies (1925) Ltd.)
The Darlington Forge Ltd.
Industrial Steels Ltd.
Taylor Bros. & Co.Ltd.
Firth-Vickers Stainless Steels Ltd. (Jointly with Thos. Firth & John Brown Ltd.)

If the interests of this group conflict with those of minority shareholders it is the latter who will suffer.

Another point is that the holding company device may enable information to be withheld from the general public. The consolidated balance sheet is not legally obligatory, nor have the methods of preparing it been perfected. A subsidiary private company in which all the shares are owned by a holding company need disclose its annual balance sheet only to the holding company: it is only public companies which are obliged to file a copy with the Registrar of Joint Stock Companies.

Co-operative Societies. Consumers' co-operative societies are associations of consumers engaged in retail trade and sharing the trading profits among their members. A number of such societies may combine to form a wholesale society, which supplies the retail societies and may engage in production. Thus the Co-operative Wholesale Society engages in many branches of production—grows wheat, makes clothing, owns ships, runs a bank, and so on.

Producers' co-operative societies are associations of producers marketing the products of their members and sharing the trading profits among them. They are more important in other countries, such as Denmark, than in Great Britain. In Great Britain the marketing of a number of commodities, such as milk and bacon, is controlled by the State through Boards representing the producers.

State Enterprises. Central and local Governments may engage in productive activity, obtaining their capital by borrowing from the public or from taxation. Thus the British Government owns and operates the Post Office, and many local authorities run tramways, provide water, gas, or electricity, and so on.

This list is not complete, but it covers the main forms of entrepreneurial organization. It is difficult to give a clear-cut definition of a firm, as of most economic terms, because the phenomena of the real world, which definitions attempt to summarize, are not clear-cut. A large business may give a very free hand to the managers of its branches or departments, and a firm may surrender much of its control over policy to a cartel. We shall regard a cartel or a producers' co-operative society not as a single firm but as an association of firms. Some of our remarks about firms will not apply to State enterprises which do not try to maximize their profits. We shall regard a group of concerns which retain their separate names but are controlled by a holding company as a single firm.

The reasoning which follows applies equally well whether the general policy of a firm is determined by one person or by a group of persons, but in order to simplify the discussion we shall suppose that it is determined by one person: the entrepreneur.

3. COSTS AND PROFITS

In ordinary speech, the costs of a firm are sometimes taken to mean only the money payments actually made by the firm in order to obtain labour, equipment, materials, and other factors. The total receipts of the firm, over a period, minus these costs are regarded as a kind of residual income. It is the earnings of the factors employed in the firm and owned by the entrepreneur himself. In other words, it is the return which he receives on his own efforts and assets in so far as they are employed in the service of his firm. It is commonly called "profits."

This popular distinction between costs and profits is somewhat arbitrary, as an example will show. Consider two exactly similar businesses. One is owned by a man who gives all his working time to managing it and who himself supplies the capital. The other is owned by a man who employs a manager, giving very little of his own time to it, and who borrows most of the capital. The profits of the first man are considerably greater, and his costs correspondingly less, than those of the second man. The discrepancy arises from the fact that, logically, the first man should count the value of his own labour (measured by what he could earn elsewhere by working as an employee—for example, as a salaried manager) and the services of his own capital (measured by what it could yield as interest if he lent it) in his costs.

Costs in the former sense of sums of money which must be paid by the entrepreneur to other people in exchange for factors of production, or for the use of their services, or for the loan of money with which he buys or hires factors, may be termed paid-out costs. The "costs" which give rise to the discrepancy just mentioned, and which measure how much the factors owned by the entrepreneur could earn if hired out and employed in other uses, may be termed other costs. A person will not, as a rule, take the risks of becoming an entrepreneur by setting up in business on his own account unless he expects that (over a number of years if not for each separate year) the total receipts of his firm will more than cover both paid-out and other costs.

The amount by which total receipts exceed paid-out and other costs, taken together, may be termed "profits" in the narrower and somewhat technical sense. Profits in this sense may be regarded as the remuneration of "pure entrepreneurship." They exist because of uncertainty and the consequent risks of business. It is the entrepreneur who bears most of these risks, and his profits will vary with his success in forecasting future changes, deciding how they will affect his business, and acting accordingly. For the sake of brevity we shall term profits in this sense "pure" profits.

Pure profits are quite often negative. Many men overestimate their own business ability and set up firms which after a time go bankrupt or, if they survive, yield their entrepreneurs a lower return than they could get by working for others and investing their capital at fixed interest. During periods of bad trade many firms fail to cover their "other" costs. The ups and downs of the trade cycle, however, affect firms in some industries more strongly than in others. A firm producing commodities, such as tobacco, for which the demand fluctuates comparatively little over time may well make some pure profits (although they may be relatively small since the risks are relatively slight) year after year, whereas a firm producing commodities, such as steel and machinery, for which the demand fluctuates widely over time may well resign itself to making losses (in the sense of negative pure profits) during bad years, expecting that large pure profits during good years will more than compensate for this.

Total pure profits, taking all firms together and good years together with bad, are almost certainly positive. In other words, entrepreneurs as a whole probably make more than they would get by working for others or by lending their capital at fixed interest instead of investing it in their own businesses. Persons with a real flair for entrepreneurship are scarce and, provided they can command sufficient capital, most of them can make much more than they would earn at other jobs. The same, of course, is true of outstanding members of other occupations such as film stars. Probably most people over-estimate the magnitude of pure profits. They do not take sufficient account of the firms which fail and of the companies which pay no dividend for years on end or are compelled to write down their capital. They do not fully appreciate the fact that the number of managers and other employees able to command sufficient capital to start on their own account, if they think that they can earn more as entrepreneurs, is fairly large. Owners of "free capital" can either act as entrepreneurs (for example, by investing in ordinary shares) or lend their money at a fixed rate of interest, and although on the whole and in the long run the former course probably gives the higher return, owing to the greater risks, competition among investors usually prevents the difference from becoming very large. For these reasons we conclude that pure profits, for all firms taken together over a long period, are almost certainly positive but are considerably smaller than many people suppose them to be.

We have seen that total costs may be divided into paid-out and other costs. They may also be divided into fixed costs which do not vary with the size of the firm's output, and variable costs, which do.[1] Given the amount of effort which the entrepreneur devotes to his firm, and the assets employed in the firm which belong to him, all "other" costs are in this sense fixed costs. They do not vary with the output of the firm; they are the same whether it is large or small. But some paid-out costs are also fixed in this sense, at least within wide limits. Thus the interest payments due from a firm to its bank or from a company to its debenture-holders, or the rent due from a farmer (who has signed a long lease) to his landlord, do not vary with the output of the firm. Expenditure on such items as the salaries of office employees, insurance of the buildings against fire or burglary, and advertising, often falls into the same category.

Both the distinction between paid-out and other costs and that between fixed and variable costs are useful provided that

[1] It will be realized that the division between the two is often not clear-cut. Suppose a shipping company decides to run an extra ship. All the extra costs thereby incurred are variable costs in so far as they would not be incurred if the ship were not run. But, once the ship is being run, these costs are "fixed" to extra passengers: the variable costs of carrying extra passengers may be very small, e.g. additional food and perhaps one or two extra stewards.

we remember that they are only rough distinctions applying to a relatively short period. Unless factor-prices change, a *substantial* increase in output can often be produced more cheaply by increasing the plant and other "fixed capital" as well as the labour, materials, and so on. A large change in output may also cause the office staff to be increased or reduced, and may lead to changes in other items of current expenditure which can normally be taken as fixed. Again, a considerable increase in output often raises the rate at which money is spent on replacing parts of the "fixed capital"—on buying new tyres for lorries, new linings for furnaces, and so on—and in keeping it in good repair. Moreover, as time goes on, "fixed capital" wears out and will not be replaced unless its expected earnings are as high as the yield obtainable by investing the money, which it costs to replace it, in some other way. In the very long run, all costs are variable.

4. THE DECISIONS OF THE ENTREPRENEUR

An entrepreneur must decide the following questions—

(1) What industry shall he enter? This is the question which confronts him at the outset, when he has made up his mind that he will do better by setting up in business for himself instead of working for others. In so far as ordinary shareholders may be regarded as entrepreneurs, they must decide in what industries they will invest, taking the risks, instead of lending at fixed interest. But the question does not disappear once a decision has been made, for an entrepreneur may think it desirable to transfer his activity or investments into another industry.

(2) What commodities or services shall he produce? Logically, this question merges into the first, for both relate to the nature of his output. But it is convenient to separate them. For a firm usually produces a number of different goods, within the same broad group of goods. The first question relates to the group—for example, pottery or machinery. The second question relates to the particular goods within the group.

(3) What shall be the size of his "plant" or plants? This term is meant to cover a "unit" such as a factory or a farm or a shop. In many cases it is difficult to say exactly what the "unit" is, but in others there is little real doubt. We treat this as a separate

question, despite the difficulty of definition, in order to stress the fact that one firm may possess a number of different "plants."

(4) What shall be the size of his firm? This question relates to the size of his output. This chapter, for the most part, assumes perfect competition; imperfect competition, or monopoly, is discussed in Chapter XV. But we may mention here that if a firm is in a monopolistic position the question of how much of a commodity it shall produce is practically identical with the question of what price it shall charge.

(5) What methods of production shall he adopt? In other words, in what proportions shall he combine the various types of labour and other factors? We discuss this under the heading of "substitution between factors."

He must also decide where his plant or plants shall be located, but we postpone discussion of this to Chapter XXV. We may say at once, however, that in this matter, as in the others, he will tend to act in accordance with the wishes of consumers. For example, less transport may be required to assemble the various materials at one point than at another. Other things being equal, he will choose the former point as a site for his plant because it will keep down his transport costs, and it is to the advantage of consumers that he should do so, for factors of production are thereby made available for other uses instead of being employed in unnecessary transport.

What considerations will guide an entrepreneur in making these various decisions? He will doubtless pay some attention to his own tastes and feelings. For example, he may prefer "being his own boss" to getting a somewhat bigger income by working for an employer or he may believe that alcoholic drink is harmful and may therefore enter some other industry although he could make bigger profits by running a brewery. He will have a certain scale of preferences as between income and leisure, and will probably content himself with a smaller income than he could obtain by devoting more time to his firm, in order to have a certain amount of leisure. If he saves, he may prefer to invest his savings in his own business although he could obtain about as high a yield if he invested them elsewhere. We shall set aside these considerations, which do not substantially affect the argument, by supposing that he has no preferences as between different fields of economic activity, and that he will neither increase nor diminish the amount of work which he devotes to his firm and the amount of other factors employed in his firm which he himself owns.

On these assumptions, he will choose whatever course promises him the greatest profits in the wide sense of "other" costs plus pure profits. In other words, he will try to get the greatest possible money income from those factors in his firm which he himself owns: that is, from the efforts which he devotes to the firm and the capital which he himself has invested in it.

This simple rule enables us to predict how an entrepreneur will behave when confronted with a given set of prices, provided that he knows, and we know, how changes in the combination of factors employed in the firm will affect its output, and provided that he does not anticipate any significant changes in relevant prices or technical possibilities. If he does anticipate changes, we can predict what he will do if we know exactly what his anticipations are.

The reader will note the great difference between the data required to predict the behaviour of a consumer, on the one hand, and of an entrepreneur, on the other hand. In order to predict how a consumer will behave, when confronted with a given set of prices, we must know his scale of preferences, for there is no accounting for tastes. But the tastes, in this sense, of the entrepreneur do not affect his behaviour. The behaviour of *all* entrepreneurs is determined by the same general principle. They will all endeavour to maximize their profits. There is no "subjective" or "psychological" aspect of the matter (apart from the relatively minor considerations which we have set aside by our assumptions) as there is in the case of a consumer. The actions of an entrepreneur are not determined by his own particular scale of preferences but by objective market facts. They therefore lend themselves to analysis far more than do the actions of consumers.

5. FIRMS AND INDUSTRIES

We define an industry as a group of firms producing similar products or rendering similar services. But it should be said at once that an "industry" in the popular sense may include firms whose products are not "similar," for they are not at all close substitutes for one another. Thus "the coal-mining industry" embraces both firms producing steam coal and firms producing household coal. These two types of coal are by no means close substitutes. The demand for one may increase while the demand for the other falls, and over a period their prices may diverge very considerably, moving in opposite directions. Indeed, fuel oil is a much closer substitute for steam coal, which is used largely in ships, than most other types of coal. It should also be said that a firm may belong to several industries at once, producing, for example, coal and steel and machinery.

Suppose there is an increased demand for the products of a particular industry. Consumers, taken together, have a stronger preference for those products, relatively to others, than before. It pays entrepreneurs to comply with their wishes. Firms already in that industry will find it profitable to expand their output, and entrepreneurs about to set up new firms will be attracted towards that industry rather than towards others. For, unless there is a good deal of "unused capacity" available for rapid expansion of output, the prices of these products will rise. The opposite, of course, applies to an industry for whose products the demand falls off. Existing firms will tend to contract their output and new entrepreneurs will tend to avoid that industry.

The number of firms in a contracting industry may diminish (apart from amalgamations) because some firms are driven into bankruptcy and some entrepreneurs transfer to other industries where they hope to make bigger profits. A firm which cannot cover its prime costs is paying out more money than it receives and sooner or later, if this continues, will be forced out of existence. The entrepreneur pays the penalty for misjudging or forecasting wrongly the wishes of consumers, or for using inefficient methods, and for entering the ranks of entrepreneurs when his services would have been valued more highly by consumers as an employee. The entrepreneurs who decide to transfer their abilities elsewhere may be among the most efficient in the industry. They may be making quite considerable profits, but now that the demand for these particular products is lower than before, they may believe that they will make still larger profits by transferring their abilities to another industry.

It is seldom that the whole group of factors constituting a firm moves bodily from one industry into another. Whether particular factors move depends largely on how "specific" they are to that industry. Plant which is suitable for only one purpose will continue, under perfect competition, to be employed for that purpose so long as it yields any net return, however small, above what could be obtained by selling it for scrap and investing the proceeds. Workers who are specialized to one industry, and would be of little use elsewhere, will remain attached to that industry even if their wages fall very low or they become unemployed. In a contracting industry there may be some reshuffle of factors among firms, the specific ones remaining in the industry, perhaps finding employment with other firms if their own cease business, and some of the non-specific ones moving to other industries. For example, if an entrepreneur moves to another industry (taking his accumulated amortisation fund, which is in the form of money or marketable securities, with him) he may sell the factory to another firm which uses it for a different purpose, and he may sell some of his plant and equipment and materials to another firm in that industry and sell the rest as scrap, while some of his workers may find jobs with other firms in that industry, some may move into various other industries, and some may remain unemployed.

The supply curve of a commodity produced under perfect competition is the marginal cost curve of the industry producing that commodity.[1] The expansion of an industry implies that its demand for particular types of labour, materials, and other factors is increasing. If it has to pay higher prices in order to obtain increased supplies of some of these factors, this will raise its marginal costs and the product will have to command a correspondingly higher price if its supply is to be increased to that extent. On the other hand, the expansion of an industry may lead to various economies which tend to reduce its marginal costs. Thus expansion due to an increased demand for its products may enable it to employ "indivisible" equipment not previously worth while. Again, the expansion of a localized industry may enable railway companies, for example, to reduce their charges owing to the larger volume of traffic. But in any event marginal cost, as we shall explain in a later section, will tend under perfect competition to equal the selling price of the product. We speak here of the marginal costs of an industry because although any single firm may take the prices of its factors as given "by the

[1] See p. 225.

market" and beyond its control, yet the simultaneous expansion of a number of firms, together perhaps with the entry of new ones, may well raise the prices of some of the factors employed in the industry.

6. THE NATURE OF THE OUTPUT

Consider an entrepreneur who is already engaged in some line of production. It may be that the demand for his products, and therefore their selling prices, are less than he had expected and his profits smaller than he had hoped. If he were just about to set up in business, he would enter a different industry. He may nevertheless remain where he is, for he has probably acquired a special knowledge of his present kind of business, and has perhaps built up a "goodwill," both of which would be sacrificed if he moved into another line.

Very few firms produce only one homogeneous product. A firm may produce only, say, shoes, but it will usually turn out a variety of styles and patterns. An entrepreneur will produce whatever assortment of products gives him the largest income, and he will meet changes in the relative demand for his different products by producing more of the goods now more in demand and less of those for which the demand has diminished. It pays him to comply with the wishes of consumers. This is true even if he is producing equipment or other producers' goods. He may sell his products to manufacturers, but their demands will reflect their anticipations of the demands of final consumers—based usually on the behaviour of the latter in the recent past. There may be many different processes and many different firms engaged in the various stages of producing a consumers' good, but always at the end of the chain are the sovereign consumers, whose anticipated preferences determine the directions taken by economic activity. An entrepreneur may decide that he can increase his profits by producing some new commodity, but in this case also his decision will turn upon his forecast of consumers' demand.

If it is easy to produce more of one good and less of another by making relatively minor adjustments to the fixed plant and equipment or using materials in different proportions, the marginal cost curves—that is, under perfect competition, the supply curves—of those goods may be practically horizontal over a certain range. Changes in demand will not appreciably alter the price but will lead at once to corresponding changes in output. But this is often not the case, as we saw in Chapter VI, section 3.

7. THE SIZE OF PLANTS

A "plant," with its equipment, stocks of materials and other goods, and workers, may coincide with a firm: a farmer may have just one farm, a shopkeeper just one shop, a manufacturer just one factory. On the other hand, one firm may control quite a number of plants. Thus some colliery companies operate a number of mines, "chain stores," such as Woolworth, run a number of shops, and some large firms, such as Unilever, control many plants of various kinds—plantations, factories, ships, shops, and so on. In Germany in 1925, 42·4 per cent of all persons occupied in industry and commerce were occupied, according to the Census, in firms with branch plants. Figures for Great Britain are not available, but many plants are controlled by holding companies and the percentage is probably quite as high as in Germany.

The size of a plant may be limited by the demand for its products. We should not expect to find an enormous factory producing only glass eyes, for the demand for glass eyes, even at a low price, is comparatively small. But the limitations imposed by the extent of total demand are much less important than those imposed by the extent of *local* demand: it is this, for example, which restricts the size of a village shop. Industries such as baking, printing, and tailoring, in which for one reason or another most plants must be fairly near the consumers, tend to have small plants distributed over space in much the same way as the population. If a commodity is heavy or bulky in proportion to its value, the advantages of large-scale production have to be considerable (as they are with Fletton bricks) to outweigh the increased costs of transport involved in supplying a wider area. Thus brick-works and breweries and furniture factories are often relatively small and distributed over space roughly according to population.

The advantages of large-scale production arise mainly, as we have seen, from the use of "indivisible" equipment. In many fields—for example, in the manufacture of steel or motor cars or ships—these advantages are so great that large plants are the rule.

In some industries integration, in the sense of carrying out a number of processes in the same plant, is often profitable. Thus in the steel industry there are economies to be gained by having coke-ovens, blast furnaces, melting shops, and rolling-mills close together, forming a single "plant." Less fuel is required if the metal is passed through its various stages without being allowed to get cold; the blast furnace gas can be utilized for the coke-ovens and the coke-oven gas can be converted into electric current for power and light. Hence most iron- and steel-works are large—partly because the greatest technical efficiency can be obtained from relatively large blast furnaces and other types of equipment, and partly because most of the works are more or less integrated.

Sometimes, however, it may pay to sacrifice some of the technical efficiency resulting from large apparatus or from integration. For example, it may pay to have blast furnaces smaller than the technically "most efficient" size if the fuel available locally could not stand the weight of the charge in a larger furnace and if better fuel would have to be brought from a long distance. Again, the by-products of coking may be utilized or sold at the mine instead of at the steel-works. A ton of coke requires about 1½ tons of coal to produce it, so that less weight is transported if coke moves instead of coal, and a steel-works may find it more profitable to buy coke than to have its own coke-ovens. In general, a plant which is not integrated can often adapt itself more readily to changes in demand for different varieties of product and to changes in relative supplies of different materials and other factors.

The size of plant which best pays an entrepreneur will tend, under perfect competition at any rate and often under monopoly, to be that which best satisfies the wants of consumers. It will pay the firm to take full advantage of economies of scale or of integration unless these are outweighed by such considerations as transport costs or the need for flexibility. If they are thus outweighed, the implication is that the wants of consumers, taking account of probable future changes, can be satisfied more fully by smaller plants.

In Great Britain, according to the 1930 Census, 75·8 per cent of all employees in Iron and Steel (Smelting and Rolling) were in plants employing over 500 workers. In Automobiles the corresponding percentage was 71·2 and in Electrical Machinery 73·9. At the other end of the scale were Bakery with a percentage of 13·0 and Furniture with a percentage of 8·4. In some industries, such as coal-mining and foundry and general engineering, there was no typical or prevailing size of plant.[1]

8. THE SIZE OF FIRMS

Two or more firms cannot both control the same plant. Hence, in industries where most plants are large, most firms will be at least correspondingly large. But small plants may be owned by large firms. The question we really have to answer is what forces limit the size of a firm. We are supposing that the amount of work which the entrepreneur devotes to his firm, and the amount of his own capital invested in it, are given, and that he wishes to maximize his profits. Why cannot he increase them indefinitely simply by expanding his output or, in other words, by increasing the size of his firm?

One reason may be that he cannot borrow the money necessary for expansion, or can borrow it only at a rate of interest so much above the prevailing rate that it would not pay him to do so. In order to expand, he will have to engage more workers and, as a rule, pay them wages before he himself is paid for the goods which they help to produce; he will have to buy more raw materials or other intermediate products such as fuel; he may have to acquire more land or buildings or equipment. All this requires expenditure; and since his own assets, which he can pledge as security to lenders, are limited, he may not be able to borrow. This point is of real importance, but it should not be exaggerated. Raw materials and other goods can usually be bought on credit; a loan can be obtained, the main security for which is the assets acquired with the loan; and an entrepreneur who has proved his efficiency by running a small business successfully can usually find a bank, or some other lender, ready to advance him money with which to expand; and if the results are satisfactory, he will usually be able to borrow more for further

[1] Most of the figures in this section are quoted from a very informative article by Prof. P. Sargant Florence entitled "Economic Research and Industrial Policy" in the *Economic Journal*, Vol. XLVII, No. 188, December, 1937.

expansion, and so on. But even if he can borrow as much as he wishes, at the prevailing rate of interest, he will not expand his output indefinitely.

If a firm continues to grow, sooner or later its output will become large enough to have a perceptible influence upon the selling price of its product. The entrepreneur will then take account of the fact that an increase in his output will lower the price which he receives for *all* the units he produces. Alternatively, he may be able to sell more at the old price only by spending more, per unit of output, upon selling costs. We have seen that the increase in transport costs, as a wider area is supplied, may limit the size of a plant. A firm may combat this by setting up new plants in other localities, but nevertheless it may have to spend more, per unit of output, upon advertising and salesmanship in order to sell a larger quantity at the old price. Again, a firm may become so large that its demand for one or more factors, such as a particular type of skilled worker, affects their price. The entrepreneur will then take account of the fact that if he employs more of this factor he will have to pay more for *every* unit of it which he employs. We return to these points in Chapter XV, which deals with Monopoly. But we may state at once an important rule, derived from the principle that an entrepreneur will try to maximize his profits. This rule is that *he will try to equate his marginal costs and his marginal revenue.* In other words, he will expand his output so long as the increase in his total costs is less than the increase in his total revenue, or receipts, due to the increase in his output. If the latter—his marginal revenue—is less than the former—his marginal costs—he will increase his profits by contracting his output. He will maximize his income, therefore, only if the two are equal. The size of his firm will be limited by the increase in marginal costs or by the decrease in marginal revenue, or both, as its output becomes larger.

Many entrepreneurs, however, do not produce enough to have a perceptible influence upon the selling prices of their products or upon the prices of the factors they employ, and yet they would make smaller profits if they increased their output. The reason for this is that an entrepreneur is limited by his own capacities. Consider, for example, a wheat-farmer. By hypothesis, the amount of work which he devotes to his farm, however big it may be, is given. This means that, after a point, his management will inevitably become less efficient. He will have to spend more time, as the farm grows in area, in moving from one part of it to another. He will have to incur extra costs in the form of book-keeping and other checks to safeguard himself from fraud by his managers. He will find it more difficult to make correct decisions as the number of decisions to be made becomes larger, for the time which he can devote to the problems of his business is given. In short, the Law of Diminishing Returns operates. As increasing amounts of other factors are combined with a fixed amount of entrepreneurship, the marginal products of the other factors diminish, although the price which has to be paid for each unit of a factor remains the same. In other words, the marginal cost of production—the increase in total costs involved in producing an additional unit (or hundred or thousand units) of output—increases.

Of course, entrepreneurs differ in capacity, so that in any industry a more capable entrepreneur will tend to control a larger firm than a less capable one. But even the most capable entrepreneur will find that, after a point, further expansion would diminish his own income: his "profits." However large a firm may be, the question remains: why is it not still larger? And the answer is always that further expansion would increase total costs more than total revenue, or receipts.

9. SUBSTITUTION BETWEEN FACTORS

Our general principle that an entrepreneur will try to maximize his own income, or "profits," implies both that he will try to produce whatever output is most profitable and that he will try to produce it at the lowest possible total cost. Hitherto we have taken this latter point for granted; we must now make it explicit.

We do not say that he will produce whatever output has the least total cost. Clearly quite a small output might have the least total cost, yet he might make greater profits from a larger output. Nor do we say that he will produce whatever output has the least average cost (per unit of output).[1] His average costs may be rising, yet it will pay him to expand so long as his

[1] It will be remembered that we are excluding from his "costs" the return on his own efforts and capital.

marginal receipts exceed his marginal costs. What we do say is that he will produce any given output in the cheapest possible way.

This means that if he can reduce his total costs, without diminishing his output, by substituting some factors for others, he will do so. His cheapest method will depend, given the technical possibilities, on the relative prices of the different factors. For example, if a machine for packing cigarettes, plus one girl, packs 10 million cigarettes a year, and if it takes five girls to pack 10 million cigarettes a year by hand, which method is cheaper will clearly depend on the relative annual cost of a machine and of a girl. If the girls must be paid £100 a year each, the machine is cheaper if its cost (including amortisation) is less than £400 a year and dearer if it is more than £400 a year. Again, if it pays him to expand his output, he will do so by hiring whatever factors enable him to produce any given increase at the least additional cost. If, for example, he begins to expand simply by hiring more of a particular grade of labour, the marginal product of that grade will fall (and the marginal products of his other factors will rise, since they are combined with a greater quantity of that grade) so that, after a point, further expansion will be obtained more cheaply by hiring more of other factors. In some circumstances considerable expansion may take place before this point is reached. If, for some reason, his plant was being worked well below capacity, he may find that the cheapest way of increasing his output until full capacity is attained is to employ mainly additional labour. Even so, he will have to decide how much more of one kind of labour, and how much more of another kind, to employ, and to what extent he will purchase more raw materials, fuel, and so on, and how much he will spend on repairs, renewals, and replacements.

Mr. R. F. Fowler gives some illustrations of the principle we are discussing in an article published in the *Quarterly Journal of Economics*, Vol. LII, November, 1937. Scrap and pig-iron can be used in different proportions as materials in the manufacture of open-hearth steel. Mr. Fowler found that "a reduction in the price of scrap relatively to the price of pig-iron leads to a greater proportion of raw material costs being incurred for scrap as compared with pig-iron." In South Wales, for example, the price of scrap in 1924 was only about 1 per cent lower per ton than the price of pig-iron. About $1\frac{1}{8}$ tons of scrap were combined with 1 ton of pig-iron. In 1935, scrap was 13 per cent cheaper, per ton, than pig-iron and twice as much scrap as pig-iron was used. Mr. Fowler also found that as the proportion of scrap consumed increases "it becomes more and more difficult to substitute scrap for pig-iron without raising costs." This, of course, is an illustration of diminishing marginal returns: the marginal productivity of scrap falls, relatively to that of pig-iron, as the proportion of scrap increases.

Our conclusion can be stated as follows.

$$\text{If the } \frac{\text{marginal product of factor A}}{\text{price of factor A}}$$

is greater than the $\frac{\text{marginal product of factor B}}{\text{price of factor B}}$ it will be to the advantage of the entrepreneur to employ a method of production which uses more of A and less of B. For example, if machines costing £400 a year add more than four times as much to the total product as girls costing £100 a year, machines will be substituted for girls. This will mean an increased demand for machines and a decreased demand for girls. The price of machines will tend to rise (unless they can be produced more cheaply on a larger scale) and the wages of girls will fall (unless they are kept up by State regulation or by their trade union, in which case their marginal product will be raised by fewer of them being employed) until their marginal products are proportional to their prices.

Under perfect competition this Principle of Substitution implies that the value of the marginal product of any factor will *equal* its price. If it were less, entrepreneurs would use less of it until the decreased demand for it lowered its price; if it were greater, entrepreneurs would increase their profits by using more of it, and their increased demand for it would raise its price. The interests of entrepreneurs and of consumers, in this respect, would be in complete harmony. The price of any factor would reflect the valuation placed by consumers on the contribution which it was making to output. Units of particular raw materials, types of labour, and other factors would be diverted towards a particular firm only if they could make a contribution to output in that firm which consumers valued at least as highly as any contribution they could make elsewhere. If an entrepreneur attempted to use so many units of a factor that some of them could produce something elsewhere which consumers valued more highly, the price of that factor would exceed the value of its marginal product in that firm, and the entrepreneur in question could increase his profits by using less of it.

10. COST OF PRODUCTION AND PRICE

A common view is that the price of a commodity—although it may vary owing to changes in demand after the commodity has been produced—is normally "determined by" its cost of production. This implies that the cost of production includes the profit of the entrepreneur, but his profit in fact may vary from time to time as a consequence of changes in price. Moreover, cost of production often varies with the size of the output, which in turn depends on the demand for the product.

The money cost of production, however defined, and whether average or marginal, itself consists of prices. It is composed of the prices of the various factors used in making the good. A complete theory of value should explain all prices, including those of gifts of Nature, labour services, land rents, loans of money, foreign currencies, and rights, as well as the prices of commodities currently produced. But the view under discussion makes no attempt to explain the prices of non-produced goods and services.

In fact, costs no more "determine" the prices of finished products than the latter determine the former. A shortage of coal-miners may raise their wages, and this may raise the price of coal. On the other hand, an increased demand for coal may raise its price and this may lead, by way of an increased demand for coal-miners, to a rise in their wages. All prices are interdependent.

The price of a good produced under imperfect competition, or monopoly, will exceed its marginal cost. Suppose, to take a simple example, that a monopolist is selling a thousand units a week at £1 per unit and that in order to sell 1100 per week he must reduce his price to 19s. The increase in his total receipts would not be 100 times 19s. but only £1045 less £1000, or 100 times 19s. *less* 1000 times 1s., that is, 900s. or £45. He will not produce this extra 100 units unless the addition to his costs is less than £45, although they sell for £95.

Let us now consider perfect competition. An increase in the output of a firm under perfect competition will not perceptibly reduce the price of its product. Its receipts will be increased by the full (present) selling price of the additional output. The marginal revenue from an extra unit will be the full price of that unit, so that the rule that an entrepreneur will equate marginal cost and marginal revenue means that he will equate marginal cost and price. *Every* firm will tend to produce that output for which marginal cost equals price. Differences in efficiency between firms will show themselves not in differences in marginal costs but in differences in output. The more efficient firm will have the larger output.

We have seen that in the long run an entrepreneur will tend to go bankrupt, or transfer to another industry, or relapse into the ranks of employees, if his receipts do not cover both his supplementary and his prime costs. But in the short run it is variable prime costs which are important. "Fixed" costs do not enter into marginal costs because they must be paid whether the output is large or small. He will expand his output so long as the price of his product exceeds the *extra* amount of money which he must pay out in order to produce one more unit of product. If the reduction in his total costs due to his producing one unit less would exceed the price of a unit, he will contract. He is maximizing his own income only if marginal cost equals price. And we may repeat that this applies to all firms and not only to some hypothetical "marginal firms." It may be that some firms will expand or contract their output by, say, a hundred or a thousand units at a time, and not by just one unit, but that in no way modifies our conclusions.

Let us take a very simple example. Suppose that an entrepreneur, growing wheat, has rented a square mile of land and has acquired a given amount of machinery, seed, fertilizer, and so on, and that in order to increase his output he must increase only the number of men he employs. Suppose the marginal product (per year) of his men varies as in the table given on page 124. Then if the wage of a man is £125 a year and the price of a unit of wheat is £1, he will employ 12 men. If he employs only 11 men, his output will be 1822 units and his receipts, therefore, £1822. One additional man would increase his output to 1950 units, adding £128 to his receipts and only £125 to his costs, thus increasing his profits by £3. But a thirteenth man would increase his receipts by only £115, whilst increasing his costs, as before, by £125. He will therefore employ 12 men, but not more than 12. In this example his marginal costs consist entirely of wages. Since men are indivisible, his costs increase, as his output expands, by jumps of £125 a year —that being the prevailing rate of wages for this type of labour. An entrepreneur who can employ men by the hour can achieve closer equality between marginal cost and price. His marginal cost will be the cost of the extra hours of labour required to produce an additional unit of product. As more labour is employed, the marginal product of labour will diminish. In other words, as output expands, an increasing number of hours' work will be required to produce yet one more unit. Marginal cost—the addition to his wages bill required to secure an additional unit of product—will therefore increase. He will expand his output only so long as the price he gets for a unit of product exceeds its marginal cost.

All this assumes not only perfect competition but also that changes in output involve changes only in the amount of labour employed, the quantities of other factors employed remaining the same. In the short run, this latter assumption may be near the truth. Expansion of output may require mainly additional labour, together, perhaps, with increased raw materials, fuel, and so on, and the loan of additional money with which to pay for these things. Any given output will be produced as cheaply as possible, so that the proportions in which different types of labour and materials are combined may change as output expands, but this does not affect the conclusion that marginal cost will tend to equal price. But it must be remembered that the longer the period under consideration the greater the number of costs—for replacements and so on—which actually have to be paid out and thus enter into marginal costs.

One further point may be added. In the short run, a firm may continue to produce although its marginal costs exceed its marginal revenue. It will do so if the loss involved in closing down temporarily and keeping its assets in good condition is greater than the loss involved in working them, and if, at the same time, it hopes that after a while the prices of the products will rise. Thus if a coal-mine is temporarily closed down, the cost of keeping it free of water and in good condition generally is relatively high: the loss from working it may be smaller. But of course if the entrepreneur is wrong in his belief that in time the prices of his products will rise (or the prices of his factors fall) sooner or later he will be compelled to close down rather than to continue paying money from his private resources to go on working at a loss.[1]

[1] "The Equilibrium of the Firm" by N. Kaldor (*Economic Journal*, 1934) deals admirably with several of the problems discussed in this chapter

CHAPTER XIV

THE MOBILITY OF FACTORS OF PRODUCTION

1. THE MEANING OF "MOBILITY"

At any moment a community has a certain quantity of factors of production. In the first place, it has a working population. This does not consist only of wage-earners. It includes also farmers, shopkeepers, workers in the professions, housewives, and indeed all whose activities contribute directly or indirectly towards the production of goods and services. In the second place, it has natural resources, including improvements of all kinds (such as roads, tunnels, and dams) made by man. In the third place, it has capital, consisting of goods of all kinds, ranging in durability from buildings to quickly perishable goods such as fish. It will be remembered that there are very many different kinds of factors of production and that we group them under these three broad headings of Labour, Land, and Capital merely for convenience of exposition. It makes little difference whether we regard, say, a canal or a bridge as falling under Land or as falling under Capital, or indeed whether or not we include all Land under Capital. The important thing is to realize how the possible output of consumers' goods and services is limited by the quantity and nature of the factors of production available.

It is true that a given quantity of factors of production may render more or fewer services. Thus a given population may perform more or less work. Some people capable of working may choose to live a life of leisure, enjoying incomes received from their ownership of property, and workers may take longer or shorter holidays, or work more or fewer hours per week. But this point is not relevant to our present problem.

Our present problem is to consider how far factors of production are capable of alternative uses. A factor capable of only one use, such as a coke-oven, is said to be completely "specific." If every factor were completely specific, a community would have little scope for choice as to what assortment of goods and services it would produce. It could indeed decide which factors were not worth utilizing, and to what extent particular factors should be worked, but that would be all. Unless it could acquire new and different factors, there would be no possibility of variation—the same factors would always produce the same products. In fact, of course, this is not the case. Many factors are capable of alternative uses, and thus a given quantity of factors can produce any one of a large number of different assortments of goods and services. Moreover, some existing factors can be converted into, or replaced by, different ones, and this increases still further the range within which the composition of the total output can be altered.

It will be remembered that in modern communities the structure of production is complex. The production of a finished commodity may involve many stages and processes, in the course of which many different kinds of factors are used. Hence we can distinguish two ways in which a given factor of production may make a different contribution to the final output. In the first place, it may continue to render exactly the same kind of services as before, but these may be utilized in a different way. For example, a typist may move from one "industry" to another without changing the nature of her work, and a blast furnace may continue to produce pig-iron but more of the pig-iron may become, say, girders and less, say, rails than before. In the second place, a factor may change the nature of the services which it renders. For example, a typist may become a shop assistant. We might then say that, whilst remaining the same person, she has become a different factor of production, and we might regard any "costs of conversion," such as the cost of training her for her new job, as an investment of capital.

We have used the term "mobility," rather than "specificity," partly because it is better known and partly because it includes the notion of geographical mobility. Changes in economic conditions may make it desirable for some factors to move from one place to another. Thus we can speak of mobility between industries, between occupations, and between places. As we have just seen, a factor may move from one industry to another without changing its occupation, and it may do so without having to move to a different place. A movement between occupations need not involve a movement between industries or places: for example, our typist may have been typing for the shopkeeper in whose shop she now acts as a saleswoman. Similarly, a movement between places need not involve a change either of industry or occupation. Any one type of mobility may be accompanied by either, or both, or neither, of the other two types.

The last two chapters have shown how the price-system provides incentives to entrepreneurs and other owners of factors to produce that assortment of goods which consumers most prefer and to change the composition of the total output in response to changes in the tastes of consumers and in the state of technical knowledge. The extent to which changes in output *are* made, as time goes on, depends upon a number of things. It depends in part upon the expectations of entrepreneurs as to how prices will change in the future. It depends in part upon how far owners of factors of production would forgo a monetary gain or incur a monetary loss rather than move their factors (which, of course, in the case of workers means themselves) to another place or occupation or industry, and upon how far their estimates of the gains or losses are correct. It depends in part upon how far State action (such as Public Assistance) discourages or encourages mobility; and so on. But the extent to which changes in output *can* be made depends upon the extent to which factors of production can be transferred to other industries or occupations or places, and upon the time required to effect such transfers. This question of the physical possibilities of mobility forms the subject of the present chapter, although we shall make some reference also to non-physical obstacles to mobility. The question is one of fact. Mobility is greater in some countries and periods than in others; we shall take our illustrations mainly from Great Britain during recent years.

2. THE MOBILITY OF LABOUR

The British Census of 1931 distinguishes about 35,000 different occupations. Some of these, such as interior decorating or dress designing or tea-tasting, require a natural aptitude possessed, in a high degree, by relatively few. Others, such as the professions or lithographic printing, require a considerable period of training or apprenticeship, in addition to sufficient natural aptitude. Any occupation, even a so-called "unskilled job" such as pick-and-shovel work, requires certain capacities; and a beginner can usually improve, perhaps quite considerably, with practice.

Nevertheless, almost any worker who is proficient at his own job could become fairly proficient at occupations demanding similar qualities, and there is usually quite a wide range of such occupations. Thus a man who is fairly efficient at tending one kind of machine could usually learn to tend other kinds of machines, a man doing work requiring mainly physical strength could usually do other jobs of a similar kind, most good chauffeurs could learn to pilot an aeroplane, and so on. And most occupations can be learnt in a fairly short time. Thus it is roughly true to say that occupations can be divided into groups. A worker can move fairly easily from one occupation to another within his group, but may have difficulty in becoming proficient at an occupation in another group demanding different qualities.

Clearly it is a simple matter for a worker to change his industry, provided that he continues to do the same kind of work and to live in the same place. And quite a number of occupations, such as those of clerks, typists, salesmen, lorry-drivers, and porters, are common to many different industries.

Movement between places, however, may not be easy. A worker may consider more than the monetary cost of moving to a new district. He may be reluctant to leave familiar scenes and friends and associations and to begin life again in a strange place. He may be still more reluctant to move to a different country, especially one with a different language and different customs.

The monetary cost of learning a new job or moving to a different place is an investment of capital. This investment may sometimes be made by the State: by providing free training or by paying the fares of workers moving to jobs in another district or by subsidizing emigration. It may sometimes be made by the employers, who consider it worth their while to train workers or to pay their fares. But usually it must be made by the worker himself. He will not make it unless he believes that the improvement in his future earnings will repay him with interest. Some workers may not have the necessary capital, and others may consider that even the probability of repayment plus, say, 10 or 20 per cent interest, in the form of increased wages for the rest of their working lives, is not sufficient to compensate them for the present sacrifice of the capital sum. It may be noted that a given prospect of increased earnings will be more likely to tempt a younger worker to move than an older one, not merely because the latter has become more set in his habits but also because he has fewer years of his working life left over in which to recoup himself for his present investment.

In a modern community, changes in demand and in technical knowledge are constantly taking place and providing incentives, through the price-mechanism, for labour to move between occupations and industries and places. There has been a marked tendency during recent years for the State to prevent or restrict entrance to certain industries: thus in Great Britain an entrepreneur may not be permitted to open a new coal-mine or to start a new bus service or to begin distributing electricity or to set up a broadcasting station or to begin growing hops for the market. Moreover, entrants to certain occupations, such as most of the professions, are required to pass some kind of qualifying test and in some cases to pay a fee. But apart from these restrictions, there are no legal obstacles to mobility within a country. Yet it cannot be claimed that movements of labour take place on a large enough scale, and sufficiently quickly, to facilitate a rapid and complete adjustment to changes in economic conditions.

A leading example of inadequate mobility is that of Great Britain during the last ten or fifteen years. Certain areas, notably South Wales, Glasgow, Lancashire, and Tyneside, are largely dependent upon "staple" industries (such as coal and cotton) which export a large proportion of their output and which have been confronted with a marked fall, especially in foreign markets, in the demand for their products. Wages in these areas have fallen below wages for comparable occupations in other parts of the country, yet the mobility of labour away from these districts has been insufficient to prevent the percentage of unemployment from being at least twice as high as in other districts, so that they are now treated as "special" or "depressed" areas. It is claimed, however, that mobility has been hindered, until recently, by a shortage of suitable houses in the more prosperous parts of the country and that it is still hindered by the fact that unemployment benefits and public assistance reduce incentives to movement.

Nevertheless, the mobility of labour *is* sufficient, in most modern countries, to make possible a very large measure of adjustment in response to changes in economic conditions. It must be remembered that it is quite exceptional for changes in conditions to require more than a quite small percentage of workers to move, in any one year, out of any one occupation or industry or district. Only that small fraction of the total working population which is most able and willing to move need do so; as a rule, complete adjustment could be achieved even if the vast majority of workers continued to live in the same place and to do the same work as before. Further, adjustment may, and often does, take place by means of a kind of "reshuffle." Suppose, for example, that a movement of population is required from the North to the South. This could be brought about by a series of ripples, constituting a general southward trend, some people in the North moving some distance southward, some people in the North Midlands moving southward, and so on. Similarly with a movement between occupations. Suppose, for example, that the coal industry is contracting and the motor industry expanding. It is possible that very few coal-miners could become proficient workers in the motor industry. In spite of this, a transition might be effected by, let us say, some coal-miners becoming builders' labourers, some builders' labourers lorry-drivers, and some lorry-drivers entering the motor industry. Finally, by far the most important influence facilitating mobility between occupations and industries, although not so much between places, is the change in *personnel* of the working population, which is constantly being diminished by deaths and retirements and increased by the flow of boys and girls entering the labour market from school or college. It is easier to decide to enter, for the first time, one occupation rather than another, than to decide to give up an occupation in which one has acquired knowledge and skill, in order to begin afresh, perhaps at a fairly advanced age, in a new field. Most of the youthful new entrants to the labour market are capable of entering any one of a number of industries and occupations, and they tend to be diverted towards those which consumers would most prefer them to enter, for it is those which offer them the brightest prospects. Here, again, the State is often helpful: children may be given "vocational tests" to discover their natural aptitudes, and parents may be advised by Employment Exchange officials and others, who know the prospects of employment and wages in different fields, into what jobs to place their children.

A few statistics will show that considerable movements of labour have taken place in Great Britain during recent years. Between July, 1923, and July, 1935, the number of insured workers attached to coal-mining fell from 1244 thousand to 939 thousand, to cotton from 568 thousand to 442 thousand, and to shipbuilding from 270 thousand to 157 thousand, whilst those attached to the distributive trades rose from 1254 thousand to 2007 thousand, to building from 716 thousand to 977 thousand, and to the motor industry from 192 thousand to 286 thousand, whilst numerous other changes also took place between industries and occupations. There was also some movement away from the depressed areas and towards the South. Thus the Census Preliminary Report, 1931 (page xiv), remarks—

> It will be observed that the counties North of Cheshire and Yorkshire inclusive have on balance lost as many as 443,000 of their population by migration during the past decennium and that from the central belt Wales has lost 259,000, the Midlands 81,000, and the Eastern region 41,000. . . . In the South-eastern section the net immigration numbers 615,000.

This movement has continued during recent years.

It may be noted that adjustment between industries and occupations is facilitated by an expanding population, for changes in the proportion of the working population attached to different industries and occupations can be brought about mainly by diverting the stream of new entrants towards those fields which are expanding, without many workers having actually to change over from one line to another. This also can be illustrated from Great Britain. In 1881 the total occupied population was 12,739 thousand, of which 1593 thousand were engaged in agriculture. Improvements in transport and in agricultural technique made it cheaper for Great Britain to buy more of the agricultural produce which she consumed from abroad instead of producing it herself. Thus in 1931, out of an occupied population of 21,055 thousand, only 1194 thousand were engaged in agriculture. A change from 1250 per 10,000 occupied persons to 567 per 10,000 occupied persons involved an absolute diminution of only 399,000 in the number engaged in agriculture, owing to the growth of population. Over this period some industries expanded greatly. For example, the numbers engaged in the manufacture of metals, machinery, etc., increased from 927 thousand to 2412 thousand, that is from 728 to 1145 per 10,000 occupied persons. These expansions took place largely by the inflow of new entrants to the labour market. A stationary, and still more a declining, population hampers adjustment, since this must take place mainly by workers leaving one kind of job and moving to another. Great Britain has been handicapped in this respect by the recent slowing-down in her rate of population growth, and this handicap is likely to increase in the future, as her population ceases to expand and begins to decline.

3. THE MOBILITY OF LAND

It will be granted that soil can be shifted, that rivers can be diverted, that minerals, once extracted, can be transported, and so on. But it will probably seem absurd to suggest that land itself can be moved from one place to another.

This is because we measure land by its area. But area, as such, is of less importance than productivity, and the productivity of a particular piece of land can be increased or diminished.

The term "land" has sometimes been restricted to the inherent and indestructible powers of the soil. But there seems little point in adopting this definition. In fact much of what is commonly called land is man-made, and it is impossible to separate "improvements" due to man from the original land. Most land requires a continuous investment of free capital in order to keep it sufficiently free from pests, or sufficiently fertilized or drained, to maintain its productivity; and as a rule additional investments will increase its productivity. The confusion between the two concepts of land is well illustrated by the story of the landowner who stipulated when leasing his land that the tenant should maintain intact the indestructible powers of the soil.

Hence if more free capital than formerly is invested in "improving" the land of one region, and less than formerly in "improving" the land of another region, the productivity of land has been increased in the former region and diminished in the latter.

But although man can do much, by irrigation and other means, to improve the natural resources of a region, he cannot give a tropical climate to land in a temperate zone, or transport minerals without first extracting them; and the uneven distribution of different natural resources over the earth's surface is a very important fact. We shall discuss its implications when we deal with the location of industry.

Some land is more or less completely "specific." For instance, much land in the North of Europe grows only forests, and the soil is not rich enough to make it worth while to clear the forests in order to grow crops. Again, much land in the interior of Australia receives a rainfall so small and unreliable that it is suited only for sparse pastoral cultivation. Most land, however, is capable of a considerable range of different uses. There is very little land which could not be made to serve as a site for buildings: witness, for example, the Ford factory which rests triumphantly on concrete piles above the swamps of Dagenham. There are few districts which could not provide some kind of golf course if the demand for it were great enough. Nearly all "arable" land is capable of growing grass and serving as pasture, and much of it could support any of several kinds of animals. Obviously the potential uses of any given piece of land are limited by its climate and by the nature of its soil, but within these limits most land is far from being completely specific. But some investment of capital is usually required in order to convert land from one use to another. Moreover, a considerable time may have to elapse before the supply of a given product can be substantially increased: for example, a rubber tree or a coffee bush takes several years before it begins to yield.

A striking example of a change in the use to which land has been put is afforded by the transfer from grain-growing to stock-raising in the United Kingdom between 1874 and 1914. Over this period, the area under wheat fell from 3·8 to 1·9 million acres and that under barley from 2·5 to 1·9 million acres, while the area under permanent grass increased from 23·7 to 27·4 million acres. Under the stimulus of a subsidy, the area under beet sugar increased from 4000 acres in 1913 to 404,000 acres in 1934. Over the same period the area under turnips and swedes fell from 1,486,000 acres to 874,000 acres.

4. THE MOBILITY OF CAPITAL

Much of the capital of a country consists of buildings and plant. It is often physically possible to dismantle plant, transport it, and set it up again in a different place, but the advantages of a change in location are seldom great enough to outweigh the cost of doing so: and it is very seldom worth while to move buildings constructed of brick or stone. Moreover, most of this fixed capital seems to be highly specific. It was designed for a particular purpose and as a rule the cost of adapting it to a different purpose would be too great to make the investment worth while. There are, of course, exceptions to this. Thus it is claimed that factories making sewing-machines can readily produce machine-guns, and that plant designed for motor cars or agricultural machinery can often be converted to the manufacture of armaments. But most fixed capital either stays where it is and does the kind of work for which it was designed or is broken up and sold as scrap.

Nevertheless, the mobility of capital is considerably greater than appears at first sight.

The "purpose" for which a building or plant was designed is often wide enough to permit considerable variation in the goods or services produced. Thus a building designed as a factory or a shop or an office will often serve equally well for any one of several kinds of factory or shop or office. Many engineering works are capable of producing a wide range of products and can readily produce more of one kind and less of another. Spindles can often be adapted to spin a finer or a coarser yarn or even to use a different kind of material.

Many raw materials and other intermediate products are used by a number of different industries, so that although the plant which produces them may be specific to that use, its products are capable of several different uses. For example, a blast furnace may produce only pig-iron, but the pig-iron may be finally transformed into part of a railway track or of a building or a ship or a motor car or a machine. In the same way the services of transport agencies, such as railways and lorries, can be used for almost any kinds of goods, and it is a simple matter to supply more light, heat, and power to some industries and less to others. Thus very considerable changes can take place fairly quickly in the composition of the final output of a country whilst most of the fixed capital continues to render exactly the same services or to produce exactly the same goods as before.

Finally, as time goes on, capital is consumed and need not be replaced in the same form. For example, an entrepreneur who wishes to keep his capital intact will set aside some of his receipts in order to replace his machinery and other equipment when it wears out. The money which he sets aside is free capital and will be used to purchase a different type of machinery or a completely different kind of plant, if he thinks that course more profitable. It is true that most buildings and many plants have a fairly long "life." Even so, the distribution of capital between industries can be changed considerably if the total amount of capital is being increased by new savings (which flow towards those industries where they can be used most profitably) just as the distribution of labour between industries is facilitated by an expanding population. Moreover, "working capital," which consists largely of stocks of intermediate products, and much consumers' capital, has a fairly short life and can readily be replaced by something different after it is consumed.

5. CONCLUSIONS

We have been considering a question of fact, namely, to what extent a modern economic system is flexible. Under capitalism, changes in economic conditions act upon the price-mechanism and provide incentives to entrepreneurs to produce more of some goods rather than of others. But this means transferring some factors of production to different uses. We have inquired how readily such transferences can take place.

Our general conclusion is that they can take place more easily than is often supposed: and this conclusion, for which we offered a number of reasons, is borne out by experience. In most modern countries some industries have waxed and others waned, and quite new industries (such as the motor car industry) have sprung up and attained a large size very quickly, with little disturbance to the economic system as a whole. But there are obstacles to mobility, and it may take some time to overcome them: in general, the longer the time which has elapsed after a change in conditions, the more complete will be the adaptation.

We have seen that adjustment is facilitated when population and capital are expanding, and that the most difficult transference to effect is often the movement of labour from one district to another. Our discussion, it should be added, has said nothing about the trade cycle. A general trade depression usually involves a marked fall in the demand for the products of the constructional industries. Large groups of unemployed may be marooned for a considerable time in districts specializing in such industries, so that problems of transference become particularly important and at the same time exceptionally difficult to solve. But we must postpone this subject to a later chapter.

CHAPTER XV
MONOPOLY

1. THE MEANING OF MONOPOLY

MONOPOLY is in some sense the opposite of perfect competition. It will be convenient to begin our discussion by stating once again what is meant by perfect competition.

An entrepreneur is acting under perfect competition when he produces such a small part of the total supply of his commodity or service that he cannot perceptibly influence its price by expanding or contracting his output. Its price appears to him as a fact which he must accept and which he cannot alter. It would be futile for him to charge more than the market price, since if he did he would sell nothing at all: there are thousands of others to whom buyers could turn instead. It would be foolish for him to charge less, since he can sell all he cares to produce at the full market price. Therefore he must, and does, accept the price as he finds it.

Of course the sum-total of the actions of all the producers of a particular good does have a powerful influence on its price. If they all produce more, the price is lower; if they all produce less, the price is higher. But no one producer can *perceptibly* influence the price—any more than one star more or less on a night of stars, one grain of sand more or less in a heap of sand, one hair more or less on most heads, makes any perceptible difference.

It is tempting to say that the opposite pole to perfect competition is absolute monopoly, and to define an absolute monopolist as one who is the sole producer of some commodity. But what is a "commodity"? Mr. Blank may be the sole producer of Blank's tea, but his product has to meet the competition of other more or less similar brands of tea. Even if Mr. Blank were the sole producer of tea he would still have to face the competition of coffee and other substitutes for tea. All commodities and services are to some extent rivals in their claims upon the limited purse of the consumer. There is no such thing as an absolute monopolist.

There is, however, a great deal of "imperfect" or "monopolistic" competition. Many firms produce a proportion of the total output of their commodity large enough for changes in their own output to have a perceptible effect upon its price: an effect which they take into account when considering what size of output will be most profitable to them. The device of trade-marks enables a firm to differentiate its products from the products of its rivals, and to fix its own price. Of course a higher price will mean lower sales, but within limits it can charge a higher price without reducing its sales to zero. The reason for this is that consumers, or at least some consumers, prefer one brand to another: they do not regard the different brands as perfect substitutes. This explains, too, why one barrister may get higher fees than another, why one cinema can charge higher prices than another, and so on. Another reason for imperfect competition is to be found in costs of transport. A colliery company, for example, could charge local consumers higher prices than those charged at the pithead by its nearest rival, provided that the difference in price (for exactly similar coal) did not exceed the cost of transporting coal from the mine of its rival to its own local consumers. In the same way some consumers may knowingly pay a slightly higher price at one shop rather than take the trouble of going to another.

As a matter of strict logic, every producer is more or less in competition with every other, any given producer must be working under either perfect or imperfect competition, and the term monopoly should be either discarded or used as a synonym for imperfect competition. Nevertheless, some producers or combinations of producers, such as Messrs. Coats, the chief producers of sewing-cotton, and the Coffee Institute of Brazil, which controls most of the coffee supply of the world, have a much greater degree of monopoly than the sellers of one brand of butter, or than any particular shop, in that they control the bulk of a commodity for which there is no very close substitute. Although our discussion of monopoly will apply, for the most part, to imperfect competition in general, we shall have in mind mainly monopolists of the former type, who enjoy a monopoly in the popular sense of the term.

2. MONOPOLY PRICE

Let us consider a monopolist who is the sole producer of some commodity and who wishes to maximize his "profits" in the sense of the money return from those factors of production, assumed to remain fixed in amount, which he himself owns and uses in his business. He can either fix whatever price he pleases or sell whatever amount (say, per week) he pleases; but he cannot sell as much as he likes at whatever price he likes. He will sell more at a lower price than at a higher price. The amount which he can sell at any given price depends upon the conditions of demand for his product, and these he cannot influence: he must accept them as a given fact.[1] They will be affected, of course, by the prices and suitability of the various substitutes for his commodity to which consumers can turn: in general, the demand for his product will be more elastic, around a given price, if fairly close substitutes are available at about that price than if they are not.

Hence it is a matter of indifference whether we ask what price he will find most profitable or what output he will find most profitable, for the amount which he can sell at any given price is determined for him by the conditions of demand. The answer to our question was given in Chapter XIII. His most profitable output will be that at which his marginal costs and his marginal revenue (or marginal receipts) are equal. The rest of this section is merely an expansion of that statement.

If he has no costs, his most profitable output will clearly be that which (supposing it all to be sold) maximizes his total receipts. After a point, further increases in his output must *diminish* his total receipts. If consumers spend more money upon his commodity, they have less to spend upon other things, so that there must be some (weekly) sum of money which is the utmost that he can obtain from consumers. A typical curve

[1] Many producers can and do raise the demand schedule for their products by such means as advertising. This fact makes no fundamental difference to our reasoning and we have therefore omitted it from the text. We can assume that our monopolist has calculated the most profitable expenditure on selling costs for any given output, and that the "demand curve" which he considers as a datum shows the sales which he expects to make at any given price if he spends whatever sum is most profitable on selling costs, and that his "cost curve" includes selling costs.

showing how total receipts vary with output (or sales) will rise to a maximum and then decline. Before this maximum is reached, the elasticity of demand is greater than unity; after it is reached, it is less than unity; and around the maximum it is equal to unity (for since the curve is neither rising nor falling it must be horizontal).[1] The marginal costs of the monopolist are zero, and therefore his most profitable output is that at which his marginal revenue is also zero—a slight increase in his output neither increasing nor diminishing his total receipts, since they are at a maximum.

Suppose now that a monopolist has costs. His marginal costs may be rising or falling or constant, but it is certain that his *total* costs will be greater for any given output than for any smaller output.[2] This means that his marginal costs will always be positive, and therefore his most profitable output will be one at which his marginal revenue is positive; it must therefore be smaller than it would be if he had no costs, since in that case, as we have seen, his marginal revenue would be zero. And even if his marginal costs are falling, there must be some point beyond which his marginal revenue would be less than his marginal costs, and beyond which, therefore, it would not pay him to expand his output.

The following table, in which the figures are of course hypothetical, shows part of the cost schedule of a monopolist and the corresponding part of the demand schedule for his product. We suppose that he would vary his output by 1000 units at a time and that his marginal costs are constant[3] at 16,000 shillings per 1000 units. His profits are maximized at a (weekly) output of 14,000 units, since at this output his marginal costs and his marginal receipts are as nearly equal as possible. If he increases his output to 15,000 units, he would increase his total costs by 16,000 shillings and his total receipts by only 13,000 shillings, thereby reducing his profits. If he reduced his output to 13,000 units, he would reduce his total costs by 16,000 shillings and his

[1] See Chapter III, section 6.

[2] He may be able, say, to produce 1000 units a week with the aid of specialized machinery at a lower total cost than 100 units per week by more primitive methods. But, if so, his cheapest method of producing 100 units per week is to use specialized machinery, even if this involves destroying the greater part of his output; and in fact it will always cost him less to produce a smaller amount.

[3] We assume a fixed charge of 300,000 shillings (per week) for equipment.

total receipts by 17,000 shillings, so that this course also would diminish his profits.

Output per Week	Price per Unit	Total Revenue	Marginal Revenue	Total Costs	Marginal Costs	Profits
	s.	s.	s.	s.	s.	s.
10,000	50	500,000	—	460,000	—	40,000
11,000	48	528,000	28,000	476,000	16,000	52,000
12,000	47	564,000	36,000	492,000	16,000	72,000
13,000	45	585,000	21,000	508,000	16,000	77,000
14,000	43	602,000	17,000	524,000	16,000	78,000
15,000	41	615,000	13,000	540,000	16,000	75,000
16,000	39	624,000	9,000	556,000	16,000	68,000
17,000	37	629,000	5,000	572,000	16,000	57,000
18,000	35	630,000	1,000	588,000	16,000	42,000
19,000	33	627,000	− 3,000	604,000	16,000	23,000

Fig. 20 shows the situation by means of a diagram. Quantities of output are measured along the horizontal axis and total receipts and total costs up the vertical axis. The curve labelled

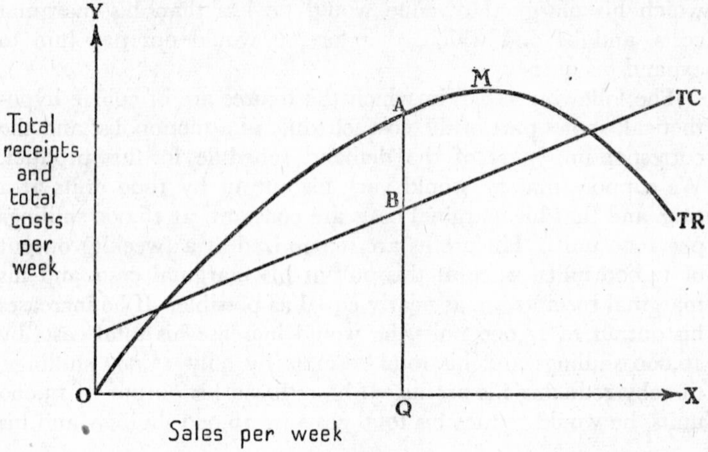

FIG. 20

TR shows the total receipts obtained from the corresponding quantity of output. It rises to a maximum at *M* and then declines. That labelled *TC* shows the total cost of each amount of output. We make it begin above *O* because we assume a certain fixed charge for equipment. It has a constant slope, showing constant marginal costs. If marginal costs were falling, it would tend to flatten from left to right, and if they were rising, it would tend to do the opposite. The object of the monopolist is to maximize the difference *AB* between his total receipts *AQ* and his total costs *BQ*. He achieves this object by producing (and selling) that amount *OQ* at which his marginal receipts and his marginal costs are equal, at which, that is to say, the slope of *TR* is the same as the slope of *TC*.[1]

The price *per unit* is not shown directly. The price per unit of any output *OQ* is the total receipts *QA* divided by the output *OQ*.

3. DISCRIMINATING MONOPOLY

Hitherto we have supposed that a monopolist is obliged to sell all his output at a uniform price per unit. He may be able, however, to divide his sales among a number of different "markets" and to charge a different price in each market. This is known as "discrimination."

Let us give a few examples. A doctor may charge a rich patient more than a poor one for an exactly similar operation. An electricity company may charge more for current used for lighting than for current used for power. A railway company may charge more per ton-mile for carrying copper than for carrying coal. A monopolist may "dump" goods abroad at a lower price than he charges for them in his home market.

All the units sold at one price are said to be sold in one "market," so that a discriminating monopolist has as many markets as he charges different prices. The same person may of course purchase from the monopolist in two or more different markets, as when a man sends two or more different commodities, charged at different rates per ton-mile, by the same railway company.

Discriminating monopoly is possible only if the goods or services sold in the cheaper market (that is, at a lower price) cannot readily be transferred to the dearer market. Thus it would hardly be possible for a firm to charge higher prices to well-dressed customers. For well-dressed persons would then either dress badly in order to make purchases or send their badly-dressed servants or friends to buy on their behalf. But a man

[1] That is, *TR* at the point *A* is parallel to *TC* at the point *B*.

cannot readily disguise his identity when he visits a doctor; copper cannot be transformed into coal while it travels by rail; the use of separate meters prevents electric current charged as being used for power from being used for lighting; and the price of goods sold abroad can be lower than the home price by the cost of transport both ways—if the difference is greater, foreign buyers can make a profit by reselling, at a price just below the home price, in the home market.

If a monopolist can divide his sales among a number of markets, between which the conditions of demand are different, he will make greater profits by charging a different price in each market. He will maximize his profits by charging such prices that his marginal costs (for his total output) are equal to the marginal receipts in each separate market. For if he does this, he will gain neither by increasing nor by decreasing his output nor yet by transferring some sales from one market to another.

A simple illustration may be useful. Suppose that a monopolist has the same cost schedule as that shown in our table, and can vary his output by 1000 units at a time, his marginal costs (for a further 1000 units) being always 16,000 shillings. Suppose that he has two markets. In one, the demand schedule is as shown in our table. In this market, therefore, he will sell 14,000 units at a price of 43 shillings per unit, his marginal revenue (from the fourteenth thousand) being 17,000 shillings. In the other market, suppose that the relevant part of the demand schedule is as follows—

Quantity	Price per Unit	Total Revenue	Marginal Revenue
	s.	s.	s.
1000	40	40,000	—
2000	30	60,000	20,000
3000	26	78,000	18,000
4000	21	84,000	6,000

In this market he will charge 26 shillings, his marginal revenue (from the third thousand) being 18,000 shillings. His total output, therefore, will be 17,000 and his total profits 602,000 plus 78,000 minus 572,000 = 108,000 shillings—these being the maximum total profits which he can obtain under the given conditions.

It should be noted that discrimination is profitable only if elasticity of demand is different in the various markets. There are doubtless many monopolists who could discriminate if they chose but who, because this condition is absent, do not find this course profitable.

As between two (or more) markets, the most profitable price will be lower in the market where the elasticity of demand is greater. The possibility of dumping on a foreign market will raise the home price if marginal costs are rising, lower it if they are falling, and leave it unaltered if (as in the above example) they are constant.[1]

4. THE FOUNDATIONS OF MONOPOLY POWER

Even a monopolist is subject to the sovereignty of the consumer. He cannot make consumers buy more of his product, at any given price, than they choose to buy. His monopoly power rests on his control over the supply of his product. It enables him to produce, and sell, whatever quantity will maximize his profits, given the conditions of demand.

If his commodity were produced under perfect competition, the quantity produced would be such that the price of the commodity equalled the marginal cost of producing it of every firm engaged in that industry, and no factors of production would be able to raise the value of their contribution to output, and earn more, by moving into that industry. But his monopoly power enables him to restrict the supply of his commodity, so that its price exceeds his marginal cost of production. A number of producers, working under perfect competition, might push their total output well beyond the point at which the elasticity of demand became less than unity. In such a case they would clearly gain if they could combine to form a monopoly and restrict their total output and thereby increase their total receipts. A monopolist, as we have seen, will always produce—if he has costs—an output smaller than that which would maximize his total receipts, for he wishes to maximize his total receipts minus his total costs. Thus the elasticity of demand for a monopolized product will always be greater than unity for the output actually produced; but the opportunities for gain by converting

[1] See NOTE at the end of this chapter.

an industry into a monopoly are particularly great when the demand for the output which would be produced under competition is relatively inelastic. In terms of our diagram, they are particularly great when the competitive output would expand beyond the maximum point M on the Total Revenue curve into the region of relatively inelastic demand.

Thus the key to the success of a monopoly is restriction of output. This keeps up the price of the commodity and enables the factors owned by the monopolist to earn more than they could earn elsewhere. But this means that owners of similar factors (or of free capital, which could be used to hire similar factors at their market price—which of course would equal their earnings outside the monopolized industry) could get a bigger income by moving their factors into the monopolized industry. If they did so, however, more of that commodity would be produced, its price would fall, and the erstwhile monopolist would earn no more from his factors than they could earn elsewhere: his monopoly would collapse. It follows that a monopoly can be maintained only if would-be new entrants can be kept out. The circumstances which prevent or deter newcomers, and thus enable output to be restricted, are the foundations upon which the power of a monopoly is based. We can classify such circumstances into three main groups.

In the first place, a monopoly may be based upon its ownership of all or most of the supply of something essential to the production of the monopolized product. This something may be a raw material—for example, the International Nickel Corporation of Canada owns most of the known deposits of nickel in the world; or it may be a secret process; or, as in the case of Charlie Chaplin, it may be a unique personality. Under this heading fall local monopolies such as that possessed by a firm which owns the sole deposit of coal in a given district.

In the second place, a monopoly may be based on the possession of an exclusive legal privilege. Thus most States, in order to encourage invention, grant patent rights which give their possessors the sole right, for a term of years, to make use of some new process or invention which they have discovered or purchased from the inventor. Again, in most countries a firm can differentiate a commodity which it produces from other similar commodities by labelling it with a trade-mark which other firms are forbidden by law to copy. Or the State may simply confer a legal monopoly in some field upon itself (for example, the French Government has given itself the monopoly of tobacco manufacture in France) or upon some firm (for example, the British Broadcasting Corporation) or upon existing producers (for example, hop-growers in Great Britain are protected by law from the entry of new producers into their industry).

Clearly, most monopolies resting upon legal privilege will have a monopoly only within the territory of their State, but within that territory they may be protected from the competition of imports by import duties or prohibitions. In general, a protective tariff, by sheltering firms within the protected area from the competition of imports, facilitates the formation and maintenance of monopolies inside the tariff wall.

In the third place, the most profitable method of production in some industries may require expensive and specialized plant and equipment. Hence the number of firms will be relatively small, and this will facilitate combination among them in order to exercise a monopolistic control over the supply of their products. This is the case, for example, in most branches of the iron and steel industry. This same circumstance may deter new firms, in the short run, from entering the industry. For fixed costs are high both absolutely and relatively to variable costs. A capitalist will hesitate before investing a large amount of capital in a highly specific form. Existing firms may be making monopoly profits, but the entry of another firm might increase output so much that the profits of all might be reduced below the competitive level—just as one shop in a small village may do well whereas two would both do badly. If the plant will last a long time, the capitalist will need to feel confident of making profits in the more distant as well as in the immediate future before he decides to erect it. Thus existing firms may for some time enjoy a monopoly based essentially upon the indivisibility of the plant and equipment needed in the industry. But they have no means of preventing new firms from entering, and hence a period of considerable prosperity is likely to tempt in new producers, thus enlarging the "capacity" of the industry. Since industries of this type, apart from public utilities, are mainly constructional industries, the demand for their products fluctuates considerably as between trade booms and trade depressions.

New firms tend to enter during a boom, and, when a depression follows, the industry finds itself with an enlarged capacity to produce but facing a diminished demand. Hence such industries tend to make monopoly profits in times of boom but to fare worse than most industries in times of depression.

The supply of transport by rail and tram, of telephonic communication, and of water, gas, and electricity, requires expensive specific fixed capital, including rails or wires or pipes by means of which the service is supplied to consumers. This tends to make such industries local monopolies and enables them to charge discriminating prices. For these reasons they are usually classed as "public utilities" by the State, which either owns them or controls their prices or profits.

These three headings cover most, although not all, of the circumstances which give rise to monopolies.

5. COMBINATIONS OF PRODUCERS

A single firm may control all or most of the output of a commodity or service, either throughout the world (as De Beers controlled diamonds) or within one area (as with Imperial Chemical Industries). Such a firm comes into existence, as a rule, by means of amalgamations. The leading firms of an industry combine together, sinking their individual identities, or one firm absorbs the others. The firm which finally emerges as the result of these amalgamations is sometimes called a "trust."

But a monopoly may consist of a combination of firms, retaining their separate identities, and uniting only for the purpose of pursuing a common monopolistic policy in their joint interests.

This common policy may consist only in fixing minimum prices which they all agree to charge. But, if this is all, the combination is not likely to hold together for long. If the distribution of orders among the firms is left entirely to consumers, some firms will receive what they consider an unduly low proportion. They will then be tempted to increase their sales by charging a lower price —either covertly, through such devices as secret rebates, or openly, by leaving the combination. Hence a combination is likely to keep together only if its members agree at the outset upon the proportion of total sales which each is to receive. They may agree also, in order to secure as far as possible that none of them evades the agreement by making undisclosed sales, or by selling below the agreed prices, that all sales must be made through a central selling agency, set up by the combination to receive all orders and all payments. Moreover, the existence of large unsold stocks leads buyers to believe that prices must fall in the future, and therefore to restrict their purchases. In order to avoid this danger, a combination may restrict the total output of its members, deciding—in accordance with its estimate of future demand—what the total output must be over the following month or quarter or year. This total output is then divided among the different firms, each receiving whatever "quota" (or proportion) was agreed upon when the combination was formed.

Even when existing producers, considered as a group, can make considerably greater profits by combining to restrict their output, negotiations to create a combination may well break down. The divergent claims of different firms must be reconciled. Firms which have produced a relatively large share of the total output in the past will demand the same share in the future. Firms which are expanding—owing, for example, to an unusually efficient management—will demand a larger share than they obtained in the past. Firms with a greater "capacity" for producing, as measured by the size of their fixed assets, such as plant, will demand a correspondingly greater share. As a rule, it will be possible to reconcile conflicting claims and to create a combination based on voluntary agreement only when the number of firms in the industry is fairly small. This is likely to be the case if there are technical advantages in large plants, as in the iron and steel industry, or if the supply of some essential raw material is confined to a few localities, as with potash or quinine, or if secret processes are used, as with dyestuffs and other chemical products. If the number of producers is large, it will be very difficult to organize them for monopolistic action unless some measure of governmental compulsion is employed. Most of the restriction schemes which have been applied to various raw materials, especially during recent years, have been organized and enforced by the State, acting in the interests of the numerous separate producers. Thus the restriction of coal output in Great Britain rests upon the Act of 1930, the output of rubber in Malaya and Ceylon was restricted (from 1922 to 1928) by an export tax on rubber, the restriction of cotton output in the United States is enforced by the Government, the Coffee Institute which controls the supply of Brazilian coffee is a Government agency, and indeed there is scarcely any such scheme, involving a large number of producers, which is not based upon legal compulsion.

The successful maintenance of a combination, once it is formed, is threatened both from within and from without. Conditions will change as time goes on, and will make it difficult for the combination to retain the adherence or "loyalty" of some of its members. Some firms will find that consumers demand more of their particular products than before and will resent having to pass on orders (in excess of their quota) to be executed by other members of the combination. Again, some firms will outstrip others in taking advantage of the progress of technical knowledge, and will conclude that they have more to gain by expanding their sales at lower prices than by continuing their membership of the combination. If the demand for the products of the industry falls considerably, the proportion of "unused capacity" will increase, and this will strengthen the desire of some firms to break away and make fuller use of their plants, thus increasing their receipts, by selling at lower prices. Hence cartels and other combinations which do not rest on Government support tend to break up after a relatively short time and to be revived only if there is a readjustment of quotas among the previous members. Such a reorganization, to be successful, must include also important "outsiders" who arose or expanded during the life of the scheme. This brings us to our second point: the danger from without.

Producers outside the combination are in a fortunate position. They can take advantage of the monopoly prices due to restriction of output by the combination whilst they themselves can produce as much as they please. The greater the success of the combination in raising prices, or in maintaining them despite falling costs, the greater is the inducement to new firms to enter the industry and to existing "outside" producers to expand their output. But as such outside output increases, the combination has to restrict its own output correspondingly more in order to maintain the prevailing prices (unless demand also happens to increase) and after a point the burden will become too heavy for it to bear. Either it will break up or there will be a reorganization and most of the outside producers (faced with the alternative of a collapse of prices) will join the combination in order that it may survive.

Many schemes for restricting output, whether supported by particular Governments or not, have broken upon this rock. For example, the Chadbourne Agreement to restrict sugar production, negotiated in 1931, covered production in Germany, Belgium, Hungary, Poland, Czechoslovakia, Yugoslavia, Cuba, Mexico, Peru, and Java. This area produced nearly half the world's sugar in 1929–30 but in 1934–35 it produced less than 30 per cent of the total output. The Agreement expired in 1935 and was not renewed. In the same way the Rubber Restriction Scheme led to a great growth of production in the Netherlands East Indies, which were outside the Scheme, and this compelled the Scheme to be abandoned in 1928. (The new Agreement of 1934 includes the Netherlands East Indies and nearly all other important producing areas.)

The United States Government still pays farmers not to grow cotton, but the present which it thereby makes to outside producers (in Brazil and elsewhere) is becoming quite expensive. In 1929–30 America produced 3·2 million metric tons of cotton, and other countries 2·5 million; in 1934–35 the corresponding figures were 2·1 million and 3·0 million.

Thus a combination can succeed in maintaining prices, for any considerable period, only if it can both maintain loyalty among its members and prevent any marked expansion of outside production or if, alternatively, the Government or Governments supporting it are prepared to shoulder the losses due to the growth of outside output (or to pass them on to home consumers).

6. ECONOMIC EFFECTS OF MONOPOLY

A full discussion of the economic effects of monopoly would occupy far more space than we can spare. On this topic, therefore, we shall restrict our own output—without, however, feeling very confident that this will make our words more valuable.

Let us first narrow the issue. Suppose that the production of some commodity, for which there is no very close substitute, is controlled by one firm, or by a combination of firms, acting as a monopolist. Our problem is to show in what respects the situation is different from what it would be if the commodity were produced by a large number of firms competing with one another.

We must begin by pointing out that in some cases this problem may not be a real one. The economies to be gained by supplying the whole market from a single "plant" may be so great that monopoly is inevitable. It is often claimed that public utilities are of this nature, so that if several firms competed with one another in supplying a district with, say, gas, the waste from duplication of plant and pipes would soon lead the different firms to combine, or one of them to oust or absorb the others. In such a case, the price charged by a private monopolist might conceivably be lower than it could be if the supply were provided by a number of competing firms; nevertheless it would be higher than his marginal cost. The question of whether the State should control such "inevitable" monopolies—in order to ensure, for example, that they expand their output up to the point at which new free capital invested in them would yield no more than elsewhere—is a difficult and controversial one into which we shall not enter. The remainder of this section leaves such cases on one side.

It is commonly believed that monopoly makes the distribution of wealth more uneven. In fact it is not always true that the monopolist is richer than the consumers whom he exploits. For example, the many small cotton-growers in the United States are poorer than most consumers of their cotton.

Monopoly may retard the application of inventions which require a new type of capital equipment. Suppose that one firm is the sole producer of a commodity, and that it is confronted with such an invention. It will scrap its existing equipment and replace it with the new type only if the cost of working the latter plus interest and amortisation upon its purchase price is less than the cost of working the existing equipment. It will install equipment of the new type side by side with the old only if the profits from the former exceed the reduction in profits upon the latter due to the increased output and consequent fall in price of its commodity. If this is not the case, it will take no action, thus withholding from consumers the benefits of the more efficient method, until some of its existing equipment wears out. But if there is no monopoly, it will be profitable for new firms to enter the industry and install the new type of equipment, for they will not be deterred by the fact that a lower price to consumers will reduce the earnings (or quasi-rent) of existing equipment belonging to their rivals.

There are a number of other possible effects of monopoly, but we shall discuss only those arising from the fact that a monopoly restricts output.

Methods of restricting output may be grouped under three heads. In the first place, some output already produced may be destroyed. Thus between 1931 and the end of 1934 the Coffee Institute of Brazil destroyed over 2 million tons of low-grade coffee. This is obviously a costly way of restricting supply, and a monopoly resorts to it only when no cheaper way is practicable. In the second place, a monopoly may leave some of its productive resources idle. Some rubber trees are not tapped, some land suitable for growing, say, cotton or sugar is kept out of cultivation, some plant and equipment is not worked. Under competition, if resources could earn anything at all they would be worked, but under monopoly they may be left idle or worked below capacity (and hence co-operating factors may be yielding constant or increasing returns) because their output would reduce the price of the product and diminish the profits of the monopoly. In the third place, there may be no visible "waste"—no productive resources being left idle and all the output being sold—but free capital and enterprise are prevented from entering the monopolized industry, although they can earn more there than elsewhere. The monopolist himself refrains from enlarging his productive resources. He employs only sufficient resources to produce whatever output maximizes his profits, and this is less than the output which would be produced under competition.

Monopolistic restriction of output has various effects. The demand for factors of production in the monopolized industry is less than it would otherwise be and this tends to reduce the price of any factor which finds one of its chief markets in that industry. Thus the monopoly in the iron and steel industry is a disadvantage to owners of mines which produce coking coal. A common effect of cartel agreements is to call "surplus capacity" into existence. Firms increase their plant in order to claim a larger quota when the cartel is reorganized. Again, when the monopoly is a combination of producers, the more efficient sources of supply often produce less, relatively to other sources, than they would produce under competition. Thus the British Coal Mines

Scheme in effect gives each mine about the same share of the total output that it had in 1928. It is certain that considerably fewer miners would have been required to produce the total output actually produced in, say, 1937 if more of that total had been produced in districts (and mines) which have increased their efficiency, relatively to others, since 1928. The World Economic Survey for 1934–5 observes (pages 96–7): "it is a curious fact that the method most generally adopted to restore a semblance of order in the markets for basic foodstuffs and raw materials has been to reduce output in the most efficient and least expensive areas of production."

At all events, monopolistic restriction of output must mean that the assortment of goods and services produced is not the assortment which consumers want most. The barriers of monopoly prevent available factors of production from being distributed among different uses in complete accordance with the preferences of consumers. Even if no goods are destroyed and no factors left idle by the monopolists, and even if all factors debarred from entering the monopolized preserves find employment elsewhere, this remains true. Some factors of production could raise the value of their marginal products by entering the monopolized fields, and this means that consumers would prefer what these factors could produce inside those fields to what they are producing outside them. In this respect, therefore, monopoly limits the sovereignty of the consumer.

We must not exaggerate the power of monopolies in the modern world. Some monopolies are operated, or closely controlled, by the State (although, on the other hand, modern States create or support a number of monopolies). Others do not try to maximize their profits because they fear that if they raise prices too much the State will intervene, or consumers will boycott their products, or inventive effort will be directed towards finding new substitutes for their products. Again, a combination of producers, as we have seen, is difficult to form and still more difficult to keep in being. Finally, every monopolist is limited by the conditions of demand for his product; these reflect the prices of substitutes, and there are few products for which some fairly close substitute is not available. Owing to these various limitations upon the scope of monopoly power, the extent to which it acts as a check upon the sovereignty of the consumer is smaller than appears at first sight. Nevertheless, the check is real and important. Monopolies often give rise to "excess capacity" and occasionally lead to the destruction of valuable products. They sometimes hold up the application of inventions and improved methods. They often increase the inequality of wealth. They make the assortment of goods and services actually produced different from what it would be under perfect competition. Thus the tendency of the price-mechanism to harmonize the interests of entrepreneurs and consumers is weakened and distorted, to a greater or less extent, by the existence of monopoly in the wide sense of imperfect competition.

NOTE

1. When the demand curve is a straight line, the marginal revenue curve will be a straight line also and will bisect a perpendicular from any point on the demand curve to the *Y* axis.

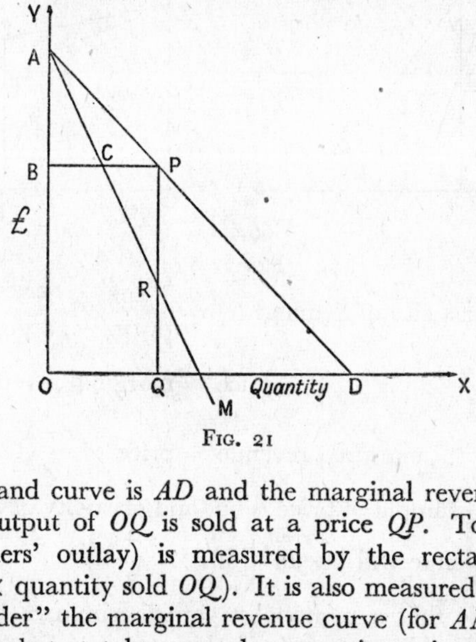

FIG. 21

The demand curve is *AD* and the marginal revenue curve is *AM*. An output of *OQ* is sold at a price *QP*. Total revenue (or consumers' outlay) is measured by the rectangle *BPQO* (price *QP* × quantity sold *OQ*). It is also measured by the area *ARQO* "under" the marginal revenue curve (for *AM* shows the additions made to total revenue by successive units of output).

Therefore these two areas are equal to one another. Subtracting the area *BCRQO*, which is common to both, the triangles *ABC* and *CPR* are equal in area and as $\angle B = \angle P =$ a right angle, and the opposite angles at C are equal, the triangles are equal in all respects.

Therefore $$BC = CP$$

(If the demand curve is not a straight line we can find the marginal revenue QR corresponding to any price P by drawing a tangent AD to the demand curve at P and proceeding as above.)

2. The elasticity of the demand curve at P is $\frac{OB}{BA}$ (as we showed in our note on page 50).

$$OB = QP = \text{price}.$$
$$BA = PR \text{ (see above)} = QP \textit{ minus } QR$$
$$= \text{price } \textit{minus} \text{ marginal revenue}.$$

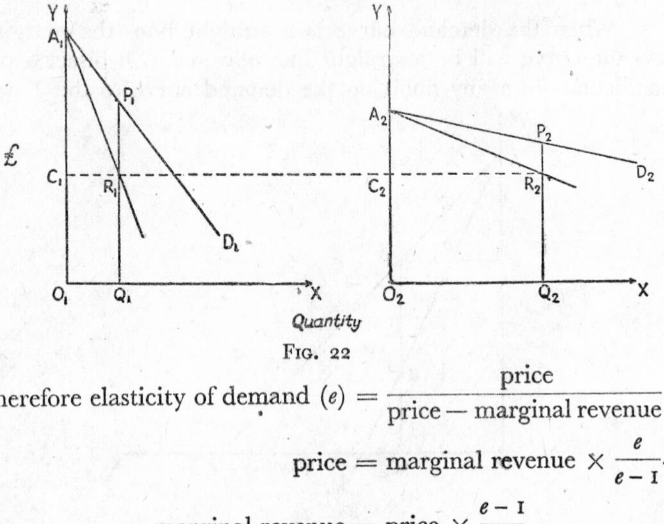

FIG. 22

Therefore elasticity of demand (e) $= \dfrac{\text{price}}{\text{price} - \text{marginal revenue}}$

or $$\text{price} = \text{marginal revenue} \times \frac{e}{e-1}.$$

or $$\text{marginal revenue} = \text{price} \times \frac{e-1}{e}.$$

Thus, for example, if price is 6d. and elasticity of demand is 2, marginal revenue will be 3d. $\left(6\text{d.} \times \dfrac{2-1}{2}\right)$.

3. Suppose that a monopolist can discriminate between two markets, and wishes to maximize his profits.

We saw (p. 210) that he must equate his marginal cost (for his total output) with his marginal revenue in each market.

He will sell O_1Q_1 at a price of Q_1P_1 in the first market and

O_2Q_2 at a price of Q_2P_2 in the second market. His marginal cost for his whole output ($O_1Q_1 + O_2Q_2$) is O_1C_1 ($= O_2C_2$) and this equals his marginal revenue (Q_1R_1) in the first market and also (Q_2R_2) in the second market.

The price in the first market is higher than in the second because the elasticity of demand is less in the first market than in the second.

4. How can we find the output OQ ($O_1Q_1 + O_2Q_2$) at which these conditions will be fulfilled if the marginal cost curve is not horizontal, but rising? By drawing the marginal cost curve and seeing where it cuts AR. AR is obtained by "adding together"

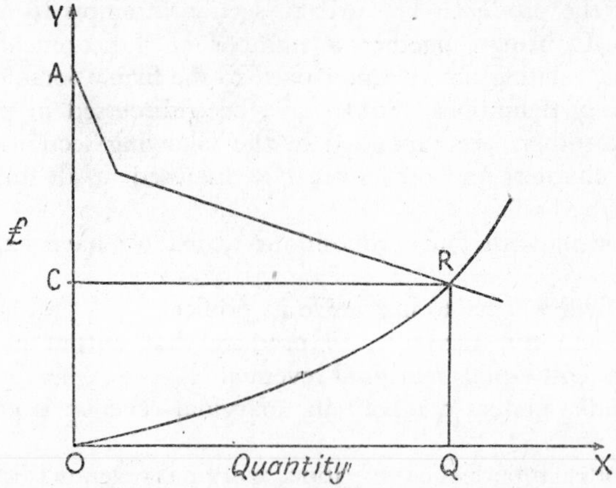

FIG. 23

the two marginal revenue curves. At a marginal revenue of so much, how great would be total sales? The answer to such questions gives us the curve AR.

With an output OQ, the marginal cost OC will equal the marginal revenue QR in each market.

In the above diagram the marginal cost curve OR is rising. The output OQ is greater than the output O_1Q_1 which would be the most profitable if only the first market were available. Hence sales to the second market means that the marginal cost (and hence the marginal revenue, and the price) is higher in the first market than if that were the only one.

If, however, the marginal cost curve were falling the opposite would be true. ("Dumping" may make possible economies of scale and so reduce the price in the home market.)

CHAPTER XVI

THE THEORY OF COSTS

1. SOME GENERALIZATIONS

THE reader, especially if he is a student, would naturally like a clear-cut theory of the relations between output, costs, and the price of the product. The present section attempts to meet his wishes. It brings together a number of "theoretical" propositions, relating, for the most part, to the firm. Some of them are merely definitions. Some have been discussed in previous chapters, others are explained in the following sections of the present chapter, and others are not discussed at all fully until later in the book.

We begin with four propositions which we have explained already.

1. A firm will try to maximize its profits.

2. It will try, therefore, to produce that output at which marginal cost equals marginal revenue.

3. Under perfect competition, marginal revenue is equal to price.

4. Under imperfect competition, marginal revenue is less than price.

The exact relation between marginal revenue and price was explained in the Note at the end of the preceding chapter. Perhaps we should add—

5. Marginal cost is the addition to variable cost associated with a small increase in output.

The total cost of producing an output O is the fixed costs F plus the variable costs V. The total cost of producing an output one unit greater $(O + 1)$ is $F + (V + m.c.)$. The fixed costs are so called because they do *not* vary with output. However great or small they are, the cost of producing the extra unit is simply the addition—*m.c.*—to the variable costs.

Next come two important propositions which state the conditions necessary for the firm to have a determinate output—instead of having an incentive to expand (or contract) its output.

6. Under perfect competition, marginal cost must be increasing.

7. Under imperfect competition, marginal cost may be increasing, constant, or decreasing; but, sooner or later, greater output must make marginal revenue less than marginal cost.

Diagrammatically—

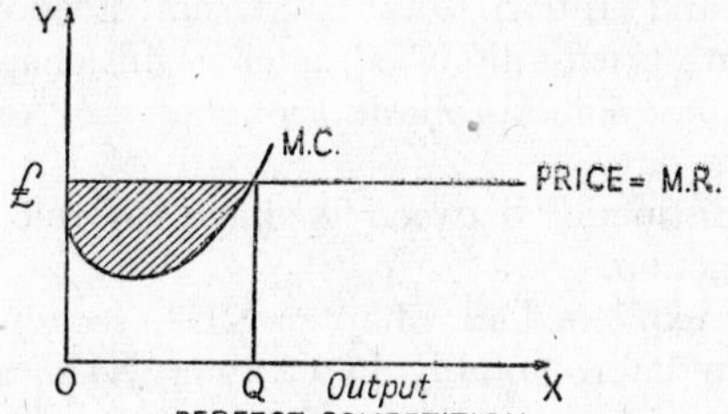

PERFECT COMPETITION

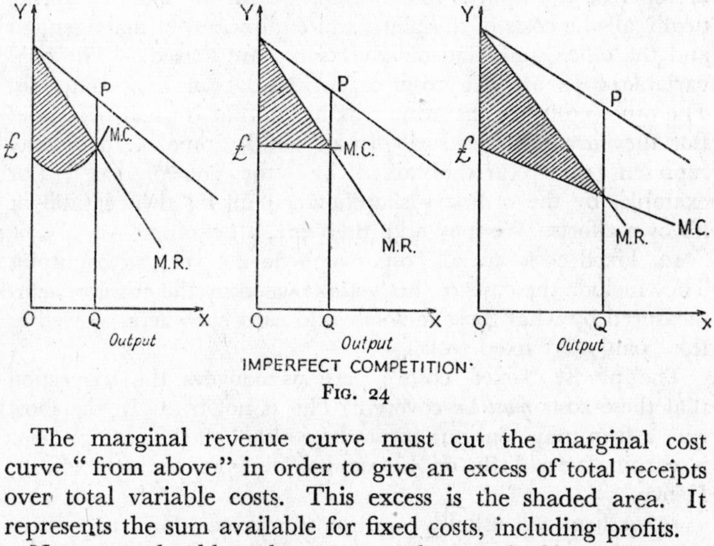

IMPERFECT COMPETITION

FIG. 24

The marginal revenue curve must cut the marginal cost curve "from above" in order to give an excess of total receipts over total variable costs. This excess is the shaded area. It represents the sum available for fixed costs, including profits.

Next, we should perhaps state *why* marginal cost may be increasing or decreasing.

8. Marginal cost may increase because of diminishing returns or (under imperfect competition) because the expansion of the firm's demand for factors raises their prices.

9. Marginal cost may decrease because of increasing returns or (under imperfect competition) because the expansion of the firm's demand for factors reduces their prices.

10. The expansion of an industry may raise or lower the marginal cost of a firm.

These propositions, as they stand, are cryptic. They are explained, and Internal and External Economies and Diseconomies are briefly discussed, later in this chapter.

Finally, come some propositions about the "fixed" or "overhead" costs.

11. The distinction between fixed and variable costs is a short-period distinction.

This was explained in Chapter XIII, section 3, and is discussed again later, notably in Chapter XIX, section 4. The longer the period, the greater the proportion of total costs which ceases to be fixed. For example, machinery wears out and must be replaced if output is to continue. But in the short run practically all the costs of the plant and equipment, of management and the office staff, and of advertising, are "fixed." The only variable costs are the costs of current labour and materials. The other costs are the same whether output is great or small.[1] But they are not necessarily "paid-out." Some of them may represent the return obtained by "the entrepreneur" (for example, by the ordinary shareholders) on his own capital or his own efforts. We may add, therefore, a definition—

12. Fixed costs are all costs which do not vary with output. They include the costs of the factors owned by the entrepreneur, measured by what those factors could earn elsewhere, as well as the "paid-out" fixed costs.

The phrase "fixed costs" perhaps conveys the suggestion that these costs *must* be covered. This is not true. In the short run, a firm may continue to produce although the entrepreneur is earning very little on his capital or from his own efforts. Hence—

13. A firm will usually continue to produce, for a time, if its prime costs are covered.

[1] This statement could be modified at some length. For example, "short-period repairs," the extra wear-and-tear of machinery caused by working it harder or working it at all, transport costs (if these are paid by the firm) on goods delivered to customers, the cost of advertising-matter included with each package, and similar items, might be classed as variable costs. But a digression on this point seems hardly worth while.

We have already discussed the substance of this proposition.[1] But the term "*prime costs*" must be explained. Prime costs are costs which must be met, in the short run, if *any* output is to be produced. They include all the variable costs and in addition some of the fixed costs: for example, the salaries of the office staff. The rest of the fixed costs are called "*supplementary costs*." But—

14. In the long run, both fixed and variable costs must be covered or a firm will go out of business.

The long run, however, may be very long. The basis of this proposition is that in the long run all costs are variable. Factors will go elsewhere if they can earn more elsewhere. If a factor can earn nothing, or relatively little, in another industry it may stay where it is despite a great reduction in its earnings. What it gets over and above the sum necessary to induce it to stay in the industry is a "*rent*," in the technical economic sense. Examples of "rents" are: the whole earnings of forest land which is useless for any other purpose; the whole earnings (above its scrap value) of completely specific plant; £500 a year of the earnings of a £1500-a-year man who would continue to do the same work at a salary of £1000 a year (but not for less). However, any particular firm must pay current prices for factors used in the industry although these prices may contain elements of "rent" in this sense. Hence—

15. Some costs contain elements of "rent." "Rents" are sums paid to factors which need not be paid in order to retain the factors *in the industry*. But a *firm* must pay current prices to obtain factors.

This is discussed in the Chapter on "Rent."

These fifteen propositions together constitute an outline of a coherent and clear-cut theory of costs. We could expand them, introducing further distinctions and definitions. Instead, we shall devote the rest of this chapter to a brief survey of the relation between output, costs, and prices in the leading fields of economic activity. This survey will afford some realistic illustrations of some of these propositions. It will also bring out their limitations.

For the real world is not clear-cut. It is full of diversity and

[1] Notably in Chapter XIII, section 3. If the fixed costs include payments to creditors (e.g. debenture-holders or banks) then whether production goes on or not depends on the attitude adopted by the creditors. Usually their best course is to come to some arrangement under which production does go on.

complications. The theory of "perfect competition" is often thought to apply to large sections of agriculture. We shall note some special features of agriculture which are of great importance but could never be deduced from the theory of perfect competition. We shall illustrate perfect competition from mining, rather than from agriculture. But, in fact, important minerals and agricultural products have been subject, in recent years, to restriction schemes. We shall therefore discuss restriction schemes, more fully than we did in the previous chapter. We have already noted that most firms produce several products; we shall illustrate how this may affect their behaviour. Perhaps the central fact which will emerge from our survey is the prevalence of imperfect competition, in a form which makes it unrealistic to speak of the "demand curve" of a firm. Rather, we shall be concerned with how customs and traditions tend to preserve "profit-margins"—and to create "excess capacity."

The golden rule, from the standpoint of social welfare, is that prices should everywhere equal (or at leas be proportionate to) marginal costs. For costs are, fundamentally, opportunity-costs; they are the values that factors could produce elsewhere. If factors (for which "costs" are paid) can produce less elsewhere, then they should move from "elsewhere" to "here," and conversely. But what if marginal costs are far below average total costs? A price equal to marginal costs would then cover only a part, perhaps well below half, of total costs. In such a case, how can the golden rule be applied? We discuss this in connection with public utilities and the two-part tariff.

Perhaps we should state explicitly that the points made in discussing one field of activity may not apply to the whole of that field and may apply to sections of other fields also. Something resembling perfect competition may prevail, to some extent, in other fields as well as in mining. "Excess capacity" is found, for example, in taxi-cabs as well as in manufacturing and retail trade; transport costs of delivering the product are important for, say, coal-mines and dairy-farms as well as for brick-works; fixed costs are relatively high in, for example, steel-works as well as in public utilities. Our aim has been to find illustrations as realistic and appropriate as possible.

Finally, we shall have enough to do to consider the relationship *at any moment* between output, costs, and prices. Technical progress, and changes in the total quantity available of different factors, are for the most part ruled out; we discuss them in other chapters. The present chapter asks only how output, costs, and prices, would change in response to an increase (or decrease) in the demand for the products.

2. MINING

Mining is usually subject to increasing costs. Suppose that there is a fairly large increase in the demand for some particular mineral. Unless this increase is expected to be merely temporary, and can be met out of existing stocks of the mineral, the result may be quite a sharp rise in price. For it may be difficult or impossible to expand output very much within a few days or weeks. Diminishing returns to labour may be very marked as more labour is employed in the existing mines, with their existing equipment. That is the short-run situation.

Now suppose that the increase in demand turns out to be permanent. The price of the mineral has risen; it is more profitable than before to produce it. Suppose that enough time passes for new shafts to be sunk, new deposits to be opened up, new equipment to be installed, and, in short, for output to adjust itself fully to the new and higher level of demand. That is the long-run situation. Even in this long run, the price of the mineral is likely to be higher than it was at first, although not so high as it was soon after demand had increased. In terms of diagrams, the long-run supply curve of a mineral is likely to be rising, although not so steeply as the short-run supply curve.

An increase in output may raise costs for either or both of two reasons. The prices of some of the factors of production employed in the industry may be forced up as more of them are required; and their physical output per unit may fall. Thus the wages of miners may rise if considerably more miners are needed. Even if the standard wage remains the same, labour-costs per ton may increase because less efficient workers are taken on. If this happens, the long-run supply curve will rise more steeply than if it does not. But it need not happen. It may be that enough additional miners, just as efficient as those already in the industry, can be obtained at prevailing wage-rates, either from some other mining industry, the demand for whose products has fallen, or from the ranks of the unemployed. Nevertheless costs are likely to be higher for our second reason: output per miner is likely to be less than before.

The fundamental reason for this is that fairly rich and accessible deposits are limited in amount. Let us take coal as an example. There are enormous "reserves" of coal in the world. But only a small part of all this coal is in thick and easily worked seams, fairly near the surface and not too far from the markets —from the places where the coal is to be used. In order to get much more coal per day from a mine already being worked miners will have to go deeper down, where the heat is so great that it reduces their efficiency, or they will have to spend more time in getting from the surface to the "faces" where they work, or they will have to tackle more difficult seams. If new mines are opened up the chances are that they will be less easy to work —otherwise they would have been opened up before. Alternatively, they may be so far from the market that the high cost of transporting the coal to the market makes them worth working only if the price of coal has risen well above its old level.

Most minerals, unlike coal, are embedded in ore, and we must therefore take account of the cost of extracting the mineral from the ore. Let us take iron as an example. The iron is extracted from the ore in a blast furnace, with the aid of coke. It may be that some deposits of ore containing, say, 25 per cent iron are easy to work. Yet it may not pay to work them if ore containing, say, 50 per cent iron is available. In the first place, to get a ton of iron twice as much ore must be mined (and perhaps transported) if the metallic content is only half as great. In the second place more coke must be used to get a ton of pig-iron from the lower-grade ore. Nowadays fairly low-grade iron-ore is mined, but that is mainly because the deposits of higher-grade ore are giving out.

Our generalization that mining is usually subject to increasing costs is valid however large the degree of monopoly in the industry may be. In fact, the output of most important minerals is now under some kind of monopolistic control. Yet perfect competition in mining is not unknown.[1] In the past, it has not

[1] Gold-mining is a special case. So long as even one government is prepared to buy unlimited amounts of gold at a fixed price, and no restriction of gold output is likely to force up that price, all gold-mining firms will take the price of gold as given.

been uncommon for a mining industry to be made up of a considerable number of firms, competing with one another, no one of which was large enough to take account of the very slight influence which changes in its own output would have upon price. For example, the thousand separate firms constituting the coal-mining industry of Great Britain were in much that position before the British Government in 1930 compelled them to form a national cartel to regulate output and prices. We shall illustrate what happens under perfect competition by considering such a firm. We shall assume that it owns only one mine.

The demand curve for its particular type of coal may slope downward quite steeply. But there are plenty of other mines producing similar coal, and therefore our firm takes the ruling price of coal as a market fact which it cannot alter. Whether it produces more or less, it will sell all that it produces at the ruling price. Hence the demand curve for *its* coal is regarded by the firm as a horizontal straight line (*DD* in Fig. 25). In technical language it considers that the elasticity of demand for *its* coal is infinite: its "average revenue" and "marginal revenue" per ton are the same—namely, the ruling price per ton.

The same thing applies to the prices of the factors which it buys. Its own demand for them is such a small part of the total demand for them that it takes their prices as given by the market.

Let us consider the short-run situation. The mine and its equipment are very specific—of little use for any other purpose. So long as the coal produced sells for more than the variable costs incurred in procuring it, the mine will be worked.[1] How much it produces per day will depend entirely on its variable costs. The firm will maximize its profits or minimize its losses by producing that output at which marginal cost is equal to price. If it produced less, it would increase its receipts more than

[1] This is not quite accurate. There may be some costs, for example the salaries of the office staff, which do not vary with output but which would be eliminated if the mine closed down. Fixed costs of this type would have to be covered as well as variable costs. On the other hand, if the mine were abandoned it would probably become flooded and useless. If the firm hopes that later the price of coal will rise again it may decide to continue pumping out water, and in general to keep the mine in a condition to be worked again even if it now ceases to mine coal from it. Should the cost of doing this be greater than the amount by which current receipts fall short of current costs it may pay the firm better to continue working at a loss.

its costs by expanding its output; if it produced more, it would reduce its costs more than its receipts by curtailing its output.

The variable costs will consist very largely of labour-costs—of wages paid to mine-workers. For the reasons we have given above, after a certain number of miners are employed an increase in their number will not increase output by the same proportion. There will be diminishing returns to labour; first marginal and then average returns will fall, as shown in the diagram on page 128. Fewer tons per miner mean a greater labour-cost per ton; first marginal and then average labour-costs will rise. These increasing costs are simply the monetary expression of diminishing returns; our diagram of page 128 must be turned upside down. The result is shown below, for each of two mines.

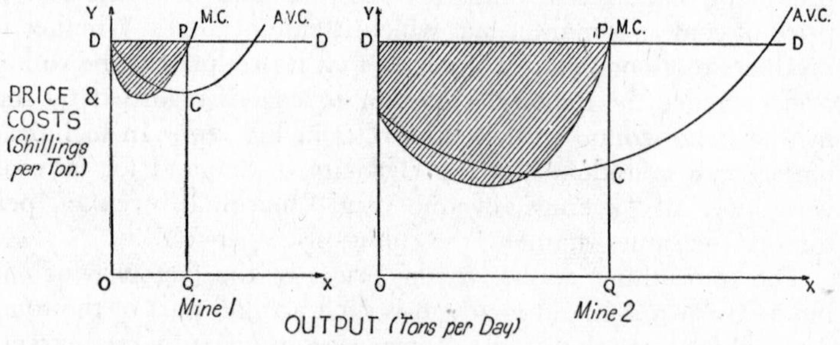

FIG. 25

The ruling price of coal is shown by the horizontal line *DD*, which is the demand curve confronting each mine for *its* coal. It is *OD* (= *QP*) shillings per ton.

The output of the mine is determined by the point *P* at which marginal cost is equal to price. It is *OQ* (= *DP*) tons per day. The total receipts per day are therefore *QP* × *DP* shillings.

The average variable cost is *QC* shillings per ton; therefore the total variable cost is *QC* × *OQ* shillings per day.

The sum available per day for "fixed costs" (including profits) is the total receipts less the total variable cost. It is therefore the rectangle *DP* × *PC*. This rectangle must be equal to the shaded area in the diagram, for the latter is the sum of the amounts by which price exceeds variable cost for each successive unit of output.

It will be noted that the marginal cost curve cuts the average (variable) cost curve at the lowest point of the latter. The reason for this is that given in the footnote on page 128. It will be noted also that we have chosen to make the marginal cost curve become almost vertical. This is likely to happen when the mine is worked nearly at full capacity. Any further increase in output will become difficult or impossible in the short run.

In the above diagram, the output (*OQ*) of mine 2 is much greater and its average variable cost (*QC*) is considerably lower than for mine 1. This does not necessarily mean that the firm owning mine 2 is more efficient than the firm owning mine 1. The differences may be due solely to the different geological structure of the two deposits. Mine 1 may contain relatively little coal but all fairly near the surface. Mine 2 may contain rich seams of coal situated at considerable depths, so that the sinking and equipment of the mine involved a large outlay of money. Doubtless it was planned from the start on a large scale, to deal with a large output. Output per miner is greater so that its variable costs per ton are lower, than for mine 1. But the initial "capital" cost was much greater. Although the firm gets a much bigger total sum per day, after paying variable costs, than the firm which owns mine 1, yet for all we know it may be getting a smaller return on its capital than it expected, whilst the small mine may be earning more than was expected.

We can now construct the short-run supply curve for this type of coal. At any given price, each of the hundreds of mines will produce a certain output, namely that output at which its marginal cost is equal to that price. By adding all these outputs together we get the total output which will be produced at that price. By doing this for a number of prices we can construct the short-run supply curve, as shown in Fig. 26.

We supposed each firm to take as given the prices to be paid per unit for the various factors. In fact, a general expansion of output, following an increase in demand, may cause some of these prices to rise. Thus the wage-rates of miners, by far the most important item in variable costs, may go up. If so, the short-run supply curve will slope upward more steeply. For the marginal cost curves of the various mines will all in fact rise more steeply than the various firms, taking wage-rates and other factor-prices as given, believe them to do.

After sufficient time has passed for output to adjust itself fully to the new and higher level of demand, the whole situation will be different. More shafts will have been sunk, new mines will have come into operation; in general terms, some existing firms will have increased their capacity and some new firms will have entered the industry. Clearly the old short-run supply curve will have become irrelevant. It will have been replaced by a new

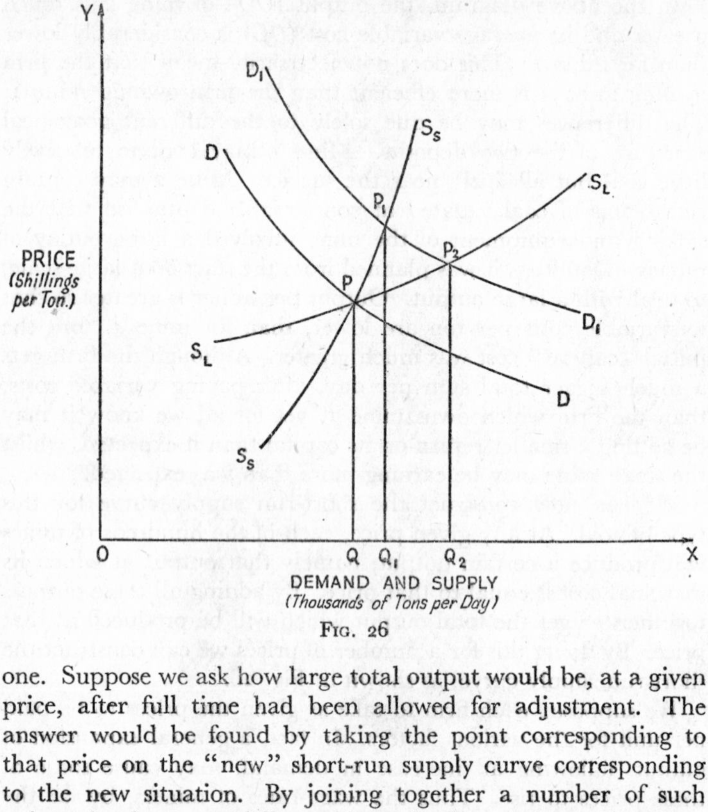

FIG. 26

one. Suppose we ask how large total output would be, at a given price, after full time had been allowed for adjustment. The answer would be found by taking the point corresponding to that price on the "new" short-run supply curve corresponding to the new situation. By joining together a number of such points (each on a different "new" short-run supply curve corresponding to the relevant situation after output had fully adjusted itself) we get the long-run supply curve. In the diagram above, the old short-run supply curve, representing the situation when the demand curve was *DD*, is shown as S_sS_s.

The long-run supply curve is shown as S_LS_L. It is more elastic—sloping upward less steeply—than S_SS_S. The new short-run supply curve, after output has adjusted itself to the higher level of demand shown by D_1D_1, is not drawn. It would pass through P_2.

The sequence of events is as follows. There is an increase in demand. The old demand curve DD is replaced by the new demand curve D_1D_1. At first price rises from P to P_1, and output expands from OQ to OQ_1, as shown by the old short-run supply curve S_SS_S. Enough time passes for the industry to adjust itself completely to the new situation. A new equilibrium position is reached with a price of P_2 and an output of OQ_2 as shown by the long-run supply curve S_LS_L.

If a decrease in demand, instead of an increase, had taken place, what would have happened? Existing mines would have reduced their output so that for each mine marginal cost again equalled price. Some mines, which now could not cover their variable costs, would have closed down at once. The short-run situation would be that at which the new and lower demand curve cuts the old S_SS_S curve. As time went on, some mines would become nearly worked out. More labour than before would be needed per ton of coal obtained. Sooner or later such mines would close down. Few if any new shafts would be sunk and no new mines would be opened up (for if it had not paid to do so before, it would not pay now, with a lower price of coal). Hence output would decline further and the price of coal would recover somewhat. The new equilibrium situation, when reached, would be that shown by a point at which the new and lower demand curve cuts the S_LS_L curve.

We can therefore make this generalization. *A change in demand will tend to cause a bigger change in price and a smaller change in output in the short run than in the long run.*

3. AGRICULTURE[1]

Almost every agricultural commodity is produced by large numbers of farmers, each of whom produces such a tiny proportion of the total that a change in his output would have a

[1] On this subject compare Chapter VI of that excellent book *The Economics of Agriculture*, by R. Cohen (Nisbet, 1940).

quite negligible effect on the price of the commodity. The same applies to changes in his demand for factors of production, such as farm labour or fertilizer. In other words, agriculture is carried on under perfect competition; each farmer takes the prices ruling in the market as given.

Further, agriculture is usually subject to increasing costs. The fundamental reason for this is that fertile and well-situated land is limited in amount. A general expansion of agriculture would mean that existing land had to be worked more intensively and, possibly, worse land brought into cultivation. There would be diminishing returns to the labour and other factors used on the land. An expansion in the output of some particular commodity might be accompanied, owing to changes in demand, by a contraction in the output of some other farm product, and factors might be shifted from one to the other without any increase in costs. For example, the demand for barley might rise and the demand for wheat fall. Some land hitherto under wheat could be sown to barley and the same farm workers and machinery could be employed. But the chances are that any considerable expansion in the output of any particular commodity will be accompanied by increasing costs due to diminishing returns. Either the land already producing it will be worked more intensively or land previously producing something else will be used to grow this commodity instead; probably both will happen. The land thus transferred is unlikely to be so suitable, in soil or climate or location, for this particular commodity as the land which was producing it before.

Nevertheless, it would be misleading to say that the diagrams explained in the previous section apply to agricultural products, and to leave it at that. For the relation between costs and output in agriculture has *four special features* which should be pointed out.

First, although agricultural output as a whole will increase in response to a general rise—due, for example, to an increase of population—in the demand for it, it will respond very sluggishly to a general fall in that demand. This is partly because land is fairly permanent. It is true that the top-soil is sometimes ruined or lost by bad farming, yet land does not inevitably become depleted, like mineral deposits, or worn-out or obsolete, like machines. And it will probably be worked so long as it yields anything at all over variable costs. Further, in many countries the family farm is the rule. The farmer and his family do most or all of the work. Even when times are bad, the farmer is usually very reluctant to abandon his farm. He may own it, and naturally will not want to sell it for a trifle or to hand it over to his creditors; he may like being his own employer; he may like farming; he may not be able to get another job which seems worth taking. Hence most farmers carry on, working as hard as, or perhaps harder than, before, despite a large fall in the prices of their products and, therefore, in their incomes. Finally, even when a large part of the labour is hired, as on plantations and large specialized farms, workers are often unable or unwilling to find different jobs and will accept a cut in their pay when times are bad.[1]

The result is that the "long run" in which output would fully adjust itself to a fall in demand is a very long run indeed. During the great depression of 1929 to 1932 agricultural output hardly declined at all despite the very heavy fall in prices. The output of manufactured products fell by more than a third, although—largely for that reason—their prices fell less than those of farm products.

Second, the farmer cannot tell in advance exactly how large his output will be. For the weather, which not even governments can control, may play a large part. How large varies between districts and products. It is greatest in districts subject to drought or extreme cold; it is greatest for tree crops and least (in temperate climes) for animals. The probable variation, from one year to another, in the yield of any product will be much greater for any particular farm than for the country as a whole, and least of all for the world, because the good yields of some farms or districts offset the bad yields of others. Thus over the years 1923 to 1935 the variations in wheat yields per acre were 4 per cent for the world as a whole, 13 per cent for Hungary, and 24 per cent for a particular farm in Hungary.[2]

Clearly this makes farming something of a gamble and

[1] In Great Britain most of the work is done by hired labour and minimum wages (£3 a week in 1942) are fixed by law. But Great Britain is exceptional in both respects.

[2] And for the United Kingdom they were 6 per cent and for Rothamsted farm 31 per cent. See Paul de Hevesy, *World Wheat Planning*, p. 735.

prevents any exact adjustment between the marginal cost of production and the output actually obtained.

Third, there is a time-lag between the "input" of factors and the corresponding output. This time-lag is greatest, and causes the most instability, for tree crops and for many livestock products. For example, a coffee bush does not begin to yield until five years after planting, and then goes on bearing for twenty years or more; "for cattle the period of gestation is

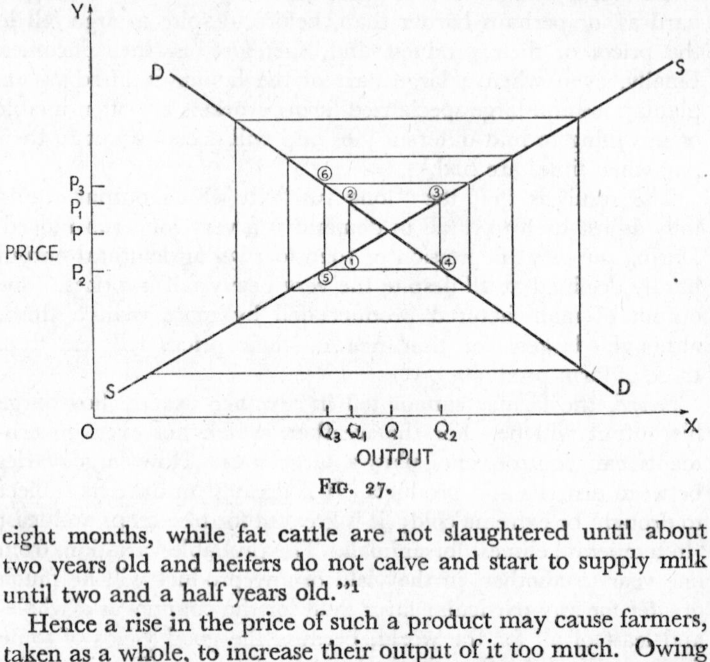

FIG. 27.

eight months, while fat cattle are not slaughtered until about two years old and heifers do not calve and start to supply milk until two and a half years old."[1]

Hence a rise in the price of such a product may cause farmers, taken as a whole, to increase their output of it too much. Owing to the time-lag, the price may remain high for some years; during this time many farmers, acting independently of one another, may take steps to increase their output; when at length the larger supplies begin to appear, in growing volume, on the market, the price of the product may fall heavily. Then farmers, as a whole, may make the opposite mistake and cut down their future output too much; in a few years, when their

[1] R. Cohen, *op. cit.*, p. 98.

decisions have resulted in a smaller output, the price may rise sharply, and the cycle may begin over again.

Hence we get "the cobweb theorem," to make our flesh creep.

If supply is more elastic than demand the fluctuations may increase in amplitude as time goes on. Suppose we begin in an equilibrium situation, with demand equal to supply OQ at a price OP. Suppose that (owing, for example, to bad weather) output falls to OQ_1 (corresponding to the point marked (1) on the supply curve). With this output of OQ_1, the price rises to OP_1 (corresponding to the point marked (2) on the demand curve). Then producers, independently, take steps to produce outputs which, after the time-lag imposed by Nature has elapsed, come on the market and aggregate, per month or per year, OQ_2 (corresponding to the point marked (3) on the supply curve). Price then falls to OP_2 (corresponding to the point marked (4) on the demand curve). Then producers, as usual independently of one another, take steps to curtail their future outputs, so that, after some time[1], total output is reduced to OQ_3 (corresponding to the point marked (5) on the supply curve). Price rises to OP_3 (corresponding to the point marked (6) on the demand curve). And so *ad infinitum.*

This, of course, is a nightmare imagined by economists rather than an account of what actually happens. Yet, in fact, there is a good deal of instability owing to these time-lags, and it is claimed that cycles of over-production and under-production (such as the alleged four-year pig cycle in Great Britain) do occur.

Fourth, it is often difficult to say exactly how much variable costs are increased or diminished by the steps which a farmer takes to increase or diminish the output of a particular commodity. If the demand for, say, bacon goes up, more pigs will be produced, and conversely. The supply of any one commodity is much more elastic than the supply (especially in response to a fall in prices) of agricultural produce in general. But many farms produce a number of different things, and do not specialize entirely on one, such as wheat, or on joint products in the strictest sense, such as wool and mutton or cotton and cotton-seed. Bacon and butter go together in Denmark: the skim milk

[1] *This* time-lag, which elapses before output is *reduced,* is not the same as the time-lag, mentioned in the previous sentence, which elapses before output is *increased.*

is fed to pigs. The dung of grazing animals may fertilize the fields where potatoes are to be planted. The tops of sugar beet can be fed to cattle. Corn crops, which take nitrogen from the soil, can be followed by leguminous plants, which put it back. Root and cereal crops use labour at different times of the year.

It follows that when a mixed farm switches over more to products more in demand, we should really take account not only of the change in the variable costs of a particular commodity which are directly associated with a planned change in its output but also of the indirect effects, favourable or unfavourable, upon the costs or outputs of other commodities produced on the same farm in combination or in rotation with this particular commodity. But these indirect effects, although often important, may be difficult to estimate with accuracy.

These four special features are not peculiar to agriculture. In any industry where fairly durable and specific equipment plays an important part the response to a fall in price may take a long time. For example, tramways or gas-works or mines or blast furnaces may be worked despite a considerable fall in the demand for their products. Some occupations, such as prospecting for gold, are more of a gamble than farming, and bad weather may seriously hamper the amount of building done. Some industrial products, such as ships (and armaments!) may have a long "period of gestation." Nearly all firms produce several products, and it is said that department stores sometimes deliberately run a restaurant or a library at a loss in order to attract customers who may buy in other departments.

Nevertheless these four features occur together in agriculture, and to a much more marked extent than any one of them occurs in most other branches of activity. That is why we chose a mineral and not an agricultural commodity to illustrate costs under perfect competition. Farmers do take prices as given; they do try to maximize their "profits"; they do respond to changes in demand for particular commodities; doubtless they try to equate the marginal cost of a commodity with its price; and it is fairly sure that the marginal cost of a commodity will rise as its output is expanded. By making appropriate assumptions, we could make our diagrams apply to an agricultural commodity. But I think the reader will agree that to do so would be somewhat unrealistic. This need not distress us. Our object is not to draw diagrams but to understand what happens in the economic world of reality.

4. COMMODITY CONTROL SCHEMES

The "cobweb theorem" paints too gloomy a picture. In fact, producers do learn something from experience. Each may produce such a small part of the total output that he could produce twice as much, or nothing at all, without perceptibly affecting prices. Yet he may not take it for granted that prevailing prices will continue for ever. He may pay some attention to what other producers are doing and may consider to what extent this is likely to change prices in the future.

Nevertheless the adjustment of supply to demand may be very imperfect. Each producer, acting independently, may be only vaguely aware of what others are doing and may give insufficient weight in his calculations to the probable results of their actions. And this is not merely a theoretical possibility. The outputs and prices of quite a number of important raw materials and foodstuffs have in fact fluctuated, in the past, far more widely than was warranted by changes in demand. Is there not a case for setting up for every such commodity a central body to act as the eyes and the brain of the "industry"?

What would such a body do? It would try to discover the conditions of demand and supply for the commodity. It would try to estimate the nature and extent of any change in those conditions. It would collect information from all producers about what they were doing and were proposing to do. It would assemble and then circulate this information. It might forecast future price movements and might give general advice to producers.

But a good Department of Agriculture, or Mines, does this already. And this alone does not prevent wide fluctuations. Clearly far more could be done if each central body, besides acting as eyes and brain, had a big stick. If it were armed with powers to compel each producer to act as it directed, it could vary total output, apart from fluctuations due to changes in the weather and other aspects of Nature, exactly as it wished.

One great danger of such a scheme is that the controlling body would act on behalf of the industry like a monopolist and would try to increase total profits by restricting output. If the demand for the commodity, before restriction, had an elasticity considerably less than one there would be considerable scope for such a policy. A smaller output might increase total receipts a good deal, besides reducing total costs. This is shown on the following diagram.

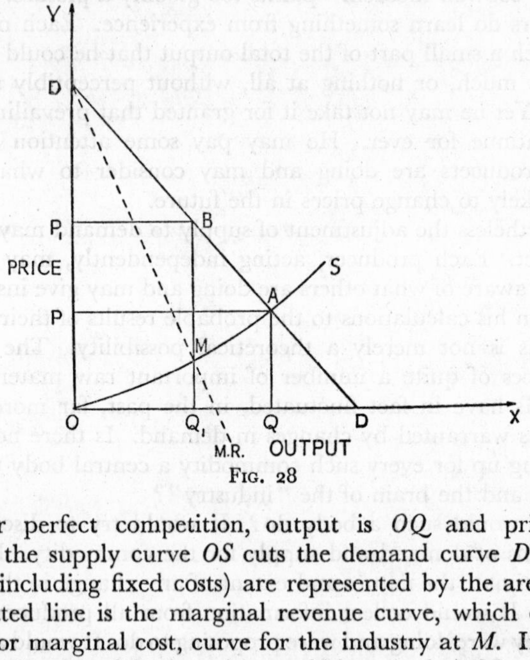

FIG. 28

Under perfect competition, output is *OQ* and price *OP*, because the supply curve *OS* cuts the demand curve *DD* at *A*. Profits (including fixed costs) are represented by the area *OPA*. The dotted line is the marginal revenue curve, which cuts the supply, or marginal cost, curve for the industry at *M*. If output were restricted to OQ_1 the price would be raised to OP_1 and total profits would be maximized. They would be represented by the area OP_1BM, which is much greater than *OPA*.

The Tin Restriction Scheme may have done something of this kind. It certainly succeeded in keeping the price of tin well above £200 a ton ever since the close of 1933 (except that it averaged only £190 in 1938) although the chairman of one of the biggest tin-mining companies in Malaya declared that "the East could produce at a profit all the tin required by the world at £100 a ton." It may be instructive to consider very briefly why this scheme succeeded in keeping up the price and, by way of contrast, why some other schemes failed.

We may note, to begin with, that the attempts at voluntary restriction made in 1930, when stocks were rising and price was falling, proved quite ineffective. Why should one mine restrict its output if the next mine, or mines in another country, did not? Further, some important low-cost producers were opposed to any kind of restriction; they thought they could do better for themselves by working to capacity than by keeping down their output for the benefit of their high-cost rivals. The Scheme which we are discussing was a compulsory scheme imposed by governments in February, 1931. This illustrates a general rule: in order to get numerous separate producers to act as directed, by a central body, compulsion by their governments is almost always necessary.

It so happened that only three governments—the British, the Dutch, and the Bolivian—between them could control most of the output. Obviously it is easier for three governments to come to an agreement than for a considerably larger number, such as would be needed to control most of the output of, for example, wheat. Further, a scheme which starts, as this did, with most of the *potential* output under control is less likely to be wrecked by the expansion of output by "outsiders." In fact, a number of outsiders (beginning with Siam in September, 1931) did join the Scheme as time went on, but they came in rather on blackmail terms. The four countries which did most of the actual restricting were Malaya, Nigeria, the Dutch East Indies, and Bolivia. They cut down their output again and again until in the summer of 1932 it was down to one-third of the 1929 level. They succeeded in raising the price of tin from about £105 a ton at the close of 1931 to over £220 a ton by the close of 1933. But the extent to which they bore the burden and other countries reaped the benefit can be seen from the following little table. In 1938,

Production of Tin (thousand tons)

	1929	1937	1938
Malaya	69	77	43
Nigeria	11	10	7
Dutch East Indies	36	40	21
Bolivia	46	25	25
Thailand	10	17	14
Rest of the world	20	38	38
Total	192	207	148

when output was being restricted rather severely, because price was falling, these four countries produced only 65 per cent of the total as against 84 per cent in 1929.

The two chief uses of tin are in cans and in motor-cars. Only about 5 lb. of tin is used in a motor-car. This costs about 4s. 6d. with tin at £100 a ton and 13s. 6d. with tin at £300 a ton. Clearly a large change in the price of tin would have a negligible effect on the price of, and therefore on the demand for, motor-cars. Much the same applies to canned goods. The contents are usually worth much more than the tin can (costing from 1 to 6 cents) which itself is made of tinplate—steel with a thin coating of tin. Even so, manufacturers would use something else instead of tin if satisfactory substitutes were available. Apparently they are not. Aluminium has partly replaced tin in some uses (notably for aluminium-foil instead of tinfoil) but not in most. Machinery could be adapted to use roller or ball bearings instead of white-metal bearings, for which there is no substitute for tin, but this would be rather expensive. A possible brake on the rise in price of a commodity may be the reclaiming of scrap. But this is not very important with tin.[1] Hence the demand for tin is very inelastic until its price becomes relatively high and so, with most of the potential output under control, the Tin Scheme succeeded (somewhat to the annoyance of the chief consuming country, the United States) in keeping up the price.

We shall not repeat what we said towards the close of Chapter XV about the social dangers of Control Schemes which act monopolistically to keep up prices, beyond repeating that in practice it is often the more efficient producers who have to restrict most, so that the supply curve *OS* in our diagram is replaced by another and steeper one, thereby reducing the "profits" area—a loss for which there is no corresponding gain to the industry as a whole.

After the war, control schemes may be set up for a number of important raw materials and foodstuffs. If these are to be effective they must be international. If they are to be operated

[1] Reclaiming is done mainly in the United States. In some years her "secondary" output has reached nearly thirty thousand tons, making her the second or third producing country, although she has no tin deposits. It is made mainly from clean tinplate clippings. Many more old cans could be treated at the plants now equipped to handle them, but in peace-time the high cost of collecting and transporting them makes this not worth while.

in the interests of society, and not merely to increase the profits of particular groups of producers, it would be well for the chief consuming countries to hold the majority of votes in each controlling body. Even so, big mistakes may be made. Governments are not always wise—witness the scrapping of a large part of British shipbuilding capacity during the 'thirties. There is a danger that changes made desirable by technical progress may be held back: every producer may be tied down, like the British coal-mines, to the percentage of the total output which he produced in some past year, and the bad policy may be followed of prohibiting or fining new entrants.

In my view, a better plan would be for one or more leading governments to hold stocks of such commodities. They should be prepared to buy without limit at a price somewhat below equilibrium level and to sell at a price somewhat above equilibrium level. Provided the limits were chosen wisely and revised from time to time to take account of technical progress and other changes, such a scheme would have a good influence in eliminating unnecessarily wide fluctuations and, possibly, in damping down the trade cycle, whilst leaving complete freedom to the initiative and efficiency of individuals.

5. MANUFACTURING

The behaviour of costs in manufacturing will vary between industries and will depend on time, place, and circumstance. Average variable costs are unlikely to rise much when output is expanded, even in the short run, and certainly not in the long run; in a number of industries they may fall.

The doctrine of diminishing returns applies to changes in the proportions between the different factors of production. An expansion of agriculture means that more men must be employed on the same land, or less suitable land must be used. There will be increasing costs due to diminishing returns to labour. Are there any "scarce" factors in manufacturing comparable in importance to suitable land in agriculture, or suitable deposits in mining?

Manufacturing uses relatively little land, and additional factory sites, almost or quite as suitable as existing ones, can usually be obtained. Existing buildings and equipment could be duplicated. It may be that additional labour, as efficient as that already engaged, could be obtained at prevailing wage-rates from the ranks of the unemployed. In the short run, however, it is quite possible that a substantial expansion would raise labour-costs. Less efficient workers may be drawn into manufacturing from other occupations, such as agriculture; there may be a shortage of certain types of skilled labour (such as the shortage of drop-forgers which hindered the increasing output of armaments in Great Britain in 1941); overtime rates may have to be paid in order to increase output quickly; and many workers may obtain increases in their rates of pay. If only a few industries expand, while others contract, some workers may move from the latter to the former and labour-costs may rise little, if at all. In the long run, after enough time has passed for youths and others entering the labour market to be diverted towards manufacturing, and for more workers to be trained to relieve the shortages of particular skills, labour-costs will not have risen much.

The main reason for diminishing returns, if they occur, may be the scarcity of good entrepreneurs. First-class business ability seems to be rare and it cannot easily be acquired by training. Some existing entrepreneurs may find it more difficult to manage their firms if these become much larger; they may even go bankrupt. New entrepreneurs coming into manufacturing from elsewhere may be less efficient, on the average, than those already established. How important these considerations are in practice is a question of fact on which opinions differ.

Our conclusion is that increasing costs due to diminishing returns may occur in manufacturing but they will be much less marked than in agriculture or mining. Particular "scarcities" of factors will be less important in the long run than in the short and less important if only a few industries expand than if there is a general expansion of manufacturing.

But increasing costs may come from higher factor-prices as well as from diminishing returns. We have seen that labour-costs may possibly increase because workers get higher rates of pay. The prices of raw materials may increase, as more of them are needed, owing to diminishing returns in the industries producing them. This may be quite important, in the long run as well as in the short.

We have now briefly reviewed the forces which may make for increasing costs. What are the forces working in the opposite direction?

To begin with, some plants may be working below capacity at the time when the demand for their products increases and their output is therefore expanded. We shall later give reasons why this state of affairs may be fairly widespread, in "normal" times as well as in bad times. Clearly average *total* cost per unit of product will fall as a plant approaches full capacity, for the "fixed costs" will be spread over a larger number of units of product. But variable costs, with which we are concerned here, may fall too. The plant may be adapted to a certain output, and average variable costs may be lowest when that output is being produced. The workers who keep their jobs in the plant may be less fully occupied, although receiving full wages, when times are slack. Some examples are given in Appendix II of that excellent book *The Economic History of Steel-Making*, by D. L. Burn. "In coke ovens the silica linings are ruined by cooling, hence continuity of work is essential; but though it is possible to reduce the pace to 30 per cent of normal, the labour force (paid mainly datal wages) remains almost unchanged, and variations occur in the yields of by-products which are on balance unfavourable. Neglecting the by-products, the main change in prime cost if the output of a modern battery of ovens fell by one half, would be a rise in average labour-cost from, say, 1s. 6d. per ton to about 2s. 9d." Again, Mr. Burn points out that "an open-hearth furnace is rarely designed to make less than 60 tons of steel at a heat"; if less is required then the rest must be stocked, as ingots, until orders for a similar steel come in. This means carrying more stock and, subsequently, additional re-heating (to heat the ingots up again in order to transform them into the required forms). Again, "a pair of rolls for heavy sections normally make upwards of 1,000 tons without being redressed. . . . If orders for a given section do not occupy a pair of rolls as long as the roll can be worked unchanged, then the cost and delay of roll changing is a heavier burden." But it may be that average variable costs rise, whether in a steel-works or in some other kind of plant, as "full capacity" is approached and less efficient equipment, previously idle, comes into operation. All we can say is that they *may* fall.

Even if there is no "excess capacity," the average variable costs of a firm may be lower when its output is greater. An increase in the demand for its product may make possible what are sometimes called *internal economies*. We discussed these in Chapter VI, section 4, and again in Chapter IX, section 5. They are economies which take place *within a firm*; they arise mainly from "indivisibilities" of one kind or another—for example, a larger and more efficient machine may be worth installing only if demand is sufficiently great to keep it fairly fully employed. *External economies* are said to arise from the expansion of a whole *industry*; a single firm could not obtain them by expanding "on its own" and therefore could not include them in its calculations. The growth of an industry—the expansion of existing firms and the establishment of new ones—often takes place in a particular district: the industry is more or less "localized." It may then pay other firms to specialize more in catering for the needs of the industry. Special banking and insurance facilities may be made available; a trade journal may be started; transport rates may be reduced owing to the greater volume of traffic; "repair shops" for its machines may be set up in the district; somebody may find it worth while to purchase from the firms in the industry by-products which were previously wasted; additional labour can be obtained when required from young people and others in the district who may have acquired, from living there, some knowledge of the customs of the industry. These and similar advantages may largely resolve themselves, upon analysis, into "internal economies" to some firm outside the industry. Thus it may pay to utilize waste products only if they are available close at hand in sufficient quantities to keep "indivisible" plant fairly fully employed. Again, freight rates may fall because existing rail or road facilities can now be used more fully. But this does not make these so-called "external economies" any the less important. It should be added, however, that the expansion of a firm may bring with it "*internal diseconomies*" such as the need for greater supervision and a closer adherence to routine and "red tape," and the expansion of an industry may bring with it "*external diseconomies*" such as greater congestion on the roads of the district and higher prices for raw materials.

We can now sum up the preceding discussion. It must be remembered that we are assuming, for the present, that no technical progress takes place. Even so, long-run marginal costs in a manufacturing industry may well be more or less constant or even falling. They may be rising (notably if an expansion of output forces up the prices of raw materials, and this is not offset by economies of scale) but they are not likely to be rising at all steeply. In the short run, they will probably rise steeply when existing plants are being worked beyond their normal capacity. But this "overcrowding" of plants is a temporary phenomenon which does not often happen. An expansion of output can usually be obtained by using some of the excess capacity already in existence. In that event, marginal costs may fall, or may rise very little.

These conclusions present us with a problem. What forces limit the size of a firm if marginal costs are not rising? The selling-price of the product must exceed the average variable cost of producing it if the fixed costs (including a "normal" rate of profit on the capital and remuneration for the services of the entrepreneur) are to be covered. But if marginal costs are not rising they will be below, or at most equal to, average variable costs. Hence it would appear that extra units of output would sell for more than their additional cost and thus increase total profits. Why are they not produced?

It may be that a firm, or group of firms, is in a monopolistic position in the sense that no other firm is producing similar commodities, or close substitutes, and that for one reason or another new firms cannot enter this field. If so, our problem is solved. The analysis of our last chapter applies. The firm will maximize its profits by equating marginal cost and marginal revenue. The former may be falling, but sooner or later the latter will be falling at a faster rate, and the two curves will intersect, as in the diagram on page 250.

Another possible explanation is that marginal selling-costs are rising. Additional units of output could be *produced* more cheaply, but the cost of *selling* them would be greater, per unit, and would more than offset the fall in marginal production costs. For example, as a local brick-works expanded its output it might have to sell to customers more and more distant from the works, so that the transport cost of delivering the bricks would rise, each extra load costing more to deliver because it had to be sent further. The cost of selling each load should be regarded as a deduction from the receipts: from the "fixed price" per load.

This is shown in the diagram on page 251. Marginal production costs are falling. The price is fixed at *OP*. The selling-cost of an additional unit is the vertical distance between the price-line and the marginal revenue curve. The latter slopes downward,

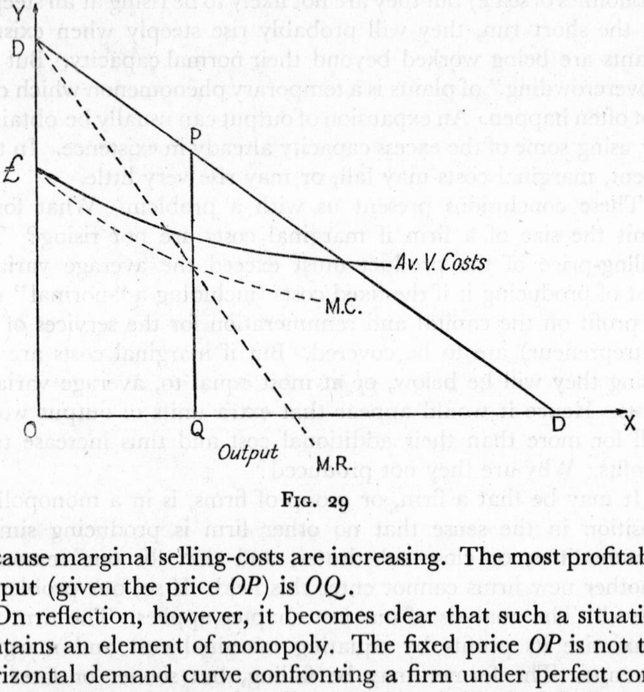

FIG. 29

because marginal selling-costs are increasing. The most profitable output (given the price *OP*) is *OQ*.

On reflection, however, it becomes clear that such a situation contains an element of monopoly. The fixed price *OP* is not the horizontal demand curve confronting a firm under perfect competition. If the firm could sell as much as it liked *at the works* at the price *OP*, why should it not make its customers pay the delivery costs? Or why should it advertise or employ salesmen? The price *OP* is fixed by the firm itself (or by agreement among the trade) and customers near the works are really being charged more, under a system of free delivery, than more distant customers.[1]

[1] Sometimes the firms in an industry agree to charge the same price for a product *plus* the cost of delivering it from some centre of production, called a "basing-point." This system was common in the steel industry. A customer living far from the basing-point had to pay the fixed price plus the freight-charge from the basing-point although in fact the goods were produced in, and delivered from, a works quite near to him.

In this example, the element of monopoly possessed by the brick-works arose from the fact that competing brick-works were some distance away, so that near-by customers could be charged more, in effect, than customers nearer to a rival source of supply.

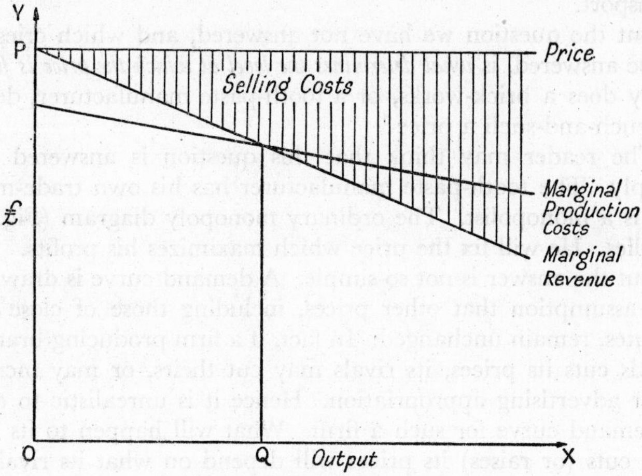

FIG. 30

During recent times there has been a growing tendency for firms to create a somewhat similar situation by "differentiating" their products from those produced by their rivals. A trade-mark or the name of the maker is attached to a commodity, and perhaps special designs or packings are used. The purpose is to convince purchasers (either the general public or other firms) that the commodity is different from, and in some or all respects better than, similar goods made by rival firms. This purpose is often promoted by advertising and the use of salesmen. Hence each "branded" good has a circle of customers more or less attached to it. A reduction in the price of a similar rival good would not draw away all, or most, of this group of customers (any more than a reduction in the price "at works" of bricks in a distant brick-works would greatly affect the local sales of the local brick-works).

The manufacturer of a branded good often considers it good business policy to fix its price (both wholesale and retail); the public becomes accustomed to this price, and the manufacturer fears that to change it in either direction might cause a loss of goodwill. Hence our diagram for the brick-works may[1] apply equally to such branded goods, except that for them selling-costs are mainly the costs of advertising and salesmen rather than of transport.

But the question we have not answered, and which cries out to be answered, is *what determines the level at which the price is fixed?* Why does a brick-works, or a tooth-paste manufacturer, decide on such-and-such a price?

The reader may think that this question is answered very simply. The tooth-paste manufacturer has his own trade-mark. He is a monopolist. The ordinary monopoly diagram (Fig. 29) applies. He will fix the price which maximizes his profits.

But the answer is not so simple. A demand curve is drawn on the assumption that other prices, including those of close substitutes, remain unchanged. In fact, if a firm producing branded goods cuts its prices, its rivals may cut theirs, or may increase their advertising appropriation. Hence it is unrealistic to draw a demand curve for such a firm. What will happen to its sales if it cuts (or raises) its prices will depend on what its rivals do and on how "loyal" the customers of each firm remain.

The true answer, which applies over a great part of manufacturing (and not only to the large and growing field of branded goods), is that given by Marshall. The current "code of trade morality" prevents a firm from selling at prices only a little above marginal costs. "Each man fears to spoil his chance of getting a better price later on from his own customers; or, if he produces for a large and open market, he is more or less in fear of incurring the resentment of other producers, should he sell needlessly at a price that spoils the common market for all."[2] The rate of profit on the turnover—the percentage "profit margin" added to average prime cost in order to arrive at the price—varies widely between industries "because it depends on the length of time and the amount of work required for the turnover."[3] For example, a shipbuilder would have to add a

[1] In fact, a firm may decide beforehand how much it will spend in selling-costs; in that event they can be considered as part of its "fixed costs." Even if it is prepared to vary them, marginal selling-costs may not be rising. The explanation which follows, in the text, covers both these cases.

[2] *Principles of Economics*, 8th edition, p. 374.

[3] *Ibid.*, p. 615.

much higher percentage than a manufacturer of handkerchiefs. "As a matter of fact there is in each trade and every branch of each trade a more or less definite rate of profits on the turnover which is regarded as a 'fair' or normal rate."[1] This is determined, assuming no great change in conditions, by the traditions of the trade. "Such traditions are the outcome of much experience tending to show that, if that rate is charged, a proper allowance will be made for all the costs (supplementary as well as prime) incurred for that particular purpose, and in addition the normal rate of profits per annum in that class of business will be afforded. If they charge a price which gives much less than this rate of profit on the turnover they can hardly prosper; and if they charge much more they are in danger of losing their custom, since others can afford to undersell them."[2]

We can supplement this by extracts from the valuable monograph on "Price Behaviour and Business Policy" (1941) written for the Temporary National Economic Committee of the United States Senate. "A materially larger sector of the price universe must be classed as insensitive to-day than was true in the earlier years of the twentieth century" (p. 19). "Business men . . . usually favour price stability" (p. xx). "Such stability may be achieved by various forms of agreement or understanding within industries" (p. 9). "The multiplication and accentuation of differences between rival products" has diverted competition from price channels (p. 10) towards "quality, performance, and style, supplemented by the use of trade-marks, brands, and advertising" (p. xxi). The result is that the prices of many products have been made "relatively stable."

The picture we now have, for a large part of manufacturing, is something like this. Marginal costs are not falling. They are, let us say, constant and equal to average variable costs. There is no monopoly in the ordinary sense of the term: new firms are quite free to enter the industry. But so long as conditions—the "methods of the trade"—do not change much, prices will be relatively stable. They will be more or less fixed by custom and tradition, perhaps supported by more direct agreements between the various firms in the industry. They will be fixed so that they cover fixed costs and yield a "normal" rate of return on the capital and efforts of the entrepreneur. Suppose that, owing

[1] *Principles of Economics*, 8th edition, p. 617. [2] *Ibid.*

perhaps to an increase in demand, they yield more. New firms can and will enter the industry until free capital and business ability can earn no more in that industry than elsewhere.

But this is not the whole story. The profit-margin—Marshall's "rate of profit on turnover"—may be high or low, within wide limits, and yet yield the "normal" rate of return on capital, and no more. Which profit-margin does yield this "normal" rate of return depends on the amount of "excess capacity" in the industry. For example, a high profit-margin may have attracted a number of firms into the industry without any of them risking a price-war by cutting the prevailing prices. The result will be a good deal of "excess capacity," so that the rate earned on the capital (used and idle together) is only the "normal" rate.

As one writer[1] puts it: "The prevalent condition of industry is neither one of pure competition nor of outright monopoly; it is one where excessive profits tend to get eliminated through competition but not one where this competition takes the orthodox form of compelling producers to reduce their profit margins; rather, selling costs and overhead costs tend to get swollen so as to absorb excessive profits."

6. PUBLIC UTILITIES

Public utilities cover an important part of economic activity. They include undertakings providing water, electricity, gas, telephone service, and rail transport. They require a relatively large amount of plant and equipment, so that their fixed costs are usually greater, and sometimes much greater, than their variable costs.

Such an undertaking is often worked below full capacity. One reason for this is that if the service is to be provided at all for a particular district, fixed capital must be provided capable of supplying more than the existing demand. For example, it may be worth while to build a railway line between two points although only a few trains a day are expected to be required. Yet, once the permanent way is there, it could probably cope with considerably more trains. Again, it may be cheaper to produce a given output—of, say, electricity—from a large plant working below capacity than from a smaller plant.

[1] N. Kaldor, in an unpublished memorandum.

Another reason for excess capacity in public utilities is that demand fluctuates over time. Unless the product can be stored (as with gas) a plant large enough to cater for the "peak" demand must have excess capacity when the demand is below this level.

Once the plant and equipment have been set up, it may be possible by means of advertising and other propaganda to raise the demand during relatively slack periods up towards the peak level and to reduce the peak level if that strains the capacity of the plant and raises marginal costs sharply. The method of charging may help to achieve this aim. Thus railways may charge cheap fares during the intervals between the rush hours, and telephone calls may be cheaper at night. If a peak occurs for electricity at certain hours a much higher rate per unit could be charged for current consumed during those periods.[1]

Variable costs are unlikely to be rising if the plant and equipment are worked below full capacity. Hence a price per unit equal to marginal cost would fail to cover the fixed costs; in other words it would cover only a part, perhaps well below half, of the total costs of the undertaking. What should be done? One course would be to charge a price per unit equal to average *total* cost. This would usually be much higher than marginal cost. But it is in the social interest that the potential demand should be met of consumers who are prepared to pay prices for extra units which cover the *extra* cost of supplying those units.

A possible solution is the two-part tariff. In Great Britain this now applies to electricity and telephone service and is employed by a growing number of gas undertakings. The consumer has to pay *two* charges. The first is a fixed charge, usually per quarter, such as the "rental" charged for a telephone. This charge does not vary with his consumption. It must be paid whether he consumes much, little, or none of the service in question. All the fixed charges, taken together, would about cover the fixed costs of the undertaking. The second is a charge *per unit* of service consumed. This covers marginal costs.

This method of charging, where practicable, seems to be the best from a social standpoint. For water, the variable charge is often nil. The marginal cost of supplying water, once all the fixed capital, including pipes, is installed, may be quite low, and

[1] On this whole subject see "The Two-Part Tariff," by W. Arthur Lewis, in *Economica*, August, 1941.

it may be thought desirable in the interest of hygiene to encourage people to use water freely.[1]

A public utility supplies services to a particular area by means of rails or cables or pipes or wires. The large amount of its "fixed capital" is specialized to that purpose. This tends to make public utilities local monopolies.

Moreover, their products are often difficult to transfer between consumers or users. This makes discriminatory charging possible. Thus an electricity company could charge the same consumer much more per unit for current used for lighting than for current used for heating or power. (The demand for electricity for the latter uses is much more elastic, owing to the possibility of using coal as a substitute.) The two-part tariff does away with this type of discrimination, but it is still possible to charge one consumer more than another for the same service. And it is difficult for railways to use a two-part tariff. Hence railways often charge more per ton-mile for valuable goods than for heavy goods such as coal or ore. (The demand for transport for the latter is more elastic because transport costs form a higher percentage of their value.)

These two features, taken together, distinguish public utilities from, for example, bus companies or shipping companies or collieries. They are the chief grounds on which the State, including local authorities, either owns and operates or closely controls public utilities.

The State often regulates their charges. This at once raises the question of how much profit they should be allowed to earn. In the United States, this has given rise to much controversy, for if charges were fixed so low as to be "confiscatory"—depriving the Utilities of part of their property—they could be declared unconstitutional by the Courts. Does a given scale of charges provide sufficient revenue to yield a fair return upon the capital? The most difficult and important of the various points involved is how to decide what is a "fair value" for the capital.

The best way to value the capital of a "going concern" is to capitalize the whole future stream of its expected net earnings.

[1] In the same way, the increased use of a bridge may increase costs by very little. It may therefore be wise to pay for the bridge out of taxation (levied partly on the owners of neighbouring land whose value is raised by the construction of the bridge) and to permit people to use it freely instead of paying a toll.

This is difficult enough. To what extent is the demand for that type of product likely to rise, or to fall, in the future? Will new substitutes be discovered? Will the cost of producing existing substitutes be reduced? If the firm meets a local demand, what is likely to happen to the numbers and wealth and tastes of the local population? Is technical progress likely to make the existing plant and equipment of the firm obsolete? If so, when? Is the cost of making renewals, repairs, and replacements likely to rise or to fall? These and similar questions must be answered before future net earnings can be estimated; and then the appropriate rate of interest, at which to capitalize, must be decided on.

But the difficulty of valuing the capital is far greater with a public utility. For its future earnings will depend on the charges which the State allows it to make, so that they cannot form the basis of valuation for the very purpose of fixing these charges.

Nor can the total value of its shares on the Stock Exchange; for this, too, will reflect expected future earnings. Hence regulatory bodies in the United States have been forced to take the cost of the plant and equipment as the basis. At once the question arises of whether the original cost or the replacement cost should be taken. The two may differ widely. Present prices of similar plant and equipment may be much higher or much lower than when the existing plant and equipment were bought and installed. And there are other complications. For example, it may be urged that the existing plant is nearly obsolete, although by no means worn out, and should soon be replaced by a more modern type. "The fact that the Interstate Commerce Commission spent years of time and millions of dollars attempting to value the railroads, and still did not arrive at a valuation which could be fully sustained in the courts, is evidence of the difficulties involved."[1]

We shall not attempt to solve these problems. But one point should be made. In economic matters, bygones are bygones. The economic problem is to make the best use of existing resources, whatever their origin or original cost. It may happen that technical progress in other directions reduces the earning-power of the assets of, say, a railway or gas company. There is

[1] A. L. Meyers: *Elements of Modern Economics*, p. 262. This book is very good, especially on imperfect competition.

no reason why the State should impose restrictions on road transport or electricity for the benefit of the shareholders in the railway or gas company. They took their risks; provided they are not penalized relatively to their rivals by State regulation they have no real grounds for complaint if their earnings are less than they had hoped.

7. MIDDLEMEN

The middleman is often an unpopular figure. The producer suspects him of getting too much for whatever work he does. The consumer, when he realizes that coal costs him about twice as much per ton as the colliery gets or that fruit costs him perhaps three times as much as the grower gets, tends to think he would get things much more cheaply if middlemen were eliminated.

Sometimes these beliefs are not without foundation. Some aspects of retail distribution, which we discuss in the following section, are often condemned as wasteful. A transport undertaking in a monopoly position may charge unduly high rates. In some branches of trade the wholesalers may form a "ring" and charge too much for their services.

Nevertheless as a rule middlemen perform useful functions. If they did not, they would not survive. Producers would cut them out by selling directly to shops or to the public, perhaps joining together (as groups of farmers have done in several countries) to form co-operative associations for this purpose.

One function of the middleman is to save producers and consumers time and trouble by bringing them together. Another may be to grade commodities. This enables consumers better to satisfy their respective tastes, and producers to get higher prices. It can usually be done more cheaply on a large scale. Alternatively many different qualities—for example of tea or tobacco—may be blended by the middlemen in order to get some particularly choice combinations. Another function may be to hold stocks, and to run the risk that they may be stolen or burned or damaged (for example, eaten by mice or weevils); or may fall in price. If retailers can quickly replenish their stocks from the wholesaler, both they and the manufacturers can hold smaller stocks. In all these functions the middleman is a specialist.

Let us consider what a manufacturer would have to do in order to cut out wholesalers and to sell direct to retailers. First, he would have to get to know the retailers, to discover the particular requirements and credit standing of each. Next, he would have to engage salesmen to call on the retailers at intervals to show samples of his goods and to take orders. The wholesaler usually does this. But he sells the goods of a number of different manufacturers, so that *fewer* salesmen are required than if each manufacturer employed his own. Further, the retailer may prefer this system. An ironmonger, for example, sells a great variety of different articles. He does not want to waste his time in interviewing a stream of salesmen from each different manufacturer of each article. He would rather deal with a wholesaler who can sell him an assortment of different things, produced by different firms, at the same time. Again, a manufacturer in, say, Birmingham, may make goods bought by, say, 200 retailers in London. If he dealt with them direct he would have to send 200 separate parcels. Transport and packing costs will be less if he sends one large parcel to a wholesaler. And the economy does not end there. True, the wholesaler breaks this large parcel up sooner or later into 200 small ones. But he gets also other large parcels of other goods from other manufacturers, so that he can still send a relatively large parcel to each retailer. This saving in transport costs is perhaps the main reason why goods may pass through several hands. On the surface it seems wasteful but it may be really the cheapest method.

Hence a manufacturer is unlikely to gain by selling direct to retailers unless his output is very large, so that his salesmen can be fully occupied; and unless his products are branded goods, which do not need grading or blending, and are (unlike coal) of a high value per ton, so that transport costs are relatively unimportant.

We may add that some manufacturers have their own shops or special retail agents as a kind of advertisement. They hope to create a belief that their products are "exclusive," and of special quality, by making them available only from their own shops or special agents. Or they may suspect that retailers, selling rival goods also, do not "push" their products enough. Hence they may sell direct although this raises selling costs for any given volume of sales.

It is interesting to recall that in 1930 Soviet Russia decided to abolish her wholesaling institutions. The factories began selling direct to the retail co-operatives. But it proved very expensive for each factory to maintain contact with all its retailers, and for goods to be handled in such small lots. Within two years wholesale institutions were back again and were recognized to be performing a useful socialist function.

Our conclusion is that in general middlemen perform useful functions and that the length of "the chain of distribution" often keeps down, rather than raises, prices to the consumer.

8. RETAIL TRADE

In Great Britain, just before the war, over two million persons were engaged in retailing. The total number of shops was around three quarters of a million—about one shop per sixty persons. On the average, there were nearly two assistants (excluding roundsmen and errand boys) per shop, but of course there were big variations. A department store, with a turnover of half-a-million or even a million pounds a year, employed a good many; most small "general" shops employed none.

The numbers of shops varied according to the commodities sold from some 100 thousand grocery-and-provision shops and some 75 thousand clothing shops to little more than 10 thousand chemists shops.

The total value of retail sales was between £2,000 million and £3,000 million a year. Perhaps a quarter of this, at least, represented the sales of department stores, multiple shops, and co-operative societies. It was these shops, rather than the more numerous private shops, which did most to keep down prices and to introduce new lines. They were strong enough to follow their own policy. Many of the smaller shops had to sell mainly branded and nationally-advertised goods, at prices fixed by the manufacturers.

The "retail mark-up," or profit-margin, varied for different goods according to the length of time an average article remained in stock and according to the risk that stock would deteriorate either physically or in appeal to customers. Thus in the United States (which took a Census of Distribution in 1930) the average ratio of retailing costs to retail prices was around 17 per cent in the grocery trade, where turnover is rapid, as against 35 per cent for jewellery, where the rate of turnover is very slow although the average value of an article is high. For fruit, where the rate of turnover is as rapid as for groceries, it was 25 per cent, owing to the risk that fruit would become spoilt. For women's millinery it was nearly 44 per cent.

Some shops, notably the big department and "chain" stores, sell more than one class of goods. Let us take a department store for illustration. This is clearly a many-product firm. Its problem is to maximize its *maintainable net* revenue. It could increase its sales in one period, by having a "sale," at the expense of its sales in the succeeding period. It has to remember that some goods which it sells are complementary, e.g. bedding and mattresses, so that for example a 10 per cent cut on *both* may give it better results than a 20 per cent cut on one alone. It must also remember that many of its goods are competitive with one another. Suppose it deals mainly with regular customers who spend a large part of their money with it. It may cut prices in one department and in consequence that department may greatly increase its receipts. But this may mean that receipts fall off in other departments. Thus women may spend more on gloves and stockings, if they are made cheaper and more attractive, but may cut down on food or other things. We have mentioned that a department—for example a restaurant or a library—may be run at a loss in order to attract customers to the store. There is also the device of prominently displaying some well-known good at less than the ruling price. The hope is that customers will come in and buy other things as well. Such a good is called a "loss leader." This practice is more widespread in America than here.

Some shops, especially during recent years, have been giving all sorts of extra facilities and service: delivery, credit accounts, rest-rooms, and so forth. But the customer who wants to buy cheaply usually can do so from "cash and carry" shops.

An important problem is that of *resale price maintenance*. This applies, of course, to branded goods, which are usually nationally advertised: for example, cigarettes, patent medicines, and toilet preparations. The manufacturer, one would think, should welcome "cut prices." He makes bigger sales and he gets the same price per unit (from the wholesaler). The customers get the goods fresher. The shops which "cut" have a bigger turnover and less idle capacity.

But the other shops object. In a provincial town all the

tobacconists, for example, might get together if a shop sold certain cigarettes at cut-prices, and might threaten the manufacturers that they would not buy unless steps were taken to cut off supplies to the cut-price shop. As a rule, the manufacturers fell into line. The Committee on Restraint of Trade (1931) accepted the argument that if a manufacturer "advertised a particular brand at a given price and if retailers, for purposes of their own, sold it temporarily at lower prices, the effect on the public would be such as to destroy the reputation of the brand." In the United States, the enforcement of minimum resale prices has been made possible by legislation. The Temporary National Economic Committee (1941) is strongly opposed to such legislation.

This leads us to the central problem of retailing—imperfect competition and excess capacity. It is easy to set up a new shop. Premises can be rented; stock can be bought on credit. The capital required has not to be tied up in durable and specific plant; it consists mainly of stock-in-trade which, at the worst, can usually be disposed of without great loss. The consequence, it is often urged, is too many shops. Certainly many shops have excess capacity—far more customers could be served by the same staff.

For more shops do not mean lower prices. An increase in the supply of retailing capacity is unlikely to reduce profit-margins; it may even raise them. Competition is imperfect. "A retail dealer," says Marshall,[1] "when once he has established a good connection has always had a partial and limited local monopoly." As a rule, a shop has its own circle of customers, who remain fairly "loyal" to it. It may be conveniently situated for them; it may grant them credit; it may be a centre for local gossip. They may rely on its reputation for goods whose technical qualities, such as durability, they must take on trust. They may take the risk of being charged more than they would have to pay at some other shop, in order to save themselves the time and trouble of seeking out the best bargains. This tendency is clearly strengthened by the growing extent to which goods are "branded" and sold everywhere at prices fixed and maintained by the manufacturers.

[1] Article on "Retail Prices," published in *Memorials of Alfred Marshall*, p. 353.

The considerations which, as a rule, prevent new shops from cutting prices may be shown by a hypothetical example. Suppose that there is a small grocery-and-provision shop at each end of a long street, and that a man starts a similar shop in the middle of the street. He can count on some customers from people who live nearer to him than to his rivals. Will it pay him to cut his prices? On some lines he cannot do this without soon being deprived of further supplies by the manufacturers. If he cuts prices on other lines, most of the customers of the other two shops will remain "loyal" to them; he will attract away only some of them. Moreover, he will risk forcing the other shops to follow suit and to cut their prices also; if this happens, all three will be in a worse position than if he had followed a policy of "live and let live." Hence he will be very likely to accept current prices and profit-margins. The consequence, therefore, of his entry into the trade will be more "excess capacity." Three shops will now be sharing the work formerly done by two.

9. THE SOCIAL CONSEQUENCES OF IMPERFECT COMPETITION

Our survey has shown that over most fields of economic activity competition is by no means perfect. In addition to restriction schemes and monopolies in the popular sense, formal or informal understandings to preserve profit-margins and to refrain from price-competition are very common, especially in manufacturing and retail trade. We must supplement our remarks on the economic effects of monopoly[1] by some discussion of how far the consequences of such understandings are undesirable, from the standpoint of the community as a whole. We shall also consider briefly what lines public policy might follow in dealing with these problems.

"Excess capacity" is sometimes inevitable; and it often carries with it advantages which partly offset, and sometimes more than offset, the waste of resources which it seems to involve. Let us take some illustrations.

We have already pointed out that a plant worked below

[1] Chapter XV, section 6.

capacity may yet produce that output at a smaller total cost than a smaller plant working at full capacity. This arises from "indivisibility." For one reason or another, the larger plant is more efficient; the next "size" which it is practicable to build does not yield the same "economies of scale."

A liner often makes a journey with fewer passengers or less cargo than it could conveniently carry. But potential passengers and shippers know in advance exactly when it will sail, and can make their plans accordingly.

The need to use certain things may occur only during certain times or seasons. It is not wasteful to have street lamps which are lit only at night or harvesting machinery which is idle most of the year. Some things are not used continuously but it is very convenient to have them available whenever they happen to be required. This applies to various things in the home, such as baths and sewing-machines and household utensils. In the same way, a firm may find it convenient to keep various things available. Some of them may be used comparatively seldom but when they are needed they may be needed urgently.

This concept of availability applies also to shop-assistants who are not fully employed all the time. A customer appreciates being served at once, and served courteously and well, instead of having to wait in a queue and then being served in a hurry.

The resources used in advertising similar but competing products appear to be wasted. In some fields, widely-advertised goods are considerably dearer than identical substances sold under non-proprietary names. For example, Bayer Aspirin, sold to retailers at 75 cents an ounce was, according to the monograph on "Price Behaviour and Business Policy," identical with acetylsalicylic acid, costing 13 cents an ounce. But a consumer often derives extra satisfaction from owning or consuming a widely-advertised product, although a cheaper product might be chemically identical or might give an equally good "performance." And newspapers and magazines often derive most of their revenue from advertisements and are therefore sold more cheaply to readers, who presumably like looking at the advertisements.

The waste in milk distribution, with several roundsmen to a street, is often criticized. But a consumer can choose the dairy she likes—for milk is not homogeneous; and the time she likes for it to be delivered; and possibly the roundsman she likes.

And so we might go on. Imperfect competition *does* usually mean some waste of resources. That is the central fact. In war-time, as we point out in the final chapter of this book, labour and other resources are urgently needed for the war effort and should not be used wastefully or below capacity. But in peace-time consumers may value the convenience and the greater freedom of choice offered to them by "wasteful" methods.

What should the State do about all this, in time of peace? This, clearly, is a very controversial question. The remarks which follow are merely my own opinions.

The most important thing is that the gate should be kept wide open for new entrants, new methods, new ideas; no special fines or taxes should be imposed upon them. The State may be tempted to restrict or penalize them in the name of "planning" or "rationalization" or "co-ordination" or "orderly marketing." It may believe that such restrictions or penalties would prevent an industry from becoming "over-saturated," that they would keep down "excess capacity" and waste. In fact, they would destroy the most powerful check on monopoly power—freedom of entry. They would prevent the fuller and more efficient satisfaction of consumers' wants; they would delay the rise of new and better methods; they would hold back the application of improved techniques.

Profit-margins are sometimes reduced. "These rates," says Marshall, "are always changing in consequence of changes in the methods of trade; which are generally begun by individuals who desire to do a larger trade at a lower rate of profit on the turnover than has been customary, but at a larger rate of profit per annum on their capital."[1] Mr. Henry Ford comes along and revolutionizes the methods of producing motor-cars. He makes himself a millionaire by charging a relatively small profit-margin on each car and selling enormous numbers at relatively low prices—made possible by mass-production coupled with a very elastic demand. The changes in "methods of trade" are seldom as spectacular as his. But the man who opens a cafetaria, the road-haulier who charges low rates for return loads, the taxi-driver who collects five passengers all going to the same football

[1] *Principles of Economics*, p. 617.

match, the author who fixes a low price for his textbook, are all, each in his humble way, doing the same kind of thing. The State should not limit entry or restrict output or fix minimum prices; nor should it give the sanction and support of law to such practices when they are carried out by a trade association. Custom and tradition may for a time maintain profit-margins and prices, but at least the gate can be kept open for newcomers, and for innovations, in every field of economic activity.

The State could do some things to lessen the extent or importance of "differentiation." For example, it could permit anybody to use any patent on paying an appropriate royalty to the owner. It need not give excessive legal protection to trade-marks and proprietary designs or brands. It need not penalize advertising—how else can innovations and new opportunities and price-reductions be brought to the notice of a wide public? —but it can make false and misleading statements by advertisers a legal offence. It can require the ingredients of such things as patent medicines to be plainly stated on the package or bottle. It may set up a Research Council, for the benefit of consumers, to make an impartial appraisal of the nature and merits of various proprietary articles.

Despite imperfect competition, the economic system does not work so very badly. In manufacturing industry in Great Britain there was an increase in average production per man-hour of 28 per cent between 1907 and 1924 and 32 per cent between 1924 and 1936. Similar progress, although not everywhere so marked, occurred in other fields of activity. There was a considerable rise in the general standard of living. The same trend will continue after the recent war, or rather after the necessary post-war period of reconstruction, provided that the State can cope with the problem of unemployment and, instead of actively fostering and supporting restrictionist practices, keeps the road clear for enterprise and initiative.

CHAPTER XVII

WAGES

1. INTRODUCTION

THE present chapter is a long one, so that it may be helpful to begin by stating the order in which different topics are treated.

The following section discusses the reasons why one worker may earn more than another who is doing exactly the same kind of work. It deals, that is, with differences in earnings within an occupation.

But differences in wage-rates within an occupation are much less significant than differences between occupations. This is the topic to which most of the chapter is devoted. After a note on independent workers, in section 3, we turn to the demand for labour in some given occupation. Here we simplify by supposing that all the workers in that occupation are of about equal efficiency and receive the same rate of pay, which we take to be a time-rate of so much per week. (As the reasons, such as differences in efficiency, for differences in pay within an occupation are discussed in section 2, we abstract from them in order to concentrate upon the more important question of why the prevailing rate in one occupation is different from that in another.) Section 4 makes two further assumptions. It assumes competition between firms both in selling their products and in bidding for their labour; and it assumes that methods of production can readily be changed. It is shown that, on these assumptions, the wages of any type of labour will tend to equal the value of its marginal product.

Section 5 considers how the situation is changed if a single firm or combine has a monopoly (*a*) in selling its products and (*b*) in purchasing a particular type of labour. Section 6 considers how the situation is changed if labour must be combined in fixed proportions with some other factor, so that methods of production cannot be freely varied.

Given the supply of labour in an occupation, its price, or wage, will depend upon the demand for it. Conversely, given the demand, the wage will depend upon the supply of that type of labour seeking employment. Section 7 discusses the influences determining the supply of labour in different occupations. Section 8 is a note on the earnings of women.

Up to this point we have supposed that the price of labour is quite free to vary. Section 9 discusses the consequences of a minimum wage, for a given occupation, which is fixed by law or maintained by a trade union. It also contains a note upon the difficulty of raising real wages all round by legislation. Section 10 considers under what conditions a trade union can raise the wages of its members. The chapter concludes with a note on unemployment.

2. DIFFERENCES IN EARNINGS WITHIN AN OCCUPATION

It will be remembered that there are many different kinds of labour. An "occupation," in the ordinary sense of the term, may include several distinct kinds or grades of labour. Obviously there are considerable differences in the kind of work done by, say, a brain specialist and a general practitioner, or by a master at a public school and a master at an elementary school, or by the captain of a large liner and the captain of a small tramp. Less obviously, a cotton operative tending mule spindles is doing a different job from one tending ring-frame spindles, and a waiter in an expensive restaurant is performing a somewhat different task from a waiter in a cheap eating-house. We therefore define "occupation" by saying that all the workers in any particular "occupation" are performing exactly the same kind of work. This sense of the term is narrower than the popular one, but it conforms to actual practice, for different occupations, in our sense, tend to receive different rates of pay.

During any given week some workers may earn more than others in the same occupation because they have a longer normal working week, or because they are working overtime, or because the others are on short-time. Apart from this, one worker may earn more than another, in the same time, because he is more efficient or more energetic. If piece-rates are paid, he will of course receive more money than the other. For example, if each is hewing coal at so much per ton and one has a bigger output than the other, he will earn correspondingly more. But in most occupations workers are paid time-rates: so much per hour or per week or per month. For in some occupations it is difficult to measure the amount of work performed by any individual; in others it is difficult to test the quality of the work done, and payment by quantitative results might lead to bad workmanship; and in others the workers object to this method of payment. Under time-rates some workers may do more work than others and yet receive only the same pay. It would cause discontent if employers paid more to those whom they believed (without any objective test) to be more efficient. Moreover, employers save time and trouble by paying a common rate to all workers of a given grade instead of making a separate bargain with each individual; in practice, standard time-rates are often fixed for different occupations by collective bargaining between employers and trade unions. In some occupations, however, it is not unusual for employers to use the objective test of seniority, paying more to workers who have been with them longer, although in fact they may not be more efficient.

Workers in one district may earn more, per hour, than similar workers in another district. It may be that such differences in money wages merely equalize "real" wages, the lower money earnings being offset by a lower cost of living. This partly explains why wage-rates in country districts are often lower than wage-rates for similar work in cities: house rents, in particular, are higher in the cities. Differences in real wages between districts are due to those obstacles to mobility, discussed in Chapter XIV, which hinder workers from moving to places where they can earn more.

Apart from differences in the amount of work done, and in location, differences in earnings within an occupation must be due mainly to ignorance. If one employer pays more than another, in the same place, for workers of equal efficiency, it would pay him to dismiss his own workers and engage those employed by his rival, at some intermediate rate of pay, and it would be to their advantage to move to him; in this way rates would tend to be equalized. Members of one occupation may be employed in several different industries, but there is no reason why employers in a prosperous industry should pay more than those in a depressed industry for exactly the same type of work.

The main purpose of this chapter is to consider why the wage-rate in any occupation is what it is, and why wage-rates are higher in some occupations than in others. We shall therefore abstract from differences in the rate of pay between workers in the same occupation and assume that a uniform time-rate prevails for any given type of labour.

3. INDEPENDENT WORKERS

A wage may be defined as a sum of money paid under contract by an employer to a worker in exchange for services rendered. There is no need for us to attempt to distinguish between wages and salaries. But the earnings of "independent" workers demand some consideration.

An independent worker is one who works on his own account and not for an employer. Whether he is a farmer or a doctor, a writer or a hawker, he is an entrepreneur. We have already argued[1] that the earnings (excluding the return on his capital) of an entrepreneur tend to be little more than those of a salaried manager or other paid worker performing the same amount and kind of work for an employer. Hence our explanation of "wages" in a given occupation will explain also the earnings of independent workers in that occupation, and we must include the latter together with wage-earners when considering the supply of labour.

The earnings of independent workers fluctuate more, over time, than those of employees, for the former are selling their services or products directly to the market, while the latter are selling them to an employer who pays an agreed rate which it is troublesome and difficult to alter frequently. Thus the gains or losses arising from changes in the prices of products accrue in the one case to the workers and in the other to the employer.

It is an important fact that many agricultural commodities are produced largely by farmers who work their own farms. When the prices of these products fall, many farmers respond by maintaining or even increasing their output, hoping that this will pay them better than temporarily leaving their land idle and seeking a different occupation. Thus the prices of such products may fall very heavily. Over the period 1928 to 1932,

[1] See pages 173–4.

the prices of many agricultural products about halved. The incomes of most farmers were greatly reduced, many thousands of them receiving less than the wages of an unskilled industrial worker. They were their own employers, selling directly to the market, and hence they could not escape the consequences of the decreased demand for their products, although they remained "fully employed." In countries, such as France and Germany, which on balance were importers of agricultural products, the farmers induced their Governments to give them some protection by restricting imports. In countries which exported agricultural products, such as the United States, the farmers appealed to their Governments for subsidies, and a number of Restriction Schemes were organized to reduce output and thus support prices. An industry such as coal-mining, in which nearly all the workers are wage-earners, offers a striking contrast. A large decrease in the demand for coal reduces the value-productivity of miners' labour but, in most countries, the miners claim that they are entitled to a certain minimum standard of living and resist any large cuts in their wages. Hence a number of pits can no longer be worked at a profit, and are closed; the diminution in the supply of coal prevents any great fall in its price; and the marginal value-productivity of coal-mining labour is kept about equal to its wage by a considerable reduction in the amount of labour employed. Broadly speaking, a marked fall in the demand for, say, wheat, cuts down the incomes of wheat-farmers, whereas a marked fall in the demand for coal causes unemployment among coal-miners. The wages of industrial workers are considerably more stable than the incomes of farmers, but unemployment is mainly an industrial, rather than an agricultural, phenomenon.

4. THE DEMAND FOR LABOUR: MARGINAL PRODUCTIVITY

The demand for labour, as for other factors of production, is a "derived demand." A consumer buys goods for their own sakes; his demand for them is ultimate. But, except in the case of personal services, an employer does not want workers for their own sakes; he wants them for the work which they perform, as measured, not by the efforts which they exert, but by the contribution which they make to his output and thereby to his receipts. Thus his demand for their services is derived from the demand of his customers for his products; he is an intermediary, buying work in order to sell it "embodied" in his products.

Workers in a particular occupation may be employed in several different industries. But we shall begin by considering a kind of labour which is demanded by entrepreneurs in one industry only. The demand for, say, coal-miners is derived entirely from the demand for coal. The sole reason why an entrepreneur employs coal-miners is that they increase his output of coal, and thereby his receipts. We have already argued that he will tend to employ additional workers only if they increase his output sufficiently to add more to his receipts than to his costs. If his output is not large enough to have a perceptible influence upon the selling price of his coal, and if the employment of additional men adds nothing more than their wages to his costs, he will tend to increase his labour force up to the point at which the addition to his weekly output arising from the employment of another miner would sell for a sum equal to the weekly wage. For if his labour force were smaller than this, he could increase his own income by taking on additional men, whose output would sell for more than their wages; and if it were greater than this, he could cut down his costs more than his receipts by dismissing some of his workers. The weekly wage of a coal-miner would equal the value of the marginal product of coal-mining labour, measured in units of "man-weeks."

The assumption that changes in his labour force alter the costs of an entrepreneur only by the addition or reduction made to his wage-bill implies that the quantity of his other factors—plant, equipment, and so on—is fixed. We know from the Law of Diminishing Returns that as more labour is combined with a fixed amount of other factors the marginal productivity of that labour, after a point, will diminish.

The curve *AB* in Fig. 31 represents the marginal productivity of labour to an entrepreneur. If wages were paid in coal, he would employ *OM* workers at a weekly wage of *OW*, and so on. His weekly output of coal would be represented by the area *OAW'M*, of which *OWW'M* would represent his wage-bill and *AWW'* the amount available for other factors (including those owned by himself). In fact wages are paid in money and not in coal, but we can still make the curve *AB* represent his demand for labour by rewriting the vertical scale, translating tons of coal into their money equivalent. For example, if coal were 15s. a ton, each unit on the vertical scale would represent 15s., and his demand for labour at a weekly wage-rate of 45s. would be *OM*, of 60s. *ON*, and so on. Clearly, a rise in the price of coal would increase his demand for labour, at any given wage-rate, and a fall in the price of coal would diminish it. Thus a rise from 15s. to

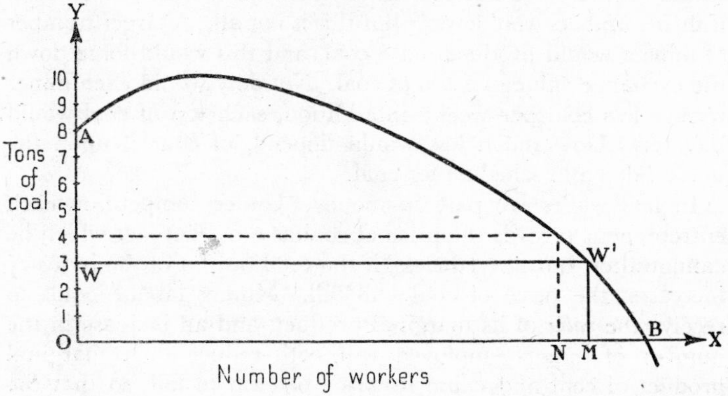

FIG. 31

£1 per ton would increase his demand for labour, at a wage-rate of £3 a week, from *ON* to *OM*. But the curve *AB* would remain unchanged.

The total demand for labour is the sum of the demands of all the different entrepreneurs. A rise in the price of coal would tend to attract entrepreneurs into the industry and a fall would have the opposite effect. But at any moment the number of entrepreneurs is given, and their combined demand for labour can be represented by a curve which adds together, so to speak, the abscissae of all the *AB* curves. For example, suppose that at a weekly wage-rate of 6 tons, one entrepreneur would employ five thousand workers, another eight hundred, another fifty, and so on, and that the sum of all these different demands was five hundred thousand workers. The curve showing the total demand for labour would indicate that at a weekly wage equivalent to 6 tons, five hundred thousand workers would be demanded.

The greater the number of workers, at any moment, attached to the industry, the lower would be the wage-rate—in terms of coal—at which they could all find employment. For the greater the amount of labour employed, in combination with a fixed quantity of other factors, in the industry, the smaller would be its marginal product of coal; and the wage-rate would tend to equal this marginal product.

Thus if wages were paid in coal, a given number of miners would each receive less coal as payment for a week's work than if their numbers were fewer. But this is not all. A larger number of miners would produce more coal, and this would force down the exchange value of a ton of coal. Not only would each miner receive less coal per week; in addition, each ton of coal would buy less. How much less would depend, of course, upon the market demand schedule for coal.

In fact wages are paid in money. Under competition each entrepreneur regards the price of coal as a market fact which he cannot alter, but nevertheless, if the total output of the industry increases, the price of coal will fall. Mining labour tends to receive the *value* of its marginal product, and an increase in the number of miners employed will both reduce their marginal product of coal and cause its price per ton to fall, so that the value of their marginal product will fall by more than the reduction in its amount. Suppose, for example, that the marginal product of five hundred thousand man-weeks is 6 tons and of six hundred thousand only 5·5 tons. An increase in the labour force from five hundred thousand to six hundred thousand would clearly increase the total weekly output of coal—it might increase it, for example, from 4·0 million to 4·6 million tons. Given the demand for coal, its price per ton would have to fall in order that 4·6 million tons, instead of 4·0 million, could be sold each week. Suppose that it would have to fall from 10s. 6d. to 10s. per ton. Then money wages would tend to fall from 63s. (6 × 10s. 6d.) to 55s. (5·5 × 10s.). The marginal product would have fallen by one-twelfth (from 6 to 5·5), its price per unit by one twenty-first (from 10s. 6d. to 10s.), and the value of the marginal product by more than one-eighth (from 63s. to 55s.).

A particular kind of labour may be demanded by several different industries, but this makes no fundamental difference to our analysis. If one worker is doing exactly the same kind of work as another, and there are no great hindrances to mobility, he will tend to receive the same wage-rate although he is helping to produce a different product. Under competition the wage-rate in such an occupation will tend to equal the value of the marginal product of that kind of labour in every industry in which it is engaged; and this will determine how many of the available workers are employed in each of the various industries. Suppose, for example, that an increased demand for the products of one industry causes the marginal product of labour in that industry to be worth more than its wage. Entrepreneurs in that industry will try to increase their own incomes by engaging more workers. But in order to attract more workers of that type from other industries they must offer higher wages. This raises the wage-rate throughout that occupation. At the higher wage-rate some entrepreneurs in other industries can no longer afford to employ as much of that labour as before. By dismissing some of their workers they raise the marginal productivity of those who remain until the value of their marginal product equals the increased wage. The dismissed workers will tend to find employment in the industry whose demand for that type of labour has increased.

It is sometimes urged that the "marginal productivity" explanation of the demand for labour does not apply to the real world, because many employers do not know by how much an additional worker (or ten, or a hundred, additional workers) would increase the total output. There is little ground for this objection. If the manager of a firm, or of a department, is at all efficient, he will always bear in mind the possibility of using more labour of one type or less of another, and from time to time he will experiment in this way and watch the results. A large firm often finds it worth while to keep cost accounts by which it can judge the effect upon output of employing more or less of a given factor. In the short run, wage-rates and marginal productivity may diverge a little. An employer confronted with a fall, which he hopes is only temporary, in the demand for his products, may retain all his workers at existing wage-rates in order to keep them together and to promote good feeling; and a rise in product-prices may not be followed immediately by a rise in wages. But entrepreneurs who do not make a serious effort to equate the marginal cost of any factor with marginal receipts will sooner or later be driven out of business by those who do.

Our analysis, however, applies only to entrepreneurs producing for the market. Modern States are large employers of labour, and within limits they can pay wages as high as they please without going bankrupt. Yet there is a connection between the wage paid by the State for a given type of labour and the marginal productivity of that labour in private industry, for the State must pay a wage high enough to attract as many workers of that type as it requires. If it pays substantially more than they could earn elsewhere, there will be keen competition to get into State employment and the tendency will be for more efficient workers to succeed. In practice, however, some jobs (especially appointments to higher-paid posts not made through competitive examination) may be secured by patronage and influence rather than on merit.

It will be remembered that in this section we have assumed that competition[1] prevails and that methods of production can readily be varied. We must now consider how far our conclusions are modified if these assumptions do not hold good.

5. THE DEMAND FOR LABOUR: MONOPOLY

In our previous discussion we supposed each entrepreneur to produce so small a proportion of the total supply of coal that variations in his output would not perceptibly affect its price per ton. If the whole output were under the control of a monopolist, who tried to maximize his profits, he would take account of the fact that an increase in his output would reduce the price he received for every ton produced. If he were to employ, say, an extra thousand men, this would increase the output of coal, bring down its price per ton, and thereby add less to his receipts than the market value of the additional output. Hence the general rule that an entrepreneur will engage additional men only if the resulting increase in his wage-bill is less than the resulting increase in his revenue means that a monopolist would lose by paying his workers the full value of their marginal product. To put the same point in another way, at any given wage-rate an industry would employ more workers if it consisted of competing firms than if it were under a monopolist. In the former case the labour force would be increased up to the point

[1] We use "competition" to mean "perfect competition" as contrasted with imperfect competition, which we call "monopoly."

at which the value of its marginal product equalled its wage. In the latter case it would be increased only up to the point at which the additional revenue due to the extra output (that is, the receipts from the sale of the extra output less the consequent reduction in the receipts from the "old" output) equalled the addition to the wage-bill.

We turn to "monopsony"—that is, monopoly in the purchase of labour (or other factors). This is much less common than monopoly in the sale of commodities. It is seldom that a firm or combine is the sole or main buyer of a particular kind of labour. When it is, it can of course offer as low a wage as it pleases, but if it pays a wage substantially below that prevailing in comparable occupations, it is very likely that, as time goes on, workers will leave it to enter such other occupations and it will not be able to get all the labour it wants. In general, the larger the number of workers it requires, the higher will be the wage which it must offer in order to obtain them. Hence it will take account of the fact that if it increases its labour force it will have to pay more not only to the additional workers but also to those it already employs—for it is rarely possible to pay different rates to men of equal efficiency working together at the same task. The marginal cost of additional workers will thus exceed their wages. This fact will tend to make its demand for labour less than it would be if that type of labour were employed also in a number of other industries, so that its wage-rate could be taken more or less as given.

6. THE DEMAND FOR LABOUR: NET PRODUCTIVITY

Our second assumption, which we must now consider, was that methods of production can readily be varied, more or less of a particular type of labour being employed in co-operation with a fixed amount of other factors.[1] This assumption is nearly always

[1] If an industry increases (or diminishes) its labour force, it will doubtless increase (or diminish) also the quantities of certain other factors which it uses. The real question, as we showed in our discussion of Diminishing Returns, is whether the *proportions* between the factors can be varied. For example, an increase of 20 per cent in the labour force, the quantity of other factors remaining the same, will reduce the marginal product of labour by about as much as an increase of 32 per cent in the labour force accompanied by an increase of 10 per cent in the quantity of other factors. (Of course the value per unit of the product would fall more in the latter case since total output would be greater.)

true. We have seen[1] that an entrepreneur will try to produce any given output in the cheapest possible way. If the price of a particular kind of labour rises (or falls) he will usually find that it pays him to use less (or more) of it, relatively to other factors, than before. It may be that in some cases very little substitution between factors is possible in the short run. For example, a plant may be designed to employ a fixed number of men. Even so, plants wear out in time and need not be replaced exactly in the same form. A change in relative factor-prices would tend to cause such plants to be replaced, in time, by plants of a different type, designed to employ more of the factors which had become cheaper and fewer of those which had become dearer. Thus it might take some time for the full effects of a rise or fall in wages to manifest themselves. But in most industries there is considerable scope for substitution between factors even in the short run.

No great difficulty is presented if labour must be combined in fixed proportions with some other factor. Suppose that for each worker there must be one machine, or a fixed quantity of raw material. An entrepreneur will treat the man plus the machine (or plus the raw material) as one unit, and if the proportion of such "units" to other factors can be varied, the marginal productivity principle still applies. Under competition the price of the unit will tend to equal the value of its marginal product. Each worker will receive this value less the cost of the machine or the raw material. This sum is sometimes called the value of his *net* product.

There is usually an interval between the payment of labour and the sale of its product, so that an entrepreneur needs "circulating capital" to advance to workers in the form of wages over this interval. If, for any entrepreneur, this interval is constant, an increase or decrease in his labour force will require a corresponding increase or decrease in his circulating capital. Hence he will not engage an additional man unless the value of the additional output covers both the wage of the man and interest at the current rate upon the extra circulating capital required. In other words, wages under such conditions would tend to equal the *discounted* value of the marginal product. But there is no reason why the interval must be constant, and therefore a given amount of circulating capital could be used to

[1] See Chapter XIII, section 9.

employ a greater or smaller number of men. (For example, £2000 advanced for three months represents the same amount of circulating capital as £1000 advanced for six months.) We have therefore ignored this complication in the preceding discussion.

7. THE SUPPLY OF LABOUR

In some or all occupations minimum wage-rates may be fixed by the State or maintained by the power of trade unions. The consequences of this are discussed in the following section. For the present we shall assume that there is no lower limit to the wage which workers are prepared, if necessary, to accept in order to obtain employment. Under such conditions the wage-rate in any occupation will tend towards that level at which all the workers in it can find employment. If it were higher than this, the pressure of unemployed workers, offering their services at less than the prevailing rate, would force it down. If it were lower than this, the competition of entrepreneurs, seeking to increase their profits by engaging more workers, would force it up. Hence, given the demand for labour in the occupation, the wage-rate will depend upon the number of workers seeking that type of work: the greater the number, the lower the wage-rate. We must therefore inquire what determines the number of workers seeking employment in any given occupation.

Logically, perhaps, we should begin by considering what determines the size of the working population as a whole. But such an inquiry would take us far afield; indeed, it would carry us well beyond the boundaries of economic science. At one time it was thought that wages had a direct influence upon the size of the working population. It was believed that a rise in "real" wages would increase the number of babies which survived and hence, in time, the number of workers, thus forcing wages down again, and that a fall in "real wages" would have the opposite effect, so that "real" wages would not remain for many years either much above or much below a given level. Some writers thought this level was that at which workers could just about subsist; others thought it was that which would provide them with the minimum standard of living which they insisted upon having. It is now generally recognized that these views are false. In modern countries birth control is widely practised, and it would be difficult to predict at all accurately the effect of a change in wages upon the number of births. Some workers earn much more than others, although their physiological needs are the same. The standard of living of any worker depends upon his wages, and not conversely. Doubtless most workers want to raise their standard of living, but unless this desire leads them to work harder or to qualify for a better-paid occupation it has no effect upon their earnings. It is true that the larger the population in any area, with given resources, the lower will be the marginal productivity of labour in general in that area, and the lower, therefore, will be the general level of wages.[1] This relative abundance of labour largely explains the low level of wages, and hence the low standard of living, in most Eastern countries; but whether a population is large or small, there are considerable differences between wage-rates in different occupations which cannot be explained by referring to the size of the population as a whole. We shall therefore assume that the size of the working population is given.

A given number of workers, however, may supply more or less work per year. One important reason for this may be variations in the amount of unemployment. We shall consider this later. The point which demands discussion at present is that workers can and do choose, to a certain extent, between income on the one hand and leisure on the other hand.

Here we meet again the concept of *a scale of preferences*. Consider, for example, a worker who is free to do as much or as little work as he pleases at a rate of, say, 2s. an hour.[2] Each day he has a fixed amount of time at his disposal to distribute between

[1] A country may be "under-populated" in that greater numbers would permit roads, railways, and other existing resources of that nature to be so much more fully utilized, and would permit so much more specialization of labour and other factors, that there would be increasing returns to labour. But most countries are not in that position.

[2] This method of statement evades a complication, namely, that the amount of work done in an hour will vary with the number of hours worked per day (and per year). In some occupations, for example, a man's total annual output may be greater with a regular nine-hour working day than with a regular twelve-hour working day. It seems probable that the very long hours worked in many British industries in the past were very wasteful, and that the legislation which reduced them both gave the workers more leisure and increased the yearly output per worker. But in countries where the normal working week is around forty-eight hours or less it is probable that a small increase or decrease in its length would lead to a roughly proportionate increase or decrease in the amount of work performed per week.

work, which yields an income, and leisure. He can increase his income only by forgoing some of his leisure, and he can increase his leisure only by forgoing some of his income. Suppose that he decides to work eight hours a day. This means that he prefers 16s. a day and sixteen hours for rest, recreation, and so on, to any other combination, such as 14s. and seventeen hours or 18s. and fifteen hours. He values his sixteenth hour of "leisure" more highly than a ninth florin, per day; on the other hand he values his eighth florin more highly than the extra (seventeenth) hour of leisure which he could obtain by forgoing it. Suppose now that his hourly rate is permanently raised to 3s. Will he work more or fewer hours per day than before? It is impossible to say. One man might respond in quite a different way from another. It is fairly certain that he would not cut down his working day so much that he earned less than before, for in that event the relative marginal significance to him of leisure (as against income) would be less than before and the extra income to be gained by giving up a given amount of leisure would be greater than before. If he were to work eight hours a day, as before, he would earn 24s. instead of 16s. as formerly, and would still have sixteen hours' leisure. The relative marginal significance of leisure, measured in hours, as against income, measured in shillings, would have increased, but his problem is how to distribute his available twenty-four hours per day, and an extra hour devoted to work now provides an extra 3s. instead of an extra 2s. as formerly. In the circumstances he might quite consistently decide either to increase or to diminish the length of his working day. Hence we cannot predict whether a permanent change in (hourly) wage-rates will lead workers to desire a longer working week or a shorter one, unless we know their scale of preferences in this matter.

Most workers are paid by the week, and apparently have no influence upon the length of their working week, which is fixed by law or by custom. But as a rule the length of the working week does correspond to the wishes of the majority of workers in that occupation. Most of them would not prefer a longer working week at the same hourly rate of pay, and expect a higher hourly rate for overtime; on the other hand they do not welcome short-time, with a corresponding reduction in their weekly earnings. And when a group of workers can succeed, owing to an increase in the demand for their labour, in obtaining either an increase in weekly wages or a reduction in hours, they demand, under collective bargaining, what the majority of them prefer. Sometimes they press mainly for increased wages and sometimes mainly for increased leisure. For example, the British Trade Union Congresses of 1936 and 1937—a time of increasing prosperity—stressed the desirability of a shorter working week more strongly than that of increased wages.

At any moment, however, the length of the working week is given. Our problem is to consider what determines the number of workers attached to each occupation.

If every worker could readily find employment in whatever occupation he pleased, the "net advantages" of all occupations would tend to be equal. Wages in some occupations might be lower than in others, but the difference would merely offset the greater attractiveness of the work, or of the conditions under which it was performed. Workers would distribute themselves among occupations in such a way that wage-rates (after allowing for other advantages or disadvantages) were everywhere the same. An increased demand for one type of labour would increase its wage, but only temporarily: for workers would leave other occupations to enter that one, thus reducing the marginal product of labour of that type. Similarly a decreased demand for one type of labour would lower its wage only for a time, for workers would leave that occupation, thus raising the marginal product of those who remained.

In fact the net advantages of different occupations are by no means equal. On the whole, the more disagreeable kinds of work are among the worst-paid, and earnings in some occupations, such as the professions, are much higher than in others. The reason is, of course, that it is difficult for most workers (or new entrants to the labour market) to enter the better-paid occupations.

The numbers in a comparatively well-paid occupation may be restricted by law. Thus a worker may be legally required to serve for a given period as an apprentice before taking employment as a journeyman, and the number of apprentices may be limited by the State. Again, the State may prevent or restrict newcomers from entering an industry which is "planned" in the sense that the State controls its total output in order to maintain the prices of its products.

Some kinds of innate ability are scarcer than others relatively to the demand for them. Thus many workers earn a comparatively low rate of wages because they lack sufficient intelligence or business ability or mechanical aptitude or artistic flair, and so on, to find employment in better-paid occupations which require one or more of such qualities in a fairly high degree.

But probably the main reason why more workers do not enter the better-paid occupations is that they lack the necessary capital. Entrance to certain occupations, such as the professions, is granted only to those who have proved by some kind of examination that they have attained at least the minimum standard of efficiency which is legally required. Thus many who may possess sufficient innate ability to enter one of these occupations are effectively debarred because they cannot afford to pay for the necessary education and training and to forgo what they could earn, during this period, by spending their time in working for pay instead of in study. Hence earnings in such occupations usually exceed earnings in occupations which require little or no training by considerably more than interest and amortisation on the initial capital outlay. Suppose, for example, that it takes a youth five years of university and hospital training to become qualified as a doctor. During this time he might have earned perhaps £750 at some relatively unskilled job, and he might have paid some £250 in fees and for books and instruments. The interest on £1000 at, say, 5 per cent is only £50 a year and the amortisation charge over a working life of, say, thirty years is considerably less. If, therefore, such a capital output brought him a return of £100 a year it would be yielding more than most investments. Yet in fact the earnings of doctors usually exceed those of relatively unskilled occupations by much more than £100 a year. And this is mainly because many young men and women who could become quite proficient in the medical profession cannot afford to make the initial investment and have no parents or friends who have both the will and the means to make it on their behalf. Hence the child of well-to-do parents begins life with a great advantage—an advantage which is lessened but not destroyed by the scholarship and maintenance grants made by the State and other bodies to enable a limited number of children to continue their studies beyond the time at which they would otherwise have been compelled to enter the labour market.

Again, a man requires capital to set up in business on his own account or to purchase a partnership in an established concern. Hence such fields are closed to the children of poor parents unless they can manage to save or to borrow enough capital, and it is not easy either to save much out of a small income or to obtain a loan without having tangible assets to serve as security for it.

Some jobs are obtained partly through "influence," and in others, such as stockbroking or selling expensive cars, a personal knowledge of fairly rich people is an asset.

We must therefore conclude that the main, although not the sole, reason why the numbers in well-paid occupations are not greater is the considerable extent to which inequality of incomes prevails in most modern communities.

8. THE EARNINGS OF WOMEN

The average woman earns considerably less than the average man.[1] This is partly because in many fields her marginal productivity is less and partly because the great majority of women are concentrated in the worst-paid occupations.

When we speak of "marginal productivity" we mean the difference made to total receipts by employing one "unit" more, or less, of a given factor. In some occupations, such as those requiring considerable strength, the physical output of a woman is less than that of a man; and such occupations may represent a larger demand for labour than those, such as the care of children, at which women are more efficient than men. In other occupations, such as waiting, or serving in shops, workers render personal services to customers. Most customers prefer to be served by men, so that a man increases receipts more than an equally efficient woman. Again, most men do not like working under a woman, so that a man in a position of authority may obtain more work from his male subordinates than an equally capable woman. Finally, most employers believe that men are more reliable than women and less likely to stay away owing to sickness or to refuse to work overtime or to leave them in the lurch by suddenly giving up their jobs. Hence a woman may

[1] Around 31s. 3d. a week, as against 64s. 6d. for men, in Great Britain in 1935. See the *Ministry of Labour Gazette*, February to July, 1937.

earn less than a man in the same occupation either because her actual output is less or because it is believed to add less, especially in the long run, to the receipts of her firm.

The other reason why women earn less, on the average, than men is that relatively few of them are in the better-paid occupations. This is partly because less is spent in educating girls than in educating boys: parents tend to invest their capital in their sons rather than in their daughters. It is partly because the general public is still rather shy of, for example, a woman solicitor or a woman doctor. Again, employers tend to think that the chief aim of a woman is to get married and leave her job, so that it would be a risky investment to train a woman for a higher-paid post in which she could not be readily replaced. Finally, many trades are closed to women, being held by law or custom (often supported by the views of the organized male workers in the trade) to be "men's jobs." Thus in Great Britain women are kept out of mining (underground), iron and steel, heavy engineering, building, most transport work, and the diplomatic service. This may or may not be socially advisable; it certainly restricts the field of employment open to women. The combined result of all these factors is that the great majority of women workers are concentrated in a few occupations where, largely for that reason, wages are low.

9. MINIMUM WAGES

So far we have assumed that the wage-rate in an occupation can vary freely in response to changes in the demand for, or in the supply of, that type of labour. We must now consider the consequences of fixing a minimum wage for an occupation. The results are the same whether the minimum wage is enforced by the State or maintained, effectively, by a trade union.

Suppose that a board is set up to fix wages in a so-called "sweated trade"—that is, one where wages are considerably lower than in most "trades" or occupations. Suppose that it fixes a minimum weekly wage considerably above the level which previously prevailed. It is by no means certain that this will prove a real benefit to the workers whom it was intended to help. Every employer in the trade is now compelled by law to pay at least the minimum wage to every worker he employs, but he is *not* compelled to continue giving employment, at this higher wage, to all his present labour force. Hence a number of workers may be dismissed; and since presumably even the low wages they received in that occupation were more than they could earn in any alternative employment open to them, they will be driven into jobs where they earn even less than they did before or—if the State permits nobody, in any occupation, to receive less than a certain minimum—they will become permanently unemployed and maintained by public or private charity.

It is conceivable that the minimum wage will be high enough to attract workers, from other employments, who are more efficient than those already engaged in that occupation. If so, employers will tend to substitute them, as far as possible, for their existing workers, and the main result of the minimum wage will be simply a redistribution of labour between occupations. Another possibility is that employers will install more labour-saving machinery and other devices, dismissing some of their workers. At the old wage, machinery costing a given sum may have been dearer than labour, but the rise in wages may make it cheaper than labour.[1] In any event, the rise in wages will diminish profits in the industries affected. Some of the less efficient employers may be forced into bankruptcy. Others may transfer their activities to a different field. As time goes on, new capital and enterprise will tend to avoid those industries, until the reduction in their output has raised the prices of their products sufficiently to make the prospects of profit there as bright as elsewhere.

Thus the probable effect of the minimum wage will be to diminish employment in that occupation. But this effect may take some time to show itself. Entrepreneurs with fixed plant may continue to work it, employing nearly as many workers as before, although they now get a smaller return from it; but when plant wears out it may not be replaced, or it may be replaced in a different form, requiring less labour. Thus

[1] This, however, does not mean that wage-fixing tends to increase the *total* capital of a country. Indeed, it is more likely—by diminishing profits and by leading to higher taxation to provide for a larger number of unemployed—to check the accumulation of capital. But it may cause the available flow of savings to distribute itself among different channels somewhat differently, some of it acting as a direct substitute for labour instead of going into, say, building, or the development of some new invention.

dismissals taking place at a considerable interval after wages have been raised may be generally believed to be due to the inefficiency of employers or to labour-saving devices and not to the minimum wage.

The extent to which a rise in wages will diminish employment in that occupation, after sufficient time has elapsed for methods of production to be changed, will vary with the elasticity of demand for that type of labour. This in turn will depend mainly upon the elasticity of demand for the products which that labour helps to produce and upon the ease with which other factors, such as machinery, can be substituted for it. If its products have to meet the competition of similar products imported from abroad, whose prices remain the same, the demand for them will be very elastic: so, therefore, will be the demand for that type of labour, and a rise in its wages will considerably reduce employment. If, on the other hand, an appreciable rise in the prices of its products will cause sales to fall off only slightly, employment *may* be reduced very little. We say "may" and not "will" because the possibility of substitution is important. An entrepreneur will try to produce any given output at the lowest possible cost, and if a rise in wages causes an alternative method of production, employing more capital, to be cheaper, he will change over to that method even if the demand for his product is completely inelastic. Where substitution is not worth while, to any great extent, the proportion of labour cost to total cost is of importance, for the smaller it is the less will be the increase in the prices of the products which would compensate employers for a given rise in wages.

We must not conclude, however, that a minimum wage must inevitably harm, in the long run, those workers whom it was intended to help. There are four ways in which it may prove of real benefit to them.

In the first place, as we have already seen, the existence of fixed and specialized plant may mean that methods of production cannot readily be changed, so that it may be possible to "squeeze" profits for the benefit of wages without thereby causing much unemployment. If a fairly small reduction in output leads to a considerable rise in the prices of the products, it is unlikely that many firms will close down, and it could be claimed that part of the increase in wages is "passed on" to the consumers of those particular products in the form of higher prices. Thus most of the workers might remain in employment, at a higher wage, for some considerable time, during which some change in conditions might occur, such as an increase in their efficiency, to increase the demand for their labour and retain them all, or nearly all, in employment.

This leads to our second point. A rise in the wages of a worker may bring about an increase in his efficiency. It may enable him to consume more and better food or other "necessaries for efficiency"; it may relieve him of some pressing anxieties about money matters and thereby raise the quality of his work; it may induce him to be more energetic or more careful in order to give something in return for the increase in his wages. Of course, if workers do more work their output increases and the prices of their products tend to fall, but on the other hand labour cost per unit of output is reduced, thereby stimulating the demand for labour relatively to other factors, so that in many cases an increase in the efficiency of workers paid on time-rates will increase the demand for them. But we feel bound to add that there seems little evidence for believing that a rise in the wages paid to the majority of workers in modern countries to-day would cause any substantial increase in their efficiency.

In the third place, some or all of the workers in a particular occupation may be "exploited" by their employers in that the latter would continue to employ them, even in the long run, if their wages were higher. But exploitation in this sense is not easy. A firm, or a combination of firms, might be the sole producer of certain commodities and yet be powerless to exploit its workers, for if the main demand for workers of that type came from other industries, where competition prevailed, it would be compelled to pay them the full value of their marginal product in those industries in order to retain their services. It is only when a firm, or a close combination of firms, is the sole or main purchaser of a particular type of labour that it possesses the power of exploitation, and even then this power is limited by the ease with which such workers could transfer to different occupations, requiring similar qualities, and work for other firms. In fact there are very few occupations whose workers are employed mainly by one firm or combine. But it may well happen that one firm is the main employer of certain types of labour in a given district. If its workers are reluctant to leave that district, even if they could earn considerably more elsewhere, they can be exploited. Nevertheless a strong check upon such local exploitation is provided by the possibility that other firms, attracted by the cheap labour, will establish plants in that district and bid up wage-rates. Again, it is conceivable that if an employer makes a separate wage bargain with each worker he may get some workers to accept less than others, whose efficiency is no greater, are receiving. But it is doubtful whether he would gain by doing this. Such workers would be discontented while they were with him and would sooner or later find a better-paid job elsewhere. Some exploitation of this kind may exist at present in the market for domestic service, but probably most housewives find that it pays them to give their servants as much as they could earn elsewhere. We conclude, therefore, that exploitation would not be common even if there were no minimum wages. In so far as a minimum wage, fixed by the State or maintained by a trade union, does abolish exploitation, it is a real gain to the workers concerned, for it raises their wages without causing many of them to be dismissed.

Finally, we must take account of unemployment benefit. It could be argued that a group of workers, taken as a whole, would not gain by a rise in their wage-rate if this caused so many of them to become unemployed that the total sum received in wages by the group was diminished. If, however, their unemployed members received every week a sum approaching in size their previous wages, provided mainly not by their fellows but by, let us say, the wealthier taxpayers, the situation would be altered. The minimum wage would have been the instrument of securing a transfer of income from the relatively rich, so that this group of workers, as a whole, might be in a better position than before.

We may now sum up. A minimum wage, above the level previously ruling, will clearly benefit those who keep their jobs. It will probably cause some unemployment—how much will depend upon the circumstances which we have named. Those who are thrown out of employment, or driven into worse-paid occupations, will lose; profits in the industries concerned will tend to diminish, for a time; consumers of products whose prices are raised will suffer to that extent; and taxpayers and others may have to contribute more than before towards unemployment benefit.

Hitherto we have considered the results of fixing a minimum wage for only one or a few occupations. It is instructive to consider what would happen if a Government insisted upon a substantial rise in the "real" wages of every worker. Suppose it were to fix a "basic" minimum weekly wage for adult males, and a lower one for adult females, say some 20 per cent above the level previously ruling for unskilled labour, permitting nobody to work for less, and were to raise wage-rates in all occupations by about 20 per cent. In order to ensure that "real" wages were raised, it would doubtless make money wages vary with the cost of living, so that if the prices of the food, clothing, housing, and other things bought by workers were to rise, their money wages would rise correspondingly.

This would close three loopholes left open when minimum wages are fixed for only a few occupations. Relatively inefficient workers, not worth the basic wage, would not be permitted to take a worse-paid job elsewhere. There would be little redistribution of labour: workers dismissed would remain unemployed. Further, a rise in prices due to a reduction of output would have much less effect in checking the diminution of profits, for higher prices would mean higher money wages. Finally, the prices of labour-saving machinery and other devices would rise nearly as much as money wages, so that there would be much less scope for checking the fall in profits by altering methods of production. The result might well be a serious check to the accumulation, and investment, of capital; after a time, the total amount of capital in the country, represented by plant, stock-in-trade, and so on, might diminish. A fall in the amount of capital co-operating with labour must mean a fall in the marginal product of labour; in the absence of wage-fixing, this would lead to a fall in wages; if real wages are maintained, it will lead to further unemployment.

Such a policy might "squeeze" owners of existing plant and other equipment, but our reasoning suggests that it might cause considerable unemployment—much more, proportionately, than minimum wages in one or two occupations only—and that the number of unemployed might increase as time went on. This would be so if the fall in profits and the increase in taxation (to provide for the unemployed) caused the total capital of the country to diminish. The history of wage-regulation in Australia, where it has been practised more extensively than in most countries, shows that the dangers of such a policy are real and have been recognized by wage-fixing authorities. On more than one occasion they have shrunk, despite or because of their desire to promote the welfare of wage-earners, from trying to discover by experiment whether the abyss of cumulative disequilibrium described above was merely a bogy created by economists.

10. TRADE UNIONS AND WAGES

Clearly a trade union will not have much power unless it includes the majority of workers in that occupation. Employers will not be greatly perturbed if only a fraction of their workers threaten to strike, provided that they can carry on with the help of the non-unionists who remain and can partly replace the strikers by workers drawn from the unemployed or from other jobs.[1] Even if a union controls nearly all the workers in one district its power is limited by the ease with which employers can import "blacklegs" from other districts. Further, the power of a union depends partly upon its funds. Its main weapon is the strike, or rather the threat to strike. If the strikers cannot support themselves and their families, they may be starved into submission: hence the importance of union funds. If workers receive unemployment benefit provided not by the union but through the State, sufficient to maintain them without any great hardship, this clearly strengthens the hands of the unions in insisting on a certain minimum wage even if this is high enough to cause some unemployment.

The consequences of fixing a minimum wage for a given occupation have been discussed. It is immaterial whether the minimum wage is fixed by some court or board whose decisions have the force of law or whether it is maintained through the power of a trade union. But our previous discussion referred mainly to a minimum wage fixed for a relatively low-paid occupation. It is interesting to consider the conditions under

[1] Hence the importance attached by trade unions to "the closed shop" (employing only union workers) and to their right to "peaceful picketing" (to keep away blacklegs) when they are on strike.

which a trade union can enforce a wage-rate considerably above that paid in comparable occupations.

Suppose that a union induces employers to agree to pay a wage-rate substantially higher than would otherwise have prevailed. This will cause some unemployment. But it may be that a change in methods of production will not be worth while, despite the higher wage; the cost of that type of labour may form only a small proportion of the total cost of the products; and the demand for the products may be fairly inelastic. Given such favourable conditions, the amount of unemployment may be small.

We may pause to point out that such favourable conditions might not last. A rise in the cost of a certain type of labour will stimulate the invention of methods, or of different types of products satisfying the same kind of want, which use less of it. Moreover, many industries employ several different types of labour. The wages of any one type may form only a small part of total costs, but if one type obtains an increase in its wages, the others will try to follow suit and the combined effect upon total costs, and thereby upon employment, may be quite large.

Assuming conditions to remain favourable, can the increased wage be maintained? By hypothesis, it is substantially above the level ruling in other occupations, requiring similar qualities. Boys leaving school will be drawn towards that occupation rather than others. Some workers in comparable jobs will try to transfer into that occupation, especially if this does not involve changing their residence. The type of work in question may be regarded as a man's job and not a woman's, but the preference of employers for male labour might be greatly weakened if they thought that women could be trained to do the work at much lower rates than those enforced by the men's union. But a large influx of new workers would tend to rob existing members of the union of their gains. The newcomers might refuse to join the union—possibly forming one of their own—and might obtain employment by accepting wages below those demanded by the union, thus throwing union members out of employment, and compelling them to agree to a lower rate. If they all joined the union, and refused to undercut, there would be a corresponding increase of unemployment, in which the original members of the union would share, and this might outweigh their gain from the increased wage and induce them to accept less.

The conclusion is that, granted that other conditions are favourable, a union is not likely to maintain such an increase in wages unless it can somehow limit the number of new entrants to its occupation. And it is not easy to do this without obtaining the sanction of the law—for example, by inducing the State to declare that a minimum period of apprenticeship must be served by new entrants and to limit the number of apprentices per journeyman. A union, like any other monopolist, can raise its price only by restricting supply.

We may add that one way of reducing supply is to adopt a "go slow" policy, under which each man performs less work per hour than before. If there is considerable unemployment in an occupation, the union may hope that this policy will "spread" the available work and create jobs, at the prevailing weekly wage, for many of its unemployed members. But the amount of work available is not fixed. A "go slow" policy raises the cost of that type of labour and thereby reduces the demand for it. This reduction may be so great that fewer workers than before are employed; how great it will be depends upon the circumstances already discussed (such as the ease with which other factors can be substituted for that type of labour). If such a policy were followed by most workers, total output would be reduced and prices would rise. Thus a union which succeeded in creating more employment for its members, at a given money wage, would have to set against this gain the rise in the cost of living due to the widespread adoption of its own "go slow" policy.

11. UNEMPLOYMENT

There are many "causes" of unemployment. To begin with, every country has some "unemployables," whose efficiency is so low that they cannot keep any job for long, and fall back upon private or public charity. But their numbers are relatively small. Again, some industries—notably docking, building, and contracting—employ casual labour: the numbers of workers employed by any one firm may fluctuate widely from one day to another, so that on any given day a considerable number of men, attached to these industries, may not find a job. Further, many industries are subject to considerable seasonal fluctuations, so that some men attached to them are out of work during their slack times.

One general "cause," which we have already discussed, is the maintenance of relatively high standard rates of wages in most occupations. These rates may be more than some of the workers—apart from the "unemployables"—are worth. Such a worker will often be out of employment. If the standard rate is a minimum, an employer who discovers his deficiencies will dismiss him; and in any event this course is simpler, and invites less misunderstanding, than offering him a wage appropriate to his efficiency. Further, the standard rate may be so high that not all the workers of average efficiency in that occupation can find employment.

As time goes on, the demand for different products is certain to change. Firms faced with a fall in demand may keep on all their workers for a time, but, unless demand revives again, they may be compelled to dismiss some of them, and some firms may close down altogether. Substantial reductions in wages might prevent much unemployment, but the workers may refuse, not unnaturally, to accept large cuts in their customary rates of pay. The question then arises of whether those thrown out of work can find employment elsewhere. Unless there is a general depression, there are sure to be some industries which are expanding. If customers spend less on some things, they have more to spend on others. But the expanding industries may be in a different part of the country, and most of the dismissed workers may stay where they are—especially if they are drawing unemployment benefit on a scale which is not too niggardly—and hope for re-employment, rather than move to a strange district in the hope of finding a job. Moreover, the expanding industries may require a different type of labour, and some of the unemployed may be too old to learn a new trade.

Changes in technique, and notably "mechanization," may be induced, as we have seen, by high wages. If they are due simply to new inventions, or to increased savings which lower the rate of interest, they need not cause unemployment. The reduction in costs will lower the price of the products, and the demand for them may be so elastic that the industry in question provides at least as much employment as before. An illustration is the motor car industry over the last twenty years or so. The number of men required to produce a car has fallen but the total number employed in making cars has considerably increased, both in Great Britain and in other countries.

As a rule, however, "mechanization" in an industry does throw some workers out of employment. But some other industries, including those making the new plant or equipment, will be expanding, and employment as a whole may increase. It is clearly absurd to claim that mechanization must diminish total employment. In most industrial countries mechanization has been going on for many years without any parallel growth in unemployment. Recent years have witnessed a considerable growth in mechanization in many British industries. It is difficult to give comparable figures of the numbers in employment at different dates but it seems broadly true, on the basis of figures given in the Abstracts of Labour Statistics, that the number of insured workers in employment was around 9½ million in 1923, and rose to some 10½ million in 1929 and to more than 12 million in 1937. Apart from the slump years of 1930–34, the growth in employment nearly kept pace with the growth in the working population, despite the progress of mechanization and the contraction of certain industries, such as coal-mining

By far the most important "cause" of unemployment, in a modern capitalist country, is the trade cycle. At the bottom of a general trade depression the percentage of workers unemployed is usually at least two or three times as high as in prosperous periods. We discuss the trade cycle in Chapter XX, section 4, but we may say a few words here about wage-policy during a depression.

This is a very controversial subject. Some economists contend that the best policy is to raise money wages in order to stimulate expenditure on consumers' goods and thereby to stimulate investment. Others believe that such an increase in the costs of entrepreneurs would lead them to dismiss still more workers, whilst reductions in wages (especially if they took place in one or two industries at a time and not in all at once) would induce firms to take on more workers and to order more equipment and materials, thus increasing investment. Probably much would depend on the beliefs and therefore the reactions of entrepreneurs. A number of economists think that, more often than not, neither increases nor decreases in money wages would have much effect and that trade depressions must be fought by other weapons.

CHAPTER XVIII

INTEREST

1. INTEREST UNDER SOCIALISM

THE question of what forces determine the rate of interest is difficult and controversial. We shall simplify the discussion by leaving out some subsidiary points and by proceeding in stages.

The first stage is to consider the part played by interest in a socialist state. The State owns all property. Nobody receives an income from interest or profits or dividends or rents. The central planning committee decides how resources shall be used. There is no unemployment.

We have met this problem before. The reader may perhaps refresh his memory by looking again at Chapter XI, section 7. We there discussed how an economic dictator would decide to what extent and in what ways he would provide for the future. That discussion must now be carried a little further.

Under socialism there would certainly be production for the future. Railways, bridges, power-stations, steel-works, machines, houses, and other durable goods would be built. How would the planning committee decide a problem such as this?

"A railway has to cross a piece of high ground. Either it may be built in the open with two steep slopes, or it may be constructed with deep cuttings and a tunnel. The first way involves greater cost *in operation* for the whole time that the line is open; the second way involves a greater expenditure of labour and materials at the time of construction. How can the authority planning the railway balance the extra annual cost of operation against the additional once-and-for-all cost of construction? If the additional construction-cost is only five times the extra annual operation-cost, it is almost certainly worth while to build the tunnel. If it is 100 times more, the tunnel is almost certainly not worth while."[1]

Presumably the planning committee would first decide how much of the community's efforts and resources are to be devoted

[1] H. D. Dickinson, *The Economics of Socialism*, p. 81.

to the future—to producing durable goods instead of to satisfying current needs. Their decision would depend largely on the general level of productivity and real income. If the level is high, as in the United States and Great Britain, the proportion of activity devoted to the future will be greater (as indeed, under capitalism, it is) than if the level is low, as in India or Italy. For at least enough consumption goods to provide necessaries for efficiency must be currently produced. A rich country, like a rich man, can save and invest more than a poor one, and thereby become richer still: to him that hath shall be given.

Having decided how much provision for the future can be made, the next question is how—in what ways—to make it. Let Mr. Dickinson, a socialist, answer this question.

"Projected works can be classified according to the number of years' purchase they require." (In the previous quotation, the tunnel was almost certainly worth while at five years' purchase and not worth while at 100 years' purchase.) "It is obvious that the community should undertake first those works in which a present outlay saves a large annual cost before proceeding with those that effect a less saving. Equilibrium is obtained by pushing the investment of resources up to the same number of years' purchase in all lines of production. The community must decide upon a certain number of years' purchase (in other words a rate of interest) and apply it as a touchstone to distinguish between feasible and unfeasible undertakings."

Thus under socialism a rate of interest would be used for purposes of calculation, although nobody paid or received interest. The rate would be determined by the productivity of "roundabout" or "capitalistic" methods of production, on the one hand, and by abstinence or thrift on the other hand. But the abstinence or thrift would be enforced from above, by the planning committee, instead of being left to the decisions of individual savers. Saving and investment would be merely two different ways of looking at the same thing—namely, the use of resources to provide for future, instead of for current, wants.

2. THE MARGINAL PRODUCTIVITY OF CAPITAL

The next stage is to consider a capitalist society from which some important influences are absent. There is no unemployment, no hoarding of money, no speculation in securities. The banking system does not expand or contract credit and the demand for money balances does not change. Entrepreneurs borrow in order to use the money in industry and trade; the money is lent to them by individual savers.

Our socialist society was a real one; it might easily exist in fact. Our assumed capitalist society is an imaginary one. We have ruled out important features, some of which, if not all, are bound to be present in any actual capitalist society. We have ruled them out in order to explain certain points without digressions or qualifications.

Why do entrepreneurs borrow? And why are they prepared to pay interest—a given percentage, per month or per year—on what they borrow? The obvious answer is that they hope to use the loans in ways that yield them a profit greater than the interest they pay. If an entrepreneur could borrow as much as he wished at the ruling rate of interest—in fact, often he cannot—he would borrow up to the point at which the marginal cost equalled the marginal revenue. The marginal cost at, say, 5 per cent would be £5 a year on each £100 he borrowed. The marginal revenue would be the increase in his receipts from using that money. So long as marginal revenue exceeded marginal cost, he would increase his net profit by borrowing more.

Why can he make a profit? The main explanation is the greater productivity of more "capitalistic" methods of production. We discussed this in Chapter X. Let us take another example. Suppose that the demand schedule for shoes is given and that shoes are made by hand. An entrepreneur realizes that if he can set up a factory to make shoes by machinery he can make them more cheaply. A given amount of labour will produce more shoes if some of this labour is first used to make shoe-machinery and to build a factory. Hence the entrepreneur is prepared to pay interest on a loan which will enable him to do this, and thereby make a profit.

Why do not the lenders set up the shoe-factory themselves, and take the whole of the profit? We shall return to this point later. Meanwhile, a partial answer is that not everybody has the qualities needed for a successful entrepreneur. Lending transfers the use of money from those less qualified to those more qualified to organize and manage industry and trade.

It is money which is lent and borrowed. The money represents command over resources. The borrower can use it to employ labour, to buy materials, and so forth. Money lent is sometimes called "free capital." It is used mainly to buy or make durable goods, and stocks of goods, used in industry and trade. These things are sometimes called "real capital."

The expected rate of profit, or marginal productivity of capital, will tend to be the same in every field of industry and trade. For if one field offers better prospects than others, new firms will enter it and existing firms already in it will expand; free capital will flow into that field rather than into others. Sooner or later, the resulting increase in output will bring down the prices of the goods or services produced in that field. An increase in shoe-factories and in the output of shoes will bring down the prices of shoes; an increase in ships will bring down freight rates. This will go on until the expected rate of profit in that field falls to the level expected elsewhere.

This result *may* be brought about more quickly by a rise in costs. Suppose that house-building, for example, offers higher prospects of profit than other fields. The percentage added each year to the total stock of houses is quite small. Thus in England and Wales the number of houses in 1931 was over 9 million; the number of new houses built during the 'twenties averaged only 150,000 a year; during the building boom of 1934 to 1938 it more than doubled but did not exceed 350,000 a year. An addition of 2 or 3 per cent a year may not appreciably reduce house-rents for some years. But if the *rate* of house-building doubles, the cost of house-building may rise, and in this way the rate of profit in this field may soon be reduced to the level prevailing elsewhere.

An important exception to the above generalization is that under monopoly the assets owned by the monopolist may yield more than the current rate of profit because free capital seeking investment cannot enter that field.

A further point is that the prospective return from some assets, such as new gold-fields or a new type of business, may be very uncertain. But investors in such fields must and do decide, after weighing the various chances of gain and loss, that on balance the prospects of profit there are as attractive as elsewhere.

At any moment, if the total amount of capital invested were greater, its marginal productivity would be lower. That is why an increase in the supply of free capital seeking investment brings down the expected rate of profit and the rate of interest. What is the underlying reason for this? It is easy to see that more capital in one branch of production will increase the output and thereby reduce the prices of the products of that branch, thus reducing the rate of profit in that field. But why should an increased supply of capital spread over all fields in accordance with the preferences of consumers reduce the general rate of profit? If it reduces the prices of consumers' goods—and whether it does so or not depends on the monetary policy adopted—it will also reduce the prices of producers' goods of all kinds. We have to explain why the physical marginal productivity of capital diminishes when the amount of it increases. At first sight we cannot explain this by the Law of Diminishing Returns. For free capital can be turned into any form, can be used to purchase or hire any type of factor, so that we are not dealing with a case in which the supply of one factor of production increases relatively to that of others. The main explanation is that some factors cannot be increased at all or can be increased only at an increasing cost. The most suitable sites are limited in number; a greater output of many raw materials can be obtained only be resorting to less accessible or less fertile sources of supply; after a point, increased fertilization of existing land yields a diminishing return and the area of fairly fertile land is limited. Nor is it possible to produce robots or slaves at will: the amount of labour done is limited. Thus an increase in the amount of capital used does in fact involve a change in the proportions of the various factors, and the resulting combinations are less productive than they would be if every factor could be increased with equal facility. In consequence, the marginal return on capital at any moment, measured by the rate of profit per £100 invested, would be greater if there were less capital and less if there were more capital. But as time goes on, the march of science and discovery reveals new ways of using capital, that is, of increasing output by the use of more capitalistic methods of production, and this tends to push up the rate of interest. The influence of this force may be greater or less than the influence of the accumulation of capital, which tends to take place as time goes on, and which of course tends to reduce the rate of interest.

3. SAVING

A person need not spend all his income on satisfying his current wants. He can save some of it. Under our present assumptions, he will lend what he saves. Every pound that he saves and lends represents the power to command resources to the value of a pound. This power he gives up, for the time being; he transfers it to the borrower. Had he spent it, he would have consumed goods and services to that value. As it is, the borrower uses it to employ labour and materials to increase the stock of real capital.

We can lay down no absolute rules as to how the amount which an individual saves will vary with his income or with the rate of interest. Different people have different temperaments. Some are naturally very parsimonious and may choose to go short even of "necessaries for efficiency" in order to save more, while others are of a spendthrift disposition and will save little or nothing even if their incomes are large. Moreover, most people are guided by their expectations of how their income will change relatively to their needs in the future. If a person expects his income to increase in the future, he will tend to save less than otherwise. If he knows that his income will cease when he reaches a certain age and is compelled to retire, he will try to make some provision for his old age. A man who expects to have children will be likely to save more for that reason, since their maintenance and education will tend to increase his expenditure in the future.

Nevertheless, experience suggests that as a rule a person will save a larger amount, and probably a larger proportion, out of a bigger income. For he need spend only a certain minimum sum on his own consumption in order to keep alive and a somewhat higher minimum in order to keep efficient. Hence a rich man has, so to speak, a bigger margin available for saving than a poor man, and in fact a country like the United States saves much more per head than a country like India, most of whose inhabitants are very poor. It is probable that a country would save less if its total income were distributed fairly evenly among its inhabitants than if the same total income were distributed unevenly. But the matter is complicated in Great Britain and some other countries by the high death duties levied on large fortunes when their owners die. It has been estimated that rich people in Great Britain, taken as a whole, do not add enough to their fortunes during their lifetimes to cover death duties. But it would be rather misleading to say that, on balance, rich people consume capital, for out of its revenue, including its revenue from death duties, the State provides for the future in various ways.

Experience also suggests that as a rule more will be saved at a higher rate of interest. Doubtless there are some persons who are so rich, and others in whom the habit of saving has become so ingrained, that their saving is almost "automatic"; they would save about the same amount even if the rate of interest were considerably higher or considerably lower (provided, of course, that a change in the rate of interest did not increase or diminish their incomes and thereby their ability to save). Some people save in order to acquire sufficient capital to provide them with a money income on which they can live when they retire or which they wish to give to their children or to use for some other purpose. If they are aiming at a money income of a given amount per year, they will save less if the rate of interest is higher: for example, if the rate of interest were twice as high, they would need only half as much in order to get a given income from the interest upon their savings. It is probable, however, that most people would save more at a higher rate of interest and less at a lower rate. A man who is prepared to forgo a certain amount of present consumption in order to obtain, say, 3 per cent would probably be prepared to forgo rather more in order to obtain, say, 6 per cent. We are fairly safe in assuming that in most countries the supply schedule of individual savings, if depicted as a curve with rates of interest measured up the vertical axis, would slope upward to the right, although probably it would slope rather steeply.

A very low rate of interest might induce some elderly people to consume their capital by selling income-yielding assets in order to purchase annuities. For example, a man of 50 with an income from property could treble that income for the rest of his life (and die leaving nothing) by selling his property and purchasing an annuity with the proceeds if the rate of interest were only 2 per cent. The lower the rate of interest, and the older the person, the greater would be the proportionate increase in his (consumed) income from doing this. Many people, however, refrain from this course because they wish to provide for their children or other heirs. In so far as more annuities would be purchased at a lower rate of interest, the amount of new savings available would be reduced by the amount absorbed in purchasing the assets sold by people about to buy annuities and this would be a restraining influence upon a downward movement of interest rates.

In modern capitalist countries a considerable amount—probably more than half—of the total saving is performed by joint-stock companies, which from time to time use part of their profits to increase their assets instead of distributing the whole amount in dividends to their shareholders. Presumably, however, most of the shareholders do not object to such action; if a majority did object, they could prevent it, and any shareholder who does not like the policy of his company can sell his shares. Hence the saving performed by companies reflects, on the whole, the desires of the individual shareholders.[1] In the same way it may be claimed that most taxpayers are in general agreement with the saving performed by a Government in spending part of its revenue upon durable assets such as roads and buildings and upon such purposes as education and research.

We have taken saving to mean net saving, over and above what is required to maintain existing capital intact. But of course everybody who owns marketable assets is free to sell some of them and consume the proceeds. A company need not set aside from its gross earnings enough money to replace all its assets when they wear out or become obsolete. A Government can borrow more than it spends on capital purposes. In short, people must constantly choose not only whether they will save more or less but also whether, and if so to what extent, they will consume their capital. The total amount which, instead of being consumed, is spent in maintaining and increasing the total stock of capital may be termed "gross saving."

[1] It should be noted, however, that some authorities do not share this view. The issue is a highly complicated one, which we have not space to discuss fully.

4. THE RATE OF INTEREST AS DETERMINED BY REAL FORCES

The reader will perceive that our imaginary capitalist society resembles the socialist society, sketched in the first section of this chapter, in that the same real forces explain and govern the rate of interest in both.

At any moment there are very many ways in which output could be increased in the future by employing capital. Many thousands of schemes would yield receipts greater than their costs if money could be borrowed for nothing. Railways could be electrified, this industry or that could be mechanized, more houses and roads and ships and other durable goods could be constructed, and all at a profit. But labour and natural resources are limited in amount, and there are also limits to the extent to which people are able and willing to curtail their present consumption in order that existing factors may be used in more "roundabout" ways. Hence it is not possible to carry out all these schemes; it is necessary somehow to choose which shall be utilized and which forgone. Under socialism, the planning committee makes the choice, using a rate of interest for purposes of calculation. Under capitalism the rate of interest cuts down the demand for loans to the amount available, thereby ruling out all schemes which are not expected to yield profit at least as great as the interest which would have to be paid on the capital employed.

Under socialism, the planning committee decides how much shall be saved. In our imaginary capitalist society, this is decided by all the people who save, each acting as he thinks best. A higher marginal productivity of capital, and therefore a higher rate of interest, is likely to induce more saving.

Under socialism, the planning committee decides in which ways savings shall be invested. In our imaginary capitalist society, this decision is taken by entrepreneurs, who seek to make profits for themselves. But they can make profits (apart from monopoly and swindling) only by using free capital in the ways which best satisfy demand. The more efficient their methods, the greater their profits.

Upon our present assumptions, the rate of interest is a price. Like all prices, it is determined by supply and demand. It is the price paid for a loan. A rate of interest of 3 per cent means that the price of a loan of £100 is £3 a year. The rate of interest ensures equality between the demand for loans and the supply of loans. Savers, by spending less than their income on consumption, release resources to be used by investors to produce new capital goods. It is true that what pass between lenders and borrowers are sums of money, but these are only the means of effecting the transfer of resources from the production of consumption goods to the production of capital goods. If an invention, or the opening up of new territories, or the discovery of new mineral resources, or the increase of population, raises the profitability of capital and thus the demand for loans, the rate of interest will rise; if the community decides to save a larger proportion of its income, the rate of interest will fall. A shift in the demand curve or in the supply curve will change the rate of interest until the demand for loans and the supply of loans, or, in other words, until investment (the value of new capital goods) and saving, are again equal.

This account of the matter is not seriously modified by the fact that entrepreneurs are not the only borrowers. Governments and other public bodies borrow, and sometimes borrow large sums, for various purposes. Some persons borrow in order to consume more than their present incomes. We need not discuss these points; the demand for loans from other borrowers can be added to the demand from industry and trade. In the same way, the fact that individuals are not the only savers—much saving being performed, as we have noted, by companies out of undistributed profits—does not seriously affect the argument.

But the whole picture is quite transformed when we remove our other assumptions, and turn from our imaginary society to an actual capitalist society. This we shall now do.

5. TYPES OF ASSETS

In an actual capitalist society, there are various kinds of assets which a person can acquire instead of spending the money on consumers' goods. We shall simplify by considering only the four main types, which may be called for brevity bonds, shares, bills, and money balances. Each type has its advantages and its drawbacks.

Long-term fixed-interest securities may be termed *bonds.* They give the holder the right to a fixed money income. Suppose that a person lends £100 to the British Government, which in return pays him £3 a year. The long-term rate of interest is 3 per cent. The lender no longer has his £100. He could have spent it; he could have kept it in his home or at his bank. Instead he parted with it to the British Government. In place of it he has a right to £3 a year. He can sell this right at any time, through the Stock Exchange, to somebody else. So long as the rate at which the British Government can borrow for a long period remains at 3 per cent, this right will be worth £100 cash. This rate may rise. Suppose it rises to 6 per cent, and is expected to remain there. The market price of a 3 per cent security of face-value £100 will fall to £50. For anybody with £50 can exchange his £50 for a fixed money income of £3 a year. Or this rate may fall. Suppose that it falls to 2 per cent, and is expected to remain there. Unless the British Government has the option of paying off the holder of such a security, by giving him its face-value of £100, the market value of this security will rise to £150, because in order to get a safe fixed income of £3 a year, a lender must now lend £150. But whatever happens to the current rate of interest, and therefore to the market value of fixed-interest securities, the man who owns such securities continues to draw the same fixed money income.

We define the long-term rate of interest, therefore, as the rate at which the British Government can borrow for a long period. It is measured, at any time, by the "yield" on long-term British Government securities, expressed as a percentage of their value. Suppose, for example, that the newspaper reports that the price of 2½ per cent Consols is 80. This means that the right to £2 10s. a year for ever, guaranteed by the British Government, sells in the market for £80. The inference is that the British Government could borrow, on long-term, at the moment by paying £2 10s. a year for each £80 lent to it. 2½ is 3⅛ per cent of 80. The current rate of interest is 3⅛ per cent.

The yield on other fixed-interest securities, such as the "debentures" issued by various firms, will be higher than this. This is because the risk of default by the borrower is greater than the quite negligible risk of default by the British Government. Yields vary also for other reasons, into which we shall not enter, such as the date when the loan is to be repaid, and the "marketability" of the security.

The advantage of a bond, then, is that it yields a fixed money income. The drawback is that its market value may fall; in other words, the current long-term rate of interest may rise.

We turn to *shares*. Some pages back we asked why lenders do not take the whole of the profit for themselves. The answer is that they often do. The owner of an "ordinary" share in a company whose capital is represented by 1000 such shares, owns one-thousandth of the assets of that company and gets one-thousandth of the profits. In contrast to the owner of a "debenture," which is a bond yielding a fixed money income, he gets a fluctuating income, a share in the profits.[1] He plays little part, as a rule, in the management of the business, which is left to a salaried and qualified manager, but he shares in the risks, and in the profits. In these respects he resembles the man who invests his capital in his own business or in, say, houses. We use "shares" as a brief term to cover "real capital" yielding profits.

Suppose a man owns a share of face-value £100 in a shoe company. In a particular year his income from it, his "dividend," may be, say, £5. Had he bought a British Government security instead, he would have received only £3. The advantage of holding shares rather than (safe) bonds is that their yield is likely to be greater. But so are the risks. For any of several reasons—changes in tastes, a fall in population, the entry of new rival firms, cheaper imports, taxes on shoes, bad management—the demand for the shoes made by that company may fall. If so, the dividend will be less; perhaps there may be no dividend at all. The value of the share will fall. Its holder will have both a smaller income and less capital.

The rate of profit per annum on capital used in industry and trade is the net yield (after deducting depreciation charges) expressed as a percentage of the current cost of the assets. Their original cost is a matter of history, without any present significance. If a firm buys a machine for £1000 and soon after the cost of similar machines falls to £800, its machine should be valued at once at only £800, and the rate of profit should be calculated on that basis.

[1] There are various "hybrids." For example, some shares give the holders the right to a fixed money income plus something extra when profits are good.

Clearly there is a close connection between the rate of profit and the rate of interest. In the absence of risks, the two would be equal. For people have the choice of taking either profits or interest, of holding either shares or bonds. Owing to risks, the rate of profit is on the average somewhat above the rate of interest. But the two tend to move together. An increase in rates of profit will tend to increase the demand for loans from industry and trade, and to raise the rate of interest; and conversely.

Short-term fixed-interest securities may be termed *bills*. A three-months' Treasury Bill for £5000 is in effect a promise by the British Government to pay £5000 in three months' time. The rate of interest on bills varies with the credit-standing of the borrower and with the length of time before "maturity": that is, before they are repaid. As a rule, short-term rates are below long-term rates. Sometimes they are far below. Thus in September, 1937, a three-months' Treasury Bill sold for about £4993⅓, giving a yield equivalent to only $\frac{17}{32}$ per cent per annum. The main reason why short-term rates are lower, as a rule, than the long-term rate is that the risk of loss from a fall in the market value of the security is much less. Suppose, for example, that a man buys a £100 three-months' bill for £99 10s. At the end of three months he will get £100. If he wants to turn the bill into money after, say, six weeks, a bank will buy it from him (or, to use the technical term, will "discount" it for him). Even if the rate of discount on such a bill has risen from 2 per cent to as much as 16 per cent, he will get £98 for it. But a man who bought Consols at £94 at the beginning of 1935 and sold them towards the close of 1937 would have had to sell them at about £76.

Hence the advantage of holding bills is that the risk of capital loss is completely avoided unless they have to be discounted before maturity; and even in that event the capital loss will be small. The drawback is that the rate of interest received is lower than on bonds.

The fourth type of assets is *money*—holdings of cash or of cash balances. The advantage of holding money is that money alone can be used to pay a money debt. The lender on short term runs only a slight risk of losing any of his money. If he can wait until the loan matures, he will get back the exact sum which he lent. But he does forgo the advantage of holding money. We may perhaps regard a short-term rate as a payment to lenders to compensate them for this sacrifice of "liquidity." If there is a general increase in the desire to become "liquid," short-term rates will rise. This happens to a marked extent during a financial panic. Firms are very anxious to borrow money on short term in order to meet their curren money obligations and avoid bankruptcy.

6. THE RATE OF INTEREST AND THE TRADE CYCLE

Nobody, so far as I know, has ever explained the rate of interest in an actual capitalist country solely on the lines which we followed when discussing our imaginary society. For the influences which we left out are often of great importance in the real world; they may, and some economists think they usually do, completely swamp the others. We must now introduce them.

This means that we must refer to the trade cycle and the banking system—topics which we deal with later in the book, and then not very fully. The alternative course would be to defer this discussion until towards the close of the book, thus splitting our account of interest into two parts. I am reluctant to do this. The reader can of course defer the present and following sections, and return to them later, if he wishes. Meanwhile, we shall be as simple as possible.

We have seen that the volume of saving depends largely on the level of income. People, and therefore countries, save more out of a large income than out of a small one. But the income of a country may be low because many workers and other resources are unemployed. If they could be employed, if slump could be transformed into recovery or boom, the national income would be greater, and so would the volume of saving. Recovery would be brought about by an increase in investment. A larger demand for free capital from industry and trade, met by an increase in the money provided by the banking system, would increase employment, thereby raising incomes and causing savings to increase. The supply curve of saving, therefore, is not independent of its own demand curve (which reminds one of the man who had to pay a higher price for a parrot at an auction sale because it had been bidding against him).

Take the opposite case. Suppose that people decide to save more. They therefore spend less. The demand for consumers' goods falls. If entrepreneurs are not prepared to increase their investment, the result may be an increase in unemployment, so that total savings (owing to the fall in incomes) are in fact no greater, and probably less, than before. The attempt to save more may bring about a slump; the industries making consumers' goods do badly, and order less machinery and equipment and materials.

This difficulty arises because the decisions to save are taken by one set of people, and the decisions to invest by another set. Saving and investment are not co-ordinated as two aspects of one and the same plan.

We have seen that the demand for loans from industry and trade, reflecting the amount of investment which entrepreneurs are prepared to undertake, depends on the expected rate of profit. This in turn depends on trade prospects. If these seem good, entrepreneurs may want to borrow a good deal. If they seem bad, some entrepreneurs may not want to borrow at all and others may not be able to borrow because potential lenders doubt whether they will be able to repay.

It follows that if fluctuations in the state of trade and the amount of unemployment are considerable, they may exert a dominating influence on the expected rate of profit and on the volume of investment and saving.

7. THE RATE OF INTEREST AS DETERMINED BY MONETARY FORCES

The demand for loans comes not only from borrowers who want the money in order to buy new capital goods or other things. It comes partly from borrowers who want to hold some of the money in the form of a balance at the bank. The supply of loans does not come only from savers. It comes also from banks which create new money and from people who decide to reduce the amount of money which they hold.

We could take account of these facts by considering the total supply of loan money, and the total demand for it, from all sources. Instead, we shall give a brief account in this section of the theory that the rate of interest equates the demand for money, meaning money balances and not loans, with the supply of money.

Let us begin with the demand for money. Most people and firms are constantly receiving money and paying out money. Nevertheless every person or firm holds on the average, taking one day with another, a certain sum of money. What determines the amount of money which, on the average, a person or firm wishes to hold?

Part of the money is held to finance current transactions. People know that they will have to make money payments in the near future. In the course of their business activities they may be suddenly called upon to make such payments. Therefore they hold money balances. Given the habits of the community, we can take the size of these balances, held for convenience, as given.

If money is held in excess of the amounts needed for these purposes, why is it held? For it is held at a cost. It could be used instead to buy securities. It could, that is to say, yield the current rate of interest. As it is, it yields nothing. It is an idle asset.

The reason is that people fear that the prices of securities may fall. A bond bought to-day at £100 may fall to £90, so that a buyer would get £3 income, say, for the year but would lose £10 of the £100 which he gave for the bond. The capital value of money, on the other hand, is perfectly safe; £100 will always be worth £100.

It is clear, however, that the reluctance of people and firms to buy securities will vary with the income which they forgo by holding assets in the form of idle money. Their demand for money as against securities will not be independent of the rate of interest. The higher the rate of interest, the greater is the inducement to hold less money and more securities, and conversely. We thus obtain a demand curve for money balances depending on the rate of interest. For interest is the price paid for money; the cost of holding money is the interest forgone by choosing to hold money rather than securities. This demand curve will be downward sloping, illustrating the fact that the lower the rate of interest, the larger will be the amount of money which people will wish to hold.

We turn now to the supply of money, in the sense of the total amount of money—coins, notes, and bank deposits—in existence. This amount is determined by the banking system. And all the money that is in existence must be held by someone.

This may seem confusing. We have just stated that the demand for money of the community as a whole depends on business habits on the one hand, and on the rate of interest and people's preferences for money balances rather than securities on the other hand. Now we declare that the total amount of money in existence, which must all be held by someone, is determined by the banking system.

This, however, involves merely an application of the general supply-and-demand analysis. If the supply of any good is independent of its price, that is, completely inelastic, all of it will be sold. Consumers will determine not the total amount which is bought, for the whole supply must be sold, but the price at which that total amount will be taken off the market. The same relationship holds here. The community as a whole does not determine the total amount of money in existence, but it does determine the price at which this money will be held. And this price, the price of money, is the rate of interest.

The rate of interest equates the supply of money as determined by the banking system with the demand for money as determined by people's habits and their preference for liquidity. If the amount of money increases, people will, in the first instance, hold more money relatively to their other assets than before. But since, before, the advantages of liquidity, derived from holding money, were just equal to the rate of interest, these advantages will now be less than the rate of interest. The relative marginal utility of holding money will have fallen, because the amount of money held is greater than before. Hence the community as a whole will try to exchange part of its money for securities. The amount of money is, of course, given. But if everybody demands securities the price of securities will go up; in other words, the rate of interest will fall. And it will continue to fall until it reaches a level at which the community as a whole is willing to hold the total amount of money in existence.

Again, suppose that the "liquidity-preference" of the community increases. This means that people's demand for money increases. Everybody will try to sell securities for money. The price of securities will fall, in other words, the rate of interest will rise. It will continue to rise until it reaches a level at which people will want to hold no more money than the amount in existence.

How does this theory manage to rule out the influence exerted on the rate of interest by the demand for loans from borrowers and the supply of loans by savers? In a progressive community, new borrowing for capital accumulation, and new lending, are taking place. What about the view that the rate of interest equates the two?

The answer given by those who hold this theory is as follows. Over a period of time, such as a year, the volume of new securities offered by borrowers and the volume of new securities demanded by savers will be small relatively to the total amount of securities in existence. A small addition both to the demand for and to the supply of securities will have no influence on their price.

An increase in the demand of borrowers will find some people willing (so it is said) to lend more, to offer more money, without a change in the rate of interest. And conversely, if saving increases, new borrowers can be found. For the demand curve for money with respect to the rate of interest is very elastic; people are willing to reduce or add to their hoards without any significant change in the price of securities. Hence, it is concluded, in the real world, where owners of wealth balance the advantages of holding securities against the advantages of holding money, the rate of interest is determined (given the amount of money) by "liquidity-preference," and not by the profitability of investment or the willingness to save.

8. THE RATE OF INTEREST AND SPECULATION

The preceding section gave a brief account of a theory which a number of economists accept. We must now point out that it needs considerable modification. Even if we accept the general standpoint that the rate of interest is a monetary phenomenon, depending on the amount of money and liquidity-preference, we cannot accept the theory just outlined as it stands.

That theory distinguishes only two types of assets—money and securities. As we have already seen, there are four main types. We must now take account of "bills": of short-dated securities, yielding a short-term rate of interest.

The term "liquidity" is ambiguous. It is often said that some assets are more liquid than others because they can be sold more easily for money. Another notion is that one asset is more liquid than another if its money value is less likely to fall. In the present context, we must insist that "to be liquid" means one thing and one alone. It means "to hold money."

Money yields no interest. The alternative, it was said, to holding money is to hold "securities"—meaning bonds. Bonds do yield interest; on the other hand, their market value may fall.

But what about bills? Bills too yield interest; and their market value, provided one can wait a little while until they mature, will not fall. One can sacrifice liquidity, and get interest, without risking one's capital, by holding bills. From this standpoint, a deposit at the Post Office Savings Bank offers the same opportunities to a relatively poor man as a Treasury Bill to a rich man.

Hence the cost of keeping liquid, the interest forgone by holding money, is measured not by the long-term rate of interest but by the short-term rate. A man who wants to safeguard the money value of his capital can do so either by holding money or by holding short-term securities. If he holds the latter he gets interest, at the short-term rate, but he sacrifices liquidity.

The long-term rate of interest is usually, but not always, above the short-term rate. The difference, over a long period, may be regarded as a "risk-premium" received by holders of bonds for taking the risk that their prices will fall.

The long-term rate of interest, as measured by the price of Consols, has in the past remained remarkably stable for a number of years at a stretch. Income has fluctuated considerably, liquidity-preference has gone up and down, banking policy has changed, but it has required an upheaval such as that caused by the "cheap money" policy adopted by the British Government in 1932 to bring about a large change in the price of Consols.

This requires explanation. The explanation is that "speculators," if we may use the term in a highly respectable sense to include banks, insurance companies, investment trusts, discount houses, and similar institutions, are at work. The majority of people who buy bonds doubtless buy them to hold. They want the fixed money income which bonds yield, and they get that whether the prices of their bonds fall or not. But there are also speculators. When the prices of bonds fall below what they have come to regard as the "normal" level, these speculators sell some of their short-term securities and buy bonds. When the prices of bonds are regarded by them as unduly high, they do the opposite.

Hence it is the short-term rate which is fundamental. This is determined largely by banking policy, by the amount of money created by the banking system; and partly by liquidity-preference. The long-term rate may be regarded as the expected average of future short-term rates (over a long period) plus a risk-premium. The long-term rate may be kept fairly stable, for several years at a time, by speculation.

9. CONCLUSIONS

We warned the reader at the outset that the subject of interest is difficult and controversial. We have felt it our duty to present both the view that interest is determined by real forces and the view that it is determined by monetary forces. Nobody, I think, would deny that in a modern capitalist society monetary influences play a large part in determining the rate of interest. Whether they completely swamp the real forces is a matter for debate.

Our own view is that for Great Britain the explanation given in the preceding section is fairly satisfactory. But it covers only three of our four types of assets. It explains short-term rates of interest and it explains the price of Consols. But the rate of profit in industry and trade, which strongly affects the prices of shares, varies much more than the long-term rate of interest. Often it is well above the latter. During a severe slump the expected rate of profit on new capital in many lines may be zero or negative. An increase in the quantity of money may, probably will, raise the price of Consols somewhat. But it will not necessarily lead to greater investment in industry and trade. The rate of interest at which firms can in fact borrow from the public or the banks, which is not the same as the yield on Consols, might have to become negative in order to induce firms to invest in more real capital.

The reader should note that the monetary theory of interest which we outlined and then modified relates to a closed community. The rate of interest within a country may be affected by borrowing from abroad or by lending to other countries.

The general level of interest rates in poor countries, which are over-populated or not developed, is well above the general level in wealthier countries. This can be explained only by real forces. The marginal productivity of capital in, let us say, Bulgaria is high because capital is relatively scarce and people are not rich enough to save much. Banking policy in Bulgaria can doubtless do something to affect interest-rates there, but it cannot enable Bulgarian farmers or factories to borrow at 3 or 4 per cent.

If important new opportunities for investment arose, similar to those provided in the past by railways or the discovery of new mine-fields, it is probable that the rate of profit would rise and that, even in Great Britain, speculators would change their views—downwards—as to the "normal" price of Consols.

CHAPTER XIX

RENT

1. RENT IN THE ORDINARY SENSE

In ordinary speech the rent of anything is a periodical payment made for the use of it. Thus the owner of a piece of land may lease it for a term of years to a tenant who contracts to pay him a fixed sum of money each year for the use of it. This fixed sum is known as the rent of the land.

The owner of any durable good may hire it out to somebody, in return for an agreed periodical payment, instead of using it himself. Thus rent may be paid for the use of a house or a machine or a refrigerator, to give only three examples, as well as for the use of land. The agreement may stipulate that the rent shall be calculated in terms of wheat or some other commodity, but as a rule rents are fixed in terms of money.

During the period of the agreement the owner is in a similar position to a person receiving a fixed income as interest. Consider, for example, a landlord who has leased his land to a tenant at a fixed annual rent. He and the tenant have made an agreement and both must abide by it. As time goes on, conditions may change. The net money yield of the land may become higher than was expected when the lease was signed. The landlord could now get a higher rent if he were free to make a fresh bargain. But he is not free to do this: he is bound by the terms of the lease. Conversely, if the net money yield of the land becomes lower than was expected, the tenant must nevertheless continue to pay the rent agreed upon. When the lease is up, the landlord can of course make a new agreement, either with the same tenant or with a new one. If the net money yield of the land is expected to be higher than when the old lease was signed, he can obtain a correspondingly higher rent; if it is expected to be lower, he must accept correspondingly less in order to get a tenant.

Clearly, changes in the net money yield of land and, in general, in the market value of the services rendered, per unit of time, by a durable good will make rents fixed by agreement in the past either higher or lower than the rents obtainable at the moment for the use of similar goods. This raises certain problems, such as those connected with the burden of fixed charges during a depression, which we need not consider here. At any moment the annual rent obtainable for a durable good will tend to equal the expected net annual value of its services.

If similar goods can be readily produced, the rent obtainable will also tend to equal the current rate of interest upon their present cost of production. If it were greater, free capital would enter that field, in order to earn more than the prevailing rate of profit, and the increased supply of such goods would reduce the value of their services. Conversely, if it were less, free capital would avoid that field, goods of that type which wore out would not be replaced, and in time the value of the services of such goods would be raised until it again became worth while to produce them.

The term rent is sometimes used by economists to denote the earnings of more or less specific means of production whose supply cannot be increased or diminished. Rent in this sense is a kind of surplus. Before considering whether all land, or some land, or any other durable good, does in fact yield rent in this sense, we shall illustrate this special meaning by a hypothetical example.

2. RENT AS A SURPLUS

Suppose that a given area of land can produce only wheat and nothing else, and that no other land can produce wheat. Suppose further that this wheat-land is homogeneous, any acre being a perfect substitute for any other. These assumptions, of course, are most unrealistic. We make them in order to illustrate the special meaning of "rent" as a kind of surplus.

If this land produces wheat without the co-operation of any other factor of production, each acre will produce a given quantity of wheat per year, and its annual earnings will be simply the value of that quantity of wheat. Thus, given the amount of wheat-land, and the amount of wheat produced by it each year, its earnings or "rent" will depend upon the demand for wheat. Since the wheat-land is homogeneous, all of it will be employed (unless it is all owned by a monopolist or unless the owners combine to act monopolistically) so that the amount of wheat forthcoming each year is fixed.

Now suppose that the amount of wheat produced in any year varies with the climate. Favourable climatic conditions result in a bigger crop. Whether the owners of the wheat-land gain or lose by a bigger crop depends upon the elasticity of the demand for wheat. They may gain or they may lose. Consumers of wheat of course gain by a bigger crop, and even if the producers lose, it is reasonable to suppose that the gain to consumers

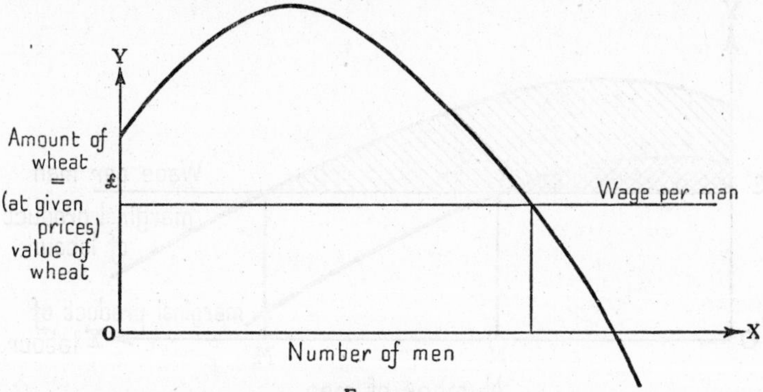

Fig. 32

outweighs the loss of producers, since the total supply of goods is increased.

In fact, however, land alone can produce very little. It needs the co-operation of other factors. Let us simplify by supposing that it needs only the co-operation of homogeneous labour. If this labour is employed mainly in other industries, the wage which owners of wheat-land must pay in order to hire it is fixed. The wage which they must pay will equal the marginal productivity of that labour in other industries.

How much of this labour will be employed per acre—or per 100 acres—of wheat-land? The more labour there is employed (up to a certain limit) the greater will be the total output of wheat. But after a point, as more labour is employed on a fixed amount of land, the marginal product of that labour will fall.[1] Thus an owner of wheat-land, regarding both the price of wheat and the wages of labour as fixed for him by the market, will

[1] See Fig. 32.

employ whatever amount of labour maximizes his own income or "rent" from his land. This amount of labour will be the amount which makes the fixed wage per man equal to the value of the marginal product of the labour.

In fact, as more men are employed upon the wheat-land, wages per man will tend to rise owing to the increased demand for labour from the wheat industry. And the prices of wheat per bushel will tend to fall, owing to the increased output of wheat. But we can suppose that this has happened in the past, and that

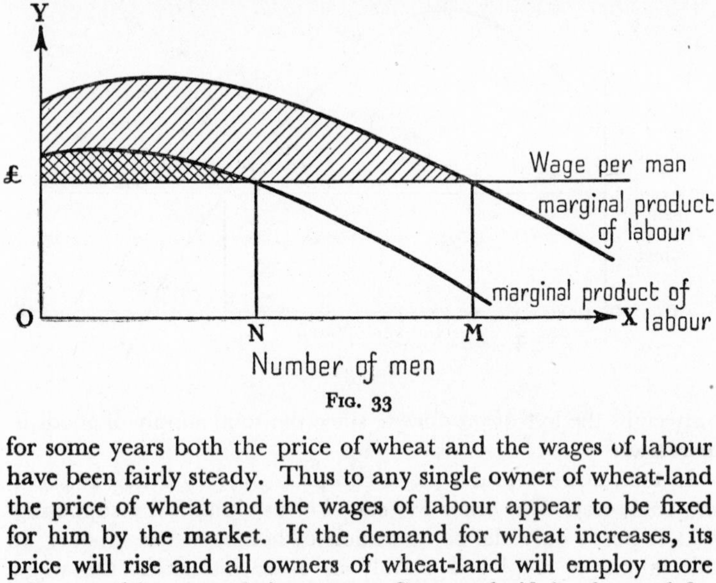

FIG. 33

for some years both the price of wheat and the wages of labour have been fairly steady. Thus to any single owner of wheat-land the price of wheat and the wages of labour appear to be fixed for him by the market. If the demand for wheat increases, its price will rise and all owners of wheat-land will employ more labour and increase their output. Conversely if the demand for wheat falls. If the wages of labour fall, owners of wheat-land will employ more labour, and conversely if they rise. In this way the preferences of consumers make themselves felt through the price-system.

Thus rent in the economic sense can be defined as a surplus accruing to a specific factor the supply of which is fixed. If the supply of wheat-land were not fixed, some of it would be devoted to other uses when the price of wheat fell and to uses requiring less labour when wages rose, and other land would be put under wheat when the price of wheat rose.

If the fixed supply of wheat-land is not homogeneous, it is easy to understand why better land will earn more per acre than worse land. It will earn more because it can produce more. In Fig. 33, the more fertile acre employs *OM* men and the shaded area represents its rent; the less fertile acre employs *ON* men and the cross-shaded area represents its rent.

And it is easy to understand why some wheat-land may be left unused. It will be left unused if the value of the wheat it produces is less than the price which has to be paid to the co-

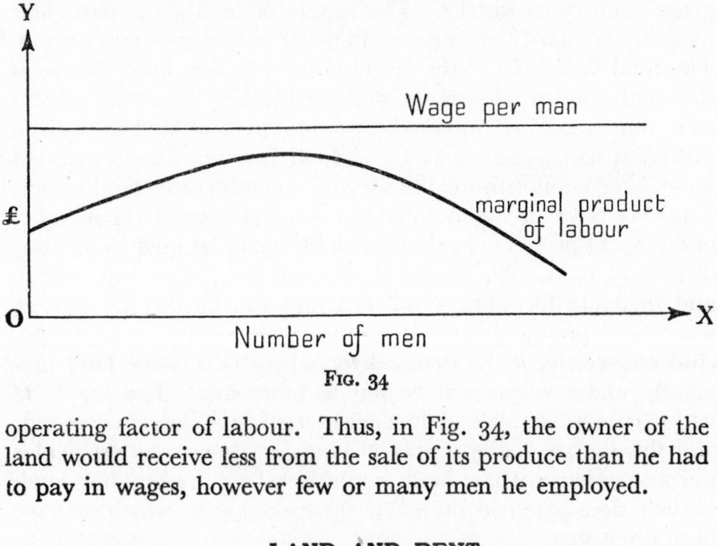

FIG. 34

operating factor of labour. Thus, in Fig. 34, the owner of the land would receive less from the sale of its produce than he had to pay in wages, however few or many men he employed.

3. LAND AND RENT

The significance of rent, in the special sense which we have just illustrated, springs from the fact that the supply of a factor which yields rent cannot adapt itself to changes in demand. The supply of such a factor will not diminish, however low its earnings may fall. It has no supply price. If the whole of its earnings, or rent, were taken away, for example by taxation, the number of units in existence would remain the same. And its supply cannot be increased. A rise in the demand for it will increase its earnings without bringing any additional units into existence, and thereby reducing towards their former level the earnings of existing units. Its earnings are a surplus, or rent, and changes in them do not lead to changes in the supply of the factor.

We must now turn to the real world and consider questions of fact. In what sense, if at all, does land yield rent? And do any other factors yield rent?

The "supply" of land, in this connection, may mean either (*a*) the supply of land for a particular purpose, such as growing wheat or serving as sites for buildings, or (*b*) the total area of land in the world as a whole, or (*c*) the total area of land in a given country or district. The supply of land for a particular purpose can fairly readily adapt itself to changes in demand. The total land area of the world is more or less fixed, but so is the total number of workers, and neither fact is very significant from our present standpoint. The total area of land in a given district is fixed, and, in so far as land in other districts cannot serve as a good substitute, this may be of considerable significance.

(*a*) We have already pointed out, when discussing the mobility of factors of production, that much land can be used in any one of several ways. An increased demand for, let us say, wheat, and therefore for wheat-land, can and will be met by turning some land previously used for other purposes into wheat-land. And conversely, if the demand for wheat falls, some land previously under wheat will be put to other uses. The supply of wheat-land is flexible and does adapt itself to changes in demand; and this is true of the supply of land for almost any particular purpose. Hence wheat-land, or pasture-land, or building-land, as such, does not yield "rent" in the special sense which we have been discussing.

(*b*) The total land surface of the world, however, is more or less fixed. This means that a permanent increase in the demand for land in general, due for example to the growth of population, would result in a permanent rise in the incomes of landowners, and a permanent decrease would result in a permanent fall in their incomes.

It is true that land can be reclaimed from the sea. Holland has reclaimed many square miles, and Capetown is about to increase its area by some 50 per cent in this way. But it is very unlikely that the land area of the world will be increased by any considerable percentage. The costs of reclaiming land are so high, even in those districts where it can be done most cheaply, that a very large rise in land-rents could take place without leading to much new reclamation.

It is also true that the productivity of land can be increased: for example, by the use of fertilizer. Free capital will be invested in this way, in response to an increased demand for the products of land, until the return on such free capital, at the margin, is no higher than the rate of profit elsewhere. But "improvements" to land are not a perfect substitute for land itself. After a point the increased application of fertilizers, or anything else, to a given area of land, yields diminishing returns. If an increased demand for agricultural products makes it profitable to invest more free capital in improving existing land, that very fact indicates that the rent or surplus accruing to the owners of land has increased. In terms of our diagrams, the increased prices of agricultural products have raised the curve showing the marginal productivity, in terms of value, of co-operating factors. The curve showing their physical marginal productivity remains the same, but a rise of, say, 20 per cent in the prices of the products raises the value of any given marginal product by 20 per cent. This increases the surplus accruing to the landowner and makes it worth his while to employ more co-operating factors, thus increasing his surplus still further.

The supply of land as a whole, then, is more or less fixed and does not respond to changes in the demand for land as a whole. Much the same is true of labour. The total number of workers available is more or less fixed. It is not in the least certain that a general rise in wages will increase the number of births and thereby, eventually, the total number of workers. Nor is it at all certain that a general fall in wages will diminish the number of births, although if the fall is sufficiently great it will doubtless eventually reduce numbers by sheer starvation. Neither acres nor workers are homogeneous, so that a general increase in the demand for labour, or for land, may bring into use workers, or acres, not worth employing before. Free capital can be invested in increasing the productivity of either labour or land and in converting one type into another; one can train an unskilled worker to become, say, a plumber and one can convert some pasture-land into, say, market gardens. The supply of either land or labour *for any particular use* can usually be increased or diminished.

Probably most changes in economic conditions increase the demand for some uses of land and diminish the demand for others. The fact that the total area of land is fixed (whilst always a limiting influence upon output) becomes significant, from our present standpoint, only when there is a permanent change in the demand for land as a whole. And the same is true, within limits, of labour. If we say that the income accruing to land as a whole is of the nature of rent, we must say the same of labour as a whole.

(*c*) Nevertheless, the geographical location of any particular acre is fixed, and this may be important. Suppose that all the land in a particular district is wheat-land. An increased demand for wheat will mean that land elsewhere is put under wheat. The landowners in that particular district may not get an appreciably larger income than before, because wheat can be grown elsewhere and sold in competition with their wheat.

But it may be that the demand for land in a particular area increases, and that land in another area will not be able to meet this demand. A leading example is the demand for sites in a given district. Thus the growth of London has raised land values in and around London. The fact that the demand for sites in South Wales has diminished has not prevented (although it may have somewhat checked) the rise in land values in London. Some people and firms may buy land in South Wales instead of in Greater London if the price difference is large enough. But land in South Wales is, for most purposes, a very imperfect substitute for land near London, and sites cannot be transferred from South Wales to London. The supply of sites in London is limited. An increased demand for them raises their value and therefore raises rents even if at the same time land values and land-rents are falling in other districts. It is true that people who want to live in London can live some distance out and spend time and money in travelling to and fro. But they will do this only if site-rents in London rise so much that they think it worth while to incur these costs.

Another important example arises from the fact that a national government may restrict the import of agricultural products. This raises the prices of agricultural products within that country and thereby tends to raise the price, and rent, of land as a whole within that country. Land elsewhere is not permitted to compete freely, for obstacles are placed in the way of its products when they try to enter.

The English classical economists laid considerable stress upon rent. That is the main reason why we have devoted a chapter to this subject. For, after all, we are only repeating from a somewhat different standpoint what we have already discussed in connection with the mobility of factors and the significance of specificity. We may hazard the opinion that the English classical economists were impressed by two facts. Landlords formed a distinct and important social class and the question whether import duties upon corn should be increased or reduced or abolished was a very live issue at the time when they wrote.

We have still to consider whether there are factors other than land which are fixed in supply, in any significant sense, and which therefore yield rent. There certainly are such factors. The owner of a mineral spring with special and unique properties, or of an historic house which people pay to visit, the Siamese twins and the Dionne quintuplets, the International Nickel Company (which owns nearly all the nickel in the world), all obtain an income of the nature of rent. And the concept of rent can be extended to include many other incomes, or portions of incomes. It can be extended to the incomes of factors which are durable, so that it takes a considerable time for their supply to diminish if their incomes fall, and which take a fairly long time to produce, so that a rise in their incomes increases their supply only after a considerable interval. We discuss this concept of quasi-rent in the next section. The concept of rent can also be extended to cover the surplus received by any given unit of a factor above its "transfer earnings." We discuss this in our final section.

4. QUASI-RENT

In the long run the earnings of durable goods will tend to equal the current rate of interest upon their current cost of production. If their earnings are greater than this, more of them will be produced, and this will bring down the prices of their products. If their earnings are less than this, they will not be replaced as they wear out—any sums set aside towards replacement being invested in other ways—and this will raise the prices of their products.

But it may take quite a long time for the supply of such a good to adjust itself completely to a change in the demand for its products. If so, the earnings of units of such a good are of the nature of rent, and have been termed Quasi-rent.

Let us consider first a fall in the demand for the products of a particular kind of good. Let us take, for example, a ship. The decreased demand for cargo-space reduces the earnings of ships below the equilibrium level, if we may use this term as a brief expression for the current rate of interest on their current cost of production. If it takes a fairly long time to reduce the number of ships sufficiently to raise the earnings of those which remain up to the equilibrium level, two conditions must be present. In the first place, ships must have a long life, so that those which wear out or sink or, in general, go out of existence in any year form only a small proportion of the existing stock. The number of motor vehicles, for example, would be reduced by a given percentage sooner than the number of ships because motor vehicles have a shorter life. In the second place, ships must be fairly specific. A fall in the demand for, say, cinemas might not reduce their earnings much if some cinemas could readily be converted into garages, and the demand for garages was increasing. A fall in the demand for one type of ship might be met by converting ships of that type into ships of other types, the demand for which had increased. But if the demand for ships in general falls and there are no other uses, nearly as profitable, to which ships can be turned, at relatively small expense, the owners of ships are helpless. Their ships must continue to be used as ships, although their earnings may be well below the equilibrium level.

There is, of course, the alternative of withdrawing the good from use—scrapping it, or laying it up, or closing it down. But it pays to continue using a durable good if the value of its product exceeds the cost of the co-operating factors—that is, more than covers "prime" or "operating" costs. Its owner prefers it to earn something, however small, rather than nothing. (We assume that its value as scrap is negligible.) Moreover, there are costs involved in closing down and subsequently restarting such things as blast furnaces and coal-mines. Hence their owners, hoping that the demand for their products will revive, may continue to work them even if receipts are less than prime costs.

Nevertheless, it should be noted that there is no hard and fast line between "supplementary" and "prime" costs. The division between them depends on the length of the period. Most equipment needs to have some of its parts replaced at fairly frequent intervals, others at less frequent intervals, and so on. This fact may mean that a good is withdrawn from use although its earnings exceed those costs which recur every week. A time may come when a relatively heavy payment for renewals, replacements, or repairs must be made if the good is to continue in use, and its owner may decide to scrap it or leave it idle rather than make this payment. On the other hand, an owner may be led, step by step, to make a series of small payments of this kind, each necessary at the time to keep the good in working order, although over a period the costs incurred add up to more than the gross receipts. This clearly depends on the foresight of owners and on whether they expect conditions to improve in the future.

The owners of durable goods (including land) may have borrowed money at fixed interest upon the security of these goods. A fall in the demand for their products may make it impossible for them both to cover their prime costs and to pay their fixed-interest charges. If this state of affairs seems likely to continue, there will probably be some kind of financial reorganization under which the mortgage- or debenture-holders consent to accept less than the fixed money income originally agreed upon.

Let us now consider a rise in the demand for the products of a particular kind of good. If the earnings of such goods remain for a long time above the equilibrium level, two conditions must be present. In the first place, such goods must take a long time to produce or a large increase in their annual output must be possible only at a considerably increased cost. Otherwise the flow of new free capital into that field would soon increase the existing stock until earnings fell again to the equilibrium level. In the second place, it must not be possible for the owners of other goods to increase their earnings by converting them, fairly quickly, into goods of this type. A rubber plantation is a good example of a good whose supply takes time to increase, for rubber trees take five years or more before they begin to yield.

Ships, to revert to our former example, take time to build. The capacity of existing shipyards is limited and additional skilled workers can be obtained, as a rule, only if wages are raised. And other goods cannot be turned into ships.

As a rule, goods whose supply will not rapidly be diminished in response to a fall in demand are also goods whose supply will not rapidly be increased in response to a rise in demand; although logically we should distinguish between these two classes, in fact they often coincide. The earnings of such durable and specific goods are of the nature of rent. The term quasi-rent is sometimes confined to the earnings of goods—machines, houses, ships, rubber plantations, and so on—but logically it applies also to the earnings of groups of workers, such as doctors, whose supply cannot rapidly be increased or diminished.

5. TRANSFER EARNINGS

Much land, many workers, and some producers' goods could be employed in any of several industries. The amount of money which any particular unit could earn in its best-paid alternative use is sometimes called its transfer earnings. If the demand for the products of a given industry decreases, that industry will tend to contract. It will contract because the earnings of factors employed in it will tend to fall, inducing some factor-units, including some entrepreneurs, to leave it and go elsewhere. The units which leave will be those whose transfer earnings are now greater than the amount they can expect to earn if they remain in the industry. Conversely, an industry expands (relatively, to others) by attracting factor-units who can now earn more in that industry than elsewhere.

Suppose, for example, that the industry is wheat-growing. Some land now under wheat could earn just a little less by being used for some other purpose, such as growing barley. Quite a small fall in the earnings of wheat-land, or quite a small rise in the earnings of, say, barley-land, will induce the owners of this land to put it under barley instead of under wheat. Some other land now under wheat could earn, say, 90 or 95 per cent as much elsewhere. A fall of 5 or 10 per cent in the earnings of wheat-land might induce the owners of this land to use it for some other purpose; and so on. At the other extreme there may be some land which is practically useless for anything except growing wheat. It would continue to grow wheat even if its earnings fell to nearly zero. The whole of its earnings, from the standpoint of the wheat-growing industry, are of the nature of rent, for they are not necessary to induce it to remain in the industry. And, in general, the excess of what any unit gets over its transfer earnings is of the nature of rent. Nevertheless, if an industry employs units of a factor with relatively high transfer earnings side by side with other units (which, when employed in that industry, are just as good as the others) whose transfer earnings are very low or zero, these latter suffer no disadvantage from being specific and enjoy an income largely of the nature of rent. For, in general, one unit will earn the same as an equally efficient unit employed in the same industry, and if a given industry must pay a certain price per unit in order to attract enough units of a given factor away from the alternative employments open to some of them, it must pay that price to specific and non-specific units alike.

The concept of transfer earnings is useful for the light that it throws on the extent to which the costs of an industry may vary with its output. For example, if an industry can expand substantially, at least in the short run, only by drawing upon particular workers and other factor-units who are getting considerably higher earnings where they are at present, the industry in question must offer them still more to induce them to move into it. This means that any substantial expansion of its output, at least in the short run, must be accompanied by considerably higher average and marginal costs per unit of product arising from the increased prices which must be paid to such factor-units, including similar units which were already in that industry.

CHAPTER XX

ECONOMIC PROGRESS

1. THE INDUSTRIAL REVOLUTION AND AFTER

EVER since the so-called "industrial revolution" took place in England in the latter half of the eighteenth century, the general trend of economic activity, at any rate in Western and Westernized countries, has been strongly upward. There has been a great increase in populations: for example, that of England and Wales grew from about 9 million in 1801 to 16 million in 1841 and over 40 million to-day. There has been a much bigger increase in the volume of production, although this cannot be measured at all accurately because new products have constantly been discovered and the proportion of total output formed by manufactured goods and by services has risen while the proportion formed by agricultural products has fallen. On the best estimate available, which is inevitably a very rough one, the volume of production per head of population in England and Wales is at present two to three times as great as it was a hundred years ago. This has brought about a very considerable rise in the general standard of living. This again cannot be measured with any accuracy. But contemporary accounts show plainly that less than a hundred years ago many English working-class families, and especially those of farm labourers, lived in what we should regard to-day as great poverty, being at times on the verge of starvation. There is no doubt that the present-day worker enjoys a standard of food, housing, and clothing, together with facilities for travel and instruction and amusement, far superior to those of his grandfather or even his father. The length of the working week, which can be measured, has certainly fallen. Factory and building workers had a working week of over sixty hours until the nineteenth century was two-thirds over; in 1913 most of them worked for fifty-four hours; to-day they work for forty-eight or less. The fall in death-rates can also be measured. The death-rate in England and Wales was over 21 per 1000 as late as 1871–80; to-day it is below 12. The high death-rates of the past were due partly to lack of medical knowledge, but partly to sheer lack of adequate nourishment. We have quoted a few figures for England and Wales. Comparable increases in population, output, and standards of living took place in most Western countries.

Without going into any detail, we may make some general remarks about this striking and quite unprecedented expansion of economic activity. We may first point out that we are not discussing something which has run its course and is now over. The growth of population in Western Europe is coming to an end but, apart from that, the broad upward trend has continued right down to the present time and is still going on. A few facts and figures will illustrate this. During the last two or three decades great new industries have come into being which make or use products, such as rubber, petroleum, motor cars, electrical apparatus, and cinematograph films, which were formerly either unknown or of relatively little importance. The world output of coal rose from a mere 12 million tons in 1800 to some 45 million in 1840, 500 million in 1890, and 1200 million in 1913. Since then, the output of coal has increased less than that of most commodities. Substitutes, such as fuel oil, have partly taken its place. Nevertheless, the world output in 1936 was 1300 million tons, while the world output of crude petroleum had grown from 20 million tons in 1900 to some 50 million in 1913 and some 230 million in 1936. The world output of pig-iron has increased from less than 200,000 tons in 1800 to some 10 million in 1870, 40 million in 1900, and 90 million in 1936. The world output of steel, owing to the increased use of scrap, exceeded the world output of pig-iron shortly after 1900 and has since grown faster, rising to more than 120 million tons in 1936. In a sense the industrial revolution was based on coal and iron. Iron was needed to make the machines and, later, to construct the railways and rolling stock, and coal was needed to provide power for the machines and locomotives. But if the output of coal and iron (together, nowadays, with that of steel and petroleum) is taken as a measure of "industrialization," the above figures show plainly that industrialization has been gathering momentum as the years have gone by.

The use of machinery driven by steam-power spread only slowly. Watt invented his steam-engine in 1776 and the rotary movement, which enabled machinery of all kinds to be driven by steam, in 1782, but in 1800 there were only 289 steam-engines in the whole of England. In 1835 there were only 123,000 power looms in the United Kingdom (as compared with nearly a million to-day) of which all but 7000 were in the cotton industry Except in the cotton industry, factory production did not become at all general until about 1840 or 1850 in England and still later in other countries.

This was partly because labour was not very mobile. In some countries most workers were bound to the soil, under some form of serfdom, until the nineteenth century was well advanced. In England they were free to move but many were reluctant to migrate northward (for the bulk of the population was in the south) and enter the factories. In the early years, Irish immigrants formed a considerable proportion of the factory hands. But the main reason for the slow growth of machine production was that progress had to take place in many different lines of activity. Decades passed before the power loom enabled the output of cloth to keep pace with the potential increase in yarn production due to improvements in carding and spinning, and still more decades passed before comparable improvements were made in the finishing processes. The early steam-engines and machines were made largely by hand. They were very defective and were often breaking down. It was not until after about 1825 that important inventions of machine tools began to revolutionize the machine-making industry, enabling accurate and reliable machines to be turned out in large numbers. Workers had to be trained to make machines, to repair them, and to use them. Moreover, the growth of machinery was partly dependent on the progress of technique in coal-mining and in smelting and working iron. Thus the complex structure of production meant that the full utilization of improved technique in one field had to await improvements in other fields. This, of course, is just as true to-day as in the past. It is also true that improvements in one line often stimulate, and sometimes assist, improvements in other lines, while these in turn may facilitate further progress in the first line. Thus the minds of inventors were turned towards the need for power looms by the improved spinning machinery. Again, the use of steam-engines for pumping water out of coal-mines cheapened coal, and cheaper coal both reduced the cost of making steam-engines and increased the demand for them.

A most important illustration of the interrelation of progress in different fields is to be found in the development of transport. Specialization between districts cannot go very far if the area of the market is restricted by the high costs of transport. Districts which cannot produce certain commodities for themselves will import only comparatively small amounts if transport costs raise their prices considerably. Most districts which can produce them will tend to do so. For the comparative advantages and consequent lower production costs of some districts—arising from a climate and soil particularly suitable for certain crops, or from the presence of coal, or iron ore, or other minerals, or from economies of scale or of concentration—will be outweighed by the high costs of sending the commodities any considerable distance. In the eighteenth century the costs of transport were very high and only quite valuable commodities were worth moving any great distance, especially by land. Improvements were made by Macadam and others in the roads, canals were built, and rivers were made more navigable, but the really big change came with the building of railways. The Stockton and Darlington railway, the first public railway to use steam locomotion and carry passengers, was opened in 1825, but the nineteenth century was half over before England had covered its area with a network of railway lines, and in other leading countries this development came still later.

The railways opened up whole continents. People could now settle in the interior instead of concentrating near the coasts and along the rivers. Crops could be grown, and minerals mined, in the interior for sale to distant markets. In 1842 the economist, McCulloch, wrote that no live cattle or salted meat was ever likely to be imported into England except from the countries round Hamburg "and the imports thence cannot be considerable." Not an ounce, he said, would ever come from South America. In 1845 Cobden pointed out that the English farmer had in effect a protective tariff of 10s. a quarter on corn, that being the cost of moving wheat from Danzig to London. The rapid growth and improvement of transport completely changed all that. The construction of railways in America and other overseas countries, together with the continuous improvements in the technique of shipbuilding, made it profitable, by the eighties, for large quantities of grain and meat to be exported to Western Europe from overseas. The same continuous reduction in transport costs gave English and other manufacturers a world market.

Continuous improvements in the technique of producing iron and, later, steel gave a great impetus to the growth of railways. The railways and rolling stock in turn demanded very large quantities of iron and steel. The increased demand made possible economies of scale in the production of iron and steel which further cheapened the prices of rails and rolling stock. Cheap transport also increased the demand for iron and steel by the expansion of manufacturing and the consequent growth in the orders for plant and equipment of all kinds, while at the same time it enabled iron- and steel-works to obtain coal or iron ore (or, later, scrap) from a distance at a lower cost than before. Thus the development of the iron and steel industry helped the development of railways and shipbuilding and conversely.

2. THE CAUSES OF ECONOMIC PROGRESS

Our brief survey of economic expansion during the last 150 years or so seems to show that the main force was the progress of technique. This conclusion is substantially true, but it requires some comment and qualification.

We may point out, to begin with, that it is misleading to think of technical progress in terms of a few striking inventions. There have indeed been outstanding landmarks such as Watt's steam-engine or the Bessemer process of making steel. But even the greatest inventors built on the work of others, and their inventions have been improved very much as time has gone on. There were steam-engines before Watt, and the efficiency of steam-engines has been continuously increased from his time down to the present day. The same applies to the technique of producing steel. Every year many thousands of inventions are made and applied throughout the various fields of economic activity. Any particular invention, taken by itself, may seem of minor importance, but taken together they continuously transform and improve methods of production or bring new products on to the market. Nowadays most discoveries and improvements are made not by isolated individuals but by teams of trained researchers working for a large firm or a Government.

Nor should we think of technical progress as applying only to manufacturing and transport and public utilities. Inventions in other spheres are also important. For example, the use of cheques, the device of joint-stock companies, and improvements in cost accounting, have all assisted the expansion of industry and trade. Again, the continuous growth of medical knowledge has considerably increased the efficiency of the working population. It should also be remembered that the laws and institutions of a country can do much to facilitate or hamper its economic progress.

It is perhaps worth repeating that improvements in agricultural technique were essential to any great expansion of industry and trade. The most urgent want is the want for food. Families with small incomes spend the greater part of them on food. So long as the labour of one family on the land provided little more than food for itself, the great bulk of the population had to be employed in agriculture. Few could have been spared from the land to produce goods satisfying less urgent wants, whatever inventions were made in other spheres. Hence the various improvements in agricultural technique, such as the discovery of the rotation of crops and of improved methods of feeding and breeding cattle, together with the supersession of the open-field system, did much to make the industrial revolution possible. As the years have passed, the technique of agriculture has been continuously improved. New varieties of crops have been discovered which are more prolific or grow faster or are better able to resist disease or unfavourable weather conditions. There have been constant improvements in methods of feeding and breeding and in the preparation and fertilization of the soil. There have been great developments, especially during quite recent years, in the use of agricultural machines such as the tractor and the "combine." Improvements in transport, as we have already implied, made available to industrial populations the products of vast areas of land overseas. We may again illustrate how progress in different spheres is inter-connected. Improvements in agriculture facilitated the movement of workers to other occupations and improvements in the production of machinery and petroleum and chemical fertilizers increased the efficiency of agriculture. It may also be noted that the continuous progress of agricultural technique, together with the low income-elasticity of demand for food, has meant that a diminishing proportion of the population—even in countries with much land, such as the United States and Australia—has been engaged in agriculture: there has been a continuous "drift to cities."

Many inventions require capital for their application. They must be embodied in such forms as railways or ships or blast furnaces or pipes and wires or machinery. It is not true that all inventions require more capital. Many of them show how existing types of machines and other producers' goods can be made more efficient, so that less capital is needed than before to produce a given output. In the same way cheaper transport may mean that a smaller number of works, situated in the most favourable locations, can produce as much as a larger number of works each supplying its own district. But the great expansion of output during and since the industrial revolution would have been impossible without a very great increase of capital, and it is usually true that increased investment is necessary for any substantial economic progress.

In the past, economic expansion has been accompanied by increased division of labour. Thousands of new occupations have been split up into a large number of processes, often with specialized machinery or equipment for each process. The widening of the market has greatly increased territorial division of labour or, in other words, specialization between districts. It is true that some inventions enable one machine or piece of apparatus to replace several specialized machines and workers. Thus pins are made nowadays by a single machine: there are no longer eighteen separate processes. But, on the whole, economic progress and greater specialization march together.

Technical progress, investment, and division of labour supplement and assist one another. Inventions often require investment, and workers trained to particular jobs, before they can be applied. The greater output resulting from their application affords a bigger margin for saving and facilitates specialization on research. Increased saving stimulates the search for new methods of using capital productively.

The general trend of economic activity has been upward, as

we have seen, for well over a hundred years. But there has not been steady and uninterrupted expansion. There have been periods when the upward movement has been less marked and there have been times when it has been reversed. What are the forces militating against economic progress?

Disasters such as floods and fires and earthquakes and dust-storms destroy or injure persons and property. But the greatest disaster of all is war. As a rule there is monetary inflation and practically full employment of labour and productive resources during a war. But a large proportion of the available means of production is engaged in war activities. Workers are taken from other occupations and put into the army or navy or air force or into factories making munitions and other war material. Hence fewer consumers' goods are produced and the general standard of living falls. The same applies, although usually to a smaller extent, to a period of intensive rearmament. A country nearly always ends a war worse equipped than before to produce goods required in peace-time. Men of working age will have been killed or wounded, so that the number of workers will be reduced more than the number of children and old people. Buildings, ships, and other assets may have been destroyed by the enemy. It is almost certain that men and materials will not have been spared from war purposes to maintain in good repair and efficiency, let alone to increase, the stock of buildings and other assets not required for war purposes.

The English classical economists believed that the growth of population would tend to wipe out the benefits of economic progress. Increased output would give a higher standard of living for a time, but this, they thought, would lead to an increase of numbers, since fewer deaths would take place from inadequate nourishment and earlier marriages would lead to more births. The growth of population would go on until the operation of diminishing returns brought down the standard of living again, despite the technical progress that had occurred, to its previous level.

This is a complex question. We have seen that in fact the standard of living in Western countries has considerably increased over the last hundred years or so, despite the growth of population. We know also that, owing mainly to the deliberate restriction of births in the past, the population of Western Europe will soon stop increasing. But it is a matter for speculation whether the volume of production per head, and the standard of living, would not be higher in any particular country if its population were smaller. On the one hand, a sudden and considerable reduction in numbers would mean more land and other assets per head. On the other hand, there might be less scope for division of labour and for economies of scale. More or less "indivisible" means of production, such as railways and bridges and power stations, would be less fully utilized. My own view is that countries such as India and China, with populations which are very large relatively to natural resources, would almost certainly have a higher standard of living if their populations were much smaller, and that this is possibly true of most countries, even including such countries as Canada and Australia. This is as may be. But even if it is right, a different point remains open, namely, whether these countries would be better off to-day if their populations had grown more slowly. This is much more doubtful. For in that event there would have been less investment and probably less invention. A rapidly growing population diminishes the risks of investment, for the demand for any particular product is likely to increase, even if it increases less than was hoped, as time goes on. It also facilitates adjustment between industries and occupations, as explained in Chapter XIV, section 2.

An important and recurring check to economic progress is provided, especially in modern countries, by general depressions of trade. The great depression which lasted from about 1930 to about 1934 will be fresh in the minds of some readers. This was the most recent and the worst, relatively to the period before it, of a whole series of depressions which have occurred at intervals in the past. It is generally agreed that these depressions, and the trade cycle of which they form part, are associated with fluctuations in the amount of investment. We must therefore consider briefly the causes and effects of such fluctuations.

3. FLUCTUATIONS IN INVESTMENT

We define investment, in the present context, as the total output of producers' goods and durable consumers' goods. Some of this output consists of renewals and replacements. Net investment is total investment less what is required to maintain capital intact. Thus, at times, net investment may be negative. For example, firms may use part of their amortisation quotas to pay dividends. But gross investment, which we are considering, is always positive.

The investible funds which are used to pay for the labour, materials, and other factors employed in producing this output come from any or all of four sources: amortisation quotas, new savings, new money, and balances previously idle. The new money may come from an increased output of gold, but under modern conditions it is usually provided by the banking system. The banks increase their loans or buy more securities, thus increasing their deposits. Such an increase in the amount of money is known as inflation and tends to raise prices,[1] thereby imposing "forced saving" on persons with relatively fixed incomes. Of course, after the new money has been spent by those who first receive it, it comes into the possession of others, and if they choose to save some of it their saving is voluntary. The term "forced saving" merely indicates that people with fixed incomes are constrained by the rise in prices to reduce their consumption. When balances of cash or bank deposits previously idle are used to buy goods and services, this also tends to raise prices.

Increased saving, or inflation, may not lead to a corresponding increase in investment. People may prefer to hold their savings in the form of idle balances. Entrepreneurs may not be willing to borrow much more from the banks, even if the latter considerably reduce the rate of interest which they charge on their loans and overdrafts. Thus the British banks reduced their rates during 1932 and 1933 without inducing entrepreneurs to borrow much more. The banks bought more securities, thereby increasing the deposits of those who sold them the securities. In this way the total of bank deposits was considerably increased. But a large part of these deposits remained idle. Their owners did not use them to buy goods and services; they did not circulate. Hence the policy of inflation, or "cheap money," failed, during these years, to give the desired stimulus to investment and activity.

The fact is that low rates of interest are not in themselves

[1] Unless unemployed men and resources are available.

a sufficient stimulus to investment. Apart from Government expenditure on public works, on which losses may be deliberately incurred in the hope of promoting a general increase in activity, investment takes place only if it seems profitable. Of course a reduction in interest rates is a reduction in costs and may lead entrepreneurs to put into operation plans which did not offer a sufficient prospect of profit when interest rates were at their former and higher level. But the expected rate of profit does not depend only on the rate of interest: it depends on the margin by which receipts are expected to exceed costs. Entrepreneurs will expand their businesses, or start new ones, only if they expect the demand for their products to increase, or the costs of making and selling them to diminish, sufficiently for them to sell a greater output than before at a profit.

The volume of investment fluctuates much more over time than the output of non-durable consumers' goods. In the past, big spurts of economic activity (apart from those taking place during a war) have nearly always been associated with big increases in the volume of investment while periods of depression have been marked by large falls in that volume. Thus in the United States at the bottom of the recent depression—in the first few months of 1933—the output of producers' goods was only a third of what it had been at its peak in 1929, whereas the output of consumers' goods was only about 15 per cent below its 1929 peak. Similar divergences occurred, although on a smaller scale, in Great Britain and other countries.

The fluctuations are most marked in the output of durable goods such as buildings and ships, and plant and equipment of all kinds. Thus it is the constructional industries, and those supplying them with materials, which show the most violent fluctuations in output and employment. It will be remembered that one reason for this is that the annual output of durable goods to provide for replacements is a relatively small proportion (varying with the life of the goods) of their existing stock. Hence a speeding-up of the replacement demand, or orders for new goods of this type from entrepreneurs who wish to increase their plant and equipment or to set up new works, will lead to a considerable increase in the activity of the constructional and allied industries, and a falling-off in the replacement demand or in other orders will lead to a considerable decrease. But anything whatever which makes entrepreneurs anticipate bigger profits will tend to stimulate investment and anything whatever which makes them fear reduced profits, or losses, will tend to check investment. This leads us to the subject of the trade cycle.

4. THE TRADE CYCLE

The trade cycle may be defined, rather baldly, as a period of prosperity followed by a period of depression. It is not surprising that economic progress should be irregular, trade being good at some times and bad at others. But it is surprising that the upswings and downswings should last for so long and should be so marked. The fact that a period of depression usually lasts for several years, during which a considerable proportion of workers and other resources are unemployed, certainly demands explanation.

Economists are not in complete agreement as to the causes of the trade cycle. Moreover, every trade cycle in the past has had some features peculiar to itself. Hence we can give only a very general account of the course and causes of trade cycles, concentrating on those features which have been common to nearly all of them. For example, we shall assume that the upswing is accompanied by an increase in the amount of money, since this has always happened in the past, as well as by a fall in the demand to hold money balances (which increases the speed at which money circulates) although the latter by itself, without any increase in the amount of money, would probably suffice to support a boom. Again, we shall assume that the prices of goods and services rise during a period of expansion or boom. This did not happen during the boom of 1925–29 in the United States, but nevertheless our explanation applies, with slight modifications, to this boom as well as to others. For the rapid growth of technical progress reduced costs, but the increase in the amount of money and in its velocity of circulation prevented prices from falling appreciably, thus raising the expected rate of profit and stimulating investment.

A period of prosperity is distinguished by an increase, and a period of depression by a decrease, in the volume of output and employment, especially in the constructional and allied industries.

This means, as we have seen, that during a period of prosperity entrepreneurs expect good and rising profits, while during a period of depression they fear losses.

We should not exaggerate the waste of resources during a depression. There is usually a considerable increase in unemployment among wage-earners. But farmers working on their own account often maintain or increase their output. Their real incomes are reduced, for the prices of their products usually fall much more than those of products whose supply has been considerably diminished. But they work themselves and their land as hard as they did before. In a predominantly industrial country, the percentage of unemployment may rise for a time above 20 or even 30. But this is a temporary peak. If we take the period of depression as a whole, the average percentage of unemployment even in an industrial country has seldom exceeded 15. It should be remembered that 5 per cent or more are often unemployed even in good times, that those dismissed are probably somewhat less efficient than those who remain, that the unemployment of plant and other resources is probably less than the unemployment of labour, and that most indexes of production and employment exaggerate changes because they give undue weight to the constructional and allied industries. We conclude that the fall in total output during a depression seldom averages as much as 10 per cent.

Of course even 10 per cent makes a big difference, and, since the waste is so obvious, economists and statesmen have devoted a great deal of attention to the search for methods of preventing and curing depressions. But we should retain our sense of proportion. Given a reasonably adequate system of unemployment relief, the bulk of the loss falls upon the receivers of profit and (in so far as debtors default) interest rather than upon wage-earners. Nowadays trade unions usually succeed in resisting large cuts in wages, so that the fall in the cost of living during a depression tends to give those workers who remain in full employment a larger real income than they enjoyed before. Moreover, in the past the rising trend of output per head has meant that each depression has taken place at a higher level of real income than the previous one. Thus in Great Britain during the last depression the real wages of workers in full employment were appreciably higher than during the previous years, and most workers drawing unemployment benefit enjoyed a standard of living which, although far below what may be regarded as desirable, was undoubtedly superior to that of an unskilled worker before the war of 1914.

We shall begin our brief account of the trade cycle with the transition from depression to recovery and expansion. In the past, recovery has usually begun with some revival of investment, although there is no reason why it might not begin with an increase in the total expenditure on consumers' goods which would induce the firms producing those goods to increase their orders for producers' goods, thus stimulating investment. The revival of investment may be due to the discovery of some important new field in which capital can be profitably employed. For example, the building of railways, the development of the gold-fields of the Rand, and the construction of plant and equipment to generate and distribute electric current, all represented big spurts of investment. Again, it may be due to Government expenditure on public works or rearmament or similar projects. If this expenditure is made with newly created money (and is not financed by increased taxation which compels taxpayers to reduce their expenditure or by loans which the lenders would otherwise have invested in industry), it will probably increase the amount of money in circulation. The wage-earners employed by the Government will spend their wages on consumers' goods and the firms supplying materials will take on more workers and will give bigger orders to the firms who provide them with their equipment. Thus employment and expenditure may increase. A "cheap money" policy may stimulate investment after a time. In particular, the demand for houses is likely to increase when rates of interest are unusually low. Moreover, the mere fact that a depression has lasted for several years may tend to promote recovery. Firms who have delayed ordering replacements will begin to feel that, judging by past experience, the depression will not last very much longer. They will therefore order replacements while prices are still low. Other firms may be compelled either to order replacements or to close down. Wages will have fallen as the depression went on. Some writers believe that reductions in wages make the depression worse because they reduce total expenditure. On the other hand, reductions in wages improve the prospects of profit and often induce firms to employ more men than they otherwise would and to order more producers' goods to be used in combination with the extra labour. On balance, reductions in wages probably stimulate activity much more often than not. They are more likely to do so if they take place, as they did in the nineteenth century, piecemeal and over time than if they are general and simultaneous. For in the latter event consumers' demand (by wage-earners) will be strongly and suddenly curtailed.

Once recovery begins, it usually gathers momentum as time goes on. The process of expansion is cumulative and self-reinforcing. At the close of a depression many workers are unemployed, many plants are working well below capacity, and so on, so that the constructional and allied industries can increase their output, when investment revives, largely by drawing upon workers and other resources previously idle. They pay out increased amounts of money for labour, materials, fuel, and other requirements. Much of this is spent by the newly employed workers on consumers' goods. This induces firms making consumers' goods to increase their equipment. Again, some of it is spent on plant and equipment by the firms supplying the constructional industries. Thus the demand for the products of those industries is further stimulated; they take on still more workers and increase their capacity; and this in turn further increases the demand for goods and services. There is thus a kind of snowball effect. An increase of output in one part of the economic system increases demand and therefore output in other parts, this in turn further stimulates the first part, and so on.

We may illustrate this from the housing boom in Great Britain. This began in the last quarter of 1932, at the bottom of the depression. The value of "plans passed" for dwelling-houses then shot upwards by a third, after which it continued to increase. The number of houses built exceeded the 1929 level by 20 per cent in 1933, by 40 per cent in 1934, and by 60 per cent in 1935. Building employed 211,000 more workers in June, 1935, than in June, 1932. But the construction and equipment of new houses give employment to workers in industries other than building. Thus, to take some leading examples, the increase in employment between 1932 and 1935 was some 21,000 in bricks and tiles, 16,000 in stoves, grates, etc., 10,000 in electrical wiring and contracting, 9000 in iron and steel tubes, 29,000 in electric cables, etc., 16,000 in furniture making, and 25,000 in gas, water, and electricity supply. Perhaps a third of the increase in employment over these years was directly due to the housing boom. Fuller employment meant that wage-earners and others had more to spend, so that the demand for consumers' goods, including houses, increased.

As recovery goes on, entrepreneurs and others become more optimistic. They see that demand has increased and they come to believe that it will continue to increase. This means that they consider that the prospect of profit has improved and is improving. They will tend to borrow more from the banks and from the public to spend in increasing their "capacity." The public, for their part, will be more willing to lend. Their desire to be liquid will have diminished with the return of confidence, and balances previously idle will be lent to industry and trade.

The increase in the amount of money and in its velocity of circulation will tend to raise prices. At first the prices of goods and services may rise little, since unemployed workers and other resources can be obtained at prevailing prices. But if the expansion goes on, a time will come when all the labour and resources which it is practicable and profitable to use will already have been absorbed. There may still be a considerable number of workers out of a job. But these will be in process of moving from one job to another, or for some reason will be unable or unwilling to move into another district or occupation where they could find work, or will be among the least efficient in their occupation and therefore not worth the standard wage for that occupation. In a rather technical sense there will be full employment. A continued increase in the amount of money or in the rate at which it circulates will then tend to raise prices—of labour and materials as well as of finished goods—rather than to expand output. Indeed, apart from technical progress or an increase in numbers or in hours of work, output can expand further only if labour and other resources are diverted from the production of consumers' goods to the production of producers' goods. Further expansion of output will then take place after an interval during which the stock of durable goods is increased.

What are the forces which bring a period of expansion to an end and usher in a period of depression?

Some writers lay much stress on monetary influences. The boom may be stopped by a deliberate reduction in the amount of money. The monetary authorities may decide to put the brake on rising prices because they fear that if they do not there will be a serious slump in one or two years' time, and they prefer a mild recession now, or if the country is on the gold standard and its prices have risen more than prices elsewhere (so that its imports rise relatively to its exports), they may deflate in order to check an outflow of gold. Or the commercial banks may restrict their loans. Thus the total monetary demand for goods and services becomes less. The expectations of entrepreneurs are disappointed. The expected rate of profit falls considerably. Pessimism replaces optimism, especially if there have been important bankruptcies; the desire to become liquid increases; investment and employment fall off.

But expansion is likely to cease even if there is no deliberate deflation. The demand for some important type of durable good, which has been increasing during the boom, may fall off. For example, so many houses may have been built that the demand for still more houses declines. This would not matter very much if the workers and other resources released from the building industry, and from industries largely dependent on it, could readily find employment elsewhere. But in fact they cannot, or at least they do not. Many workers are reluctant to learn a new occupation or to move to a new district. Hence there is a decline in the demand for consumers' goods and in the derived demand for producers' goods. Moreover, some important financial firms may have lent imprudently to builders. If the buildings cannot be sold or let, and the builders cannot repay, some of these firms may be forced into bankruptcy, thus giving a shock to confidence and thereby increasing the desire to be liquid. Again, suppose that the Government has embarked on a large rearmament programme. At first, the firms who have obtained contracts to supply the Government will give increased orders to the constructional industries. But when they have sufficiently enlarged their capacity, their orders will fall off, although the Government demand for armaments continues. In so far as the engineering, iron and steel, and similar industries expected the demand from these firms to be maintained, they will be disappointed. In any event they may be compelled to dismiss workers, and these may not readily find jobs elsewhere.

The rise in costs may tend to stop the expansion. Interest rates tend to rise as profits increase. Wage-earners demand and obtain increased wages after the cost of living has risen appreciably. After full employment, in the technical sense, has been reached, "bottle-necks" appear. The supply of certain materials, or of certain types of skilled workers, cannot be increased quickly, and the prices of those available may rise quite substantially in response to the increased demand. Hence some entrepreneurs may find that they have been too optimistic. They had not anticipated that costs would rise so much; their expected profits become smaller or turn into losses; some of them may be forced into bankruptcy and others may contract their output.

It will be remembered that the rate of expansion of output must slow down after the idle labour and other resources worth employing have been absorbed. But the output of the constructional and allied industries, up to this point, will probably have been considerably more than was required simply to provide for replacements. Part of it will have gone to increase the plant and equipment of other industries. This part will no longer be demanded when these other industries cannot further increase their output. Thus activity in the constructional and allied industries will not merely stop increasing—it will actually diminish, and perhaps considerably.

Some writers maintain that people and firms save a larger proportion of an increased income. Hence the increase in incomes during a boom causes a diminishing proportion of total income to be spent, thereby reducing the derived demand for producers' goods and checking investment. This is possible, but in such a case we should expect the boom to end with interest rates at a low level. In fact the opposite is much more frequent. It may well be urged that in the later stages of a boom, when wages have increased, the prices of ordinary shares have risen, and optimism has grown, the proportion of income spent will again rise. If the banks are unwilling to increase the supply of money still further, rates of interest will rise. The consumers' goods industries will tend to draw labour away from the constructional and allied industries, which will be faced with a rise in wages and in interest charges together with a reduced demand for their products. In such circumstances the end of the boom may be marked by failures in these industries.[1]

We have been covering controversial ground, but we hope that we have demonstrated possible ways in which a boom may collapse and turn into a depression. After this has happened, the process of contraction tends to be cumulative and self-reinforcing in just the same manner as the process of expansion. A fall in the output of some industries reduces demand and output in others; pessimism grows and spreads; the desire to be liquid increases and leads to a growing volume of idle balances withheld from expenditure. This continues until something happens to improve the prospect of profits sufficiently for investment to revive a little, after which recovery may slowly gather momentum.

[1] In general, an increase in the quantity of capital goods tends to lower their marginal productivity, thereby reducing the demand for investible funds and the rate of interest. But the opposite may happen if specific capital goods have been produced in the expectation that the demand for their products will be greater than in fact it proves to be. Suppose, for example, that a large hydro-electric plant has been constructed and that the demand for electric current is much less than was expected. The plant is there; its owners will try to get as big an income from it as possible, although they cannot get as much as they had hoped; it will probably pay them to reduce considerably their charges for electric current, in order to keep the plant fairly fully utilized. This will stimulate the demand for electric motors and other equipment to use electric current. In this way the production of some capital goods (on over-optimistic expectations) may stimulate, instead of checking, the demand for others—namely, for those needed to complete the processes begun by the former. If this happens in several important industries a boom can end with a shortage of capital, and high rates of interest, even if there is no monetary deflation.

See Hayek. "Investment that Raises the Demand for Capital," *Review of Economic Statistics*, Vol. XIX, No. 4, November, 1937.

BOOK IV

MONEY AND BANKING

CHAPTER XXI

THE NATURE AND FUNCTIONS OF MONEY

1. INTRODUCTION

THE modern economic world is based on division of labour. Few people, except farmers, produce for themselves as much as one-tenth or even one-hundredth of the goods which they consume. Most production takes place for the market; the products are sold and the producers buy what they want with the proceeds —in effect, they exchange their products against others. Moreover, the production, and the distribution to consumers, of most commodities involves a long chain of processes and the co-operation of many different factors of production. A society organized on these lines could not exist unless it used money. Hence it is quite unreal to compare a modern community with an imaginary community which resembles it in all respects but does not use money, for such a community is not possible. In the same way it is somewhat illogical to distinguish certain "functions" performed by money. All these so-called "functions" of money are simply different, but related, aspects of the fact that the use of money is essential to a community based on complex division of labour and exchange.

Nevertheless it will be convenient to make our discussion follow the traditional lines. Writers on the subject usually assert that money has four functions. It serves as a medium of exchange, as a measure of value, as a standard for deferred payments, and as a store of value. We shall discuss the role of money under these four headings, except that we shall use the phrase "a liquid asset" instead of "a store of value." This discussion will at the same time explain the nature of money, for "money is that money does." The present book, however, continues to assume a closed community, with a single monetary system. Problems arising from the existence of several countries, with different currencies, are postponed until the following book.

2. MONEY AS A MEDIUM OF EXCHANGE

Exchange without the use of money must take place by barter. The main difficulty of barter is that it requires "a double coincidence of wants": a man must find another who both has what he wants and wants what he has. This is seldom easy even with finished commodities. Thus a story is told—typical of many others—of a traveller in Africa who wished to obtain a boat. The owner of the boat was willing to part with it but wanted ivory in exchange. The traveller had no ivory. He found a man who had ivory and wanted cloth. He himself had no cloth. But he had wire, and he found yet another man who gave him cloth for his wire, so that he could then exchange the cloth for ivory, and finally exchange the ivory for the boat. Clearly trade under such conditions must be very restricted in scope, and just because it would be so restricted it is probable that there would be few generally accepted market values, and that a good deal of time might therefore be spent in bargaining. A further point is that some goods (such as boats) cannot be divided into portions without destroying their utility; hence the owner of such a good could not exchange part of it against the goods of one man, part against the goods of another, and so on. Most exchanges in the modern world are not exchanges of finished commodities. How, for example, would wages be paid under barter? The employer might, where possible, pay his workers by giving them a share of what they had helped to produce, leaving them to barter the wheat, or coal, or yarn, or whatever it might be, as best they could, in order to obtain what they themselves wanted. Clearly this plan could not be followed in the case of workers engaged in supplying transport facilities or other services or in producing indivisible and valuable goods such as battleships. An alternative plan would be for the employer to barter his products for goods which his workers, and shareholders, and suppliers of raw materials, wanted. But this discussion need not be prolonged; its purpose is merely to show that a modern economy could not well continue without the use of money.

Money overcomes the difficulties of barter by serving as a general medium of exchange, or means of payment. Money is something which everybody prerepared to accept in exchange for goods or services. A person will accept money in payment, not because he necessarily wants money for its own sake but because he knows that other people in turn will accept it from him in return for the goods and services which he himself requires. Hence money has been defined as "generally acceptable purchasing power" and when this aspect of money is under consideration the monetary unit is called a unit of currency because it "runs" from hand to hand. The use of money thus greatly facilitates exchange and leads, under competition, to market prices, thus avoiding much waste of time in bargaining. Further, whatever serves as money can be made divisible: for example, in Great Britain we have shillings and pence as well as pounds.

3. MONEY AS A MEASURE OF VALUE

When something comes to serve as a generally accepted medium of exchange, it is natural to express values, to make contracts, and to keep accounts in terms of that something. The advantage of this is not merely that everything has a price—that is, a value in terms of money—instead of having a separate value in terms of each of the many commodities against which it might exchange. The use of money as a measure of value immensely facilitates economic calculation. A consumer with a certain money income is confronted with money prices, and these enable him to decide which assortment of goods and services he wants to buy. The changes in the demands of consumers affect prices and thereby induce entrepreneurs to produce more of the goods for which demand has increased and fewer of the goods for which demand has decreased. An entrepreneur knows the market price of each factor of production. He can therefore plan the location of his establishment, the size of his output, and his methods of production in such a way as to maximize his profits. This means that factors are directed towards those uses in which their products have the greatest value. If, to revert to a simple example, a piece of land yields a greater money return under wheat than under barley this means not only that its owner will gain more by using it for wheat but also that consumers prefer it to be used for wheat. Such calculations, however, would be much more difficult and much less accurate if there were no common measure for comparing values and costs. The "price-mechanism" under such conditions would work only roughly and cumbersomely. At present, entrepreneurs take the risk that prices will change to their disadvantage. Under barter, this risk would be much greater owing to the difficulty of calculating and forecasting exchange ratios between the goods they produced and the various goods which their employees and their suppliers demanded in payment. Hence there would be much less division of labour.

The monetary unit for purposes of calculation is called "the unit of account." Normally the unit of currency and the unit of account are the same, for clearly the use of money as a measure of value springs from its use as a medium of exchange. It is possible, however, for the two units to be different, provided that an exchange ratio between them can be somehow established. Thus in Germany in 1923, when prices were rising very rapidly, contracts were often made in terms of Swiss francs or United States dollars. When the time for payment arrived, the payment was made in marks, the number of marks given being the number required to equal the specified sum of francs or dollars at the rate ruling at the time in the foreign exchange market. The mark remained the unit of currency but the unit of account was the franc or the dollar.

4. MONEY AS A STANDARD FOR DEFERRED PAYMENTS

Contracts, including loans, are usually made in terms of money. This is because people believe that the value, or purchasing power, of money is not likely to change much during the period of the contract. If people fear that the value of their money may change considerably, they tend to make contracts in terms of something else, which they expect to remain fairly stable in value. We have already noted that in Germany in 1923 many contracts were made in francs or dollars, although the national unit of account was the mark. During subsequent years, many contracts made both in Germany and in certain other countries contained a "gold clause" intended to protect the creditor against a fall in the gold value of the currency in question. In effect, the debtor agreed to pay a sum of money equal at the time of payment to an amount of gold specified in the contract.

If there were no money, lending of all kinds would be much

restricted owing to the risk that the value of the commodity in terms of which the loan was made would change considerably. This was illustrated during the years 1932 to 1936 by the relatively small amount of international lending. Thus, for example, few British investors bought French Rentes even when they yielded nearly twice as much as Consols. For it was feared that sooner or later the exchange value of the French franc would fall—as indeed it did, when the franc was devalued in September, 1936.

Clearly there is little justification, from the standpoint of logic, in treating this "function" of money separately from its function as a measure of value.

5. MONEY AS A LIQUID ASSET

Since money is the general medium of exchange, capable of discharging any economic obligation, every individual and firm will want to hold a certain amount of money. Such a holding, or reserve, of money will be constantly diminished by payments-out and replenished or increased by receipts. If a person knew exactly what sums of money he would receive, and at what times, he might conceivably arrange his money expenditures in such a way that he paid out money almost as soon as he received it, never holding any appreciable amount of money for more than a day or two. Many wage-earners behave something like this, paying their rent, buying groceries, and so forth, on their pay-day or soon afterwards, and retaining very little money in their pockets or their homes. But firms, including banks, cannot forecast their money receipts as accurately as wage-earners, and most people like to keep a certain reserve of money to meet unforeseen contingencies.

Another reason for holding money, rather than investing it, is that the money value of stocks and shares, or other assets, may fall. Hence anybody who fears that his creditors may demand money payment from him in the near future will tend to be deterred from purchasing assets which might have to be sold at a loss in order to meet their claims. The more readily an asset can be turned into money, without having to be sold for less than its present value, the more "liquid" it is said to be. Hence, by definition, money is the most liquid of all assets. We shall return to this point when we discuss the demand for money.

6. KINDS OF MONEY

At different times many commodities have served as money, from cattle and knives to sea-shells and rum. Usually, in the past, the commodity which came to be used as money was generally desired for its own sake by the members of the community which so used it. Even so, the fact that it was used as money tended to increase its value by increasing the demand for it.

It is by no means essential, however, that the commodity used as money should be valuable as a commodity and desired for its own sake. Thus in Great Britain £1 notes, costing less than a penny to produce, are quite satisfactory as money and purchase anything worth £1. They are accepted in payment because everybody believes that he too will be able to use them to discharge his obligations and to purchase goods and services.

Gold and silver have probably been used as money for some five thousand years. They are fairly generally desired for their own sake—although their exchange value would be considerably lower if they were not widely used as money. They are durable and divisible and homogeneous and not too heavy or bulky to serve as a medium of exchange. Moreover, their annual supply from the mines is only a small proportion of the total stock in existence, so that considerable fluctuations in their value, arising from changes in the total supply, are much less likely than in the case of perishable commodities of which the annual supply is greater than the total stock.

At first, gold and silver seem to have exchanged against goods without being coined. This meant that everybody who received gold or silver in payment had to satisfy himself as to the weight and fineness of the metal which he received. Later, the invention of coinage saved him this trouble. A coin is a piece of metal whose weight and fineness are certified by whoever makes the coin. A bank-note convertible into gold is a promise by the bank which issues it to pay on demand, in exchange for the note, a stated weight of gold (usually in the form of a gold coin or gold coins).

Money is sometimes classified into commodity money, metallic money, and representative money (such as paper notes, whether or not they are convertible into gold).

The money used for small change is sometimes called "token money" when, as is usually the case, its metallic content is worth less than its face value. Thus a shilling contains (in 1939) less than two pennyworth of metal. It has been called "a note printed on silver." Such coins circulate because everybody will accept them. Naturally the Mint which issues them makes a profit (sometimes called seigniorage). On occasions, a rise in the price of silver has caused some silver coins to be worth more as metal than as coins, and they have tended to disappear from circulation to be melted down and sold as metal. This happened to British silver coins in 1920. The Coinage Act of that year, therefore, reduced the fineness of the silver used from 925 to 500 thousandths.

It is sometimes claimed that under modern conditions money, and especially paper money, serves as a medium of exchange because it is legal tender. It is contended that people accept it because the Government compels them to do so. Certainly the fact that money can be used in payment of taxes tends to make it acceptable. But money can be generally acceptable without being legal tender. For example, the chief medium of exchange in parts of Northern Africa has been for many years the "Maria Theresa" dollar, which the London and other Mints continue to provide, in response to the demand for it, bearing the date 1780. This dollar has never been legal tender and its metallic content has often been worth much less than its face value. On the other hand, the fact that certain money is legal tender will not suffice to make it generally acceptable as a measure of value if people expect a considerable change in its value. A strong Government may force its subjects to use its money, by imposing heavy penalties on those who disobey, but it is difficult to continue forcing people to accept money which they distrust. If it is possible, without penalty, something else will be used as a measure of value, as in Germany in 1923.

CHAPTER XXII

BANKS

1. BANK-NOTES

A BANK-NOTE is a promise made by a bank to pay a stated sum of money on demand. Thus a £5 note issued by the Bank of England is a promise by the Bank of England to pay the holder of the note £5 on demand. Before the war of 1914, anybody who presented such a note to the Bank of England was entitled to receive five gold sovereigns in exchange.

The gold certificates issued by the United States Treasury are in effect receipts for gold which has been deposited with it. Unlike most bank-notes, they are "backed" 100 per cent by gold. In the same way, a bank might accept deposits of coin or bullion, giving its receipts in return. If such receipts were promises to pay the stated amount of coin or bullion to anybody presenting them to the bank, they would be bank-notes. These receipts, or bank-notes, might pass from hand to hand among the public, being accepted as equivalent to coin. But if the bank kept coin or bullion on its premises to the full value of the receipts, or notes, which it had issued, so that these notes were "backed" 100 per cent by coin or bullion, it would be acting like a safe-deposit company. And in order to cover its expenses it would have to charge its depositors for keeping their coin and bullion for them.

But it is possible and usual for a bank to issue notes to a value greater than that of the metal which it holds. Day by day, people may present notes and receive the stated amount of coin or bullion from the bank in exchange. But day by day other people may deposit coin or bullion with the bank, receiving its notes in exchange. Provided that the bank always keeps a reserve of coin and bullion on the premises sufficient to meet any excess of payments-out over payments-in, it fulfils its promise to give cash to any holder of its notes who demands cash in exchange. Its notes circulate among the public, and everybody who holds one of its notes, instead of going to the bank and demanding cash for it, is in effect lending that amount (free of interest) to the bank. The bank may put its notes into circulation not only by giving them in exchange for cash deposited with it but also by lending them to people who want to borrow money, or by using them to buy securities. In this way the bank may derive an income from the interest which it receives from its borrowers or upon the securities it has bought. At the same time, it adds to the existing means of payment by providing bank-notes which pass from hand to hand, among the public, and serve as substitutes for cash.

Thus it is clear that a bank could "create credit" in the sense of putting into circulation notes to a value greater than the value of the coin or bullion which it held as "backing" for them. In the past, many banks have been permitted to create credit in this way. For many years, however, most countries have given their central banks a monopoly of the right to issue notes. Thus in England only the Bank of England may issue notes. Its notes are legal tender and, together with coins, constitute the "cash" of England. Since September, 1931, the Bank of England has been relieved of the obligation to give gold in exchange for its notes, and although a £1 note, for example, bears the legend that the Bank of England promises to pay the bearer the sum of £1 on demand, this has no meaning. In fact, in 1939 the market value of the gold held by the Bank of England exceeded considerably the face value of its notes in circulation; nevertheless they were not convertible into gold. Even when a central bank is obliged to give gold on demand in exchange for its notes, they need not have a 100 per cent gold backing. It is usually required by law to keep a certain percentage[1]—for example, 35 per cent in France and 40 per cent in the United States—of gold coin and bullion as backing for its notes, and although this legal minimum is often considerably exceeded, it is probable that a much smaller percentage than the legal minimum would in fact suffice to enable it to fulfil its promise to give gold to everybody presenting its notes, for these circulate and are accepted as money. Indeed, a central bank requires a gold reserve mainly to provide

[1] The Bank of England is an exception. "Peel's Act"—the Bank Charter Act of 1844—laid down the rule that all notes except a maximum and limited number, known as the "fiduciary issue," were to be backed £1 for £1 by gold. Since then this rule has been followed, but the fiduciary issue was greatly increased in 1928, when £1 and 10s. "Treasury Notes" were transferred to the Bank. (But see pages 385–386.)

gold for payments abroad, since its notes circulate only in its own country.

These remarks on central banks and their gold reserves have been somewhat of a digression: we shall return to this topic later. Our main object has been to show how banks can create credit, and in the past have created credit, in the sense of increasing both the amount of money and the supply of loans, by putting their notes into circulation. At present, in most developed countries, the chief means of payment is not the bank-note but the cheque. In Great Britain and the United States about 90 per cent in value of all payments are made by cheque; and in other countries, where the habit of using banks is less widespread, the proportion of payments made by cheque, although not so great as 90 per cent, is quite substantial. Our remarks on bank-notes were made mainly as a prelude to a discussion of cheques.

2. CHEQUES

A cheque is an order on a bank to pay a stated sum of money to the person named as the payee, or to the bearer of the cheque. The bank will obey this order if the drawer of the cheque—the person who signs it—has a sufficient sum standing to his credit at the bank to cover the amount named in the cheque, or if the bank has given him the right to "overdraw" to that extent. Otherwise the cheque will be returned to the person who presented it marked R/D (Refer to Drawer) or N.S.F. (Not Sufficient Funds).

Thus anybody who accepts a cheque in payment of money due to him runs the risk of having the cheque returned to him by the bank on which it is drawn because the drawer has not sufficient funds at the bank to cover the sum named. Hence most people do not like to part with goods or services in exchange for a cheque signed by somebody who is a stranger to them. They prefer to wait until the bank has paid the sum named in the cheque before delivering the goods or rendering the services. There is the further risk that, even if the cheque is a good one, the bank may fail before it has paid the sum named. Bank failures have been very rare in Great Britain during recent decades, but in certain other countries such as Germany and Austria some important banks failed during the recent depression, and the number of banks—many of them small—which failed in the United States was very large.

This leads us to questions of definition. Clearly we should distinguish between means of payment which are generally acceptable and those which are not. In England, the former consist only of notes issued by the Bank of England and silver and copper coins issued by the Mint. We shall call them "cash." A bank which undertakes to repay deposits undertakes to repay them in cash. Means of payment include all substitutes for cash, ranging from cheques to the paper tokens accepted in payment by the refectory of a particular college and current only there. But cheques are so important quantitatively, and are such close substitutes for cash, that it is usual to define "money" as cash plus cheques (or bank deposits). Since the question is purely a verbal one, we shall follow the customary practice.

3. BANK DEPOSITS

A deposit with a bank may be on current account or on deposit account. In the United States the latter kind of deposit is called a "time deposit" and in some countries it is called a "fixed deposit." Deposits of this kind usually bear interest and can be withdrawn only if the depositor has notified the bank of his intention beforehand. In England the period of notice usually required is seven days, but as a rule a bank will permit a customer to withdraw without giving notice. The proportion of current accounts to deposit accounts is significant in that the owners of deposit accounts presumably do not intend to draw upon them in the near future. Thus, during the depression, when people were less anxious to invest and wished to remain more "liquid" than before, the proportion of such deposits to total deposits rose: from 45·9 per cent in 1929 to 50·5 per cent in 1932. Only current accounts are subject to cheque, but since deposit accounts can be withdrawn after due notice, and in practice—as a rule—almost at once, we shall assume, in order to simplify the discussion, that all deposits are subject to cheque.

When A draws a cheque in favour of B, B usually "pays in" the cheque to the credit of his account at his own bank, which collects the sum due from the bank on which the cheque is drawn. A's deposit with his bank is reduced, and B's deposit with his bank is increased, by the sum named in the cheque; the total of bank deposits remains the same. Hence it is bank deposits, rather than cheques, which constitute the means of payment: a cheque is an order by the drawer to his bank to reduce his deposit by that amount in favour of the payee. The total volume of cheques drawn over a period depends on how rapidly bank deposits are "turned over"; people hold money in the form of bank deposits and not in the form of cheques.

4. THE ORIGIN OF BANK DEPOSITS

Clearly a bank deposit could originate in the payment of cash, to that amount, by the depositor to the bank. The depositor might feel that his money was in safer keeping with the bank than at his home; and he might find it convenient to make many of his payments by cheque rather than in cash and to "pay in" cheques which he received, letting his bank collect the amounts and add them to the sum standing to his credit, instead of collecting them himself.

It is conceivable that a bank might act like a cloakroom. It might keep a little safe for each customer, and all the cash which he paid in, or which the bank collected on his behalf, might be put in the safe. In this way, people could pay one another by cheque and the corresponding amount of cash could be moved from one safe to another by the bank or banks concerned.

A bank which did this would probably find that it always had a large amount of cash on its premises. All the time, it would be paying cash across the counter to customers who wanted to withdraw some of their deposits, and it would constantly be paying cash, on behalf of its customers, to other banks in favour of whose customers its own customers had drawn cheques. But on the other hand it would all the time be receiving new deposits of cash across the counter, and from other banks whose customers had drawn cheques in favour of its own customers. The amount of cash in any particular safe might fluctuate considerably from day to day, but when the amount to the credit of some customers was low the amount to the credit of other customers would probably be high, so that day in and day out the total amount of cash in the bank would be large and would not fluctuate very much.

Under these conditions, it is quite likely that it would occur to the banker to lend out the greater part of the cash on his premises. Instead of keeping a separate safe for each customer, he could lump all the cash together, and although he lent out most of it he could still retain enough to enable him to pay on demand (to his customers or, on behalf of his customers, to other banks) all the cash which in fact he would be asked to pay.

A necessary condition for this, it will be noted, is that cash is homogeneous. A depositor who took the number of a pound note which he paid into his bank would have no cause to feel aggrieved if he saw that note in circulation the next day. For his banker would have another pound note ready for him, if he wanted it; and one pound note is as good as another. Another necessary condition is that only a small proportion of the total deposits are likely to be withdrawn in cash at the same time. Suppose the banker decided, on the basis of his past experience, that 10 per cent of his total deposits was an adequate reserve of cash. If—owing, say, to a rumour that the bank was likely to fail—there was a "run on the bank," a large proportion of his depositors demanding repayment in cash, the cash would not be there. The banker might protest that he was perfectly solvent and that, given sufficient time, he could call in his loans, sell his investments, and thus meet his debts, yet his reputation as a banker would be gone, for he would have failed to fulfil his obligation of paying cash on demand.

The banker would receive interest on the loans which he made with his depositors' money and hence he might be able to pay interest (at a lower rate) to his depositors. For a deposit of money with a bank is not like the deposit of an article at a cloakroom: it is really a loan to the bank, and it is generally understood that the bank will re-lend most of the money.

The money which the banks lend will be used by the borrowers to make payments. Suppose, for the moment, that there is only one bank. The people to whom the money is paid may be customers of this bank, and may pay it in again to their credit. In the course of time, the same note or coin might pass and repass several times across the counter of the bank, being deposited by one customer, lent to a borrower, deposited by another customer, and so on. Thus in time the total deposits of the bank might considerably exceed the total amount of cash in the country. This would be quite all right, provided that the bank kept a sufficient reserve of cash to meet all demands for cash which were in fact made upon it. Against its liability to depositors it would hold partly cash and mainly other assets such as debts due to it by people who had borrowed from it.

In fact, when a bank makes a loan it does not usually lend actual cash. Instead, it gives the borrower the right to draw cheques upon it, although he has made no corresponding deposit. For example, a bank may grant its depositor A the right to overdraw his account up to the value of £1000, A agreeing to pay a certain rate of interest on the amount which he in fact overdraws. A proceeds to draw cheques, to pay for goods and services which he requires or to pay his creditors, if he has run into debt, and the people who receive his cheques probably pay them in to their own banks, to be added to their deposits. Thus the deposits of these people are increased, and nobody's deposit is reduced, by the grant of the overdraft or loan to A. It is in this way that "loans create deposits." Of course, the same thing happens if the bank, instead of granting a loan to A, purchases securities and pays for them with its own cheque. The seller of the securities "pays in" this cheque and thereby increases his deposit with his own bank, which may or may not be the bank which drew the cheque. Most of the increase in the total deposits of British banks which has taken place during recent decades has come about through the granting of loans or the purchase of securities by banks. The extra deposits have been virtually created by the banks themselves.

5. THE LIMITATIONS ON THE POWER OF BANKS TO CREATE CREDIT

We have just seen that a bank may receive interest simply by permitting customers to overdraw their accounts or by purchasing securities and paying for them with its own cheques, thus increasing the total of bank deposits: that is, "creating credit." This seems a very easy way of making profits. Yet the rate of profits in banking is no higher than in other branches of industry. The banks have expenses—for premises, equipment, and staff—and their power to create credit is limited.

It is limited by their obligation to pay their depositors cash on demand. This means that they dare not let their reserve of cash fall below what they consider a safe level. In Great Britain during recent years the banks have considered that 9 or 10 per cent of their deposits is the minimum below which their cash reserves must not fall. Since additional loans or purchases of securities would increase total deposits they would thereby reduce the banks' reserve of cash (assuming it to be near the minimum, and to remain the same in amount) below this minimum percentage.

In order to expand credit further, therefore, the banks must either increase the absolute amount of their cash reserves or permit them to form a lower percentage of deposits than they previously considered the lowest compatible with safety.

Let us suppose, to begin with, that there is only one bank (with numerous branches) in the country but that it cannot increase or diminish the total amount of cash in the country, the supply of cash being controlled by the Government. At any moment, all the cash in the country is divided between the bank and the public. The bank cannot permanently increase its holding of cash by forcing the public to hold less. It can temporarily obtain more cash—by selling securities to the public or by requesting some of its customers to repay their loans or overdrafts in cash—but it will be unable to keep this extra cash and use it as a basis for credit expansion. For the public has the whip-hand of the bank in that it can always replenish its holdings of cash by withdrawing deposits in cash. Thus, assuming that total deposits exceed the total amount of cash in the country, the public can always hold as much of the total cash as it wishes. If the public's demand for cash remains the same as before, and the total amount of cash in the country is not increased, the bank will be powerless to bring about a permanent increase in its cash reserve.

Suppose that the total cash in the country is £500 million, of which (taking one day with another) half is held by the bank and half by the public, and that bank deposits amount to £2500 million. The bank could expand credit, and thereby increase its deposits, by £250 million only if it was prepared to let its cash reserve of £250 million form only one-eleventh instead of one-tenth of its total deposits. But it might be unable to achieve even this result. For the amount of cash which the public wants to hold tends to vary with the level of prices. If prices rise, firms and individuals tend to keep more cash than before in their safes or tills or pockets. The expansion of bank credit from £2500 million to £2750 million might well send up prices and so cause the public to want to hold, say, £275 million instead of £250 million as formerly. This would leave only £225 million for the bank, and that would be little more than 8 per cent of the deposits. Hence, if it was prepared to reduce its cash ratio to 9 per cent, but not lower, it could not expand credit by as much as £250 million.

Thus the total of bank deposits may be said to depend on three things, namely—

(1) the total amount of cash in the country,

(2) the amount of cash which the public wishes to hold,

(3) the minimum percentage of cash to deposits which the banks consider safe.

The total amount of cash in the country can be increased only if the monetary authorities (whom we have supposed to be the Government) decide to increase it. The public's demand for cash may be diminished by a fall in population or by a change in the public's monetary habits: for example, groups of wage-earners who had previously been paid in cash might come to be paid by cheque and to use cheques to make payments which they previously made in cash. The bank might feel, at a time of general prosperity and optimism, that a lower percentage than usual would be quite safe. But if none of these factors changes, the total amount of bank credit cannot increase.

The fact that there are several different banks does not make any substantial difference to the argument. Its implications are discussed in the following section.

We may add that the controversy as to whether the inflations in Germany and other countries during and after the war of 1914 were "due" to an expansion of bank credit or to an expansion of the note issue is rather like the controversy as to whether the hen or the egg came first. In fact, expansions of bank credit came first, but the enlarged volume of bank credit could not have been maintained, still less increased, without the subsequent creation of additional cash, in the form of notes issued by the Government or central bank, to enable the banks to keep their customary proportion of cash to deposits.

6. BANK CLEARING

Consider a particular bank, let us say, for example, the Midland Bank. Suppose that it has about one-fifth of the total bank deposits. Every day its customers pay in cheques to their credit, and the chances are that about four-fifths of these cheques will be drawn upon other banks. The Midland Bank could of course collect the cash due to it, on those cheques, from the other banks. But the customers of the other banks will pay in cheques to their credit and presumably the average total value of these cheques will be about four times as great as that of the cheques paid in to the Midland Bank, and the chances are that about one-fifth of them will be drawn on the Midland Bank. Thus the Midland Bank will have to pay the other banks about as much cash as they have to pay to it.

Obviously a convenient arrangement would be for each bank (in any town) to send a clerk to meet clerks from other banks at a central office or "clearing house." Each bank could then give the Midland Bank the cheques which it had received drawn upon the Midland Bank, the Midland could reciprocate, and so on. If at any such "clearing" the Midland Bank owed, say, the Westminster Bank more than the Westminster Bank owed it, it could pay the difference in cash. Such clearings do take place every day (and in large towns two or three times a day) but the differences are not paid in cash. In England most important banks themselves have deposits with the Bank of England, and settle their differences at the clearing by cheques drawn on the Bank of England. Thus, if the Midland Bank owes the Westminster Bank £50,000, on balance, at any particular clearing, it gives the Westminster Bank a cheque drawn by itself on the Bank of England for £50,000. The Midland Bank's deposit at the Bank of England is reduced, and the Westminster Bank's is increased, by £50,000. The banks consider their deposits with the Bank of England as equivalent to cash, for they can withdraw them in notes or coins at any time.

Clearly the equilibrium position for any bank is that it neither gains nor loses cash, over a period, at the clearing. If it habitually gains cash, it will expand its loans, so that more cheques will be drawn upon it, until its percentage of cash to deposits falls to whatever it considers the lowest consistent with safety.

Conversely, if it habitually loses cash to the other banks, it will be compelled to contract its loans, so that fewer cheques are drawn upon it.

If all the banks decide to expand credit, and keep in step with one another, no bank will lose cash to other banks at the clearing, and the limits to credit expansion will be simply those which we discussed in the previous section, on the assumption that there was only one bank.

Suppose that one bank only, say the Midland Bank, decides to expand credit. It will soon be checked by the loss of cash to the other banks at the clearing. If it expands its loans by £10 million, and has about one-fifth of the total deposits, the chances are that its new borrowers will pay four-fifths of their cheques to people who are customers of other banks, so that the Midland Bank will lose about £8 million cash to other banks at the clearing. Suppose that it had £400 million deposits and £40 million cash (including, of course, its deposits with the Bank of England) and that the other banks, taken together, had £1600 million deposits and £160 million cash. The Midland Bank, let us say, is prepared to let its reserve ratio fall from 10 per cent to 9 per cent. The other banks, taken together, wish to maintain the ratio of 10 per cent. The Midland Bank cannot expand its loans by £40 million, in the hope that this will increase its deposits to £440 million, leaving its cash at £40 million. For the result would be to expand its deposits to about £408 million and reduce its cash to about £8 million, since about four-fifths of the cheques drawn by its new borrowers would come into the possession of depositors of other banks. But, by gradual expansion, an equilibrium position might be reached with its deposits at about £411 million and its cash at about £37 million, the total deposits of the other banks being £1630 million and their cash £163 million. For, as the other banks acquired more cash from the Midland Bank, they would gradually expand their loans or investments.

One conclusion which emerges from all this is that although 90 per cent in value of all payments are made by cheques it is the quantity of cash which is really important. For so long as the banks maintain their conventional reserve ratio they can increase their deposits only if the amount of cash in the country increases or the public's demand for cash diminishes.

CHAPTER XXIII

MONEY MARKETS AND CENTRAL BANKS

1. INTRODUCTION

THE previous chapter gave a general discussion of banks and of the forces determining the volume of bank deposits or "bank credit." The present chapter is largely descriptive. It is concerned mainly with facts and figures relating to British banks and the London money market.

An account of the British banking system inevitably involves some discussion of the London money market and of the Bank of England. A money market is a market for short-term loans. Most of the money lent on the London money market is supplied, directly or indirectly, by the British commercial banks. It is they who, by buying Treasury bills, lend the British Government most of the large amount of money which it borrows on short term. It is they who supply the discount houses and bill brokers, by lending to them on short term, with most of the money which they use to buy Treasury bills, bills of exchange, and Government securities. The banks regard their short-term loans to the money market and their holdings of Treasury and other bills as their most liquid assets with the exception, of course, of cash. We must therefore give a brief account of discount houses and bill brokers and of accepting houses (who, by "accepting" bills —which means, in effect, guaranteeing they will be paid—make them more marketable) and we must say something about Treasury bills and bills of exchange.

We must also discuss the central bank: the Bank of England. A banking system can flourish without a central bank. But where there is a central bank it can, if it chooses, control the volume of bank credit—and, incidentally, affect short-term and possibly long-term rates of interest—by causing the amount of cash available for the commercial banks to increase or to diminish. The Bank of England, as we shall see, is in a position to do this.

When Great Britain was on gold, the immediate object of the

Bank of England was to maintain an adequate reserve of gold and, at any rate before 1914, it responded to the danger of a drain of gold by raising its bank rate. But Great Britain has been off gold since September, 1931, and our discussion in the present chapter describes the situation since that time. We consider the gold standard in a later chapter. For the present we leave international complications out of account.

Since we devote most of our illustrations to the British banking system it may be well to point out the chief respects in which other systems are different. In the first place, the volume of Treasury and other bills in London is greater than in most centres. These bills are treated by the banks as relatively liquid assets which (together with their short loans to bill brokers) supplement their cash reserves, forming a second line of defence. The banks therefore can and do maintain a smaller reserve of cash against their deposits than they would have to maintain if such liquid assets were not available. In countries with less developed money markets the banks maintain a higher ratio of cash to deposits than in England.

In the second place, the intervention of the discount houses and bill brokers between the central bank and the commercial banks is peculiar to England. In other countries the commercial banks borrow, when they need more cash, directly from the central bank. In England they never do this. Instead, they call in their short loans, thereby constraining the bill brokers to borrow from the Bank of England in order to repay them.

In the third place, England has greatly developed branch banking. A few large banks with numerous branches do the great bulk of the business and hold most of the total deposits. The banking system of the United States is in marked contrast. There, widespread branch banking is forbidden by law and there are many thousands of independent banks, although the Federal Reserve system has done much (since it was set up in 1914) to "pool" and centralize the cash reserves of its member banks. Branch banking enables a large bank to use its cash reserves more effectively, distributing them among its branches according to the demand for cash in different places. It also facilitates loans from one part of the country to another: some of the deposits of a district with a relatively small demand for loans can be lent, in effect, to other districts where the demands for loans are greater. On the other hand, all loans of any size require the prior sanction of the head office, so that a local manager cannot use his discretion as much as if his branch were an independent bank. Moreover, the failure of a large bank with numerous branches would mean widespread distress and alarm, whereas the failure of a few local banks might have little effect outside their own districts.

2. THE ENGLISH COMMERCIAL BANKS

The five biggest English banks are the Midland, Barclays, Lloyds, the Westminster, and the National Provincial. These, together with six others, are known as the London Clearing Banks because they alone are members of the London Clearing House; other banks do their clearing through one of these. The remaining English banks are of minor importance, but many foreign and Dominion banks have offices in London and the banks of Scotland and Northern Ireland do a good deal of business.

The main items on the "liabilities" side of a bank's statement of accounts are capital paid up, reserve fund, and deposits ("current, deposit, and other accounts"). In October, 1937, the combined capital of the London clearing banks aggregated some £77 million and their reserve funds (accumulated out of undistributed profits) some £58 million. These sums belonged to their shareholders. In addition, there were substantial concealed reserves in that some of their assets (notably investments and premises) were shown below market value; these may have been in the neighbourhood of £100 million. The bulk of their resources, however, were deposits, amounting to some £2312 million, and these of course belonged to the depositors and not to the shareholders.

The policy of an English commercial bank may be regarded as a compromise between three conflicting aims. In the first place, the bank wants to make as good profits as possible for its shareholders. In the second place, its funds belong mainly to its depositors, so that it cannot afford to risk losing some of them by investing them in risky enterprises without adequate security even if this course seems likely to yield high profits. In the third place, it has undertaken to repay depositors in cash and it must therefore keep a certain proportion of its assets in cash or in forms which can readily be converted into cash without appreciable loss. The distribution of its assets will reflect its compromise between these three aims of profits, security, and liquidity.

In October, 1937, the main[1] items on the "assets" side of the statements of the London clearing banks, taken together, were as follows—

	£ million
Cash	234
Money at call and short notice	165
Bills discounted	296
Investments	639
Advances to customers	984

These items have been given in order of liquidity. The order of profitability is exactly the reverse. Advances are the most profitable, yielding (in 1937) around 4 to 5 per cent, while cash, of course, yields nothing at all.

Cash is, by definition, completely liquid. Rather more than half this item consists of notes and coin, the rest being deposits ("Bankers' Deposits") with the Bank of England, which the banks regard as completely equivalent to notes and coin. The percentage of cash to deposits varies somewhat between individual banks and from one time to another, but for all the banks together it is seldom shown as less than 10 per cent and seldom rises much above 11 per cent.

Money at call and short notice has been lent mainly to discount houses and bill brokers and partly to stockbrokers. (The banks also lend for longer periods to stockbrokers, but these loans are included in their advances.) This item constitutes the most liquid part, after cash, of the bank's assets, for some of the loans can be recalled on demand and the rest within a few days. In 1937 the banks obtained only ½ to 1 per cent on this item, which usually is equivalent to around 6 or 7 per cent of their deposits.

Bills discounted become liquid as they mature. They consist mainly of Treasury bills, for the volume of commercial bills has shrunk greatly during recent years. In 1937, Treasury bills yielded little more than ½ per cent and three months' trade bills

[1] We omit liabilities of customers for acceptances, indorsements, etc. (£116 million), balanced, of course, by a corresponding item of the same value on the liabilities side. We omit also balances with and cheques in course of collection on other banks, items in transit, bank premises, and investments in affiliated banks and subsidiary companies.

2 to 2½ per cent. Bank bills yielded little more than Treasury bills, but the commercial bills held by the banks were mainly trade bills and not bank bills. Bills usually amount to between 12 and 20 per cent of deposits.

Investments consist mainly of British Government securities, which during recent years have yielded little more than 3 per cent and which may fluctuate in value from time to time. The banks follow the aim of security by restricting their investments to those which are "gilt-edged" and not risking their depositors' money in speculative shares. In the past, investments have usually varied between 14 and 17 per cent of deposits, but during the last four or five years before the outbreak of war the proportion was much higher: in October, 1937, it was over 27 per cent.

Advances to customers, by way of loan or overdraft, are the most profitable but the least liquid item, for although an overdraft may nominally be repayable on demand it is often difficult to get it repaid at short notice. In general, the English banks aim at providing industry and trade with working capital only, and seldom lend for more than six months. In the past, some continental banks have provided particular firms with long-term loans. But such banks had a much greater capital relatively to their deposits than English banks, who seldom do this: the long-term loan of £3 million made by Lloyds Bank to Stewarts and Lloyds in 1932 was quite exceptional. The English banks try to protect their depositors by obtaining adequate security for their advances. But sometimes a security which seemed adequate at the time falls heavily in value; the customer cannot repay; and the banks are left with "frozen" assets. This happened to a number of bank loans during the depression following the war of 1914–18. Advances in the past have usually amounted to more than 50 per cent of the deposits, but during recent years the proportion has fallen considerably below this.

A comparison with October, 1931, is interesting. The total deposits of the London clearing banks at that time were only £1724 million; their investments were £304 million and their advances £910 million. The "cheap money" policy pursued by the Bank of England and the Treasury since then has considerably increased the volume of deposits, but the corresponding change on the assets side has taken the form mainly of a great increase in investments, owing to the lack of sufficient safe borrowers to maintain the customary ratio of advances to deposits.

It should be noted that the published statements of the banks include a certain amount of "window-dressing": that is to say, the amount of cash shown exceeds the amount normally held. Each of the big banks makes up its accounts on a different day of the week, calling in short loans for that purpose. The bill brokers repay one bank by borrowing from the other banks. At the end of the half-year, when all the banks make up their accounts on the same day, different measures are needed. We shall see later what these are.

3. BILLS

We use the word "bills" as a general term for negotiable documents which embody the promises of borrowers to repay short-term loans. The main types are promissory notes (little used in England), bills of exchange, and Treasury bills.

In the United States it is not uncommon for a customer who borrows from a bank to give the bank his "note." This is a signed promise by the customer to pay the bank a stated sum—the amount borrowed plus interest—on a stated date. It is known as a promissory note. A bank wishing to increase its cash reserve can discount such notes (or, strictly, re-discount them, for the bank has already discounted them for its customers) with the Federal Reserve Bank of its district. The notes then carry the guarantee of the bank which re-discounts them, as well as of its customers.

In Great Britain, loans and overdrafts granted by the commercial banks are not embodied in negotiable documents. A bank which makes a loan often safeguards itself by taking over the custody, but not the ownership, of stock exchange securities or other titles to assets belonging to the customer, to a value greater than the amount of the loan. If the customer does not repay, the bank has the right to sell this "collateral" and thus recoup itself, handing over to the customer any excess which remains after it has done so. If the customer does not "put up" sufficient collateral, the bank usually demands the guarantee of a third party that the loan will be repaid. But the loan does not give rise to any document of the nature of a bill.

A bill of exchange is an order by one person (or firm) to another to pay him some definite sum of money at a specified future date. The person giving this order is called the "drawer" of the bill. If the other person signifies his agreement by signing the bill, he is said to "accept" it. The bill is negotiable: that is to say, the drawer can transfer it to a third party, who then has the right to the money when the bill falls due for payment. He can transfer it by "indorsing" it, that is, by signing his name on the back of it; he then becomes liable for the sum named if the acceptor fails to keep his promise. In the same way, the third party can transfer it to a fourth, and so on.

A bill can be sold, or, to use the technical term, "discounted," at any time before it matures—that is, falls due for payment. Suppose that a bank discounts a bill of face value £1000 which has three months to run at a rate of discount of 4 per cent per annum. It gives £990 now for the bill (since 4 per cent per annum is 1 per cent for three months). It is clearly making a loan, which will be repaid plus £10 when the bill matures. The present value of the bill depends partly on the length of time it has to run. For example, the above bill will be worth £995, assuming the rate of discount is still 4 per cent, after half the three months have elapsed.

But the present value of a bill also depends partly on the credit standing of the persons or firms whose names appear upon it and who are therefore responsible for seeing that it is paid. A bill bearing only the names of firms whose credit standing is not generally known to be high is usually discounted by the bank of the drawer, which holds it until it matures, and it is discounted at a relatively high rate. Most of the bills in the London money market bear, in addition to the names of the firms concerned, the name of a well-known bank or accepting house and are known as bank bills (the others being known as trade bills). By thus "accepting" the bill, the bank has given its own guarantee that the bill will be met at the due date. This raises the present value of the bill; in other words, the bill can be discounted at a considerably lower rate.

For many years London has been the leading international market for first-class bills of exchange. It attained this position owing partly to the large and widespread foreign trade of Great Britain (for these bills mostly have their origin in foreign trade transactions) and partly to the presence in London of several firms of merchant bankers with important foreign connections. The credit of these firms—for example, Barings, Rothschild, and Schroeder—was, and is, very high, and their acceptance of a bill meant that it could readily be discounted in either London or some foreign centre. They are now known as accepting houses. They sometimes act as "issue houses," raising relatively large loans in London on behalf of foreign Governments or other important clients. They accept deposits, both from their foreign clients and from British firms, and use the money to buy bills or Government securities or to make short-term loans. They accept bills for their clients, receiving a commission (usually of 1 to 2 per cent) for giving their guarantee that the money will be paid when the bills mature and thereby raising their present value and making them readily discountable. Usually they are safeguarded by receiving possession of documents such as bills of lading, invoices, and insurance policies giving them control over the goods, or by collateral security deposited with them by their clients. Since 1918, the practice of granting reimbursement credits has sprung up. For example, a foreign bank will be given a credit of, say, £500,000 by an accepting house. The foreign bank then instructs its clients to draw their bills upon the accepting house. The foreign bank makes itself liable for their payments and probably the accepting house is secured against its contingent liability by securities deposited with it by the foreign bank. The leading English commercial banks have themselves done an increasing amount of acceptance business since the last war. Towards the close of 1937 their total acceptances exceeded £100 million.

A bill is considerably more liquid than a bank loan made for the same period. For the borrower may urge his banker to renew the loan on the ground that he cannot immediately find the money conveniently, but will be able to do so later. The banker may lose a good customer if he refuses; and, further, the loan may not be adequately backed by collateral, or the collateral may have fallen in value considerably since the loan was granted, so that the bank may not be able to obtain repayment in full even if it hardens its heart to the customer's appeal. A bill, on the other hand, is virtually a written promise to pay at a specified future date, and if the promise is not kept the credit of the bank (or firm) which accepted it is destroyed. Hence bills are nearly always met, except in quite exceptional circumstances, whilst loans and overdrafts are frequently renewed even when the bank would prefer not to renew them. It has been said that the first duty of a banker is to realize the difference between a bill of exchange and a mortgage. The former is very liquid; it is highly probable that the money will be forthcoming when it matures. The latter is much less liquid; if circumstances arose in which the property had to be sold, it is likely that a good deal of other property would be offered for sale, owing to those same circumstances, at the same time, thus forcing down its price below the face value of the mortgage.

Governments often borrow on short term. Their revenue, especially from income tax, fluctuates considerably over the year, so that they are sometimes constrained to borrow, in anticipation of revenue, to meet current expenses. Moreover, short-term rates are often lower, and sometimes much lower, than long-term rates. A small part of the short-term or "floating" debt of the British Government sometimes consists of advances, called Ways and Means advances, made by the Bank of England, but the great bulk of it consists of Treasury bills. These are three months' bills issued by the British Government (in amounts of £5000 and £10,000) and payable on the due date at the Bank of England. They are an extremely liquid form of investment. Nobody doubts that the money will be forthcoming on the due date, and therefore a Treasury bill can be readily discounted if the holder requires cash sooner than he had expected. When the Treasury issues these bills, it invites tenders for them. Banks and other would-be buyers state how many they are prepared to take, and at what price, and the bills go to the highest bidders. Towards the close of 1937, there were some £900 million of these bills outstanding, and their average rate of discount was little more than ½ per cent: that is to say, the average price paid for a £5000 bill was little lower than £4993 15s. Some of these bills were not put up for tender but were issued direct ("through the tap") to various Government Departments which had balances to invest for short periods; most of the rest were held by banks. Every week, Treasury bills to the value of about £45 million were issued to the market, and every week a somewhat similar volume of bills fell due for payment. Ever since the last war, the volume of Treasury bills in the London money market has been greater than the volume of commercial bills, and since 1931 they have swamped the latter in importance.

The bank rate of a central bank is the minimum rate at which it will discount first-class bank bills, accepted payable by a leading bank or by one or more firms of equally high standing. A central bank will usually discount only Treasury bills or first-class commercial bills; in other words, it will usually refuse ordinary trade bills. Moreover, a number of central banks normally discount only bills with less than, say, two months to run.

4. THE LONDON DISCOUNT MARKET

The dealers in bills on the London market comprise three large discount houses—namely, Alexanders Discount Company, The National Discount Company, and The Union Discount Company—with a total capital (including reserves) of about £7·5 million, twenty bill brokers with a total capital of over £7 million, and nine "running brokers" who are pure intermediaries with little capital of their own.

The discount market is much more important in London than in any other centre, and the practice followed by the English commercial banks of calling in their loans to the discount market instead of themselves borrowing from the central bank is peculiar to England.

We may perhaps be permitted to use the term bill broker to include discount houses. Clearly a bill broker can discount bills with his own capital. Having the bills, he can then use them as security on which to borrow money at call or short notice from a bank. Having borrowed this money, he can then discount some more bills, borrow more money on the security of the bills, and so on. Thus the greater part, by far, of the funds utilized by a bill broker are provided on short loan by the banks. Most bill brokers also accept deposits. The capital of some bill-broking firms is as much as a tenth of the money which they borrow from the banks and from their depositors, but in some cases it is only a twentieth or a thirtieth. They may use some part of their funds to buy Government securities, particularly short-dated ones.

Bill brokers do not hold all the bills which they discount until they mature. They resell some, at a slight profit, to the banks. They can do this because any given bank likes to arrange its holding of bills so that about the same amount of money falls due for payment every day (or, rather, more falls due at times when it knows that it will have to make unusually large payments out) and likes not to hold too many bills bearing the same signatures. A bill broker is a specialist in bills and knows the credit standing of the various firms responsible for paying the bills. He himself, except in the case of running brokers, guarantees payment of the bills which he re-sells to the banks. Hence the banks are prepared to discount them at a fraction of 1 per cent less than he did—in other words to buy them from him at a slightly higher price than he paid for them.

Thus bill brokers make their profits by discounting bills and holding them and perhaps buying some Government securities and holding them, receiving a rate of interest higher than the rate which they pay for the money which they borrowed from the banks and, to a less extent, from their depositors. They also make profits by re-selling some of their bills to the banks.

When a bank wishes to replenish or increase its cash it usually calls in some of its loans to the discount market. The bill brokers may be able to borrow the money from another bank. But if all the banks are calling in their short loans at the same time, this is not possible. The bill brokers are then constrained to obtain the money from the Bank of England, either by obtaining an advance (usually at ½ per cent above bank rate) or by re-discounting some of their bills. At such a time the market is said to be "in the Bank." But of course the banks cannot permanently increase their cash reserves in this way. If the bank rate is maintained at a level which makes it unprofitable for bill brokers to borrow from the Bank, they will not do so for longer than they can help. When they repay, deposits are thereby transferred from the commercial banks to the Bank of England. Similarly, when bills re-discounted by the Bank mature, the deposit of whoever pays the money is reduced and the money is paid by his bank to the Bank of England. In this way bankers' deposits at the Bank of England are again reduced.

Since 1931 the volume of trade bills has become small[1] and the

[1] Foreign-drawn bills fell from about £500 million in 1929 to about £150 million in 1936–37. See *The Economist*, 26th March, 1938, p. 689.

bills held by the discount market are now mainly Treasury bills. The yield on these is exceedingly low, and, in order to keep their businesses alive, the bill brokers have been obliged to increase their investments in long-dated securities.

Treasury bills are offered for sale by tender on Fridays, and tenderers can specify the day in the following week on which they wish their bills to be dated. When the banks call in their loans at the half-year to increase their cash for window-dressing purposes, if the end of the half-year falls in mid-week, it is possible for the holders of Treasury bills to arrange that their bills maturing that week mature in the first half of it, while the new bills they are taking up are dated and paid for in the second half. The Treasury is thus compelled to borrow from the Bank of England and the money market is supplied with funds to meet the calls of the banks without itself having to borrow much from the Bank of England.

5. CENTRAL BANKS

Most countries, nowadays, have a central bank.[1] The main task of the central bank is to carry out the monetary policy of the country or, more accurately, to take from time to time whatever measures seem appropriate to ensure that the course of events in the monetary sphere conforms as closely as possible to this policy. A central bank nearly always pays good dividends to its shareholders, for it usually has the profitable privilege of holding the deposits of the Government. But its primary purpose is not to make profits. It follows whatever course is considered best for the country, even if its profits are thereby reduced.

Nowadays Governments and central banks are usually in agreement as to the general monetary policy which should be pursued, and work closely together to make it effective. The Government can help in various ways. For example, the tone and substance of speeches by ministers may induce the business community to be more enterprising, or more cautious; the volume of Government loans raised or repaid or converted during

[1] The United States is divided into twelve districts. In each of these there is a Federal Reserve Bank, holding the central reserve and acting as a central bank for its district. But the activities of these twelve are controlled and co-ordinated by a single body, the Federal Reserve Board, working in close co-operation with the United States Treasury.

any period may affect rates of interest; the sums spent on public works may influence activity and employment; the extent to which imports of commodities or international movements of capital are restricted will affect the general monetary situation. Naturally it is usually the Minister of Finance (called in Great Britain the Chancellor of the Exchequer) and two or three of the chief permanent officials in his Department who play the greatest part, on behalf of the Government, in conferring with the governor or directors of the central bank as to what should be done from time to time.

It may happen, however, that the Government and the central bank do not agree upon policy. There may well be a conflict at certain periods between the immediate interests of the Treasury, which is about to borrow money and therefore wishes to keep interest rates down, and the views of the central bank, which may believe that interest rates should be maintained or raised. Again, the Government may wish to borrow more from the central bank than the latter thinks desirable. If the Government cannot be persuaded to change its attitude, its will must ultimately prevail. If the governor of the central bank maintains his opposition, he will be constrained to resign and will be replaced by somebody more amenable.

The rapidity and ease with which the Government can override the wishes of the central bank when there is a serious difference of opinion between them varies from one country to another. In New Zealand, for example, the central bank is practically the puppet of the Government. In some other countries it has been thought desirable to enable the central bank to enforce a period of delay or to compel the Government to pass special legislation before submitting to a policy which it considers unwise. For this reason, most central banks are not owned by their Governments. The Government may hold some shares and usually has the right to nominate some directors, but as a rule the bulk of the shares are in private hands.

A country may pursue any of several broad monetary policies. It may decide that the best way to promote prosperity is to maintain an international standard, such as the gold standard. In that event, the main reserve of gold (or silver, or foreign exchange, according to the standard adopted) is held by the central bank and its actions are largely directed towards maintaining an adequate reserve. The main alternative policies are to try to keep the general level of either commodity prices or money incomes fairly stable, or to take whatever monetary measures seem most suitable from time to time to promote activity and employment and to avoid a general slump. Our present purpose is not to discuss the merits and defects of alternative policies but to show in what ways a central bank can try to make effective whatever policy has been decided upon.

When a central bank is not deliberately pursuing an active policy, it responds to a fall in short-term interest rates by reducing its bank rate—the minimum rate at which it will discount first-class bills—because it is useless to keep it high above market rates, and it responds to a drain of cash by raising its bank rate. The drain may be external. If the country is on the gold standard, its exchange rates may tend to fall, leading to a withdrawal of gold from the central bank. Or the drain may be internal. In most countries except England the commercial banks borrow at times from the central bank. If they borrow so much that its cash reserve falls below what it considers a reasonably safe level, it raises its bank rate to induce the commercial banks to borrow less.

But we are concerned with an active, deliberate policy. In pursuance of such a policy, a central bank exerts its influence mainly by causing the amount of money in the country to increase or diminish. An increase in the amount of money is usually associated with lower rates, especially short-term rates, of interest. If the extra money gets into circulation through increased loans and overdrafts granted by the commercial banks, this usually implies that the latter have reduced their rates to induce entrepreneurs and others to borrow more from them. It is usually hoped that the extra money, whether it gets into circulation via bank loans or via Government spending or by some other route, will tend to raise money incomes and prices and to stimulate economic activity. A diminution in the amount of money, on the other hand, is usually accompanied by higher rates of interest and tends to reduce money incomes and prices and to check economic activity.

It may be wondered why a central bank ever reduces the amount of money, since this tends to depress business and to cause unemployment. It may do so because a reduction of money incomes is necessary to safeguard the gold reserve and to keep the country on the gold standard. It may do so because people fear an inflation and action of this kind is needed to restore confidence. Or it may do so during a boom because it thinks that unless the boom is checked now it will develop later into a serious slump.

How can a central bank alter the total amount of money in the country? It usually has a monopoly of the issue of bank-notes. If its bank-notes were the chief means of payment it could simply issue more notes (putting them into circulation by buying securities or discounting bills) when it wanted to expand the volume of money and withdraw notes (by selling securities or reducing its holding of bills) when it wanted to contract the volume of money. But the chief means of payment, in most modern countries, is the deposits of the commercial banks. How can the central bank alter the total of bank deposits?

Commercial banks often keep a fairly constant proportion between their cash and their deposits. If their cash consisted entirely of notes issued by the central bank, a change in the total volume of these notes would lead to a change in the total of bank deposits. For presumably the public would for some time want to hold about the same value of notes as before, so that extra notes issued by the central bank would nearly all find their way into the cash reserves of the commercial banks, while notes withdrawn from circulation by the central bank would correspondingly deplete the cash reserves of the commercial banks. Thus, if the latter kept a proportion of cash to deposits of 1 to 10, every increase of £1 million in the note issue would lead to an expansion of £10 million in bank deposits and every decrease of £1 million in the note issue to a contraction of £10 million in bank deposits.

The actual position, in most countries, is slightly more complicated than this. Most central banks are required by law to keep a minimum percentage of gold (or silver, or foreign exchange) against their notes. Hence they can expand their note issue only if they acquire more gold. But they can nevertheless cause large variations in the total of bank deposits even if their note issue does not change. For the commercial banks usually hold considerable balances with the central bank. In some countries the commercial banks are compelled by law to do this; in others they do so by custom. The practice is convenient for them, since a balance due at the clearing from one commercial bank to another can be settled by a cheque on the central bank. The commercial banks treat their deposits with the central bank, which we shall call bankers' deposits, as cash. The central bank can readily vary the total of bankers' deposits. When it buys securities or bills, it pays for them with its own cheques, and the sellers deposit these cheques with their own banks. Conversely, when the central bank sells securities, the buyers pay by cheques on their own banks and this diminishes bankers' deposits by that amount. Such purchases and sales of securities, by the central bank, resulting in an expansion or contraction of bank deposits (of ten times the expansion or contraction in bankers' deposits if the commercial banks maintain a ratio of 1 to 10 between their cash and their deposits) are usually described as "open-market operations" because the central bank buys or sells in the open market.

Most central banks publish their bank rate, which they may vary from time to time. This, it will be remembered, indicates the rate at which they will discount first-class bills. A rise in the bank rate is often followed by a rise in other short-term rates, including the rates charged by the commercial banks on loans and overdrafts. If so, it results in a fall in bank loans and therefore in the volume of bank deposits. Similarly, a fall in the bank rate is often followed by a fall in other short-term rates and an expansion in the volume of bank deposits. But this need not happen. If the change in the bank rate does not reflect or anticipate a change in interest rates due to a change in the state of supply or demand in the loan market, it may not affect other rates at all. Of course, if the bank rate is reduced to such a level that it is cheaper to borrow from the central bank than from other lenders, the central bank may be flooded with requests for loans and will probably be compelled to raise its rate again. But a reduction in the bank rate from, say, 6 per cent to 5 per cent at a time when other short-term rates were all well below 5 per cent might have no effect at all. *A fortiori*, a rise in the bank rate from 6 per cent to something higher at such a time might have no effect whatever on the market. The fact is that changes upwards or downwards in the bank rate, so long as it remains above the market rate of discount on first-class bills, will lead to changes in other rates only if lenders or borrowers in a monopolistic position choose to alter their rates accordingly. There is, however, the further point that such borrowers or lenders, and notably the commercial banks, may raise their rates when the bank rate is raised because they fear that they themselves may have to borrow from the central bank in the near future. Often the central bank takes further measures to make its new rate "effective." It engages in open-market operations, and it is these which are important, rather than the bank rate. A reduction in the "cash" (including bankers' deposits) of the commercial banks compels them to reduce their loans and raise their rates; an increase in their cash induces them to do the opposite.

In addition to open-market operations and changes in its bank rate, a central bank can exert its influence by making its wishes known to financial houses. It usually has great prestige, so that it is often heeded. But it will seldom succeed in inducing banks and other financial firms to forgo for long profits which they could make quite legally by disregarding its desires.

We shall now illustrate these general statements by an account of the control exercised by the Bank of England.

6. THE BANK OF ENGLAND

The Bank of England has virtually a monopoly of the note issue. The Treasury issued £1 and 10s. notes during the last war, but these were amalgamated with the note issue of the Bank by the Act of 1928. Certain banks in Scotland and in Northern Ireland have the right to issue notes, but since all their notes except £4·3 million must be backed, pound for pound, by Bank of England notes, this is of minor importance. The Mint provides silver and copper coins: the face value of the coins in circulation is now rather more than £50 million. Thus the great bulk of the "cash" of the United Kingdom consists of Bank of England notes.

The Bank can issue notes to the value of the gold coin and bullion which it holds, valued since 1939 at the current market value, plus a further amount known as "the fiduciary issue" backed only by securities.[1] Between the Act of 1928 and the summer of 1931 the maximum laid down for the fiduciary issue was £260 million; it was then raised to £275 million; reduced again to £260 million legally and £250 million in practice; and

[1] Plus silver up to a maximum face value of £5·5 million.

raised in 1939 to £300 million. The Bank always issues notes to the maximum permitted value; those which do not go into circulation remain as a reserve in its Banking Department. Thus on 10th November, 1937, it held £326 million of gold and bullion and had therefore issued notes to the value of £526 million of which £485 million were in circulation and £41 million held as a Reserve in its Banking Department.

The Bank can temporarily increase its fiduciary issue with the permission of the Treasury. It was formerly thought that this power would be used only in case of something approaching a financial panic, when firms want to increase their holdings of cash. But a temporary expansion of £20 million was authorized to meet the seasonal expansion of the note circulation at Christmas, 1937, and it seems likely that the use of this expedient may become a part of the bank's regular procedure at such times. Any central bank must control the note issue if it is to have full power over monetary policy. It could not command the situation if other banks were free to vary the amount of cash. But the active measures of control taken by the Bank of England consist mainly of varying its bank rate and engaging in open-market policy in such a way as to cause bankers' deposits and therefore the total deposits of the commercial banks to vary, rather than of varying its note issue.

The commercial banks maintain a fairly constant ratio of "cash" (including their deposits with the Bank) to deposits. But the Banking Department of the Bank holds the central reserve of cash and can and does vary its own proportion of cash to deposits within wide limits. It is prepared, for example, to make bankers' deposits vary considerably whilst its own holding of cash remains about the same. It thereby causes total deposits to expand or contract by nine or ten times the amount of the expansion or contraction in bankers' deposits.

The activities of the Bank are best illustrated by reference to one of its weekly returns. We give below the return for the week ended 10th November, 1937,[1] showing the various items to the

[1] On 23rd August, 1939, notes in circulation were £508 million and in the Banking Department £38 million. Gold coin and bullion amounted to £246 million (at 148s. 6d. per oz. fine). The fiduciary issue was £300 million. "Other Government securities" held against it were £284 million and "other securities" £4 million. The remaining items were not substantially different from what they were on 10th November, 1937.

nearest £1 million and omitting the small item of £9360 of silver coin held in the Issue Department as part of the security for the fiduciary issue.

ISSUE DEPARTMENT

		£ Million		£ Million
Notes Issued:			Government Debt	11
In Circulation		485	Other Governmentt Scurities	188
In Banking Department		41	Other Securities	1
			Amount of Fiduciary Issue	200
			Gold Coin and Bullion	326
		£526		£526

BANKING DEPARTMENT

		£ Million			£ Million
Proprietors' Capital		15	Government Securities		104
Rest		3	Other Securities:		
Public Deposits		31	Discounts and Advances	8	
Other Deposits:			Securities	21	
Bankers	91				29
Other Accounts	36		Notes		41
		127	Gold and Silver Coin		2
		£176			£176

We have already discussed the Issue Department. The net profits on the note issue go to the Exchequer.

All the shares of the Bank are in private hands. This accounts for the £15 million—actually £14,553,000—known as proprietors' capital. The "Rest" is the name given to the reserve fund accumulated out of undistributed profits. The Public Deposits are those of the British Government. They include the Exchequer Account, the Paymaster-General's Account, from which supplies are issued to the spending departments, and many accounts in connection with the National Debt, the collection of taxation, and Government funds of various types. The sums received and disbursed by the Government are so large that they would exercise a disturbing effect upon the money market unless the Bank were able to offset such possible disturbances if it wished.[1] The very important item of Bankers' Deposits has already been

[1] But it has done little recently. It seems more interested in the stability of total deposits than of Bankers' Deposits. The banks seem to do the offsetting by varying the amount of "window-dressing."

explained. It includes only the deposits of British banks whose main business is conducted in England. Other Accounts include balances maintained by foreign central banks, colonial banks, British banks operating mainly abroad, merchant banks and financial houses, and Indian and Colonial Governments.

Against these liabilities the Bank holds assets consisting of Government Securities, Other Securities, and Cash. Government Securities include only direct obligations of the British Government. Treasury bills acquired by the Bank on its own initiative and not presented to it for discount and any temporary Ways and Means Advances made to the Exchequer fall under this head. Thus it is this item which increases when the Bank pursues an expansionist open-market policy and buys Treasury bills or other Government securities, and which decreases when it follows the opposite policy.

The item of Other Securities is divided into two. Discounts and Advances comprise Treasury and other bills brought to the Bank for discount and advances made by the Bank to the discount market and to private clients. It is this item which increases when the market is "in the Bank." The other head, called "Securities," includes such stocks as first-class Indian, Dominion, Colonial, and foreign securities and commercial bills bought by the Bank on its own initiative.

We have already explained the notes. The gold and silver coin consists almost entirely of silver coin. The ratio which these two items bear to the total deposits of the Bank is usually known as the Proportion. In the above return, the Proportion is 26·9 per cent.

When Great Britain was on the gold standard, the policy of the Bank was directed towards protecting its gold reserve. Since September, 1931, this has not been so. The Bank is no longer compelled to give gold in exchange for its notes, and it acquired a very large gold reserve during recent years.

The "cheap money," or expansionist, policy followed by the Bank during recent years is brought out clearly by a comparison of the return for the week ended 11th November, 1931, with the one shown above. At the former date, the Bank held only £121 million of gold. Its total note issue was only £396 million, of which £357 million was in circulation. Its holding of Government securities was only £55 million and bankers' deposits were only £60 million. The bank rate was 6 per cent; it was reduced by stages to 2 per cent, where it has since remained,[1] in the summer of 1932. The great increase in its gold enabled it to expand the note circulation; its open-market purchases increased bankers' deposits; and the result, combined with lower rates of interest, was a great expansion in the deposits of the commercial banks.

An increase in public deposits tends to reduce bankers' deposits, for taxpayers and others draw cheques on their own banks in favour of the Government when they make payments to it. Such an increase, when foreseen, is often offset. For example, the Government issues fewer Treasury bills. An example of an increase which was not offset occurred during September and October, 1937. The following figures of the deposits of the Bank explain themselves.

	8th Sept., 1937. (£ Million)	27th Oct., 1937. (£ Million)
Public Deposits	12·0	32·2
Bankers' Deposits	105·6	87·7
Other Accounts	36·3	36·6
Total	153·9	156·5

The market is usually "in the Bank" around the turn of the year, when the commercial banks follow the absurd practice of "window-dressing," calling in some of their short loans to show in their statements of accounts higher cash reserves than they normally hold—the normal ratio is about 9 or 9½ per cent of deposits. The Bank apparently will not lend an appreciable sum to the discount market for less than a month or so, so that the effect of "window-dressing" on its item of Discounts and Advances takes some time to disappear. Thus on 23rd December, 1936, this item was £6·4 million. On 30th December it had risen to £17·5 million. It had not fallen back to normal before 10th February, when it was again £6·5 million.

We may perhaps conclude with a caution as to the limitations of monetary policy. It is relatively easy for the Bank, by buying bills or securities on the open market and allowing its Proportion to fall, to reduce short-term rates of interest and to increase

[1] Until it was suddenly raised to 4 per cent, owing to the grave risk of war in August, 1939.

bankers' deposits and thereby to increase by nine or ten times as much the total volume of bank deposits. But, to quote the wisdom of the people, you can lead a horse to the water but you cannot make him drink. Industry and trade may not be willing to borrow much more from the banks even at lower rates. In any event, the banks have to meet their operating costs, and they earn little or nothing on some of their assets, so that they are reluctant to reduce their rates on advances below a minimum of about 4 per cent. Hence the extra money may be created mainly by the purchase of additional investments by the banks, and most of it may remain idle. This was more or less the position in Great Britain after 1931 until the housing boom (due partly to low rates of interest) stimulated activity. In such circumstances, direct spending by the Government is often advocated in order to put the extra money into circulation.

It is possible, however, to give the horse only a limited ration of water. By raising the bank rate and reducing the amount of money the Bank can deflate, or so it may seem, as much as it wishes. But here too there are difficulties. The ultimate object of deflation is to reduce money incomes and costs. If most of the workers are strongly organized and resist any substantial reduction of wages, a firm policy of deflation may indeed reduce money income, but not labour costs, by means of a great increase in unemployment. In such circumstances, such a monetary policy—whether or not it would be best in the long run—would probably be abandoned or reversed owing to the great public outcry against it.

CHAPTER XXIV

THE VALUE OF MONEY

1. INTRODUCTION

We are now in a position to consider the causes of changes in the value of money: that is to say, in the purchasing power of a unit of currency over "things in general." The value of money may be regarded as the reciprocal of the general level of prices: for example, if the general level of prices has doubled, this means that the value of money has halved. The measurement of changes in the value of money presents difficulties. A discussion of these is postponed until the final section of this chapter. For the present, we need only point out that "sectional price-levels" often vary relatively to one another. For example, the prices of most ordinary shares may rise considerably (as in 1928 and 1929 in the United States) while the prices of commodities remain fairly stable, and wages may rise or fall relatively to the "cost of living."

A considerable change in the value of money usually has important consequences. We postpone a discussion of these until the last section but one.

The forces affecting the value of money, as of anything else, can be grouped under the two categories of supply and demand. After a note on monetary theories in general, and another on the quantity theory, we turn to the forces affecting the supply of money and the demand for it. These sections are comparatively brief because for the most part they simply repeat and generalize what has been said before. The supply of money in a particular country depends on its monetary and banking system. The previous chapter described at some length the monetary and banking system of Great Britain and showed the forces affecting the supply of money in Great Britain during recent years. The situation when a country forms part of a gold-standard or similar international monetary system is discussed in Chapter XXVIII. The demand for money, as for anything else, depends largely on the alternatives available. The main alternative to holding money is investing it. We discussed this in the chapter on Interest. Of course, at any moment all the existing stock of money is being held by different firms and institutions and individuals. But a community as a whole can always make its stock of money as large or as small a proportion of its total assets as it wishes. For an increase in its demand for money shows itself in a fall in the value of other assets, and conversely.

2. MONETARY THEORIES

The student of monetary theory soon finds that there seem to be many different theories as to the forces which determine the value of money. But this conflict of opinion among economists is largely apparent rather than real. Most economists would probably agree upon the reasons for any particular change which had occurred in the value of money, but some would phrase their explanations in different terms from others. The differences between them are mainly differences in the mode of approach and in terminology rather than fundamental differences of analysis.

A leading illustration of this is the apparent divergence between those who speak of the velocity of circulation of money and those who speak of the demand for money. An increase in the velocity of circulation—that is, in the rapidity with which units of currency pass from hand to hand—means that people are more willing than before to spend or invest money instead of holding it. But this means that their demand for money to hold has decreased. Hence those who use the former term are discussing just the same phenomenon as those who use the latter.

We have decided to use the term money to include bank deposits as well as cash. Some writers prefer not to include bank deposits but to regard them as substitutes for money. Thus we should regard an increase in bank deposits as an increase in the supply of money, but they would regard it as tending to decrease the demand for it in the same way as increased substitutes for anything tend to diminish the demand for it. But we should all agree that the consequence would be a tendency for the value of money to fall.

Some writers take the value of money to mean its purchasing power over commodities only, or over consumers' goods and services only, defining it as the reciprocal of "the general level of commodity prices" or of "the cost of living" instead of including everything against which money exchanges. We know that only a small part of total money payments are made against consumers' goods. Thus the quantity of money and its velocity of circulation may both increase—as in the United States from 1925 to 1929—and the result may be a great rise in the prices of stock exchange securities and a considerable rise in the prices of factors of production without any rise in the prices of commodities or in the cost of living. But writers who follow the above practice are usually well aware of this, and bear in mind that they are discussing a sectional price-level. Some of them point out that it is important to distinguish between "the financial circulation" —the stream of money payments made against stocks and shares and similar paper titles—and "the industrial circulation."

Another source of ambiguity is the concept of "the quantity of money." It is generally agreed that an increase in the quantity of money tends to raise prices and a decrease to lower them. But suppose that the central bank decided to print more notes and that these extra notes simply lay idle in its vaults, without causing anybody to change his actions. These extra notes would have no influence upon prices. We could say either that the *effective* quantity of money had not changed or that the increased supply of money had been exactly offset by an increased demand for money on the part of the central bank. Probably the latter is the more appropriate. For the banks might increase their deposits by purchasing securities and the additional deposits might remain idle, or the central bank might increase the amount of notes "in circulation" and yet the extra notes might not in fact circulate: they might be hoarded. It is simpler to take the total amount of money in existence as one of our data and then to consider what proportion of it is "hoarded" than to deduct the estimated amount hoarded and to speak of the remainder as the amount of "effective" money. But clearly the two methods should both lead to the same result.

3. THE QUANTITY THEORY OF MONEY

The best-known theory of the value of money is the Quantity Theory, which declares that the value of money depends upon its quantity. In its most rigid form, this theory asserts that any given percentage increase or decrease in the quantity of money will lead to the same percentage increase or decrease in the general level of prices.

This conclusion springs from the belief that money is only a kind of counter or ticket serving as a medium of exchange and that therefore the actual amount of money, provided there is enough to enable it to do its work, does not matter. It assumes that if a community had twice as much money all prices would be twice as high, that if it had only half as much money all prices would be half as high, and so on, so that the purchasing power of the total amount of money would always be the same. In other words, it assumes that the elasticity of the demand for money, in terms of other things, is always equal to unity, and that the "demand curve" for money remains unchanged.

This assumption seldom corresponds to reality. The demand for money frequently changes, and this may lead to considerable changes in prices even if the quantity of money remains constant. Moreover, any considerable change in the quantity of money is likely to cause a change in the demand for it—that is, in the total purchasing power of the total amount of money.

For example, during the German inflation after the last war, the quantity of money was increasing rapidly and prices were rising. People expected this movement to continue and in consequence their demand for money diminished. They tended to avoid holding depreciating marks, or claims to marks, and tried to change their marks at once into goods or shares or foreign exchange. In the language of some writers, there was a great increase in the velocity of circulation of marks. The result was that, owing to the general expectation that prices would continue to rise, prices in fact rose much more rapidly than the quantity of money was increased. Thus the volume of the note issue increased from 81 milliard paper marks in December, 1920, to 116,000 milliard in August, 1923, but its value in gold marks fell from 4800 million to 116 million.

Any general trade depression affords an illustration of a considerable fall in prices due to an increase in the demand for money rather than a diminution in its supply. The amount of cash and the volume of bank deposits were both increased substantially in Great Britain after 1931, yet for some years most prices remained well below their pre-depression level. This was because the public feared, for some time, that the depression would continue. People therefore refrained from spending more or from substantially increasing their investments in industry. In other words, their demand for money was greater than it had been before the depression and therefore prices were lower despite the increase in the quantity of money.

Nobody to-day holds the quantity theory in its rigid form. But a number of writers set out some more flexible version, which takes account of changes in other influences as well as in the quantity of money. The version put forward by Professor Irving Fisher is so well known that we shall give a brief critical account of it.

Over a period, a number of transactions take place in which money is exchanged against other things. To take a simple example, on a very small scale, these transactions may consist of the sale of 40,000 loaves of bread at 6d. a loaf, the sale of 100 shares at £1 a share, and the sale of the services for one week of 100 men at £3 each. The total money payments during the period must equal the total value of the things exchanged against money—in this case, of £1000 for the loaves, £100 for the shares, and £300 for the wages, making £1400 in all. Professor Fisher denotes the total quantity of things exchanged against money—the "volume of transactions"—by the symbol T and defines the symbol P in such a way that P multiplied by T is the total value of all the transactions. P is thus the general level of prices at which these transactions are effected; $\frac{1}{P}$ is the value of money.

We have seen that the total value of these transactions, TP, must equal the total money payments made. But, over the period, some units of money may not be exchanged for anything else, while other units may change hands a number of times, being used for a number of transactions. The total quantity of money in existence may be termed M and the average number of times which a unit of money changes hands during the period, in paying for other things, may be called the velocity of circulation of money and may be denoted by V. Thus the total value of money payments is M multiplied by V. This gives us the "equation of exchange," namely

$$MV = PT$$

This equation is perhaps useful in demonstrating that if the quantity of money is increased and V and T remain unchanged (or if V divided by T remains constant), the general level of prices must increase by exactly the same percentage. If, for example, double the stream of money meets the same stream of other things, against which it exchanges, the average prices of these other things must double.

But in reality, as we have already remarked, a change in M is almost certain to cause changes in V and T, and in some monetary and banking systems a change in P may lead to a change in M. The four elements in the equation are interrelated; it is not true that M alone will change, causing a corresponding change in P.

Moreover, there seems no need to break away from the general theory of value, when we discuss the value of money, by introducing the concept of "velocity of circulation." Instead of speaking of an increase or decrease in the velocity of circulation of money, we can speak of a decrease or increase in the demand for money.

We shall therefore consider first the forces determining the supply of money, which will be different according to the monetary and banking system of the country under consideration, and then the forces determining the demand for money.

4. THE SUPPLY OF MONEY

The ways in which means of payment come into existence and go out of existence, and the extent to which the supply of them will change when conditions change, depend upon the monetary and banking system and the policy of those who control it. If a country is on the gold standard (or on any other international standard) it must keep its price-level in line with the price-levels of other countries on the same standard. We shall consider this subject later. Let us think of an isolated country.

Suppose the country uses a commodity, let us say gold, as money. Suppose the only money consists of gold coins. The total stock of gold in existence will be large relatively to the annual output of gold from the mines, so that considerable changes in the total stock of monetary gold will not be likely over fairly short periods. There may be an industrial demand for gold as well as a monetary demand. If so, some of the gold in existence, and part of the annual output, will not be available for monetary purposes. In fact, the monetary demand for gold is far more important than the industrial demand, and if the former were to disappear the value of gold would fall very heavily.

The "price" of an ounce of gold is fixed if gold is used as money, and if the gold-mines are working under competition the marginal cost of producing gold will equal its price. An improvement in the technique of gold-mining or the discovery of new deposits, which could be worked profitably, would lower the marginal cost of production of gold and would cause the output of gold to increase to a level at which marginal cost again equalled the fixed price. Conversely, the exhaustion of the better deposits would raise marginal cost and diminish the output.

This situation would remain essentially the same if a central bank bought and sold gold at a fixed price and issued paper notes backed 100 per cent by gold. Instead of a given number of gold coins being in circulation, the same number of paper notes would be in circulation at any time.

The situation would be fundamentally altered, however, if the central bank could issue paper notes to a *greater* value than the gold in its vaults. New money could then come into circulation not only by new gold being mined and exchanged for notes but also by the central bank printing more notes (without receiving additional gold) and using them to purchase something or lending them to borrowers, who would spend them. Each note might be convertible into gold at the central bank and yet the public might hold considerably more notes than were backed by gold without wishing to change them into gold. Under these conditions, the amount of notes in circulation would depend (within wide limits) upon the discretion of the central bank. If the bank thought it unwise to increase the supply of money despite an increased output of gold, it could keep the volume of its notes constant by, for example, selling securities and thus taking notes out of circulation equal to the number which it had to put into circulation owing to its purchase of gold. Again, it could increase its note issue and put the extra notes into circulation even if the output of gold remained the same or diminished. Provided the public continued to accept the notes, without wanting to convert them into gold, there would be no upper limit to the quantity of money unless a limit was set by a law forbidding the bank to issue more than a given number of notes not based on gold, or compelling it to maintain a minimum percentage reserve of gold against its notes.

Now suppose that there are other banks which receive deposits upon which cheques can be drawn: this is of course the actual situation in modern countries. Means of payment now include bank deposits. The banks hold a reserve of "cash," consisting, say, of notes (of the central bank) plus deposits with the central bank, against their deposits. They can increase their deposits by increasing their loans and they can diminish their deposits by lending less freely. When a new loan is created, deposits will increase by that amount and when an old loan is paid off deposits will diminish by that amount. There is no reason why the banks should keep a constant percentage of cash to deposits (although they tend to do so in Great Britain). When trade prospects seem bright and there is a general optimistic outlook the banks may lend more freely, reducing their percentage reserve of cash, and when prospects seem gloomy they may follow the opposite policy. Even if they do keep a constant percentage reserve of cash, it is in the power of the central bank to increase or decrease their holdings of cash and thereby lead them to expand or contract their loans and deposits.

Thus there may be times when the banking system as a whole wants to increase the supply of money. It can always do this by purchasing securities. The sellers of these securities find their deposits increased. But if these additional deposits are left idle, only the prices of securities will be raised. In order to raise the prices of other things, the banks must induce borrowers to borrow more, spending the money upon expanding their businesses. If the expected rate of profits is above the rate charged by the banks to borrowers, there will be no difficulty in finding borrowers. But if it is not, then the banks must lower their rates in order to induce entrepreneurs and others to borrow more. If entrepreneurs and others think that the trade outlook is gloomy, enough additional borrowers (able to offer adequate security) to bring about an appreciable rise in the price-level may not be forthcoming. It may be that the rate charged by the banks would have to be negative in order to increase substantially the volume of bank loans. At such times, the banking system may do its best to increase the supply of money but its efforts may meet with no response; it may indeed increase the supply (by purchasing securities) but this may be offset by a corresponding increase in the demand for money by the public. Some writers urge that during such times of depression Governments should bring about an effective increase in the supply of money by spending more upon public works, unemployment relief, and so on, or by reducing taxation, thus deliberately creating a budget deficit. Even such a policy might not succeed in raising the price-level—if the public distrusted it, the public might offset the efforts of the Government by increasing its own demand for money. Other writers believe that a better remedy would be to reduce costs and thus make the expected rate of profit higher. Against this it is argued that some costs, and, in particular, wages, are very difficult to reduce. We express no opinion here upon this controversy. Our only object has been to show the forces which determine the supply of money.

5. THE DEMAND FOR MONEY

The concept of the demand for money has been mentioned before.[1] If the total amount of money in a country is given, then at any moment all of it must be somewhere—in pockets, in tills, in the vaults of banks, and so on. The total amount of money, no more and no less, must be demanded, in the sense that all of it must be held somewhere by somebody. But the value, or purchasing power, of this amount—the demand for money in terms of other things—may change.

An increase in the demand for houses—the stock of houses being given—shows itself in an increase in the value of houses. An increase in the demand for money shows itself in an increase in the value of money—i.e. a general fall in prices, as during the depression. The demand for money *increases* during a depression: that is why the price-level falls, although the quantity of money may be increased. For the demand for money is a demand *to hold* money rather than other assets.

Most people and firms (including banks) are constantly receiving money and paying out money. Apart from hoarders, people hold very different amounts of money at different times.

[1] Chapter XVIII, section 7; and Chapter XXI, section 5.

Wage-earners paid on Fridays have more money on Friday nights than on Thursday nights. Nevertheless every person or firm holds on the average, taking one day with another, a certain sum of money. What determines the amount of money which, on the average, he wishes to hold?

If he did not hold money, he could either spend it or invest it. It is easy to understand why people prefer holding money to holding large stocks of goods which may deteriorate in quality. The question is why they do not invest this money and get interest on it until the time comes when they want to spend it. One reason is that it is costly and troublesome to invest small sums for short periods. Another reason is that people are not sure of how much cash they will need in the near future, and like to keep a certain amount of cash or bank deposits as a liquid reserve against possible unforeseen contingencies. Finally, they fear that the prices of securities may fall. Thus people and firms tend to keep a certain proportion of their assets in the form of money. An increase in the practice of offsetting by book-entry debts due from A to B by debts due from B to A (a process which is carried to the limit when firms engaged in different stages of producing the same finished commodity amalgamate) would reduce the demand for money; if more wage-earners were paid by cheque they would keep some of their money in the form of bank deposits and not of cash, and this would enable the banks to expand their total deposits without reducing their percentage reserve of cash, and so on.

Now suppose that people think that the rate of profits is rising. They will want to keep a smaller proportion of their assets in the form of money, since investment is more profitable than it was before and the need for liquidity is no greater. Investment will increase. Purchases by entrepreneurs and others who get command of the new capital will increase and this will tend to raise prices. Although the total amount of money may remain the same, its value will fall. Thus the desire of the public to hold a smaller proportion of their assets in the form of money will be fulfilled. Each may hold as much money as before but its value will be less. In the same way if people think that the prices of commodities are going to rise they will try to hold more commodities and less money, and the increased purchases of commodities will send up their prices and reduce the value of a given amount of money.

In other words, when people think that investment is more profitable and that prices are going to rise their "liquidity-preference" diminishes: they want to hold a smaller proportion of the total value of their assets in the form of money. When they think the opposite, their liquidity-preference increases. The proportion of deposit accounts to current accounts tends to grow. Their liquidity-preference, together with such things as the amount of integration among businesses, the extent to which book credit is used and the extent to which cheques are used—things which do not change much over short periods—determines the demand for money. This together with the supply determines the value of money. But it should always be remembered that sectional price-levels may show divergent movements, especially in periods of rapid change.[1]

6. THE EFFECTS OF CHANGES IN THE VALUE OF MONEY

Although we cannot measure changes in the value of money with absolute accuracy, such changes are often sufficiently marked to leave no room for doubt or dispute. We know that they have occurred and we know roughly how large they have been.

At times they have been very large indeed. During and after the last war a considerable rise took place in the price-level of most European countries. The rise in Germany reached an astronomical height. In the summer of 1923 most prices, in terms of German paper marks, were many million times higher than they had been a few years earlier. Again, the Great Depression of

[1] In Chapter XVIII we found that according to one school of thought the demand for and supply of money determine the rate of interest. We now say that they determine the price level. Those who believe in the former view may nevertheless hold the latter view also, explaining the apparent inconsistency on the following lines. The rate of interest, they might argue, is the link between the quantity of money and the price level. There is no direct relation between the quantity of money and prices; what affects prices is not the quantity of money (M), but total spending (MV). And total spending will normally increase only if there is an increase in the production of new capital goods, either because entrepreneurs believe that the profitability of capital has increased or because the rate of interest has fallen. An increase in the quantity of money, for example, will, in certain circumstances, lower the rate of interest and thus increase investment and raise the general level of prices. The demand for and supply of money thus determine both the rate of interest and the general level of prices.

recent years led to a very considerable fall in the general level of prices. The extent of this fall differed between countries. Some countries left the gold standard in order to lessen the fall in prices in terms of their own money. Moreover, the fall in interest rates was reflected in a rise in the prices of fixed-interest securities issued by "safe" borrowers. Nevertheless it is beyond dispute that between, say, 1928 and 1932, the general level of prices fell, in terms of gold, by something between one-third and one-half. Changes of anything approaching this order of magnitude have very important consequences.

Suppose that the value of money is falling or, in other words, that the general level of prices is rising. Some prices will rise faster than others. As a rule, the prices of commodities will rise faster than wage-rates—the prices of labour services. This will increase the value of the marginal products of all types of labour. If previously a number of workers were unemployed, many of them will be reabsorbed into employment, and overtime may be worked. Profits will increase. The prices of ordinary shares and of capital goods will tend to rise. Those who borrow at fixed interest will gain if they use the money to buy goods which they resell on a rising market, or to produce goods which have risen in price with the aid of factors of production whose prices have risen less. Those who lend at fixed interest will lose, since the purchasing power of their money will be less when it is repaid than it was when they lent it. The increased rate of profits, while leading to a rise in the price of ordinary shares, will depress the prices of securities yielding fixed rates of interest. The "burden of fixed charges" upon entrepreneurs will be lessened, since although the money amount of the charges will remain the same the receipts of the entrepreneurs will increase. People holding money or claims to fixed sums of money will clearly lose by a fall in the value of money; under this head come all receivers of fixed incomes.

There will also be effects on the structure of production, as we saw when discussing the trade cycle. If the rise in prices is due to increased supplies of money which are spent by entrepreneurs, the demand for producers' goods will expand relatively to the demand for consumers' goods, and the structure of production will become more capitalistic.

The social and political consequences of a considerable fall in the value of money may be very important. For example, the marked rise in the price-level during the sixteenth and seventeenth centuries played a considerable part in bringing about the transference of power in England from the King to Parliament. The income of the monarchy was more or less fixed, but its expenses rose with the rise in prices, so that taxation had to be increased, and Parliament could insist upon concessions in return for increased grants to the monarchy. Again, many observers contend that the post-war German inflation practically wiped out the "middle classes" and thereby paved the way for the rise of National Socialism.

When the value of money is rising, the effects are exactly the opposite of those we have just described. In particular, if wage-rates are at all "sticky" (as they usually are) the values of the marginal products of labour will diminish and unemployment will increase. At the bottom of the Great Depression, the total number of unemployed workers in the leading industrial countries exceeded 30 million.

7. THE MEASUREMENT OF CHANGES IN THE VALUE OF MONEY

If tea costs 2s. a lb., the value of £1 in terms of pounds of tea is 10. If the price of tea rises to 2s. 6d., the value of £1 in terms of pounds of tea falls to 8. The change can be expressed by saying either that the price of tea has risen by 25 per cent or that the value of money, in terms of tea, has fallen by 20 per cent. Since money serves as a general measure of value we always tend to think of the change in the value of the commodity in terms of money, which we call its price, rather than of the change in the value of money in terms of the commodity.

We can measure the change in the value of money, as between two dates, in terms of a *group* of commodities, such as foodstuffs. Suppose that we know the retail price of every kind of foodstuff at each of the two dates. There are several different ways in which we can compress all these facts into a single figure showing the percentage change in what may be termed the "price-level of foodstuffs" between the two dates; and the different ways may give different results. We can illustrate this briefly by taking a "group" of two commodities, bread and tea. Suppose that the price of bread has fallen from 6¼d. to 6d. per 4 lb. loaf and that the price of tea has risen from 2s. to 2s. 6d. per lb. One way of measuring the change in the price-level of the group is to add together all the percentage changes and divide by the number of commodities. In this case, this gives a result of minus 4 plus 25 divided by 2—that is, a rise of 10·5 per cent. But this method gives the same importance or "weight" to every commodity. Suppose that at the former date 30 loaves were consumed for every pound of tea consumed. We could measure the change in the value of a collection consisting of 30 loaves plus 1 lb. of tea. Such a collection cost 17s. 7½d. at the former date and 17s. 6d. at the latter date, so that this method (of "weighting") gives us a fall of 0·7 per cent. We may know, however, that at the latter date only 20 loaves were consumed for every pound of tea consumed, and the cost of *this* collection has *risen* from 12s. 5d. to 12s. 6d. Thus our result may vary according to the "weights" which we employ.

We may further illustrate this point by considering the temporary but spectacular rise in the price of metals which took place early in 1937. The following table gives prices per ton at each of three dates—

	11th Mar., 1936	10th Feb., 1937	10th Mar., 1937
	£	£	£
Steel (Bars) . .	10	10·5	12
Copper (Electrolytic) .	40	61	77
Lead (Pig) . . .	19	29	37 5
Spelter (G.O.B.) . .	16	23	36
Tin (Ingots) . .	215	237	301

On 10th February, 1937, the percentage increase in the price of steel, as compared with 11th March, 1936, was 5, of copper 52, of lead 53, of spelter 44, of tin 10. If we add these together and divide by five, we find that the average rise was 33 per cent. On 10th March, 1937, the percentage increase in the price of steel, as compared with 11th March, 1936, was 20, of copper 92, of lead 97, of spelter 125, and of tin 40, If we add these together and divide by five, we find that the average rise was 75 per cent. These results could be expressed in the form of a series of index numbers, as follows—

INDEX OF METAL PRICES

11th March, 1936	100
10th February, 1937	133
10th March, 1937	175

But the relative importance of these five metals is no the same. The world output of tin in 1935 was only 145,000 metric tons. That of steel was over 100 million metric tons—about 700 times as great; and that of each of the other three was roughly 10 times as great. We can apply these "weights" by calculating the cost of a collection consisting of 700 tons of steel, 10 tons of copper, 10 tons of lead, 10 tons of spelter, and 1 ton of tin, on each of these three dates. On 11th March, 1936, it cost £7965; on 10th February, 1937, it cost £8717, having risen by 9 per cent; and on 10th March, 1937, it cost £10,206, having risen by 28 per cent. Thus an index constructed in this way would show a considerably smaller rise than the one given above, and would read as follows—

INDEX OF METAL PRICES

11th March, 1936	100
10th February, 1937	109
10th March, 1937	128

But an index weighted differently—according, say, to production in a different year or to consumption in a particular country—would yield a different result.

Clearly it is possible to measure, by whatever method seems most appropriate, the changes over time in all kinds of "sectional price-levels." Thus we can measure the change over time in the cost of a group of raw materials, or mineral products, or manufactured goods, or export commodities, or commodities sold at wholesale, or commodities sold at retail. We can combine groups together. For example, *The Economist* index of British wholesale prices shows that on 21st September, 1931, when Great Britain left the gold standard, the price-level of cereals and meat was 64·5 per cent, that of other food 62·2 per cent, that of textiles 43·7 per cent, that of minerals 67·4 per cent, and that of miscellaneous goods 65·8 per cent, of their 1927 level. The price-level of all these groups combined was 60·4 per cent of what it was in 1927. Nor are we confined to commodities. We can group together any things which money can buy. Thus we can measure the changes over time in the "price-level" of stocks and shares, or of house-rents, and we can combine the changes in different kinds of wage-rates in order to measure the change in "the general level of wage-rates." It is usual, in order to facilitate comparisons, to show the results in the form of "index numbers." The cost of the group at some date, known as the "base" date, is denoted by the index number 100, and the cost at other dates is expressed as a percentage of the cost at the base date. Thus the cost of the collection of foodstuffs used by the British Ministry of Labour to measure changes in the retail price-level of foodstuffs was 223·8d. on July, 1914, the base date, and 354·6d. on 1st January, 1929, so that the index number for the former date is 100 and for the latter 159, since $\frac{354\cdot6}{223\cdot8} = \frac{159}{100}$. The same method can be used to measure differences in the value of money between different places.

The value of money in terms of one group of things may, and often does, move in a different way from its value in terms of another group of things. For example, the "cost of living" (retail foodstuffs, house-rents, clothing, and so on) may rise or fall relatively to the general level of wages, the price-level of stocks and shares may rise or fall relatively to wholesale commodity prices, the price-level of exports may rise or fall relatively to that of imports. Such divergences often indicate important economic changes, and it is essential for anybody who wishes to apply economic analysis to the study of current problems to know them and to appreciate their significance. Indeed, these sectional price-levels, and the divergences in their respective trends, are far more significant than some all-embracing index purporting to measure changes in the value of money in terms of *all* things against which money exchanges. In my judgment, such an index, although logically the only one which could measure changes in *the* value of money, as against "things in general," would relate to such a hotch-potch that it would be of little use.

One difficulty of compiling an adequate and accurate index even of a sectional price-level may be the practical one that statistics of prices are costly to collect. The task is usually undertaken by Governments, but no Government attempts to collect data relating to all the many thousands of different things which are sold for money every day. It is easy to obtain the prices of goods dealt in on organized markets, but it is more difficult to get satisfactory figures for goods sold retail. Thus an index which attempts to measure changes in "the cost of living" may be defective either because the prices of goods which are not included vary differently from those of goods which are, or because the prices collected are not the prices at which most of the goods are in fact sold. But this difficulty is a relatively minor one, and does not seriously impair the reliability of most existing indexes.

The real difficulty about index numbers is often called "the index-number problem," and there is no possible way of surmounting it. It is the difficulty of deciding what things should be included and how they should be weighted. We shall set out this difficulty under three headings, but all three relate to what is essentially the same problem.

In the first place, different persons buy different things and hold different assets. Hence a given change in prices will affect one person differently from another. Thus a cost-of-living index number based on the consumption of "typical" working-class families at a particular date may have little relevance to middle-class families or to working-class families whose consumption is appreciably different from that of the "typical" family. Moreover, as time goes on, the same person may change his habits, owing to changes in his wealth or tastes. The cost-of-living index number prepared by the British Ministry of Labour is based on the consumption of a typical working-class family in 1904. By 1938 it was admittedly out of date. The consumption of a typical working-class family was considerably different from what it had been in 1904. A new index, based on present consumption, is to be compiled. But there is no way of making a really satisfactory comparison between the cost of living in 1904 and the cost of living in 1938, for consumption habits have considerably changed over this period.

In the second place some things may be sold at one time or place and not at another, and must therefore be excluded from the data. Thus many new things, such as motor cars and radios and artificial silk and electrical apparatus and visits to cinemas, have entered the circle of exchange during the last few decades. Even if a commodity has the same name, it may be quite different in style and quality. Artificial silk stockings are not the same thing as woollen stockings; 1938 motor cars are not the same thing as 1928 motor cars; and so on. The clothing and houses of the Tropics are not the same as those of more temperate regions. This means that comparisons between times or places in which the collections of things sold for money are markedly different have little significance. This same difficulty arises over short periods also, since some things are widely sold only at certain seasons. It is for this reason that the British Ministry of Labour is constrained to exclude fruit and vegetables, other than potatoes, from its cost-of-living index number.

In the third place, both relative prices and the relative quantities of different things coming forward for sale may differ as between the times or places which are being compared. If the price of every individual thing were, say, 10 per cent higher at one time or place we could say that the general level of prices was 10 per cent higher, since *any* collection of things would cost 10 per cent more. Again, if the relative quantities of different things were exactly the same, we could base our index upon quantities of different things combined in these fixed proportions. But usually relative prices move in a different way from relative quantities sold. As time goes on, various changes take place. Tastes, in the narrower sense, may change: for example, English people now drink considerably less beer and spirits than some years ago, and women spend more time and money in beauty-parlours. The age-composition of the population may change: the declining proportion of children in Great Britain has caused the sales of such things as perambulators and baby foods to diminish. The real income of the population, or its distribution among persons, may change: an increase in real income, such as has taken place in most countries during recent years, will induce people to buy what used to be considered luxuries (for example, motor cars, radios, refrigerators, vacuum cleaners, and fruit and butter) rather than bread and the coarser kinds of foodstuffs, of clothing, and so on. Technical progress may reduce the prices of certain goods, and in consequence people may buy more of them. In times of depression, the demand for "gilt-edged" securities tends to rise and the demand for ordinary shares to fall; in times of boom the opposite takes place.

The same difficulty emerges if comparisons are made between

places. For example, the British inquiry into the *Cost of Living in German Towns*, made before the last war, concluded that the goods and services habitually consumed by German workmen cost about a tenth more in England than in Germany, whereas the goods and services habitually consumed by British workmen cost about a fifth more in Germany than in England.

This difficulty means, as we saw in our examples of bread and tea, and of metals, that one set of "weights" may yield quite a different result from another. Various compromises are possible. For example, we could average the results obtained from different sets of "weights" or we could draw up a table of "equivalents," postulating, for example, that 50 litres of *vin ordinaire* (the main drink of the French workman) are equivalent to 1 lb. of tea (the main drink of the British workman) or that 1 lb. of butter (the consumption of which has greatly increased in Great Britain during recent years) is equivalent to 2 lb. of margarine. But clearly no such compromises are really satisfactory and we must resign ourselves to the fact that any measure of differences in the value of money between times or places will be more or less arbitrary and inaccurate.

BOOK V
INTERNATIONAL TRADE

CHAPTER XXV

THE THEORY OF INTERNATIONAL TRADE

1. INTRODUCTION

We must now take account of the fact that the world is divided into a large number of countries between which trade and investment and migration may take place.

Clearly this fact does not in any way upset the conclusions which we have already reached. For example, the Law of Diminishing Returns, or the fact that output can be increased, up to a point, by greater specialization, by the use of more capitalistic methods, and by improvements in technique, is obviously valid however few or however many countries there may be in the world. Similarly, the fact that price tends to equate supply and demand, that an entrepreneur tends to equate marginal cost and marginal revenue, that the price of a factor-unit, under competition, tends to equal the value of the marginal product of that factor—these are general propositions which apply wherever there is capitalism; they are equally valid in France or in Japan or in the county of Somerset. Why, then, need we take account, for the purpose of economic analysis, of national boundaries?

Perhaps the main reason is that labour and capital move less freely between countries than within a country. Workers are often reluctant to move to a different country, especially if the language and ways of living are different, despite the attraction of higher wages. Owners of capital often think that it is more risky for them to invest abroad than at home. Further, national Governments often place obstacles in the way of movements of labour and capital across their boundaries. Thus, nowadays many Governments restrict both the immigration of labour and the export of capital. We have already seen that it is not always easy for factors to move from one district to another within a country, but in fact movement between countries may be so much more difficult that a special theory of international trade is empirically justified.

Moreover, a national Government may take various measures in pursuit of a national economic policy. Thus it may impose duties or quotas on imports or it may control the purchase and sale of foreign exchange. The present book makes some study of the economic effects of such measures. It also considers the main problems arising from separate national currency and banking systems.

2. THE LOCATION OF INDUSTRY

Trade between countries is clearly just a special case of trade between regions. Queensland, for example, supplies New South Wales with bananas. She did so before 1901, when Queensland and New South Wales were separate countries and the trade was therefore called international. The federation of the Australian states in 1901 made not the slightest difference to the relative advantages of Queensland in the production of bananas. Lorraine supplied iron ore to the Ruhr before 1914, when both districts formed part of Germany. The restoration of Lorraine to France made this trade international but it did nothing to change the comparative advantages of Lorraine in the production of iron ore. From the standpoint of economic geography, national boundaries are arbitrary. But in practice a national Government may restrict the movement of goods from another country into its own whilst it does not restrict the movement of goods from one district to another within its own territory. We need, then, to begin with, a theory of the location of industry. Why do different districts specialize in the production of particular goods and services? What are the underlying conditions which make it more profitable for an entrepreneur to set up an establishment (to produce particular goods) in one place rather than in another?

The main reason why different districts specialize in different products is that factors of production are distributed in unequal proportions over the surface of the earth.

This is obvious in the case of those factors usually grouped under the heading of land or natural resources. Some districts, for example, have a climate particularly suitable for certain products. Other districts possess minerals which are not found elsewhere, or which are not so accessible elsewhere. It is easy to understand why Italy exports citrus fruits, why Canada exports furs, and why Great Britain exports coal.

Different kinds of labour also are unevenly distributed, relatively to other factors. For example, trained chemists are relatively abundant in Germany and therefore Germany exports chemical products. Again, contrast Japan and Australia. Japan has a population of nearly 70 million and an area of only 147,000 square miles, of which over half is forest and less than a fifth can be cultivated. Australia has a population of less than 7 million and an area of 3 million square miles, the greater part of which (although arid) is suitable for sparse pastoral cultivation. In Japan, agriculture is very intensive—the number per square mile is large—and the main products are rice and silk. Her main manufactured products are textiles, produced largely with the aid of automatic machines and relatively unskilled female labour. In Australia, agriculture is extensive and her chief product is wool, which requires a high proportion of land relatively to labour.

In terms of costs, our principle implies that a factor which is relatively abundant in a given district will be relatively cheap there. Hence goods requiring a relatively large proportion of that factor can be produced more cheaply in that district than elsewhere.

We need not inquire why factors are distributed territorially as they are; this is a question falling mainly within the provinces of economic geography and economic history. To give just one example, the five towns in Staffordshire specialize in pottery, but their clay comes from Cornwall. And the reason is that in the eighteenth century there was suitable clay in Staffordshire; the industry expanded greatly; Staffordshire clay-beds became quite inadequate to supply its needs, but the skilled workers were now in Staffordshire and so the industry continued there, importing its clay from Cornwall and elsewhere.

The question of why workers of a given type do not move to districts where they are relatively scarce and therefore might earn more has already been discussed. Climate, obviously, cannot move.

This, then, explains why certain goods are produced more cheaply in some districts than in others. It explains why an entrepreneur may find it cheaper to set up a factory in one place than in another.

The main reason, to repeat, for the location of industry is the fact that factors are distributed in unequal proportions over the surface of the earth. Australia can produce wool cheaply because wool requires a high proportion of land to labour, and in Australia land is relatively abundant and therefore relatively cheap, while labour is relatively scarce and therefore relatively dear. We may note further that this explains differences in the method of production of the same commodity in different districts. In England, for example, land is scarcer relatively to labour than in new countries so that cultivation is more intensive. The yield of wheat per acre is much greater in England than in overseas countries; the yield per man is less. Again, England has a relative abundance of skilled cotton operatives; she therefore spins, on the whole, finer yarns, and uses more Egyptian cotton and mule spindles than, say, India or Japan.

There are, however, some further observations which should be made about the location of industry.

In the first place, given the distribution, purchasing power, and purchasing habits of the population, costs of marketing must be considered. District A may produce a commodity more cheaply than district B but may be unable to compete in the B market with producers in B owing to the cost of transporting the commodity from A to B. The cost of transport does not vary directly with distance. Sea transport is especially cheap, and this tends to locate export industries near ports.

In the second place, some materials lose weight in the process of manufacture and hence transport costs can be avoided by manufacturing near the source of the material. The leading example, of course, is coal, which loses all its weight when it is used as fuel. To use the coal on the spot saves the cost of transporting it because its weight adds nothing to the weight of the products which it is used in making. When there are several materials, located at different points, works will tend to be located where the total costs of transport of the materials are lowest. Thus blast furnaces will tend to be near the iron ore, as in Lorraine and the English Midlands, rather than near the coal, if the iron content of the ore is low. For if the iron content is, say, one-third, 3 tons of iron ore plus about 1½ tons of coal are needed to produce 1 ton of pig-iron. Assuming the markets to be equally far from both the coal and the ore, locating the blast furnaces near the ore rather than near the coal saves $1\frac{1}{2}x$ ton-miles of transport (x being the distance in miles between the coal and the ore) for every ton of pig-iron produced.

In the third place, there may be economic advantages in integration.

In the fourth place, there may be a gain from using indivisible specialized equipment, which requires a large output to make it worth while. A country like South Africa or New Zealand does not provide a large enough market to make worth while the conveyer-system used in the mass production of motor cars or the specialized equipment used in producing certain heavy steel parts. Hence such goods tend to be made near the big markets, in Western Europe or the United States, and exported all over the world.

In the fifth place, there is the gain from concentrating an industry in an area. A leading example of this is the Lancashire cotton industry. There is a constant supply of skilled labour available; subsidiary industries are close at hand so that machinery can readily be replaced or repaired; the banks understand cotton and the financing of its importation and manufacture; the transport system is constructed to serve a localized industry, and so on. These gains are important although the indivisible units of equipment are relatively small.

3. THE GAIN FROM INTERNATIONAL TRADE

If the whole world were one country, there would be no difficulty in realizing how consumers gain by different goods being produced in different places. We have seen that, under competition, goods are produced where their costs of production plus marketing are lowest. Consumers benefit by this, since any other arrangement would raise costs and therefore prices.

But in fact the world is cut up into countries with different Governments and different currencies. This does not in any way alter our reasoning but it does make advisable a different statement of the problem. We have to show how a country may gain by importing goods which it could produce for itself.

Let us simplify a little by supposing that there are only two countries, A and B, and that factors of production cannot move from one country to another: only goods can move.

(1) A can produce, say, tea but not linen. B can produce linen but not tea. Here trade gives both countries the possibility of consuming a good otherwise unobtainable. A merchant can leave A with a cargo of tea, exchange it for linen in B, and sell the linen in A for enough to replace the money he spent on the tea and on the voyage and give him a profit for himself. The producers of tea in A are not injured: they produce as much tea as before, only some is now consumed abroad. Similarly with the producers of linen in B. The consumers in A gain because they prefer to buy some linen and less tea, and the consumers in B gain because they prefer to buy some tea and less linen.

(2) Now suppose that both countries can produce both tea and linen but that A can produce tea more cheaply than B and B can produce linen more cheaply than A, owing to differences in climate and soil. For example—

X factors produce	100 tea in A
	50 linen in A
X factors produce	50 tea in B
	100 linen in B

Suppose trade takes place, A specializing in tea and B in linen. 2 *X* factors in A produce 200 tea. 2 *X* factors in B produce 200 linen. The total output of these 4 *X* factors is now 200 tea + 200 linen whereas before it was 150 tea + 150 linen. The manner in which the gain is divided between the two countries A and B will depend on the terms of trade—on the rate at which tea is exchanged for linen. Suppose, to give a simple illustration, that this rate is 1 unit of tea against 1 unit of linen. (Actually, any rate between 1 tea to 2 linen and 1 tea to $\frac{1}{2}$ linen would be profitable to both, although naturally the greater the amount of linen obtained for a unit of tea the greater is the relative gain of A.) Then A might exchange, for example, 80 tea against 80 linen, so that A would now have 120 tea and 80 linen while B would now have 80 tea and 120 linen.

(3) Now suppose that A can produce both tea and linen more cheaply than B but that its comparative advantage is greater in tea. A given number of workers in A, with the aid of climate and other factors, can produce *either* 200 units tea

or 200 units linen *or* 100 tea + 100 linen, and so on—an extra unit of tea "costing" a unit of linen. In fact A—self-supporting —produces 150 tea plus 50 linen.

In country B the same quantity of factors can produce *either* 80 tea *or* 160 linen *or* 40 tea + 80 linen, and so on, an extra unit of tea "costing" 2 units of linen. In fact B—self-supporting—produces 40 tea + 80 linen.

Now suppose that trade takes place, A specializing on tea and B on linen. For example, A gives 45 tea for 60 linen. Therefore A has 155 tea + 60 linen and B has 45 tea + 100 linen. Clearly both countries have gained by specializing and exchanging.

4. THE PRINCIPLE OF COMPARATIVE COSTS

In our first two examples, country A enjoyed an absolute advantage over country B in the production of tea. In our first example, this advantage was immeasurably great, since country B was supposed incapable of producing any tea at all. In our second example, country B was capable of producing tea, but fewer factors of production were required to produce a unit of tea in A than in B. In both examples, country B enjoyed an absolute advantage over country A in the production of linen. In our third example, country A enjoyed an absolute advantage over country B in the production of both tea and linen. But this advantage was greater in the production of tea than in the production of linen. To put the matter from the standpoint of country B, country B had an absolute disadvantage in the production of both commodities, but her disadvantage (relatively to country A) was less in linen than in tea. Both countries gained, therefore, by entering into trade with one another, A specializing in the production of tea and B in the production of linen.

All these three examples fall under one general principle: the principle of comparative costs. This principle states that a country will gain by specializing in the production of those commodities in which its comparative cost advantage is greater (or in which its comparative cost disadvantage is less), exporting these commodities in exchange for commodities in which its comparative cost advantage is less (or its comparative cost disadvantage is greater).

In fact, the absolute money cost of producing a commodity

in a country which exports it is always lower than in a country which imports it. Why, then, do we bother about this principle of comparative costs? Why do we not simply say that goods will be produced where the money costs of production (and marketing) are lowest?

The reason is that this statement, although true, is merely superficial. Money costs of production are made up of prices

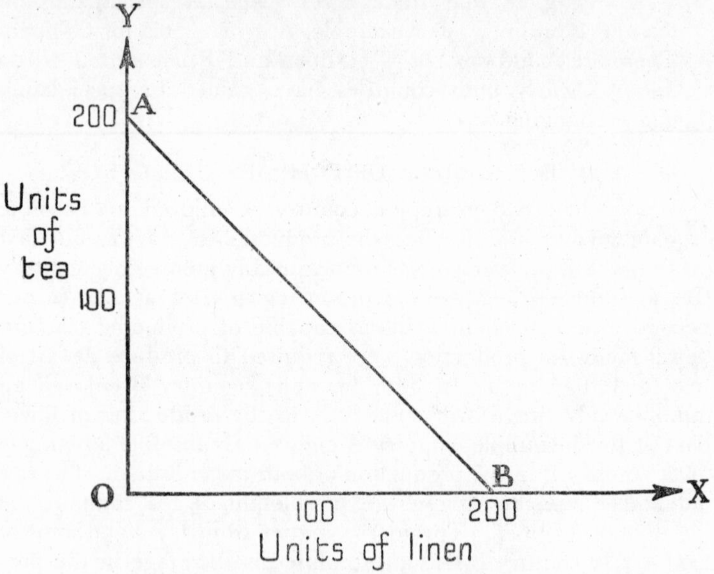

FIG. 35

paid to various factors. These prices are different from what they would be if there were no international trade. The existing factor-prices, and therefore the existing money costs, in a country are partly the *result* of international trade. The principle of comparative costs gives us a *fundamental* explanation of why trade takes place.

The "costs" to which this principle refers are not money costs. As we have stated the argument, the term costs seems to relate to the quantity of factors required to produce a unit of tea or linen. But in fact we have been using the term in the sense of "opportunity-costs."

It will be remembered that any community must somehow decide what goods to produce with its available factors of production. If it decides to produce more of some goods, it must divert more factors of production towards those industries, and must therefore produce less than before of other kinds of goods. In order to produce more tea, it must produce less linen, and conversely.

Let us revert to our third example. In country A, the opportunity-cost of producing one unit of tea is one unit of linen. If

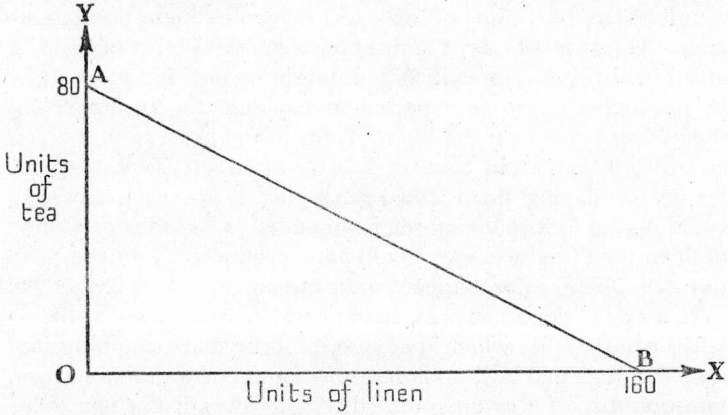

FIG. 36

country A is producing both tea and linen, and wishes to produce one more unit of tea, then it must produce one unit less of linen, and conversely. In Fig. 35, the line *AB* shows all the various combinations of tea and linen which country A can produce with its available factors. It can produce either 200 units of tea (per unit of time) and no linen, or 200 units of linen and no tea, or it can divide its 200 units as it pleases between tea and linen.

In country B, the opportunity-cost of producing 1 unit of tea is 2 units of linen; to put the same thing in other words, the opportunity-cost of producing a unit of linen is half a unit of tea. Country B can produce any combination of tea and linen lying on the line *AB* in Fig. 36.

Clearly the opportunity-cost ratios (shown by the slope of

AB in the two diagrams) are different in the two countries and it is this fact, and this fact alone, which makes it profitable for them both to specialize and to trade with one another. However many or however few factors may be required to produce a unit of linen in A, those same factors could produce, alternatively, a unit of tea. And (ignoring costs of transport) country B will be willing to give anything below 2 units of linen in exchange for 1 unit of tea, because country B needs as many factors to produce 1 unit of tea for herself as to produce 2 units of linen. Hence trade at any ratio between 1 unit of tea for 1 unit of linen and 1 unit of tea for 2 units of linen will be profitable to both countries. At a ratio of, say, 1 unit of tea against 1½ units of linen, a given quantity of factors in A can obtain 50 per cent more linen by producing tea to be exported in exchange for linen than by themselves producing the linen. And, in the same way, a given quantity of factors in country B can obtain 33⅓ per cent more tea by producing linen and exchanging it for tea than they could obtain by producing tea for themselves. For every 3 units of linen they produce, they could have produced 1½ units of tea; but they obtain in exchange 2 units of tea.

It may be wondered why many countries produce for themselves commodities which they also import. If the comparative-cost situation makes it advantageous for them to import a certain quantity of a given commodity, why does it not pay them to obtain all that they require of that commodity from abroad, instead of producing some of it for themselves?

The main answer is that the assumption, which we made in order to simplify the exposition, that the opportunity-cost ratio in a country is constant, may not be correct. For example, some soils and climates in A may be less suitable for tea-growing (relatively to flax-growing) than others. Hence, after a point, further expansion of tea-growing may involve increasing costs in terms of linen-production forgone. In terms of the diagrams, *AB* may be a humped curve, as in Fig. 37, and not a straight line. In that event, the production of tea will be expanded only up to the point at which further factors can obtain more linen by producing it directly than by producing tea (under less advantageous conditions at the margin) and exchanging it for linen.

Thus country A, under international trade, may produce *OT*

tea and *OL* linen. Let us ignore costs of transport. The slope of the curve at *P* will represent the exchange-ratio between tea and linen. By giving up the production of 1 unit of tea she can produce, say, $1\frac{1}{2}$ additional units of linen. (This is shown by the dotted lines.) Hence 1 unit of tea must exchange for at least $1\frac{1}{2}$ units of linen (otherwise A would produce more linen than *OL*) but not for more than $1\frac{1}{2}$ (otherwise A would produce more than *OT* tea). The corresponding diagram for country

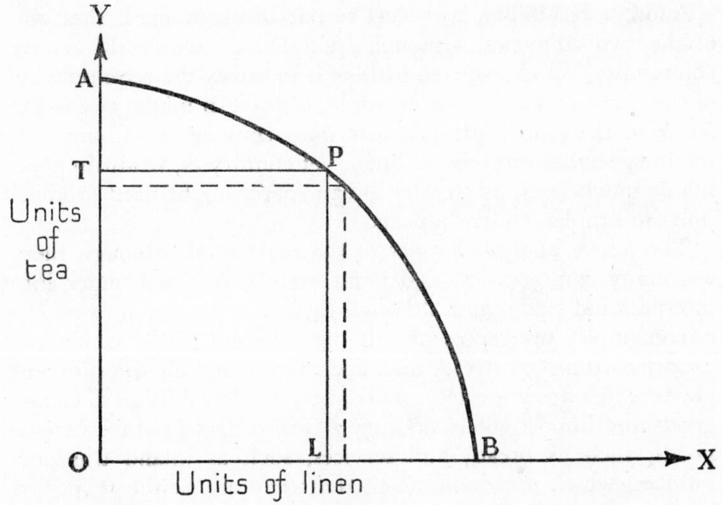

FIG. 37

B would show that the slope of the corresponding point *P* was the same as for A—in equilibrium, opportunity-cost ratios equal exchange-ratios between tea and linen and are the same in both countries.

A minor point is that relative costs of transport make it advantageous for one part of the country to import the commodity which another part exports. Thus Hamburg imports coal from Great Britain, whilst the Ruhr produces coal not only for home consumption but also for export. The cost of transporting coal by sea from England to Hamburg is considerably less than the cost of transporting it from the Ruhr to Hamburg. Again, the commodity imported may differ from the commodity produced at home, although both bear the same name in popular speech. Thus France imports a far greater quantity of wine than she exports, but the wines which she exports are of a finer quality, on the whole, than those she imports. Again, a country may decide that it is "desirable" to produce certain goods at home, although it could obtain them more cheaply from abroad. Thus Great Britain subsidizes the home production of beet-sugar, although she can and does import sugar much more cheaply than she can produce it.

Another possibility, to revert to our illustrations, is that one of the two countries, although specializing completely in one commodity, yet exports too little of it to satisfy the requirements of the other country. For example, country B might possess far fewer workers and other factors than country A. Country B might specialize entirely on linen, yet country A, whilst importing as much linen as country B can spare, might itself produce linen to supplement its imports.

The above analysis applies to the real world although there are many commodities, and not merely two, which enter into international trade, and although there are many countries. In our example, tea represents all the different goods which are exported from country A and linen represents all the different goods which are imported into country A. In addition to export goods and import goods, country A will in fact produce various goods, such as bread, and services, such as inland transport services, which are domestic in that they are neither exported nor imported. It is possible to arrange all these different goods in order, placing first that good in producing which the comparative advantage of A is greatest, placing second whichever of the remaining goods A enjoys the greatest comparative advantage in producing, and so on, ending with the good which A has the least comparative advantage—or the greatest comparative disadvantage—in producing. If costs of transport are taken into account, the various export goods will come first on the list, next the domestic goods, and finally the import goods. Exactly where the dividing lines will come, and exactly how much of each good A will export or import, will depend on the world demand for the various goods as well as on their comparative cost of production. Similarly, when there are more than two countries, we cannot say exactly which goods A will export and which goods she will import without knowing the comparative-cost situation in all the countries and the total demand for the different goods. We can be sure, however, that A will have a greater comparative advantage in any good which she exports than in any good which she imports, and will therefore obtain a larger real income by specializing and engaging in international trade than she could obtain if she were self-sufficient. And this, of course, applies to every country and not only to A.

Thus, Great Britain, for example, obtains a much greater quantity of foodstuffs such as wheat and of raw materials such as wool and timber by using some of her factors of production to produce, for example, coal and machinery and textile goods for export than she could obtain if she used these factors to produce all the wheat and wool and timber which she required. Her exports are exchanged for such foodstuffs and raw materials, produced in countries which have a comparative advantage, relatively to Great Britain, in producing them.

5. THE TERMS OF TRADE

A country which engages in international trade produces goods and services, some of which are consumed at home, the rest being exported. Let us call the former H and the latter E. In return for her exports she obtains imports, which we shall call I. She prefers the assortment of goods $H + I$ to any assortment which she could produce herself. This follows from our arithmetical example, which shows that she could obtain more of every single good by engaging in international trade. The same conclusion follows from the fact that a firm which engages in exporting and importing can obtain greater profits by selling the export goods abroad and buying imports, to sell at home, with the proceeds, than it could obtain by selling the former goods to home consumers. Home consumers prefer the imports to the exports, and therefore pay more for them. If the "exports" were sold at home, their prices would be still lower at home, and if the imports did not come in, the prices of home-produced substitutes for them would be still higher.

But the extent to which A gains by international trade may vary with what are called the terms of trade—that is, with the rate at which her exports exchange against imports. Let us revert to our third example. For country A, the opportunity-cost of producing 1 unit of linen is 1 unit of tea. She will therefore be prepared to exchange some tea for some linen at any rate which gives her more than 1 unit of linen for every unit of tea exported. For country B, the opportunity-cost of producing 1 unit of tea is 2 units of linen. She will therefore be prepared to exchange some linen for some tea at any rate which gives her 1 unit of tea for less than 2 units of linen. This means that the terms of trade between the two countries will lie somewhere between the opportunity-cost ratio in each. One unit of tea, that is, will exchange for more than 1 unit but less than 2 units of linen. Exactly where the ratio will lie between these two limits will depend upon the relative demand for tea as against linen in both countries.

As time goes on, a change in the terms of trade may take place. The last column of the following table shows how the terms of trade of Great Britain have changed since 1924. For example, the price-level of British imports in 1933 was only 55 per cent as high as in 1924. The price-level of British exports was also lower than in 1924, but only 33 per cent lower. Hence a given quantity of British exports in 1933 exchanged for about 23 per

AVERAGE STERLING PRICES: 1924 = 100

	(1) Imports (net)	(2) Exports	(3) (2) ÷ (1)
1913	62	52·5	85
1924	100	100	100
1925	99	97	98
1926	90	92	102
1927	87	87	100
1928	88	86	99
1929	84	84	100
1930	76	83	108
1931	62	74	119
1932	58	69	119
1933	55	67	123
1934	56	68	121
1935	57	68	119
1936	60	69	115
1937	69	75	109
1938	64	76	119

cent more imports than in 1924. The reader should be warned, however, that a table such as this can practically never give an exact measure of the changes in the terms of trade, owing to "the index-number difficulty": the composition of both imports and exports changes over a period.[1]

If a change in the terms of trade is due to a change in demand, the country whose exports are now demanded more strongly will gain. Take Australia as an illustration. Australia exports mainly wool and wheat. If the demand for wool and wheat increases, as it has during recent years, and the prices of the goods which Australia imports rise less, or do not rise at all, then clearly Australia can obtain more imports than before in exchange for a given quantity of wool or wheat. The marked fall in the price-level of British imports after 1929 reflects the heavy fall in the prices of most foodstuffs and raw materials in the first years of the great depression. This, more than anything else, enabled the great bulk of the population of Great Britain to maintain a higher standard of living during the depression than they had ever enjoyed before, although at the same time it increased the number of unemployed attached to her export industries. But of course these years were, conversely, very hard for the overseas countries which specialized in foodstuffs and raw materials.

The consequences of a change in the cost position, associated with a change in the terms of trade, are less clear-cut. Thus, if the coal deposits of Great Britain become more difficult to work, because the more accessible coal has already been removed, the people of Great Britain will probably be worse off than they would be if their coal resources were easier to work, yet Great Britain may well get a higher price for her coal, on the world market, than before. Conversely, if technical progress in, say, the manufacture of motor cars enables more cars than before to be produced from a given amount of factors, the net effect will probably be to increase the real income of the country specializing in cars and exporting them, although she will get a lower price than before for her cars.

[1] The table has been calculated from statistics published by the Board of Trade, but the latter, with commendable caution, has twice changed its base year: first to 1930 and then to 1935. We have taken 1924 as the base year throughout. This enables us to make comparisons, but increases the margin of error.

Finally, the significance of a change in the terms of trade will clearly be greater for a country which exports a relatively large proportion of her output than for one which exports a relatively small proportion. Empirically, a small country is likely to export a larger proportion of her output than a large country, because she is less likely to possess a wide range of climates, soils, minerals, and other factors.

6. INTERNATIONAL TRADE AND PRICES

We must now inquire how the prices both of goods and services and of factors are affected by international trade. Goods which enter into international trade have a world market. This means that the price of such a good in a country which imports it equals its price in the exporting country plus transport costs and importers' profits, and tariff charges, if it is subject to duty. Suppose, for example, that the rate of exchange between United States dollars and British pounds is 5 dollars to the pound. Then a good costing, say, £1 in Great Britain, which is exported to America, will cost 5 dollars plus transport and other charges, in the United States; and conversely a good exported from the United States which costs 5 dollars there will cost £1 plus transport charges, etc., in Great Britain.

But what about factor-prices?

Let us consider particularly labour. We have seen that labour is more abundant relatively to land in Japan than in Australia. Therefore wages (for workers of equal efficiency) will be lower relatively to rents (for land of equal quality) in Japan than in Australia. In the absence of international trade, these relative differences would be greater. By hypothesis, labour cannot move from Japan to Australia. But goods embodying a high proportion of labour to land can and do move from Japan to Australia (and elsewhere). This makes the abundance of labour in Japan less than it would be if Japan were self-supporting, for the foreign demand for Japanese exports increases the demand for Japanese labour relatively to the demand for Japanese land. Conversely, the export of wool and wheat and meat from Australia tends to make land in Australia less cheap, relatively to labour, than it would otherwise be. Hence restrictions imposed by other countries on Japanese exports tend, in addition to reducing the general gain from international specialization, to reduce wages in Japan. True humanitarians, distressed at the low standard of living in Japan, would be doing a great disservice to Japanese workers by urging other countries to refuse their products on the ground that Japanese labour was "sweated." They would best help the Japanese workers by urging that Japanese goods should be admitted freely and that immigration of Japanese workers into countries where labour is relatively scarce should be permitted. The flow of Japanese goods into Australia and other countries where labour is relatively scarce will tend to raise the price of land there relatively to the price of labour. But it is almost certain that, under international trade, real wages in Australia and similar countries will be higher. For, as we have seen, international division of labour increases the total real income of every country which takes part in it, and the increase—as compared with the state of isolation—is usually very considerable. It is most unlikely that labour will not get a good part of this increase, although it cannot be denied that particular groups of workers, whose skill consists mainly in producing goods which are displaced by substitutes imported from Japan, may suffer. But some groups of workers or of property-owners must suffer from any change in economic conditions, even if the change is of great benefit to the community as a whole.

Let us now consider the absolute height of factor-prices, using our third example for illustration, and considering wages. Country A is more efficient in everything than country B. But the prices of all international goods are the same, allowing for costs of transport, etc., in both A and B. The difference in efficiency shows itself in the higher level of factor-prices in country A. To simplify the illustration, let us take account only of labour. Suppose that both countries use the same currency, and that, after the international trade has been established, the daily wage in B is 10s. A worker in A, we assumed, can produce $\frac{200}{160}$, or 25 per cent more, linen, or $\frac{200}{80}$, or 150 per cent more, tea than a worker in B. His daily wage, therefore, will lie somewhere between 12s. 6d. and 25s. Its exact level will depend on the terms of trade. Suppose, as before, that A exports 45 units of tea and receives in exchange 60 units of linen. Suppose that it takes one day's labour in B to produce a unit of linen. Then the price of a unit of linen is 10s. and since 60 units of linen (£30) buy 45 units of tea the price of a unit of tea is £$\frac{30}{45}$ or 13s. 4d. Our example assumed that the quantity of labour required to produce 160 units of linen in B can produce 200 units of tea in A. Therefore, with constant opportunity-costs, if 1 day's labour in B produces 1 unit of linen and earns 10s., 1 day's labour in A will produce $\frac{200}{160}$, or $1\frac{1}{4}$, units of tea and will earn $1\frac{1}{4}$ times 13s. 4d., or 16s. 8d. The difference in wages between the two countries is the result of the fact that other factors, such as favourable climate, are more abundant in A than in B and that therefore a given worker can produce more in A than in B. If A and B were different districts in the same country, we should expect that workers, attracted by the higher wages, would move from the less-favoured into the more-favoured district. But by hypothesis A and B are separate countries and factors of production cannot move between them.

These differences in money wages between the two countries are the result of international trade, and not the cause of it. If each country was self-supporting, it could pay whatever money wages it liked. But a day's wage in B would not buy more than 1 unit of linen or $\frac{1}{2}$ unit of tea—because in B it takes a day's labour to produce either 1 unit of linen or $\frac{1}{2}$ unit of tea. In A, by the same reasoning, the wage paid for a day's labour would purchase either $1\frac{1}{4}$ units of linen or $1\frac{1}{4}$ units of tea. By international trade, real wages in both countries have been raised. A day's labour in B receives 10s., which will purchase either 1 unit of linen or $\frac{3}{4}$ unit of tea. A day's labour in A receives 16s. 8d., which will purchase either $1\frac{2}{3}$ units of linen or $1\frac{1}{4}$ units of tea. It would clearly be stupid for workers in A to protest against the import of linen from B on the ground that it was produced with cheap labour. Of course, the money cost of production of linen is less in B than in A. In B the cost is only 10s.; in A it would be 16s. 8d. for $1\frac{1}{4}$ units, that is, 13s. 4d. for 1 unit. But the workers in A would lose if imports were prohibited, for—as we have already shown—the real income of A is increased by international trade.[1]

[1] It is conceivable that workers might benefit from a tariff if the goods excluded competed with goods involving a high proportion of labour and consumed mainly by landlords and capitalists. But this is of little practical significance.

7. MOVEMENTS OF FACTORS BETWEEN COUNTRIES

Our discussion of comparative costs assumed that factors of production do not move from one country to another. In fact, some workers do emigrate and some capital is invested abroad. We must therefore consider the main consequences of such movements.

If there were no money costs, and no other hindrances of any kind to check the migration of labour, workers would move from low-wage districts into high-wage districts until the net advantages in any given occupation, for workers of equal efficiency, were the same all over the world. We say the "net advantages" because if there were differences between countries in the cost of living, or in the length of the working week or in other working conditions, there would be differences in money wages to compensate for these other differences. Of course, some workers would still earn more than others. But this would be because, owing to their natural aptitudes, training, capital, influence, or luck, they were in better-paid occupations, or because they were more efficient than the others at the same job. It would not be because they lived in a different country.

In the same way, if capital could move perfectly freely, there would be no difference between countries in the rate of interest on loans made for any given period, after allowing for the risk of default. The free movement of capital would make wages somewhat less unequal between countries. For capital would tend to flow towards countries where efficiency-wages were low. This would raise the marginal productivity of labour in those countries, whereas the marginal productivity of labour in the countries from which the capital came would be less than if it had been invested at home.

But if the present obstacles to territorial mobility of labour were not removed, substantial differences in wage-levels between countries would continue to exist. For workers would continue to be far more numerous, relatively to land and other natural resources, in some countries than in others.

It is quite fantastic to suppose that natural resources such as land, climate, and mineral resources, could be freely transferred from one country to another. If they could, and if capital also were completely mobile, international trade would almost disappear. It would continue only in so far as some countries had so small a population, and were so distant from other markets, that it paid them to import goods produced elsewhere on a large scale with the aid of expensive indivisible plant or equipment. The movement of goods is, in a sense, a substitute for the movement of factors. If factors could move freely, there would be no need for goods to move, and each country could be self-supporting without thereby reducing its real income. But, of course, natural resources cannot move. Hence even if labour and capital were perfectly mobile a good deal of international trade would still be advantageous. Tropical countries could export tropical products, countries with rich deposits of particular minerals could export those minerals, and so on.

In actual fact, the movement of workers between countries has seldom exceeded 1 per 1000 of the world's population in any given year. It is impeded by the money costs of migrating, the reluctance of workers to go to a strange country, their ignorance of conditions abroad, and the restrictions on immigration which a number of Governments have imposed, especially during recent years. Over a fairly short period, it is much nearer the truth to suppose that labour does not move at all between countries than to suppose that it is perfectly mobile.

Emigration has had very little effect on the dense populations of Eastern countries, although the movement of Chinese into Manchuria after the last war at times reached nearly a million a year. Their populations remain much larger, relatively to their resources, than those of Western countries, and this is perhaps the main reason why their standards of living are so low.

Some movements between "old" countries have been large enough to be significant. Before the last war, there was a seasonal movement every year of nearly a million Poles and others into Germany during the beet and potato harvests and there has long been a considerable seasonal movement of Italians and Spaniards into France to help pick the grapes. After the last war, there was a striking influx, mainly from Poland, Italy, Belgium, and Spain, into France. The number of foreigners in France rose from 1½ million in 1920 to some 3 million in 1930. Incidentally, France sent many of these back to their own countries during the depression.

The big trend, however, for more than a hundred years has

been from Europe to "new" overseas countries. Most of these migrants—no less than 34 million between 1821 and 1920—were absorbed by the United States, although at times the rate of entry into other new countries has been very high: for example, between 1903 and 1914 some 2½ million entered Canada. During the nineteenth century, the great majority came from the United Kingdom, Germany, and other countries in North-west Europe, but during the decade or two before the last war increasing numbers were coming from Southern and Eastern Europe, the numbers from Italy alone reaching nearly 400,000 a year. Nevertheless we may hazard the view that the only country whose numbers were very considerably affected by emigration was Ireland, whose population fell from over 8 million in 1814 to 4½ million in 1900. Even at its peak, just before the war of 1914, the total emigration from Europe was little more than a million a year. Since the war, owing largely to the restrictions on entry into the United States and other countries, the movement has been much smaller, and during the depression there was a small net movement away from some "new" countries, such as Canada and Australia.

As a rule—the great wave of emigration from Ireland between 1845 and 1855, due largely to the potato famine, being a notable exception—migration has tended to increase when conditions in the receiving countries were prosperous rather than when conditions at home were bad, and most immigrants have entered relatively unskilled occupations while the workers already in the country of immigration have moved up in the occupational scale.

At present, some countries, such as Australia and the Argentine, are obviously under-populated *relatively* to others. But whether such a country would gain, from its own national standpoint, by an increase in its numbers is quite a different question. Immigration would tend to raise land values but to lower the wages of workers with whom the immigrants directly competed.

If the combined real income of a country of emigration and the country of immigration remained the same, migration would tend to equalize wages and to diminish international trade. But this condition has not been fulfilled during the economic expansion of overseas countries. The migration of labour has usually been accompanied by a migration of capital; the development of the new countries has increased international trade; and the improved distribution of labour and capital relatively to natural resources has increased real incomes, including wages, in the countries of emigration as well as in the overseas countries. Moreover, the development of the latter has on the whole increased and cheapened the supply of foodstuffs and raw materials required by the former, whilst expanding the market for their manufactures; that is to say, it has tended to turn the terms of trade in favour of the old countries.

The movement of capital between countries has been of considerable importance in the past. "New" countries overseas have been developed partly with the aid of loans from Western Europe and, in recent times, the United States, and these loans have stimulated exports from Great Britain and other lending countries. During the period 1925 to 1929 a number of borrowing countries, including Germany, enjoyed boom conditions based largely on their expenditure of money borrowed from the United States and other lending countries. Nevertheless the existence of separate national States provides a considerable barrier to capital movements and such movements between countries, taking the world as a whole, have been less than is often supposed. They have been hampered by the reluctance of capitalists to invest in a country which they do not know and to run the risks of default or confiscation. The total value of British foreign investment in 1939 was about the same as in 1913, namely, around £4000 million. This was more than the foreign investments of all other countries put together, yet it was only about a fifth of the total value of the capital invested in Great Britain. During recent years several European countries have forbidden the export of capital, and a considerable amount of "refugee" capital has been moving from one centre to another seeking security rather than a higher rate of interest. For example, a good deal of French capital was transferred to London because its owners feared that the franc would fall in value. The big increase in the note issue of the Bank of England during 1932–7 was permitted partly in order to offset the hoarding of these notes by Frenchmen and others.

CHAPTER XXVI

BALANCES OF PAYMENTS

1. THE MEANING OF A BALANCE OF PAYMENTS

When the value of a country's imports exceeds the value of its exports over some arbitrary period, usually one year, the "balance of trade" of that country is said to have been adverse or unfavourable or passive. The extent to which it has been adverse is measured by the "excess of imports." The amount of this excess, however, will depend partly on what is included in imports and exports, in this connection, and on the method of valuation. Countries which produce and export gold and silver usually include them in their recorded exports (and imports) but other countries often show movements of gold, and sometimes of silver, separately, so that their "imports" and "exports" relate only to merchandise or to merchandise plus silver. Again, some countries—notably the United States, Canada, and South Africa—value their imports f.o.b.: that is, at their value when they leave the countries from which they are sent. Most other countries value their imports c.i.f.: that is, at their value on arrival. Clearly the former method shows a greater excess of exports, or a smaller excess of imports, than the latter.

When a country has an excess of exports its balance of trade is said to be favourable or active to that extent. The terms "favourable" and "unfavourable" (or "adverse") are a survival from the days when it was thought desirable for a country to accumulate gold. A favourable balance was taken as an indication that gold would be imported and an unfavourable balance, it was thought, would probably have to be met by an export of gold. In fact, a growing adverse balance of trade is sometimes a sign of prosperity. For example, when an old country like Great Britain is increasing her imports more than her exports, this may mean that she is buying more materials from abroad owing to greater activity at home and that in the near future the countries which supply her with raw materials and other goods will increase their demands for her exports.

In any event, the balance of trade does not tell the whole

story. For many years Great Britain has had a large excess of imports. This is largely because some of her inhabitants are entitled to receive considerable sums as interest or dividends on their overseas investments, and because British firms render shipping, insurance, banking and other services to foreigners. These payments are made, in effect, in the form of goods: hence the excess of imports. Clearly we can get a complete picture only by taking account of all transactions, and not only of those included in the recorded estimates of imports and exports.

The balance of payments of a country, if complete and accurate, would include all payments made during the period by foreigners to residents—all such payments are called "credits" —and all payments (known as "debits") made during the period by residents to foreigners. The term "residents" includes all persons, Governments, firms, institutions, and other bodies, whatever their nationality, within the country. Similarly a "foreigner" is anybody, whatever his nationality, outside the country.

It may be wondered why a country is usually chosen as the relevant area for which to construct a balance of payments. Why not take a group of countries, such as Scandinavia, or a district, such as Cornwall? The main reason is that a country usually has its own monetary and banking system. Hence when a foreigner wishes to make a payment to somebody in a given country he cannot simply send his own money or cheque, for as a rule his money will not be acceptable in that country. He must therefore obtain money of that country, or get his bank to do so for him, giving his own money in exchange. The opposite of course applies to payments made by residents to foreigners. Under free exchange rates, the exchange value of a currency tends to be such that the amount demanded on the foreign exchange market equals the amount supplied; under fixed exchange rates, changes in the balance of payments tend to influence the level of money incomes and of interest rates within the country in question. We shall consider these matters later. We mention them now to show why the balance of payments is important.

Few countries give anything like a complete and detailed estimate of their balance of payments. Perhaps the fullest is that given by the United States, of which we reproduce a specimen, together with one for the United Kingdom, in the following section.

2. ESTIMATES FOR THE UNITED STATES AND THE UNITED KINGDOM

The following is the official estimate of the United States balance of payments for 1936. It is in millions of dollars.

Item	Receipts from Foreigners for "Exports" (Credits)	Payments to Foreigners for "Imports" (Debits)	Net Credits (+) or Debits (−)
Trade and service items—			
Merchandise	2456	2422	+ 34
Merchandise adjustments	66	41	+ 25
Freight and shipping	68	129	− 61
Tourist expenditures	125	497	− 372
Immigrant remittances	5	115	− 110
Charitable, educational, and other contributions		32	− 32
Interest and dividends	568	238	+ 330
War-debt receipts	1		+ 1
Government transactions (excluding war-debt receipts)	30	96	− 66
Miscellaneous services	164	66	+ 98
Total trade and service items	3483	3636	− 153
Gold and silver—			
Gold exports and imports	28	1144	− 1116
Gold earmarking operations (net)			+ 86
Gold movements (net)			− 1030
Silver exports and imports	3	183	− 180
Total gold and silver movements (net)			− 1210
Capital items—			
Long-term capital movements	3475	2717	+ 758
Movement of short-term banking funds (net)			+ 404
Miscellaneous capital items (net)			− 12
Paper currency movements	57	35	+ 22
Total capital items (net)			+ 1172
Residual item (net)			+ 191

Most of these items explain themselves. "Merchandise adjustments" cover purchases and sales of such things as ships and bunker-fuel, smuggling, and estimated over- or under-valuations. The debit side of immigrant remittances represents sums sent home by immigrants in the United States: thus 13·5 million dollars were sent to Greece and 8·2 million to Italy. "Miscellaneous services" include 110 million dollars on the credit side for motion pictures' royalties received from foreigners, as against 6 million dollars paid for the use of foreign films, a credit of 20 million dollars for taxes, fees, and commissions paid by foreigners in connection with their transactions in American securities, and payments made and received for insurance services. The very large imports of gold will be noted. When gold in the United States is bought by foreigners (as by the central bank of China, which was paid in this way for its exports of silver to the United States) and is therefore "earmarked" as belonging to them, this is equivalent to an export of gold, although the gold remains in the United States, for it is a sale of gold to foreigners. "Paper currency movements" means what it says: there was a net export of dollar notes from the United States during 1936.

The United Kingdom estimate shows "balances" only and no capital movements. The following is taken from the *Board of Trade Journal* for 25th February, 1937.

	1936 £ Million
Excess of imports of merchandise and silver bullion and specie[1]	347
Estimated excess of Government payments made overseas	2
	£349
Estimated net national shipping income	95
Estimated net income from overseas investments	195
Estimated net receipts from commissions, etc.	30
Estimated net receipts from other sources	10
	£330
Estimated total debit on items specified above	19

[1]

Imports	£ Million	*Exports*	£ Million
Merchandise	848·9	Merchandise	501·1
Silver bullion and specie	17·1	Silver bullion and specie	18·1
	£866·0		£519·2

"Government transactions" include receipts and payments in respect of loans between Governments (e.g. in 1934 the Government of South Africa repaid £7½ million of war debt) and on account of the overseas activity of the Admiralty and other public departments. "Shipping income" requires a word of explanation. Suppose goods are brought to the United Kingdom in British ships. The payment for freight is an *internal* payment made by a British importing firm to a British shipping company. But the goods are valued c.i.f., therefore the payment for freight should appear on the credit side, in order to offset the freight charges which are, but should not be, included in the value of imports. Hence the whole of the receipts of British shipping firms in respect of overseas transactions are included in this item, plus disbursements by foreign ships (for bunkers, stores, port dues, commissions, etc.) in British ports and minus disbursements by British ships in foreign ports.

"Income from overseas investments" consists of the income from long-term investments abroad less sums paid to foreigners as income on their long-term investments in the United Kingdom. War debt payments are excluded. Roughly £100 million of the receipts are interest payments fixed in sterling. The rest is mainly dividends. When a foreign loan is raised in the United Kingdom it appears as a debit item, for that amount of sterling is made available to the borrowers, who use it to buy goods or foreign exchange on other countries. Interest payments and repayments of capital are of course credit items. If a country borrows about the same sum each year paying, say, 5 per cent, after twenty years its external interest payments exceed its new foreign borrowing. Several countries are in this position.

"Net receipts from commissions, etc.," include charges in respect of acceptance credits, discounts on foreign bills, bank interest, commissions and other charges on new issues paid by overseas borrowers, merchanting commissions on overseas produce, brokers' commissions, insurance remittances from abroad, and earnings on exchange transactions. It thus consists largely of the earnings of the City of London on its foreign transactions.

"Receipts from other sources" include such items as tourist expenditures (a net debit of some £2 million), film royalties (a net debit of £5 million), sales of second-hand ships, emigrants' remittances, and expenditure by foreign Governments on their diplomatic and consular services in the United Kingdom.

3. THE DEFECTS OF SUCH ESTIMATES

The estimates of most countries are incomplete. The British estimate quoted above could be supplemented by a net debit on account of gold movements, but the *Board of Trade Journal* warns us that the recorded excess of imports over exports of gold bullion and specie—£227·5 million—is a figure to which little significance should be attached, mainly because it takes no account of "earmarking" operations. Something is known about capital movements. The value of new overseas loans floated on the London market in 1936 is estimated by the Midland Bank at £26 million. The United States Department of Commerce gives the net inflow of funds from the United Kingdom during 1936 in connection with transactions in United States securities at 218 million dollars. Lord Kindersley estimates sinking fund and maturity repayments to the United Kingdom during 1936 at no less than £107 million. But the capital movements which are not known—for example, the movements of "refugee" capital into or out of the United Kingdom—may be so large that the Board of Trade is probably well advised to exclude all capital movements from its estimates. We should be clear, however, as to the meaning of this. It means that the published estimate is quite useless as an indication of the net credit or debit on transactions as a whole.

Even complete and careful estimates, such as those of the United States, are admitted to have a substantial margin of error, for it is difficult to make an accurate estimate of items such as tourist expenditures or to keep track of all the multitudinous capital transactions.

Sometimes goods are known to be wrongly valued. For example Australia " dumps " sugar on the British market. For several years she has sold her sugar at about half the price ruling in Australia. But she values it at the latter price, and not at the price she receives.

Some items may be included wrongly, since they involve no transfer of money. Thus household requisites brought by immigrants into the United States are included in imports. In the same way, "American corporations operating properties in foreign countries often import the produce of their operations and employ all or a large part of the proceeds in meeting administration expenses of their home offices." As the United States Report points out (on page 16) such imports—of copper, sugar, petroleum, and so on—either should not be included in imports, since they are not paid for, or should be offset (but are not) by a corresponding increase in the credit item of "interest and dividends," for they represent a direct return on American foreign investments.

Finally, it should be noted that estimates relate, for the most part, to the transactions recorded and not to the payments made. Thus an import entering a country in 1936 would be included in the 1936 estimate, although payment for it might have been made before 1936 or might not be made until after 1936.

4. HOW DOES A BALANCE OF PAYMENTS BALANCE?

An exchange always has two sides. Every amount of foreign currency bought must be sold by somebody. Over any period, however short, the total amount of sterling sold on the foreign exchange market equals—in fact, *is*—the total amount bought. In this sense the balance of payments always balances. But this sense is not helpful.

A multitude of international transactions is constantly taking place. Most of the people concerned know little about the balance of payments and care less. Firms export or import to whatever extent pays them best; investors, taking account of risks of all kinds and of expected yields, invest abroad rather than at home if they think they will get a higher return abroad; people go abroad for their holidays when they wish, and spend as much as they please; firms employ foreign ships or insurance companies if they are cheaper and give equally good service; and so on. *A priori*, there is no reason whatever why the total "credit" payments received by a country over a year should equal the total "debit" payments which it has to make.

Suppose, then, that over a year the payments actually made by a country exceed the payments which it actually receives. By hypothesis, these extra payments are made, and are made in foreign currency. How are they made?

Suppose that this happened to Australia. The Australian

banks hold considerable sterling balances in London. Payments abroad made by Australians reduce these balances, and payments by foreigners to Australians increase them—assuming that all such payments are made through Australian banks. Thus the result of an excess of payments over receipts would be a corresponding diminution in the amount of the sterling balances held by Australian banks in London.

Let us be clear as to what happens. When an Australian draws a cheque to settle an internal transaction, the Australian who receives the cheque pays it into his bank, and the total amount of bank deposits in Australia remains the same. When an Australian makes a payment overseas, he draws a cheque in favour of his bank, which pays out a corresponding amount of sterling in London. Thus the total of bank deposits in Australia is reduced and the amount of sterling held by Australian banks in London is correspondingly reduced. Every Australian may have met his obligations in full, and yet in a sense the current payments made by Australia overseas exceed her current receipts from overseas. The extra amount of sterling due from Australians as a whole actually comes out of the sterling balances held by Australian banks in London.

We have chosen Australia because what may be called "the foreign balance" is held by Australian banks almost entirely in the form of sterling balances in London. The same applies to a number of other overseas countries. Great Britain, however, (and to a less extent certain other countries, such as the United States and France) is an important financial centre. British banks therefore hold comparatively few assets in the form of foreign currency. Hence a net debit in the balance of payments shows itself mainly in the form of an increase in the sterling balances held by Australian and other banks in London—for a net debit of Great Britain obviously implies a net credit to one or more other countries.

Clearly, if all the facts were fully known, such a net debit could be made to appear, for book-keeping purposes, as a balancing item. In the case of Australia, this item might read "decrease in short-term lending by Australia—i.e. decrease in sterling balances held by Australian banks in London." In the case of Great Britain, it might read "increase in short-term indebtedness of Great Britain—i.e. increase in sterling balances held by foreign banks, etc., in London." Thus, on paper, the balance of payments of a country could always be made to balance exactly.

5. METHODS OF CORRECTING AN ADVERSE BALANCE OF PAYMENTS

If a country continued to have a net debit, its balance of payments might be made to balance on paper, but the position would be one of disequilibrium—it could not go on indefinitely. For example, the sterling balances held in London by Australian banks might fall to zero. We must therefore consider what steps may be taken, and by whom, to prevent such a position from arising or to reverse it after it has arisen.

Let us keep to the example of Australia. It is in the interests of the Australian banks to prevent such a situation from going too far. For if they have no sterling balances, they cannot carry on their business of foreign exchange; and if they regard their sterling balances as "cash," their "cash position"—that is, their ratio of cash to deposits—has worsened.

Their most obvious remedy is to charge a higher price, in Australian money, for drafts on London. This will tend to check imports to Australia, since importers will now have to pay a larger amount of Australian money for the same foreign goods. In the same way, it will tend to check tourist expenditure abroad by Australians, investment abroad by Australians, and certain other debit items. On the other hand, it will tend to stimulate exports from Australia, since for every pound sterling or dollar received abroad the Australian exporter will get a larger amount of Australian currency than before; and it will also stimulate certain other credit items. Thus the flow of sterling into the balances held by Australian banks in London will increase, and the flow of sterling out of those balances will diminish.

This is the method of letting the exchange rate depreciate. Except in very unusual circumstances, complete adjustment of the balance of payments can be achieved by this method alone. There is no need for money incomes within the country to be reduced at all—although, of course, if they are reduced, the amount of exchange depreciation required will be less than otherwise.

Now suppose that the central bank of Australia wishes to keep the rate of exchange with sterling at a fixed level. The same argument would apply to a country which wished to remain on the gold standard, for that implies keeping its rate of exchange fixed with all countries on the gold standard.

The central bank must now take action. It must be prepared to supply sterling (or gold) at the fixed price in Australian currency which it is trying to maintain. But how can it prevent its sterling reserves (or gold reserves) from falling to zero? By reducing the total money income of Australia, and thereby reducing the monetary demand in Australia for imports. If the reduction of income involves a reduction in costs, as is very probable, this will tend to stimulate exports. The reduction in money income may be brought about in various ways. In general, the method is to reduce the "cash" of the banks, thereby causing them to reduce their advances (by raising interest rates or by rationing their loans) and thereby their deposits. Usually the central bank itself raises its bank rate and takes steps to make the rise effective. This process of reducing the money income of a country by monetary and banking measures is known as deflation.

We may note that the amount of exchange depreciation or deflation needed to correct a continuous adverse balance of payments will vary with what may be termed the Marginal Propensity to Import of the country in question. If imports have to be restricted by, let us say, 10 per cent (other things remaining the same), it may require quite a small fall in the exchange rate or in the total money income of the country to bring this about. This is likely to be so when a large proportion of the imports is more or less of luxuries. On the other hand, a very large fall—of much more than 10 per cent—may be required. This is likely to be so when imports consist largely of essential foodstuffs and raw materials, as in the case of Great Britain and indeed most West European countries.

We may also note that it is alleged that wage-earners object to a reduction in money wages much more than to a rise in the cost of living. If this is so, a country with a large proportion of wage-earners which chooses the path of deflation may find it difficult to reduce money wages. The result will be that the reduction in the total money income of the country is brought about partly by the growth of unemployment. In general, deflation is easier in a country such as Poland, with a large proportion of agricultural workers and a small proportion of wage-earners, than in an industrial country. Nevertheless the view, held by Lord Keynes and others, that wage-earners will accept a considerable rise in the cost of living without demanding increased money wages but will resist any attempts to cut their money wages, may not be quite true. It is interesting to note that in the country where wage-earners are perhaps most highly organized—namely, Australia—a cut in money wages of no less than 26 per cent, made by the Commonwealth Arbitration Court, was accepted almost without a murmur.

We have mentioned two methods—exchange depreciation and deflation. Others are possible, of which the most important are (1) devaluation—that is, remaining on the gold standard but at a lower parity, (2) restriction of imports by tariffs, import quotas and prohibitions, and other methods, and promotion of exports by export bounties and other methods, and (3) foreign exchange control. The following chapters discuss all these five methods. Some of them may be, and have been, used in combination. For example, exchange depreciation may be combined with some deflation, some exchange control, and some restriction of imports. But it is impossible both to let the exchange rate depreciate and to keep it fixed—a country must choose one or the other unless it formally escapes the dilemma by keeping its exchange rate nominally fixed by exchange control while in fact letting it depreciate.

CHAPTER XXVII

FREE EXCHANGE RATES

1. INTRODUCTION

THE question to which we now turn is what are the forces which determine the exchange value of a currency whose rates of exchange are quite free to vary. Such a currency, of course, is by definition not linked to gold or to any other standard. It consists, let us say, of inconvertible paper. Sterling has been more or less in this position since 21st September, 1931, but it has not been quite free to vary since the setting-up of the Exchange Equalization Fund, and the Currency Agreement with France, the United States, etc., reached in October, 1936, has had a stabilizing effect.

Clearly, as time goes on, such a currency may rise in terms of some foreign currencies and fall in terms of others. Thus in 1932 sterling rose considerably in terms of yen but fell in terms of gold-standard currencies. Let us suppose, for purposes of discussion, that all other currencies remain stable in terms of one another. We can then represent the rest of the world by one other country—let us call it France.

The value of sterling (taking sterling to be the inconvertible currency in question) in terms of francs will depend upon the demand for sterling, coming from people who offer francs in order to obtain sterling, relatively to the supply of sterling coming from people who offer it in order to obtain francs. The sterling-franc rate will tend to be that which equates the supply of sterling and the demand for it.

But before discussing the influences affecting the foreign demand for a currency (relatively to the supply of it on the foreign exchange market) we must consider briefly the Purchasing Power Parity Theory. For this Theory claims to show that the rate of exchange between two currencies will always tend to vary with their respective purchasing powers. Granted that the exchange rate will tend to equate supply and demand, it will also tend —it is claimed—to equal what may be termed the Purchasing Power Parity between the two currencies.

2. THE PURCHASING POWER PARITY THEORY

This theory has two main forms.

(*a*) In its narrower form it simply asserts that the prices of internationally traded goods will be the same everywhere, allowing for costs of transport: that these goods, in fact, have a world market. This is a truism. The price of raw cotton is the same in Liverpool, Le Havre, Bremen, Genoa, etc. Of course within a country (as distinct from at the port) price may be increased by import duties. Suppose that costs of transport are ignored. Then a bale of cotton may cost, say, £10 at Liverpool and 1000 francs at Le Havre: £1 = 100 francs. If we know any two of these three facts we can deduce the third by simple arithmetic. If the third fact is different from our deduction, there is a chance for profitable arbitrage by somebody. Suppose, for example, that a bale of cotton costs £10 in Liverpool and 1000 francs in Le Havre and that the franc is 120 to the £. Then by paying 1000 francs in Le Havre for a bale and selling the bale in Liverpool one gets £10 which can be exchanged for 1200 francs, yielding an arbitrage profit of 200 francs! *A priori*, given these three facts—

1 bale = £10
1 bale = 1000 francs
£1 = 120 francs

(and assuming costs of transport are negligible) we know this situation will not last, but we cannot say whether it will be adjusted mainly by a fall in the English price of cotton—

1 bale = £8⅓
1 bale = 1000 francs
£1 = 120 francs

or mainly by a rise in the French price of cotton—

1 bale = £10
1 bale = 1200 francs
£1 = 120 francs

or mainly by a rise in the exchange value of the franc—

1 bale = £10
1 bale = 1000 francs
£1 = 100 francs.

Actually there are few opportunities, as a rule, for even a small margin of arbitrage profits. Sellers in the exporting centres sell wherever the price is a fraction higher and international prices appear to adjust themselves very rapidly on the basis of prevailing exchange rates.

This truism—that certain goods have a world market—therefore throws little light on the causes of changes in exchange rates.

(*b*) The Purchasing Power Parity Theory in its wider form is perhaps best stated in the words of Cassel. It goes back at least to Ricardo but it was popularized by Cassel following the last war. He writes—

> Our willingness to pay a certain price for foreign money must ultimately and essentially be due to the fact that this money possesses a purchasing power as against commodities and services in that foreign country. On the other hand, when we offer so-and-so-much of our own money, we are actually offering a purchasing power as against commodities and services in our own country. Our valuation of a foreign currency in terms of our own, therefore, depends mainly on the relative purchasing power of the two currencies in their respective countries.

It is very difficult to compare the purchasing power of, say, pounds in England with that of francs in France. The assortment of goods and services bought and consumed in one country is different from the assortment bought and consumed in another country. For example, the French workman drinks wine and the English workman tea; the French consume more veal and the English more mutton. Even if we could take only goods consumed in both countries, some of these goods would have a higher price (at the current rate of exchange) in France and some would have a higher price in England. These differences arise from costs of transport, tariffs, taxation, and so on, and there is no reason whatever why they should cancel out. In general, a country with a high tariff will have a higher price-level than a country with a low tariff.

This means that the theory cannot be applied to absolute levels of prices. But it can be, and has been, applied to changes in price-levels. This is the way in which Cassel and others have applied it. To take a simple example, if over a period the price-level in France doubles, owing to inflation in France, and the price-level in England remains the same, the purchasing power parity is twice as many francs as before to £1 sterling. This assumes that other things—relative costs of transport, tariffs, and taxation—remain the same.

The Purchasing Power Parity Theory was used after the last war by Cassel and others to demonstrate that the fall in the exchange value of the German, Austrian, Polish, and other currencies, was due mainly to inflation in those countries. At the time, this demonstration was doubtless useful, because many responsible people refused to believe that it was inflation which was sending up prices and forcing down exchange rates. Cassel writes—

When two currencies have undergone inflation, the normal rate of exchange will be equal to the old rate multiplied by the quotient of the degree of inflation in the one country and in the other. . . . If, for instance, the inflation in A has reached the ratio of 320 to 100 and the inflation in B the ratio of 240 to 100, the new exchange rate (taking the quotation of A's currency in B's currency) will be $\frac{3}{4}$ of the old rate.

The rate calculated by the above method must be regarded as the new parity between the currencies, the point of balance towards which, in spite of all temporary fluctuations, the rate will always tend.

We may take an illustration from Keynes's *Tract on Monetary Reform*. Taking 1913 as equal to 100, in May, 1923, the *Economist* price index number was 164 and the United States Bureau of Labour Index Number was 156. $\frac{156}{164} = \frac{95 \cdot 1}{100}$. The purchasing power parity of the pound therefore was 95·1 per cent of 4·866 dollars. The actual rate was almost exactly this.

It is from discussions on the Purchasing Power Parity Theory that we derive the concept of a possible difference between the internal and the external purchasing power of a currency. For example, when the actual exchange value (or external purchasing power) of the franc was below its purchasing power parity, this tended to stimulate exports from France. If the two had been equal, there would have been no abnormal stimulus, for although French exporters would have obtained more francs than before for each pound's worth of goods exported, their costs would have risen in the same proportion.

But in fact actual exchange rates often diverge very much from purchasing power parity, calculated in the manner described. This can be seen at once by looking at the statistics and graphs given in the writings of Cassel, Keynes, and others.

On its record in the past, the purchasing power parity is a very dubious guide. I think it would baffle anybody to calculate the actual sterling-dollar exchange rate over the last few years if he knew only the changes in internal purchasing power in the two countries. Consider, for example, the following figures—

COST OF LIVING INDEX NUMBER (1924 = 100)

Date	Great Britain	United States	Dollars per £
December, 1930	87	90	4·86
„ 1931	84	80	3·37
„ 1932	81	74	3·28
„ 1933	81	76	5·12
„ 1934	81	80	4·95
„ 1935	84	83	4·93
„ 1936	87	85	4·91

In any particular case, the divergence between purchasing power parity and the actual rate may be merely temporary (due, for example, to speculation) and equilibrium may be equality between the two. Even so, we cannot say *a priori* whether this equality will be attained mainly by movements in the price-level of country A, or in the price-level of country B, or in the exchange rate. Adherents of the Purchasing Power Parity Theory often seem to imply that it will be the last (if neither country is inflating nor deflating) but that need not be so and often is not so. Moreover, the true equilibrium is often *not* an equality between purchasing power parity and the actual rate. For there may have been changes in transport costs, tariffs, etc., and there may have been a change in the terms of trade.

3. INFLUENCES AFFECTING EXCHANGE RATES

Probably the best way to explain movements in foreign exchange rates is to say that a free exchange rate will always tend to equalize the supply of and the demand for a currency on the foreign exchange market, and to say that the main influences affecting supply and demand are—

(*a*) Monetary policy.

(*b*) Capital movements, including speculation.

(*c*) The demand from country B for goods of country A, and conversely. Fundamentally, country B demands the goods of country A by offering its own goods in exchange. The "demand curve" of country B which we have in mind does *not* show the volume of A goods demanded by B at each of a series of money prices. It shows the volume demanded (and therefore the volume of its own goods which it would supply in exchange) at each of a series of "terms of trade."

We shall say a little about the first two of these three influences and then we shall discuss the third more fully.

(*a*) Monetary Policy

We have discussed this in connection with the Purchasing Power Parity Theory. For example, if Great Britain were to inflate and to raise prices, the foreign demand for sterling at the old rate of exchange wouid fall, because fewer goods could be bought in England than before with a given amount of sterling. As English prices would be higher, while prices in other countries remained the same, the British demand for foreign currencies at the old rate of exchange would increase. Thus the exchange value of sterling would fall. Of course the same reasoning applies if Great Britain inflates more, or deflates less, than other countries. But, as we have seen, other forces may change also, so that the actual rate at any moment may diverge considerably from the purchasing power parity at that moment.

(*b*) Capital Movements

If country A is exporting capital to country B, this will clearly increase the supply of A's money offered against B's money and will tend to raise the exchange value of B's money, even if no inflation or deflation is taking place in either country. Over a short period, when it is feared that one currency or another will fall considerably in exchange value, quite large movements of capital may take place, not for long-term investment, but in the hope of making a gain or avoiding a loss on exchange movements. The Bank for International Settlements and others have attempted to estimate the amount of this "refugee" capital liable to move, seeking greater security rather than a higher interest rate, from one centre to another. But—in the absence of legal restrictions—the *potential* amount of such capital is almost unlimited, because citizens can "flee" from their own currency. Over a short period, speculative short-term movements of this kind may be so great that they far outweigh movements of goods in their effect on the demand for a particular currency or on the supply of another.

An interesting illustration of the effects of speculation is provided by the exchange value of the Chilean peso between 1878 and 1892. There was in Chile a sharp division between foreign trade centres and the rest of the country. Hence any gradual emission of currency could be readily absorbed in the interior of the country without materially altering the exchange rate. Thus there was virtually no correlation between the increases in the circulating medium and the exchange rate. In fact, the only thing which gives a high correlation with the variations in the exchange rate over this period is the military history of Chile. By observing a graph of foreign exchange movements it is possible to tell the exact dates of Chile's victories and defeats in her disputes with Peru, Bolivia, and Argentina. The sharpest single variation was in August, 1879, when the Chilean peso rose from 25 pence to 36 pence without any alteration either in the balance of payments or in the quantity of currency. This jump was due entirely to the capture of two enemy warships by the Chilean navy.

(c) Reciprocal Supply-and-Demand of Goods and Services

Let us simplify by supposing that England exports, and can export, only coal, and that France exports, and can export, only wine. Let us begin with the balance of payments in equilibrium. Every day England exports, say, 10 tons of coal and imports, say, 20 gallons of wine. Let us suppose that all transport charges can be neglected. The price of a ton of coal is, say, £1. The price of a gallon of wine is, say, 50 francs. The rate of exchange therefore must be £1 = 100 francs.

In order to avoid complications due to monetary policy, let us suppose that each country keeps its factor-prices constant and that no changes take place in relative supplies of factors, technical knowledge, and so on, and that changes in the output of coal or wine do not appreciably affect the price of coal in sterling or the price of wine in francs. A ton of coal always costs £1 and a gallon of wine always costs 50 francs.

Now suppose that for some reason the French demand for

British coal increases. In order to get more sterling to buy more coal, France must sell more wine in England. But the English demand for wine has not changed, so that in order to sell more wine in England the sterling price of wine must be reduced. This comes about through a rise in the exchange value of sterling. The value of sterling is pushed up by French people wanting to buy more coal, and this enables English people to buy wine more cheaply. The French exporter still gets 50 francs a gallon, but this 50 francs represents less sterling than before.

Suppose, for example, that the new equilibrium rate of exchange is £1 = 120 francs, and that at this rate 15 tons of coal a day are exported. It follows that 36 gallons of wine are imported. The terms of trade have moved in favour of England. One ton of coal used to exchange against 2 gallons of wine. It now exchanges against $2\frac{2}{5}$ gallons. The terms of trade, that is, have improved by one-fifth. And the value of sterling has likewise increased by one-fifth, for £1 now commands 120 francs instead of 100. The rise in the value of sterling simply reflects the improvement in the terms of trade.[1]

This example demonstrates a fundamental defect in the Purchasing Power Parity Theory of foreign exchange. In so far as this theory merely asserts that the prices of goods which have a world market tend to be the same (allowing for transport charges) in different centres, it is a truism. The price of a ton of coal is £1 in England, and 120 francs in France, and the rate of exchange is £1 equals 120 francs. Given any two of these data, the third can be obtained by simple arithmetic. But in so far as the theory says more than this, and asserts that a change in the rate of exchange reflects a corresponding change in the relative purchasing power of the two currencies *over goods in general*, it may not be true. In our illustration, the price of nothing in England is changed except the price of wine, which is now 8s. 4d. a gallon instead of 10s. The price of nothing in France is changed except coal, which is now 120 francs instead of 100 francs. If the great bulk of the goods sold in either country are home-produced, there has been very little change in the two price-levels, and yet the rate of exchange has altered by one-fifth. The Purchasing Power Parity Theory, in its wider

[1] This is true only if the change in the terms of trade is due solely to changes in demand, as distinct from changes in costs.

form, takes no account of changes in the terms of trade due to real changes in demand.

A good illustration of this point is the fall in the exchange value of the yen after 1931. Japan returned to gold in January, 1930, at the pre-war parity, equal to 2s. per yen. In September, 1931, Great Britain left gold. The yen rose to over 3s. Japan left gold at the end of 1931. By the middle of 1933 the yen fell to about 1s. 2d. and remained there.

Why did the yen have to depreciate so much more than sterling? Only partly owing to inflation. At the end of 1935 wholesale prices in Japan were only 37 per cent and retail prices only 16 per cent above the low levels of the second half of 1931. The main reason is to be found in the adverse change in the terms of trade, largely due to the great fall in the American demand for Japanese silk.

JAPAN (10th December, 1931 = 100)

	1933 Av.	1934 Av.	1935 Av.
Export Goods .	138	132	134
Import Goods .	171	187	196

In Great Britain, on the other hand, the terms of trade became much more favourable.

4. EXCHANGE EQUALIZATION FUNDS

A country may decide not to leave its exchange rates entirely to the free play of supply and demand. It may therefore establish, usually under the control of the central bank, an exchange equalization fund.

Great Britain was the first country to set up such a fund. It began in June, 1932, with assets of about £150 million in Treasury bills, augmented in April, 1933, by a further £200 million of Treasury bills, and in June, 1937, with yet a further £200 million, and it is still in active existence.

Its main object, the Chancellor declared, was to offset purely speculative movements in sterling exchange rates whilst allowing "real" causes to affect the long-term trend. The Fund was to smooth out temporary fluctuations. In particular, it was to offset inward and outward movements of "refugee capital." In the absence of control, an inward movement of such capital, seeking a safe temporary resting-place, might raise the value of sterling very considerably. Later, the withdrawal of this "hot money" would have the opposite effect. The Fund can prevent or lessen these disturbing ups and downs. When capital is moving in, the Fund can and does provide the extra sterling required by selling some of its Treasury bills. It parts with sterling and acquires the foreign money which is being offered against sterling. In practice, it then uses this foreign money to buy gold. When an outward movement of capital takes place, the Fund can meet it by releasing some of its gold, getting back sterling in exchange.

At any moment, therefore, part of the assets of the Fund consists of sterling, in the form of Treasury bills, and the rest of gold. If it were to try to offset a continued tendency for sterling to rise, after a time all its sterling assets would have been turned into gold, and it would then be unable to keep sterling down unless its sterling resources were replenished—for example, by a further issue of Treasury bills. In the same way, it could not continue to keep sterling up after it had parted with all its gold unless—for example, by raising a foreign loan—it could replenish its gold. Its power to keep sterling down is limited by the extent of its sterling assets, and its power to keep sterling up is limited by the extent of its foreign assets.

The British Fund has at times exerted a downward and at times an upward influence on the exchange value of sterling but its net effect since it began operations has probably been in a downward direction, for the gold which it holds represents a demand for foreign currencies which it exerted in the past and which would not otherwise have existed. Thus the Fund has made a profit, but against this must be set about £10 million a year. For, in consequence of the various funding loans which have been issued during the past few years, the total of Treasury bills in the hands oi the market is only about the same as it was before the Fund was started. The cost to the Treasury of holding the gold acquired by the Fund must therefore be estimated on the basis of the long-term interest rate. On this basis, it amounts to some £10 million a year. In other words, if there had been no Fund, the Treasury would not have needed to raise some £350 million of long-term debt.

Some other countries, notably the United States and France, have established similar funds. The United States is—in a sense—on gold, but wishes to exercise some control over its exchange rates with countries that are not on gold.

CHAPTER XXVIII

THE GOLD STANDARD

1. TYPES OF GOLD STANDARD

It is often said that it would be a great simplification and improvement on the present state of affairs if all the countries of the world, or at any rate the leading countries, could share a common currency. It is pointed out that if each English county had its own separate currency, trade and investment would be considerably hampered. Why then, it is urged, should each leading country have its own particular currency? Would not economic progress be greatly promoted if some genius could invent an international money and persuade all the leading countries to use it?

Those who speak in this way do not realize that the gold standard virtually does what they are asking. In effect, every country on the gold standard is sharing a common currency. Each country has its own banking system, and one calls its currency units pounds, another dollars, another francs, and so on, but a country which stays on the gold standard thereby gives up the privilege of following whatever monetary policy it likes. It has decided that, on balance, the benefit to international trade and investment of stable rates of exchange is worth the sacrifice of its independence in the sphere of monetary policy. It has tied its currency to gold, and so has every other gold-standard country; all such currencies are thereby tied to one another; the purchasing power of gold, and hence of every such currency, depends on the supply of gold and the demand for it throughout the world; and commodity price-levels in all gold-standard countries tend to rise and fall together. We shall develop and qualify these statements later in this chapter. It seemed desirable, by way of introduction, to stress the point that the gold standard virtually provides an international money.

A country is on the gold standard when the purchasing power of a unit of its currency is kept equal to the purchasing power of a given weight of gold. There are various ways of achieving this result. We shall describe the three main ways under the headings of (*a*) the full gold standard, (*b*) the gold bullion standard, and (*c*) the gold exchange standard.

(*a*) The Full Gold Standard

This is in operation when the currency of a country consists mainly of coins containing gold equal to their face value, and when gold can be minted into such coins, without charge and without limit, and the coins can be melted down or exported without restriction. Before the war of 1914, the United Kingdom was on the full gold standard. Gold sovereigns circulated freely. The sovereign *was* a definite weight ($113\frac{1}{623}$ grains) of pure gold plus a little alloy, of negligible value, to make the coins more durable. Eleven-twelfths of the weight (123·27447 grains) of a sovereign was pure or "fine" gold; the other twelfth was alloy; the coin was said to consist of gold "eleven-twelfths fine." Anybody was free to melt down and export sovereigns, so that the purchasing power of a sovereign could never be appreciably less than that of 113 odd grains of fine gold. We may state the same facts in terms of ounces. Four and a quarter sovereigns contained an ounce of fine gold. Hence 4¼ sovereigns—or £4 5s. in British money, since Bank of England notes (of which the lowest denomination was £5), silver and copper coins, and cheques could all be exchanged for sovereigns—could never buy appreciably less than an ounce of fine gold. On the other hand, the British Mint would always turn gold into sovereigns without charge. In practice, gold was usually sold to the Bank of England which acted as agent for the Mint. The Mint would pay the full price of £4 5s. (or, to be accurate, about a halfpenny less, for 4¼ sovereigns contained a shade more than an ounce of fine gold), but, in order to avoid delay, sellers usually preferred to sell to the Bank, which paid them a trifle less: £3 17s. 9d. instead of £3 17s. 10½d. per ounce $\frac{11}{12}$ths fine. Hence the purchasing power of an ounce of fine gold could never be appreciably less than that of £4 5s. of British money.

(*b*) The Gold Bullion Standard

This is in operation when the central bank or the Treasury of a country is always prepared both to buy and to sell gold at a fixed price and there are no restrictions on the import or export of gold. The United Kingdom was on the gold bullion standard from April, 1925, when she returned to gold, until September, 1931, when she again went off gold. The Bank of England was prepared to buy any amount of gold at £3 17s. 9d. per ounce $\frac{11}{12}$ths fine and to sell it, in minimum amounts of 400 ounces, at £3 17s. 10½d. per ounce. Hence "convertibility both ways"—of gold into currency and of currency into gold—was maintained, and the sterling price of gold, just as before 1914, seldom varied by more than a penny from its fixed price of 84s. 11½d. per fine ounce. Gold coins, however, were not in circulation: the currency consisted mainly of paper notes. The gold bullion standard, it is claimed, economizes gold, for all the monetary gold in the country can be held in the central bank, and none of the precious metal need be employed as currency. This was considered an advantage a decade or so ago, when a shortage of gold was feared, but during recent years there seems to have been too much rather than too little gold, and some economists advocate a return to the full gold standard. They argue that the reintroduction of gold coins would absorb some of the present large stock of monetary gold and would make the working of the gold standard more automatic.

(*c*) The Gold Exchange Standard

A number of countries, such as Australia and India and Denmark, have close commercial relations with Great Britain. Most of their external debt is fixed in sterling, or Great Britain is their main purchaser, or supplier, or both. Such a country may decide that its best monetary policy is to keep the exchange value of its currency more or less stable in terms of sterling. We may perhaps term such a country, without implying any inferiority of status, a satellite country of Great Britain in the monetary sphere. The United States, France, and some other countries also have their satellites.

The monetary authorities of the satellite country may reserve themselves full liberty to vary the rate of exchange with the "planet" country as and when they please. They may merely keep it stable, or more or less stable, so long as it suits them, without giving any kind of guarantee that they will continue to do so. Most of the countries in the so-called "sterling bloc" were in this position before the war.

But the central bank or Treasury of a satellite country may formally undertake to keep the exchange value of its currency fixed in terms of the planet currency. The currencies of India and Egypt, for example, are linked in this way to sterling.

Whether the link is *de jure* and firm, or *de facto* and flexible, the central bank or Treasury must keep a reserve of sterling in Great Britain (assuming its currency to be tied to sterling) and must be prepared to diminish this reserve by selling sterling or to increase it by buying sterling. If it formally undertakes to buy and sell bills or drafts upon London at a fixed rate, it is formally on a sterling exchange standard. If sterling is on gold, this means that it is on a gold exchange standard.

This practice enables it to keep its main monetary reserve in the form of interest-bearing assets, such as gilt-edged securities or Treasury bills, in London instead of in the form of gold in its own country. But it also entails the risk that these assets may fall in value relatively to gold. In particular, it entails the risk that the "planet" country may suddenly leave gold or devalue. The sterling assets held by other countries fell considerably in value, relatively to gold, when Great Britain left the gold standard in September, 1931.

2. THE RULES OF THE GOLD STANDARD

The gold standard, in any of its forms, provides practically fixed rates of exchange between the countries on it. For if the currency of each country is convertible into gold, or into a gold-standard currency, at a fixed rate, and conversely, it follows that the currencies of these countries are convertible into one another at practically fixed rates. If £1 and 4·866 dollars can both be exchanged for the same amount of gold, and conversely, then the exchange value of £1 cannot long remain above or below 4·866 dollars by more than the relatively small cost—usually well below 1 per cent—of sending gold from New York to London or from London to New York. And this means that the price of any good in dollars cannot long exceed or fall short of $\frac{4866}{1000}$ of its price in pounds, plus or minus tariff and transport charges and importer's profits. It means, that is, that a country on the gold standard cannot raise or lower commodity prices, in terms of its own currency, as it pleases. It can indeed do something, as we shall see later, by changing its duties or other restrictions on imports. Apart from such changes, commodity prices in that country must move in harmony with commodity prices in other gold-standard countries.

A country with free exchange rates, of course, is in no way subject to such restrictions. It can follow whatever monetary policy it pleases. If it wishes, it can increase the quantity of money and thereby raise commodity prices almost to any extent, or it can keep its general level of commodity prices fairly stable, or reduce it, whatever may be happening elsewhere. Other things remaining the same, changes in the internal purchasing power of its own currency units, relatively to those of other countries, will be reflected by changes in its rates of exchange. But a gold-standard country is debarred from independent action of this kind. It must keep its rates of exchange with other gold-standard countries practically fixed.

Let us suppose that week by week the debits of Great Britain exceed its credits. The "foreign balance" of Great Britain will diminish and the sterling balances held by banks of other countries will increase. British banks will tend to quote drafts and bills on other centres at a premium and foreign banks will tend to quote drafts and bills on London at a discount. In other words the exchange value of sterling will tend to fall.

If the exchange value of sterling were quite free to vary, it would fall sufficiently to restore equilibrium in the balance of payments. The prices of imported goods would rise in terms of sterling and this would check imports. The prices of British exports would fall in terms of other currencies and this would stimulate exports. But if Great Britain is on the gold standard this cannot happen. After sterling has fallen below "the gold export point" relatively to, say, the dollar, persons in Great Britain can pay their creditors in the United States more cheaply by sending gold than by buying drafts or bills on New York. In practice, it is usually the banks who ship gold. The British banks do so to restore their balances abroad. Other banks do so to reduce their swollen London balances and to restore their cash position at home, for their deposits will have been increased (since an export to Great Britain results in an increase in their sterling balances and a corresponding increase in the deposit of the exporter). In any event, gold leaves Great Britain.

The export of gold from Great Britain is in itself a credit item. Hence the deficiency in the British balance of payments might be filled, week by week, by the export of gold. But Great Britain does not produce gold. Sooner or later, if the deficiency continued, all the gold would go. The Bank of England would then be compelled to suspend gold payments, for it would have no gold. Great Britain would be off the gold standard. Clearly the position could not be remedied by importing gold. The imported gold would be a further debit item and would have to be paid for. Its re-export would simply offset this extra debit by an extra credit and the initial deficiency would remain.

This brings us to "the rules of the gold standard." We can best explain these rules, in general terms, by considering what would happen if all the gold in Great Britain consisted of gold coins in circulation. Gold coins would be exported, and the quantity of money would be thereby reduced. The prices of internationally traded commodities could not fall relatively to their prices elsewhere. But money incomes would fall and this would reduce the prices of "domestic" goods and services such as houses and railway rates and labour services. The fall in money incomes would reduce total money expenditure, including expenditure on imports. The fall in money costs would stimulate exports. In so far as they were not fixed by contract, like external interest payments, other debit items would tend to diminish and other credit items to increase. For example, British tourist expenditure abroad would fall relatively to the expenditure of foreign tourists in Great Britain, and investment abroad would become less profitable than before relatively to investment at home. In this way equilibrium would be restored in the balance of payments. The working of the gold standard would be automatic, requiring no intervention by the monetary authorities.

In fact, a modern country has a superstructure of paper notes and bank deposits based upon its stock of monetary gold, and most or all of this stock is held by the central bank or the Treasury. The rules of the gold standard require the monetary authorities, when confronted with an actual or even an imminent export of gold due to an excess of debits over credits which seems likely to continue, to take action resulting in an adjustment similar to that which would come about automatically if the only money were gold coins. They must try to bring about a fall in money incomes and money costs. The usual method is to raise the bank rate and possibly to supplement this by selling securities on the open market, thereby reducing the quantity of money.

Conversely, countries which are in the opposite position and are therefore receiving gold should do their part in bringing about an adjustment by increasing their money incomes and money costs. A defect of the gold exchange standard is that it may throw the whole burden of adjustment on the satellite country. For example, if the balance of payments of Egypt is adverse, the sterling balance held in London by the National Bank of Egypt will diminish, but this need not cause any monetary expansion in Great Britain or elsewhere. Egypt may have to make the whole adjustment if the exchange value of her currency is to remain fixed at 97½ piastres to the pound sterling. But if Egypt were on the gold standard proper, she would export gold and this gold would lead to monetary expansion in the countries receiving it.

If every country on the gold standard followed the rules, the distribution of the total stock of monetary gold among the various countries would depend mainly on the monetary and banking habits and the value of production in each country. For example, in Great Britain the use of cheques is more widespread and the volume of notes and bank deposits is normally much greater, relatively to the gold basis, than in France. Great Britain would therefore need much less gold than France—in fact, perhaps a quarter or a fifth as much—as a basis for the same national income. But of course the national income of one country, measured in some common monetary unit, is different from that of another. The national income of a country, in this context, may be defined as the value of its production plus any sums received from abroad as income on its foreign investments, or as reparations or gifts, and minus any sums paid abroad for the same purposes. It is the total sum which the country can spend or invest during the period, whether at home or abroad, without either borrowing or parting with some of its assets. A country with, say, twice the national income of another will tend to hold twice as large a stock of gold if the normal proportion of gold stock to money income is the same in both countries. But if this proportion is twice as high in the latter country each will tend to hold the same stock of gold, and if it is four times as high the latter country will tend to hold twice as much gold as the former. An increase in the value of production in one country, relatively to others, will tend to attract gold to that country and a decrease will make it tend to lose gold. Movements of this kind are constantly taking place, without arousing any comment, between different districts in the same country. Some leading causes of such gold movements between countries are discussed in section 4. But we must first explain why and how a country may choose not to follow the rules of the gold standard.

3. THE GOLD STANDARD IN PRACTICE

If there were no banks and all money consisted of gold coins, an adverse balance of payments would automatically tend to reduce the amount of money in a country, and thereby its national income, and a favourable balance would tend to do the opposite. In a modern country, however, the central bank can influence the size of the total money income. The central bank, or whatever the monetary authority may be, of a country on the gold standard may decide, in certain circumstances, not to follow the rules. Hence the distribution of gold among countries may diverge, and perhaps widely, from what it would otherwise be.

The central bank of a country which is receiving a large inflow of gold may fear that if it permits this inflow to exert its full influence on incomes and prices the consequence would be a short-lived inflationary boom followed by a depression. It may therefore decide to "sterilize" the extra gold. It is especially likely to come to this decision if the influx is due largely to an inflow of capital which is likely to be withdrawn some time in the near future. The United States received a large inflow of gold during recent years, due largely to the influx of foreign capital to purchase American securities. Clearly the buyers of these securities might decide at any time to sell them, taking their profits or cutting their losses, and to withdraw their capital. Hence the United States has not permitted this influx of gold to send up incomes correspondingly. It has increased its proportion of gold stock to money income, first by compelling the banks to keep bigger reserves and then by locking away the gold purchased by the Treasury, and keeping it out of the banking system. In the same way, during the last years before the war, Great Britain, although not formally on the gold standard, received a large influx of gold, due partly to the inflow of refugee capital, liable to be withdrawn at any time, from France and elsewhere. Her total stock of gold (including that held by the Exchange Equalization Fund) was worth around £800 million in 1939; at the end of 1931 her gold stock was only £121 million. This influx of gold was not permitted to have anything like its full effect on the level of incomes. Part of it was "sterilized" in the Fund. The Bank of England officially valued its gold at the old price of 84s. 11½d. per fine ounce instead of at the market price of around 140s., and even so greatly increased its proportion of gold to notes and deposits.

The central bank of a country which is tending to lose gold, because its balance of payments is adverse, may decide not to follow the policy of deflation indicated by "the rules." It may fear that deflation would increase unemployment and lead to bankruptcy and distress. It may therefore reduce the proportion of gold stock to money income, keeping the latter fairly constant despite the loss of gold. Great Britain was in this situation, and the Bank of England acted in this way, during the period 1925 to 1931, and especially after 1929. Sir Ernest Harvey, Deputy Governor of the Bank of England, said in his evidence before the Macmillan Committee (Q. 353), "You will find if you look at a succession of Bank returns that the amount of gold we have lost has been almost entirely replaced by an increase in the Bank's securities."

As a rule, however, this alone will not suffice, for the central bank will not be prepared to part with enough gold to fill the gap, month by month, in the balance of payments. It will therefore resort to other measures or persuade its Government to do so.

One such measure is to borrow from abroad, either on long term or on short term. It may be possible, by raising the bank rate or persuading other countries to lower theirs, to attract short-term capital without permitting the rise in the bank rate to reduce money incomes. If the central bank holds balances abroad, it can let them run down. If foreign banks hold balances in that centre, as they do in London, the central bank may persuade them to permit their balances to increase without withdrawing gold; in effect, to make a short-term loan. But all these are clearly stop-gap measures which do not solve the long-run problem if the balance of payments continues to be adverse. Money income is being maintained only by borrowing or by reducing foreign assets.

If the country does not wish to leave gold or to devalue (that is, to reduce the gold parity of its monetary unit) but nevertheless wishes to avoid deflation, the Government must interfere with the flow of investment or foreign trade. It may forbid foreign investment by its nationals, thus reducing its debits. The Bank of England, besides resorting to most of the measures already named, at times placed an unofficial ban on lending money abroad. But such a ban is not likely to be very effective.

The other alternative is for the Government to impose tariffs or other restrictions on imports, thus reducing debits, and perhaps to supplement this by subsidies on exports.

But clearly the only course for a country in such a position which wishes to remain on the gold standard without interfering with foreign trade or investment, and without living on its capital or on loans from abroad, is to deflate, reducing its money income.

4. THE CAUSES OF GOLD FLOWS

Any change which would raise or lower the exchange value of a currency if its rates of exchange were quite free to vary will have the same tendency if the currency is on gold, and will therefore tend to bring about an inflow or outflow of gold. We shall discuss briefly the main types of changes, under the headings used in the last chapter: monetary policy, capital movements, and reciprocal supply-and-demand of goods and services. We shall assume that previous to the change the balance of payments was in equilibrium and that the total stock of monetary gold remains the same.

(1) Monetary Policy

Suppose that country A inflates and other gold-standard countries do not. Incomes rise in A and the amount of money spent on everything, including imports, increases. The rise in incomes—assuming full employment before the inflation—is a rise in factor-prices, that is, in costs, so that exports fall off. The country loses gold and this makes it reverse the inflation. All gold-standard countries can inflate or deflate together, provided they keep pace, without causing gold flows, but one country alone cannot do so. If A holds a considerable proportion of the total gold stock, it can cause, by itself inflating, some inflation in other countries, based on the gold they receive from A. But it can do this only if it is prepared to reduce its ratio of gold to national income, and if other countries do not reduce their ratios it will be checked after a time, for it will not be prepared to go on increasing its income on the basis of a diminishing stock of gold.

(2) Capital Movements

Suppose that A begins to lend so much per month abroad. This will make its balance of payments adverse, leading to an outflow of gold. If A follows the rules, this will reduce its money income, checking its imports and stimulating its exports, until it develops a monthly surplus of exports over imports (or, more accurately, of credits over other debits) equal in value to the monthly sum it lends abroad. The country receiving the loan will have an inflow of gold which will raise its money income until it develops a corresponding surplus of imports. Of course, the increased exports of A need not go to the borrowing country: the transfer may take place via third countries. Interest receipts by A, and repayments to A of loans which it made in the past, will have the opposite effects.

(3) Reciprocal Supply-and-Demand of Goods and Services

This is subject to many influences, several of which may change simultaneously. Apart from changes in monetary and trade policy, the main possible changes are in population, capital, technique, and demand. We shall discuss them under those headings. It should be remembered that it is always changes *relatively* to other countries, and not absolute changes, which are important in this context.

(*a*) Changes in Population

Suppose that there is a considerable increase—say from immigration—in the population of A, and not of other countries.

If monetary and banking habits in A do not change, the demand for money in A will increase. Incomes and prices in A will therefore tend to fall. Its exports will be stimulated and its imports checked. Gold will flow from other gold-standard countries to A and will stay there. Incidentally the terms of trade will probably become less favourable to A. For she is likely to offer more of her exports on the world's markets, thus depressing their prices, and to demand more of other countries' export goods, thus raising their prices. The volume of international trade is likely to increase.

(*b*) Changes in Capital

Suppose that the people of A save more than before, investing at home, so that the capital in A increases relatively to that in other countries. After a time, this will lead to an increase in the volume of output. The export industries will probably share in the increase of capital and therefore of output. Hence the prices of A's export goods will fall and, assuming that the foreign demand for them is fairly elastic, the total value of A's exports will increase. But the total value of A's imports is unlikely to rise as much. For by hypothesis the output of A's domestic goods—which will be to some extent substitutes for imports—will have increased and their prices will have fallen; but the prices of imported goods will not have fallen. Hence A has an excess of credits over debits and acquires more gold from other gold-standard countries until her increased monetary stock of gold enables her to have a bigger money income than before whilst retaining her old proportion of gold to money income.

(*c*) Changes in Technique

A very similar analysis applies when greater technical progress occurs in A than in other countries, assuming that it affects the export industries of A (and the domestic industries of A whose products are substitutes for imports). It may be the result of chance: for example, inventions may be made which apply to the export industries of A more than to other industries. Or, more probably, technical progress in A may go hand-in-hand with an increase of capital in A. What will happen?

The prices of A's export goods will fall. If the foreign demand for them is fairly elastic, foreign countries will spend more money than before upon them. But A's demand for imports will fall, at first, because her money income remains the same and her domestic goods fall in price whereas her imports do not. Hence gold will flow to A. Then her demand for imports will recover —partly because her money income will be larger and partly because money costs elsewhere will probably fall (since factor-prices elsewhere will probably fall). In the new equilibrium A will have more gold and a bigger money income than before, the terms of trade will be somewhat less favourable to A than before, and the volume of international trade will be greater than before.

Another gold-standard country, say B, will be somewhat better off than before if she follows "the rules"—namely, allows gold to flow out and deflates, reducing her money income by reducing factor-prices and not by creating unemployment. B will have a lower money income than before but her home-produced goods will be correspondingly cheaper and she will obtain more imports than before for any given quantity of exports.

(*d*) Changes in Demand

Suppose that there is a fall in the foreign demand for the export goods of country B. This may be due simply to a change in the tastes of foreign consumers. It may be due to the fact that foreign countries place greater restrictions than before on the import of B's products. It may be due to changes in knowledge which enable countries to substitute home-produced goods for goods which they previously imported from B or which enable, for example, 9 tons of coal to do the work previously done by 10 tons. (This will diminish the amount of coal required if the elasticity of demand for coal is less than unity.) Or it may be due to a change in relative factor-supplies abroad which make the comparative-cost conditions less favourable to B than before.

B may be able to lessen the fall in demand for her exports by changing their composition. But in any event, the tendency will be for B to lose gold until the consequent reduction in her money income cuts down her demand for imports to the value which she can pay for.

5. THE MONETARY POLICY OF THE GOLD-STANDARD SYSTEM

We have been considering what forces determine how a given stock of monetary gold is divided among the various countries. The money income of a country, as of any area, equals the value of its production plus its net income from foreign investments or minus its net interest payments made abroad. But its money income in the sense of the amount available for expenditure of all kinds will be increased by inward and diminished by outward movements of capital. The "rules" are designed to give each country that money income to which it is entitled *relatively to other countries*. If a country is losing gold, that is a sign that its money income is too large relatively to the money incomes of other countries, and should be reduced. If its monetary authorities intervene to maintain its money income, despite the tendency to lose gold, they probably do so by inducing inward movements of capital which would not otherwise have taken place or restricting outward movements, as explained in section 3. The theory of the gold standard, as we have outlined it, relates to the *relative* incomes of the various countries.

There remains the question of what forces determine the *absolute* levels of money incomes within the gold-standard system. All the countries in this system are virtually sharing a common currency, based on gold. An increase in the stock of monetary gold tends to raise money incomes and prices within the system as a whole. So does a general fall in the demand for money or, in the language of some writers, an increase in the velocity of circulation. Technical progress tends to increase output and to bring down prices but not money incomes. The opposite changes tend to have the opposite effects.

These tendencies, however, can be modified or counteracted by the central banks or other monetary authorities. There is no reason why the gold-standard system as a whole should not pursue its own monetary policy just as fully as an isolated country. The "rules" relate only to relative incomes. All gold-standard countries can inflate or deflate together, reducing or increasing their ratios of gold stock to money income, without impairing the stability of their exchange rates with one another. And in fact gold has long been a "managed" currency: changes in the supply of gold or in the demand for money have not been permitted to exert an uncontrolled influence on incomes and prices within the gold-standard system.

The various monetary authorities might meet together from time to time to decide on an agreed policy for the system as a whole. During the inter-war years there were some meetings between representatives of leading central banks or Treasuries in order to "co-ordinate" their monetary policies. For the most part, however, each monetary authority did what it could to raise or lower prices or incomes or to keep them stable, as it thought best, whilst remaining on gold. In such circumstances the country with the biggest income can exert the biggest pull. That country was the United States.

From about 1924 to 1929 there was a very considerable increase in the output of the United States. This was due to the growth of investment and the progress of technique. It tended to reduce commodity prices, not only in the United States but in all gold-standard countries. But the monetary authorities of the United States seem to have aimed at keeping the general level of commodity prices fairly stable. They therefore permitted a very considerable increase in money incomes. In the autumn of 1927 the Bank of France began to withdraw some of its accumulated sterling balances from London. Great Britain sought international co-operation in order to avoid reducing her money income by deflation. The Federal Reserve Board lowered discount rates, thus relieving the strain on Great Britain by further increasing the quantity of money, and money income, in the United States. This gave a fresh impetus to the American boom. Wages were rising in the United States, but not as much as output per worker.[1] Stable selling prices coupled with lower costs per unit produced, owing to technical progress, mean increasing profits. From 1924 to 1929 profits in the United States about doubled. The continued expectation of rising profits reduced the demand for money: people wanted to invest in stock exchange securities rather than to keep their assets more liquid. There were thus all the symptoms of a boom, except that commodity prices remained fairly stable.

[1] From 1923–5 to 1929 pay-rolls divided by the index of production declined nearly 10 per cent. See H. Barger in the *Journal of Political Economy*, December, 1935.

Moreover, from 1925 to 1930 the United States lent over 6000 million dollars overseas. This enabled the borrowing countries, mainly in Central Europe and South America, to maintain or increase their money incomes without losing gold.

The American boom ended with the collapse of security prices on Wall Street in October, 1929. There was a great increase in the desire to be liquid rather than to invest and commodity prices began to fall, which meant that they fell not only in the United States but throughout the gold-standard system. After a time, American investors practically stopped lending abroad. The boom conditions which Germany and some other countries had enjoyed, partly on the basis of loans made to them by the United States or Great Britain, came abruptly to an end. Such countries now had to create an export surplus to cover their interest and repayments due to foreign creditors. Most countries exporting mainly agricultural products had been borrowing and were doubly hit, for the prices of their exports, which had already fallen somewhat since 1928, fell heavily and at the same time their inflow of loan-money dwindled. There were considerable defaults on debts due abroad. Countries such as Australia and the Argentine felt that they could not face the drastic reduction in money income which would have been necessary to enable them to remain on gold, and they left the gold standard. Great Britain followed their example in September, 1931, and was herself followed by a number of other countries.

We shall not discuss what monetary policy an isolated country, or the gold-standard system as a whole, ought to follow. The foregoing brief remarks are intended merely to show that much of the criticism which has been levelled against the gold standard, on the ground that it worked badly during the 'twenties and led to the great depression, is really without foundation. The gold standard did not work badly. It was badly worked. Some countries, notably Great Britain, did not follow the rules. Other countries overborrowed. The Federal Reserve Board—urged in 1927, as we have noted, by Great Britain—followed an inflationary policy, and by its foreign lending permitted borrowing countries to do the same. Thus the monetary policy of the gold-standard system as a whole was, admittedly, a bad one. But this is not an argument against the gold standard as such.

The world's monetary stock of gold has grown from just over

600 million ounces of fine gold at the end of 1931 to nearly 800 million at the end of 1936. 35·3 million ounces were produced in 1936 as against 22·4 million in 1931. This was due partly to gold discoveries in Russia (whose output is estimated, not very reliably, to have grown from 1·7 million ounces in 1931 to 7·4 million in 1936) but mainly to the rise in the price of gold. Gold-producing countries have left the gold standard and the value of their currencies has fallen in terms of gold. The rise in the labour and other costs of gold production has been less than the rise in the price of gold and this has led to an expansion of output. The world stock of monetary gold measured in dollars or sterling has more than doubled since 1931, for the price of gold in dollars or sterling has risen by 60 to 70 per cent. This means that if there is a general return to the gold standard the leading countries will have to agree upon the absolute levels of money incomes desired and make their monetary arrangements conform to this joint policy. Probably they will want to avoid the inflationary effects which would result if the greatly increased stock of gold were permitted to produce a corresponding increase in money incomes. The United States and Great Britain were virtually "sterilizing" a great deal of gold before the war, and would doubtless have continued to do so.

6. THE MERITS AND DEFECTS OF THE GOLD STANDARD

The great advantage of the gold standard is that it provides practically fixed rates of exchange between the countries on it. This is a very real boon to traders and investors, for it removes the risk of loss from fluctuations in the exchanges. Hence it greatly facilitates international division of labour and international investment. The gold-standard system as a whole gains by having virtually a common currency in the same way that a country gains by having a single currency instead of a separate one for each of its various local areas.

Of course any international standard would achieve this result. Indeed, it could be achieved simply by an agreement between the various Governments to keep exchange rates fixed at a given level. But the only common standard at all likely to be accepted by most important countries is the gold standard.

The gold standard, however, loses most of its virtue if traders and investors fear that it may not be maintained. The stimulus which it gives to foreign trade and investment depends on their confidence that exchange rates will in fact remain stable. For example, on 1st October, 1936, the French franc was devalued. Its gold equivalent was to be between 43 and 49 milligrammes of gold $\frac{9}{10}$ths fine, instead of 65·5. One of the strongest arguments for devaluation was that for months or even years there had been a general distrust of the franc. It was thought that France would not be able to remain on gold at a parity of 65·5 milligrammes. It was hoped that devaluation would end this uncertainty. In fact it did not, for traders and investors feared—rightly, as it turned out—that the big rise in labour costs due to the Blum policy would make it impossible for the franc to be held even at its new and lower level. In the same way, the agreement reached in October, 1936, between the Governments of the United States and Great Britain is virtually an agreement to keep the dollar-sterling exchange rate fairly stable. But either Government can depart from it at a day's notice, so that it has inspired much less confidence than if Great Britain had returned, like the United States, to a *de jure* gold standard. Again, a Government which says that it is on the gold standard but reserves the right to change the gold parity whenever this seems desirable, or which fixes a wide margin (within which the exchange value of its currency can vary) between the price at which it will buy gold and the price at which it will sell gold, will not create confidence that its exchange rates will remain stable. The case for the gold standard is a case for a strict *de jure* gold standard, with each country following "the rules" so that no gold-standard currency becomes distrusted.

Obviously the benefit of stable exchange rates provided by the gold standard varies with the number of countries on it. If only one country were on gold, no exchange rate would be stable.

A defect of the gold standard, with banking systems as they are, is that gold movements lead to changes in interest rates, so that investment is stimulated or checked solely in order to expand or reduce money income.

Some arguments against the gold standard spring mainly from misunderstanding. Thus it has been urged at times that gold is "maldistributed" between countries when its distribution is due to the fact that some countries, like France, maintain a large ratio of gold stock to money income, or to the fact that the growth of the gold exchange standard has resulted in the transference of gold to two or three leading centres, or to the fact that the value of output has increased much more in some countries than in others. Again, it is sometimes claimed that the proper working of the gold standard requires creditor countries to continue lending to borrowing countries even after it has become clear that the latter are in difficulties because they have been living partly on foreign loans and that they may be unable to pay interest on their existing external debts.

On the other hand, the claim that the gold standard prevents inflation is false. It is true that a country cannot remain on gold and at the same time raise its prices relatively to other gold-standard countries. But the system as a whole can inflate, as we have seen. Moreover, although the total stock of monetary gold does not change very much over a short period (since gold is very durable) the demand for money in gold-standard countries may change greatly within a very short time. It is an illusion to think that the gold standard ensures a stable price-level or prevents booms and depressions. The monetary policy of the gold-standard system, like that of a country with an independent currency, may or may not be wise.

The general case for free exchange rates is that a country on gold cannot follow an independent monetary policy. In particular, at times it may be compelled to deflate quite considerably in order to stay on gold. Deflation is usually unpopular. It increases the relative burden of fixed charges, such as interest on the National Debt and on mortgages and debentures. It reduces expected profits and checks investment. If wage-rates are fairly rigid, deflation may lead to a considerable increase in unemployment. Many countries left gold after 1929 rather than face the drastic deflation which would otherwise have been necessary. A country with an independent currency need never deflate. It can correct an adverse balance of payments by letting the exchange value of its currency fall, without reducing incomes in terms of its own monetary unit. Nevertheless free exchange rates cannot secure full employment if occupational wages are rigid and there are obstacles to the mobility of labour, nor can they prevent a fall in real income if a country is faced with a fall in the demand for its exports. They give a country a free hand to fix its own level of prices and money incomes at the cost of restricting international trade and investment.

7. DEVALUATION

At this stage, we may remind the reader that we concluded the chapter on Balances of Payments by pointing out that there are five methods by which a country can try to correct an adverse balance of payments. These five methods are, briefly, exchange depreciation, deflation, devaluation, exchange control, and restriction of imports. We may also remind him that nearly all the difficulties associated with balances of payments arise from the existence of separate national States with separate currency and banking systems.

The last chapter discussed free exchange rates, under which the first method is adopted. The present chapter has discussed the gold standard, under which the second method is adopted. The next chapter gives a general discussion of exchange control: the method adopted by countries which wish nominally to stay on gold without following the rules of the gold standard. The final chapter gives a general discussion of restrictions on imports. The present section discusses briefly the third method, namely, devaluation.

A country which does not wish to deflate sufficiently to remain on gold at its existing parity but wants nevertheless to retain the advantage of stable exchange rates provided by the gold standard may decide to devalue its currency. To devalue is to reduce the gold parity of its currency. A country may devalue overnight, or it may leave the gold standard and return to it, at a lower parity, after an interval of months or years.

If all the countries on the gold standard were to devalue at the same time and to the same extent, their rates of exchange with one another would remain as they were before. The price of gold, and the value of existing stocks of gold in central banks and elsewhere, in terms of the devalued currencies, would rise at once. For to devalue is to fix a higher price for gold in terms of one's own currency. Thus the "profit" on the French devaluation of 1st October, 1936, amounted to between 16 and 17 milliard francs (of which 10 milliard were transferred in gold to the French Exchange Equalization Fund). Such a "profit" is of course only nominal in so far as the gold does not buy more goods than before on the world's markets but it may make a welcome contribution to the budgets of the devaluing countries.

The rise in the nominal value of stocks of monetary gold makes possible, if desired, a considerable expansion of bank credit without reducing the customary ratio of gold stock to money income. The United States left gold in the spring of 1933, returning early in 1934 at slightly under 60 per cent of the old gold parity, largely in order to pave the way for a rise in her internal incomes and prices.

The rise in the price of gold will probably lead to an expansion in the amount of gold produced. The price of gold rises at once in terms of the devalued currencies but the costs of producing it probably rise less. Hence output tends to expand (although it should be noted that in South Africa the first effect is some reduction in output owing to lower-grade ore being worked) until, under competition, the marginal cost of producing gold rises sufficiently to equal the new and higher price of gold.

During recent years a number of currencies have been devalued, some of them more than once, although there has been no simultaneous devaluation by all gold-standard countries acting in concert, and exchange rates between them have therefore varied considerably from one time to another. The world stock of monetary gold, measured in dollars or in sterling or in francs, has more than doubled since 1931, and the annual output has increased by more than 50 per cent.

Suppose now that only one country devalues. The exchange value of its currency, relatively to other gold-standard currencies, will be correspondingly reduced. This will tend to stimulate its exports and other credit items and to check its imports and other debit items. If its balance of payments was continuously adverse before the devaluation, it will now tend to become less adverse or to become favourable. We may note, however, that this did not happen in the case of France, who was unable to stay on gold even at the lower parity adopted on 1st October, 1936. This was largely due to the very considerable rise in labour costs which took place at the same time and counteracted the stimulus to exports. It was partly due to the fact that the bulk of French imports came in under quota, and therefore imports were not restricted by the reduced exchange value of the franc.

Devaluation gives a country, provided that most other countries do not follow its example, the relief of a reduction in its exchange rates whilst enabling it to remain on gold. But the advantages of remaining on gold are secured only if there is general confidence that the country can and will maintain the new parity. If a currency is devalued again and again in the course of a few years, traders and investors cease to have confidence in it. Devaluation is a serious step which fails in its purpose if it is lightly undertaken only to be followed by a fresh devaluation later.

CHAPTER XXIX

EXCHANGE CONTROL

1. THE MOTIVES FOR EXCHANGE CONTROL

DURING the Great Depression, a number of countries adopted, and most of them still retain, a system of controlling all foreign exchange transactions: a system far more complete and far-reaching than mere intervention in the foreign exchange market by an Exchange Equalization Fund. We shall discuss this system mainly with reference to pre-war Nazi Germany, but most of our remarks will apply to other countries which have adopted it as well as to Germany.

Germany has developed this system so thoroughly that the German Government, through the Reichsbank, has almost complete control of foreign trade. No German can import without a licence. Hence the Government can give precedence to materials required for armaments and other imports deemed essential, whilst restricting imports of goods, such as luxury articles, which it considers less important. Goods coming from certain countries can be favoured as against goods coming from others. Particular kinds of exports, or exports to particular countries, can be subsidized to a greater or less extent. Hence exchange control, together with the power to vary import duties and railway rates, has become the handmaid of politics. It is an instrument of central planning.

It was adopted in the first place as an emergency measure. In the summer of 1931, after the German banking crisis, the Reichsbank was left with a very depleted and quite inadequate gold reserve of something over a milliard marks. Some 3 milliard marks of short-term credits had already been withdrawn since the beginning of 1931 and further withdrawals were almost certain. German securities and other assets were being sold and converted into foreign exchange. Germany was facing a flight from the mark.

The orthodox course—if she wanted to stay on gold at the existing parity—was to deflate vigorously, hoping that high rates of interest would deter capital from leaving and perhaps even attract some from abroad. But deflation could not have coped with the immediate danger of a flight of capital and would have increased unemployment. Another possible course was to go off gold and let the exchange value of the mark find its own level. But the general public remembered the hyper-inflation in Germany after the last war, and associated a fall in the exchange value of the mark with inflation. This course, therefore, might well have created panic and confusion due to a general belief that the purchasing power of the mark would depreciate. Moreover, it would have increased the apparent burden of fixed charges expressed in other currencies and payable abroad, for more marks would have been needed to provide a given sum in dollars or pounds or francs.

Similar arguments applied against devaluation. Later, it was doubtless realized that although a sufficiently large devaluation might maintain equilibrium in the balance of payments and permit exchange control to be abandoned, the consequent all-round stimulus to German exports would enable creditor countries to claim and possibly to seize, by means of payments agreements, a much larger share of the sums due to them. Much of the loans made to Germany before the slump had been malinvested. It was most unlikely that Germany would be able to meet her interest and repayment charges in full. It happened that exchange control enabled her virtually to default on most of her foreign debts on the ground that foreign exchange was not available to permit the money to be transferred. And exports could be directed mainly towards non-creditor countries.

Thus exchange control began in the summer of 1931, with 13 milliards of short-term credits due for repayment in the near future, with interest due on a long-term debt aggregating nearly 20 milliard marks, with the gold reserve extremely low, and with a flight from the mark gathering force. It was adopted to give temporary relief and it has become a leading part of economic policy.

2. THE METHODS OF EXCHANGE CONTROL

The object of exchange control, as we have seen, is to prevent a flight of capital and to prevent the gold reserves of the central bank from becoming further depleted—indeed, if possible, to increase them—without deflating and whilst nominally maintaining the exchange value of the currency. At this exchange value, the demand for foreign exchange greatly exceeds the supply. Exchange control, therefore, must restrict the demand for foreign exchange whilst endeavouring to increase the amount of it supplied.

The most rigid method is to compel all foreign exchange transactions to take place through a central office, under the control of the central bank. Thus anybody can obtain any quantity of marks, giving foreign exchange in return, at the official rate. But no German can obtain foreign exchange, giving marks in return, without special permission. This is given for "essential imports"—the amount of foreign exchange to be doled out to purchase any particular foreign good, and the importers who are to receive it, being determined by consultation with the various Chambers of Commerce in Germany. A little foreign exchange may be given, at the official rate, to Germans wishing to travel abroad; and some is used for paying Government debts abroad, wholly or in part.

We may perhaps supplement this general account by naming certain measures taken to restrict the demand for foreign exchange and to prevent a flight of capital through evasion of the regulations. It will be appreciated that foreign merchants would be glad to buy marks at, say, 20 to the pound instead of about 12 to the pound in order to use them to pay for German goods which they would import or had imported. On the other hand, German importers (unable to obtain sufficient foreign exchange from the central office) might make good profits if they could obtain more foreign exchange, even at a rate of about 20 marks to the pound. Again, foreign owners of assets frozen in Germany might be glad to recover their capital even at this rate. Hence there is clearly an incentive for people to exchange marks for foreign exchange at a rate considerably lower than the official rate. Hence a "black bourse" arises. A perfect system of exchange control exercises such vigilant supervision, and enforces such heavy penalties for illegal dealings, that a black bourse cannot flourish. The purchase of foreign securities by nationals is made illegal. The export of, say, German notes is prohibited (since foreign exchange would be given for them which might otherwise come to the central office) and in some countries the re-import of such notes is also prohibited. Imports are scrutinized to make sure that the German importer has not induced his foreign supplier to invoice the goods above their actual price and to invest the difference (abroad) on his behalf. Foreigners are not allowed to sell their German assets and convert the proceeds into foreign exchange.

The treatment of short-term credits due to foreigners deserves special mention. The foreign short-term debt of Germany in 1931 was about 13 milliard marks. About half of this (consisting of acceptance credits and bank advances granted to German banks and business firms by foreign banks and finance houses) came under the "Standstill Agreement." The creditors agreed not to press for more than a very moderate rate of repayment, and to go on re-lending the money, which by a useful fiction continued to be treated as self-liquidating. As time went on, this indebtedness was considerably reduced, by creditors accepting payment at a discount and by the depreciation of the pound and the dollar. It is now below 1·0 milliard marks. Similar agreements were made with some other short-term creditors (who had lent, for example, to German municipalities) and the rest were forbidden—by unilateral action on the part of the German Government—to withdraw their capital in foreign exchange. In these ways, the demand for foreign exchange was restricted.

As to the supply of foreign exchange, it was decreed that all foreign currencies and values held by nationals were to be sold to the monetary authorities; similarly with the proceeds from goods and services exported. Of course, there was a strong tendency to evasion, for more marks could be obtained for foreign exchange by selling it illegally. An obvious form of evasion is to quote lower prices for German exports than the prices actually paid—the German exporter thus getting foreign exchange without the knowledge of the central bank. In order to counter this, there is Government supervision of export prices.

3. BLOCKED ACCOUNTS

Exchange control created a large number of blocked accounts. A blocked account is a deposit in marks at the Reichsbank in favour of a foreigner. But the foreigner who owns it is not allowed to draw upon it, or is allowed to do so only to a limited extent and for a specified purpose, such as to cover his personal expenditure whilst travelling in Germany. The account remains "blocked."

These accounts arose in various ways. For example, German importers who were quite solvent might be refused foreign exchange to pay for goods which they had already received. They paid in marks, but these marks went into blocked accounts in the names of their creditors. Again, many payments due on foreign debts were blocked. Thus when in June, 1933, the German Government announced that it would be forced to suspend the transfer of payments on all foreign debts except the Dawes and Young loans, the sums due were paid into blocked accounts in the names of the creditors. Short-term credits and sales of securities and other assets held in Germany by foreigners also gave rise to blocked accounts.

The existence of these accounts enabled Germany to subsidize certain exports at the expense of foreign creditors. Some of the latter were prepared to cut their losses by "selling" their accounts to the Reichsbank in return for their own currency, taking, say, 40 per cent less than they were entitled to receive if the exchange value of their marks had been calculated at the official rate. The "profits" on such sales constituted a fund out of which the Reichsbank subsidized selected German exports.

During recent years blocked accounts have been diminishing. Their aggregate value in 1936 was only around 500 million marks. Foreigners have become wary of selling goods or otherwise giving credit to Germans without some kind of guarantee that they would be paid in their own currency. German exports are now subsidized mainly out of a fund created for the purpose by a special tax imposed on all German industry, and the great bulk of the foreign trade of Germany takes place under clearing agreements or payments agreements.

4. CLEARING AGREEMENTS

Exchange control gave rise to many clearing agreements. These were usually insisted upon, in the interests of their nationals, by countries exporting to a country practising exchange control. We can take the Swedish-German Agreement of 1st September, 1934, as an illustration.

Swedish exporters to Germany had not been paid in full in their own currency but partly in blocked mark accounts. This naturally discouraged further exports to Germany. But in 1933 the export surplus of Germany to Sweden was 90 million marks. Germany needed the balance of foreign exchange resulting from her trade with Sweden to pay for raw materials from other countries, with whom she had an import surplus. This placed Sweden in a strong bargaining position. She could, and did, insist on a clearing agreement by which she hoped to get payment for goods already delivered and for goods delivered in future and also to secure a larger share of the interest payments due from Germany to Swedish creditors.

Under the terms of this Agreement all payments made by Swedes for goods imported from Germany were to be made in Swedish currency into a special fund at the Swedish central bank. Out of this fund the claims of Swedish exporters to Germany were to be met. The balance was to be divided between the Reichsbank and specified Swedish creditors of Germany, those who had subscribed to the Dawes and Young loans taking precedence, and the total sum available to such creditors varying with the size of Germany's export surplus to Sweden.

On the whole, such agreements have disappointed the creditor countries. Their exporters, feeling assured of payment, have increased their deliveries to the other country. If the latter has inflated, or has diverted exports to countries from which it could get more foreign exchange, or if the rate of exchange fixed in the clearing agreement has been the official one whereas previously transactions took place in fact at a lower rate, the export surplus of the exchange-control country has been much less than was anticipated and exporters in the other country have had to wait a long time for payment. Thus Switzerland concluded a clearing agreement with Turkey, an exchange-control country, in March, 1934. During the preceding twelve months her exports to Turkey were 63 per cent of her imports from Turkey. For the following six months they were 188 per cent. Again, German purchases from Yugoslavia increased so much, under the clearing agreement between the two countries, that Yugoslavia found herself by 1935 with a large balance owing to her from Germany, and her national bank was compelled to grant premiums to Yugoslavs purchasing goods from Germany in order to reduce this balance. Discontent with clearing agreements has led to some development of what is termed "private compensation." This is virtually barter. Traders in two countries are allowed to make their own arrangements for exchanging goods. Naturally a country with exchange control dislikes this system, for it gives it no foreign exchange and partly prevents it from influencing the nature and direction of foreign trade. Nevertheless such countries have been constrained to acquiesce in some arrangements of this kind in order to get imports which foreigners would not otherwise have supplied.

5. PAYMENTS AGREEMENTS

A payments agreement is an improved type of clearing agreement. Under agreements of the old type, exporters to an exchange-control country had to wait their turn to receive payment out of the fund created by the payments of their fellow-countrymen who had imported from that country. They sometimes had to wait many months. Their working capital was thus tied up and uncertainty as to when they would receive payment discouraged further transactions.

The agreement of November, 1934, between Great Britain and Germany limits the latter's imports from Great Britain in any month to 55 per cent of the value of her exports to Great Britain during the last month but one. Apart from a sum earmarked at the beginning to clear off existing commercial debts, the surplus 45 per cent is partly used to pay certain interest and other charges, the rest being placed at the free disposal of the Reichsbank. Thus a German importer who has been granted a permit to import from Great Britain and to get foreign exchange for that purpose knows that he will in fact get the required amount of sterling in two months. The British exporter can be assured of payment in two months by his German customer (assuming of course that he is solvent) and both parties can use the ordinary facilities of the banking system to obtain overdrafts or discount bills in order to finance the transaction. There is direct contact all the time between buyers and sellers and the latter must pay attention to the credit standing of their customers instead of relying upon the administrative arrangements made by their Governments.

In these ways payments agreements are an improvement on the old type of clearing agreements. Both, however, are directly due to exchange restrictions and reflect the disadvantages of that system. In some countries, it has led to considerable corruption among the host of officials administering it. Everywhere it has diverted foreign trade from the channels indicated by the comparative-cost situation. Germany, for example, has bought goods from countries other than those which produce them most cheaply because she could "pay" by giving a credit at the clearing instead of actually providing foreign exchange, and other countries have bought from her rather than elsewhere in order to get something in return for their previous sales to her. There is no doubt that exchange restrictions have considerably kept down the volume and altered the directions of world trade.

CHAPTER XXX

IMPORT DUTIES AND QUOTAS

I. ARGUMENTS FOR PROTECTION

COMPLETE freedom of foreign trade is quite exceptional. Nearly every country has always imposed restrictions on at least some of its imports, although the nature and extent of these restrictions have varied between countries and have been different at different periods. Various forms of restriction have been practised. For example, importers have been forced to comply with burdensome administrative regulations, railway rates on inward movements of goods have been made higher than on outward movements, unnecessarily severe rules imposed in the alleged interests of health and hygiene have kept down imports of live animals and other goods, and, as we have just seen, exchange control permits the Government to curtail imports as it wishes. But the most usual devices have been to impose taxes known as "duties" or "tariffs" on some or all imports or to restrict the quantity imported to a stated maximum fixed by a "quota." This maximum may be nil: that is, the import of some goods may be prohibited. Our discussion will be confined mainly to import duties and import quotas.

Import duties imposed by a country on goods which it does not produce or accompanied by equivalent "excise duties" on similar goods produced at home are said to be "revenue duties." The British duties on tobacco are an illustration. If the quantity imported and consumed is not appreciably reduced by the duty, the demand being fairly rigid, there is little diversion of productive resources within the country. But if imports and consumption are considerably curtailed, fewer factors of production are employed in the export industries, for in the long run to curtail imports is to curtail exports. We shall be concerned mainly with "protective" duties, designed to encourage the production of similar domestic goods.

The support given to Protection springs partly from a belief, which has persisted through the centuries, that it is desirable to stimulate exports and curtail imports. At first sight this belief seems very odd. The standard of living depends on goods produced for home consumption and imports; exports are consumed by foreigners. If it were somehow possible for a country continuously to get more imports in return for fewer exports, one would expect its citizens to welcome the scheme instead of trying to do the opposite. In the past, however, an export surplus has often been desired as a means of obtaining gold. Moreover, at times when there is heavy unemployment in the export industries, the desire to stimulate exports is quite understandable. Bounties or subsidies have often been granted on exports. For example, after the last war most leading countries subsidized their shipping. But export bounties cost a Government money, whereas import duties bring it revenue, so that the latter have been much more popular than the former.

Some arguments for Protection which carry much weight with the general public are mainly fallacious. A leading example of these is the argument that imports from countries with low wages should be taxed in order to prevent the standard of living of workers in the home country from being reduced. We exposed the fallacy of this contention in Chapter XXV, section 6. Again, those concerned with a particular industry may urge that protection against competing imports would enable that industry to expand. Nobody disputes this. But the real question is whether it would be desirable for the country as a whole to bring about an expansion of that industry at the cost of a contraction in the export industries. The expansion of industry A will doubtless increase the purchasing power of its workers and shareholders, but if consumers spend more on the products of A, they will have less to spend on other products, including imports, and foreigners will therefore have less to spend on the exports of that country.

Some arguments for Protection are based mainly on non-economic considerations. Thus a country may stimulate its iron and steel industry in order to be better prepared for war, or may protect agriculture because it is thought desirable to maintain a fairly large agricultural population. An economist can only point out the sacrifice, in the form of a standard of living lower than it would otherwise be, entailed by such policies, leaving statesmen or citizens to decide whether the sacrifice is worth making.

Some arguments for Protection are based on economic analysis. For example, it has been urged, and rightly, that import duties or taxes on exports tend to turn the terms of trade in favour of the country imposing them. They may enable that country to take fuller advantage of its monopolistic position as a seller or buyer. Thus the export taxes imposed on rubber, under the Rubber Restriction Scheme, by Malaya doubtless enabled her to get more in return for her rubber than she would otherwise have obtained. Again, the restrictions imposed on the import of agricultural products by most countries in Western Europe during the Great Depression undoubtedly kept down the prices of such products[1] and turned the terms of trade further in favour of the countries importing them—although most of the benefit of this went to Great Britain, since such countries as France, Germany, and Italy cut down their agricultural imports to very low levels. It should be remembered, however, that the terms of trade of a country are merely the relation between two sets of world prices: those of the goods it exports and those of the goods it imports. It is seldom that one country alone can exert a considerable influence on relative world prices. Moreover, its loss from the restriction of international division of labour may be greater than its gain from improved terms of trade. Another famous argument is that in favour of protecting "infant industries" which are suited to the country but which require a period of help during which they can establish themselves against existing foreign competitors and become sufficiently strong to dispense with further aid.

Nevertheless, tariffs for which there is a case on theoretical grounds have seldom worked well in practice. The imposition of duties by one country often leads to retaliation by others. Infant industries practically never grow up but on the contrary demand increased protection. A protective tariff usually gives rise to "log-rolling," pressure on the Government by vested interests seeking more protection, and, in some countries, a good deal of corruption. Whatever may be said for protection in theory, free trade seems best in practice, and there is always the general case for free trade, which few people without economic training really understand: namely, that it promotes

[1] On the world market. Their prices were much higher inside the "protecting" countries.

international specialization and thereby enables the productive resources of a country to be put to their most advantageous uses. But the case for Protection as an emergency measure deserves special mention.

2. PROTECTION AS AN EMERGENCY MEASURE

Great Britain might possibly have adopted Protection in 1930 or 1931, before she left the gold standard, as an emergency measure. She had an adverse balance of payments which seemed likely to continue for some time. One possible course was to reduce her money income. But it was widely believed that money wages were fairly rigid. It was thought that wage-earners would not object to a rise in the cost of living but would resist any considerable cuts in money wages. It followed from these assumptions and from the fact that the demand for imports was fairly rigid, that the orthodox policy of deflation would have led to a big increase in unemployment. Another possible course was to leave gold and let the exchange value of sterling fall until equilibrium was restored in the balance of payments. But Great Britain is very dependent on international trade and has large foreign investments. She therefore wished, if possible, to stay on gold. Another alternative was to devalue. But this would have broken a tradition of over two hundred years. In the circumstances, the imposition of tariffs appeared to some to be the least of several evils. Tariffs would have cut down the demand for imports, thereby reducing or eliminating the adverse balance of payments. They would thus have enabled Great Britain to retain or acquire more gold than otherwise, and to maintain her money income by permitting the cost of living to rise.

In fact Great Britain did not adopt this solution. She did not impose a general tariff until March, 1932, after she had left gold. At that time, therefore, the above argument for tariffs did not apply. The balance of payments could have been kept in equilibrium solely by permitting the exchange value of sterling to fall to the required extent. The new tariffs kept sterling higher than it would otherwise have been but they discriminated against particular imports, whereas if equilibrium had been secured through the exchange rates alone consumers could have chosen for themselves what imports they would dispense with.

During a depression public opinion often swings more strongly towards increased Protection as a palliative. There may be heavy unemployment and it may be possible to reduce it by protecting home producers against competing imports. Fuller employment may be deemed worth the rise in the cost of living due to Protection. Increased activity in the protected industries might even stimulate investment and promote recovery. The case for Protection seems to be strengthened if the competing imports are being sold at prices which can scarcely be profitable to the foreign producers.

It was on such grounds that most countries considerably increased their Protection during the first years of the Great Depression. In particular, the main agricultural countries of Western Europe greatly restricted their imports of foodstuffs in order to protect their farmers against imports whose prices had fallen to around half of what they had been in 1928.

One can sympathize with the desire for Protection as a depression measure. But once import restrictions are imposed, they tend to remain. It is difficult to remove them, in the face of protests from the producers affected, when the emergency has passed. In practice, increased Protection by one country often breeds increased Protection by others. Agrarian protection in Europe, which still remains, has stimulated manufacturing in the overseas agricultural countries. The rise in the cost of living recently in France, and to a less extent in Great Britain, has in fact led to demands for higher money wages and may lead to greater unemployment. It is probable that the world would have been more prosperous if countries had resisted the temptation to increase Protection and had fought the depression in other ways.

3. EFFECTS OF IMPORT DUTIES

As we have seen, a country on the gold standard which imposes tariffs can thereby acquire more gold, maintaining both its money income and its commodity prices (except those of its exports) at a higher level than they would otherwise be. A country with free exchange rates can of course have whatever money income it wishes. If it imposes tariffs, these raise the prices of the taxed imports, but whether they affect money incomes and the general price-level, and if so in what direction, depends on how they affect the demand for money in that country.

An import duty resembles an indirect tax. The price of the taxed commodity will always be higher inside the taxing country, by the full amount of the duty plus transport charges, than on the world market. If, as is usually the case, the taxing country takes only a small part of the total world supply of the commodity, the consequent reduction in its demand will have a very slight effect on the world price: that is to say, consumers in the taxing country will bear nearly the whole of the incidence of the tax. But if the taxing country takes a considerable part of the world supply, and if in consequence of the duty its demand is considerably curtailed, the result may be an appreciable fall in the world price of the commodity: that is to say, an appreciable part of the incidence of the tax will be borne by foreign suppliers.

The extent to which the protected home industry expands will depend partly on the elasticity of the home demand for the protected commodity and partly on the extent to which the costs of that industry increase (owing to the difficulty of getting sufficient suitable skilled labour or suitable soils and so on) as it expands. If some imports continue to come in, this shows that further expansion of the home industry would lead to a further rise in costs and would not be profitable unless the import duty was increased so that the home price could be raised.

4. IMPORT QUOTAS

An import quota lays down the maximum amount—not value—of the commodity which may be imported during a given period. For example, the French import quota for butter in the last quarter of 1931 was 12,000 quintals.[1] The British import quota for bacon is 10,670,000 cwt. a year less the expected British production and less the expected imports from Empire countries: practically speaking, the quota applies only to non-Empire countries and in particular to Denmark. Import quotas during the recent depression were first resorted to by France in 1931. Since then the system has been greatly extended and developed in France: most of her imports are now subject to

[1] A quintal is one-tenth of a metric ton.

quota. It has also been adopted, to a greater or less extent, by many other countries and especially by European countries.

A "global" quota, which simply restricts the total amount to be imported of a given commodity, does not work well. Goods arrive at the frontier after the quota is filled and must be refused, importers are not certain of getting supplies, and countries from which only a little has been imported before the quota is filled complain of unfair treatment. A quota is therefore usually divided among the supplying countries. The amount allotted to each is usually fixed according to the proportion which imports of that commodity from that country have formed of the total imports of it during previous years. The distribution of the total quantity imported among different importers is usually determined by the Government, or by a Chamber of Commerce acting on its behalf, which distributes import licences. If so, imports are allowed to enter only if an import licence is produced. But sometimes a Chamber of Commerce or some other responsible body in the exporting country restricts the amount sent by issuing export licences without which the commodity cannot be exported to the quota country.

Under a system of import duties the tax payments on the goods imported swell the revenue of the taxing Government. Under the quota system the difference between the home price (which is raised by the restriction of imports) and the world price tends to go to the importers. But if the exporters are organized, and if they hold export licences while the importers in the quota country bid against one another to get imports, this difference goes to the exporters. Denmark has gained in this way from the British quota on bacon, but this "gain" has been offset, in recent years, by the drastic limitation imposed by Great Britain on the entry of Danish bacon.

Quotas are alleged to have certain advantages over duties. Home producers know exactly what quantity of imports will come in. It is said that quotas are more flexible than duties, as they usually can be adjusted by the administrative authorities without resort to legislation. It is also said that quotas arouse less protest than duties from consumers, and—because they can readily be altered—are more suitable as bargaining counters in negotiating trade concessions with other countries.

Certainly quotas have the "advantage" that they enable a

country to increase its Protection even when it has bound itself by trade agreements not to raise its import duties. Moreover, quotas enable a country to evade the Most Favoured Nation clause. This clause is a feature of most trade treaties. It prevents discrimination in that if duties are reduced to one country they must automatically be reduced to all other countries enjoying most-favoured-nation treatment with the country reducing them. But a quota is necessarily divided among the various supplying countries in a somewhat arbitrary way.

A disadvantage of quotas is that they give more power to administrative officials and may lead to corruption. Moreover, unless the quota Government puts up import licences to auction —a course which seems never to be adopted—it loses revenue which it would have obtained from equivalent import duties. Above all, an import quota cuts off a country from the world market in that commodity. Under a stable import duty, if costs of production fall in exporting countries imports increase and the price in the home country falls. This cannot happen under a quota, for the amount to be imported is fixed. Under a quota the price of the commodity may be falling in the world market and rising (owing to increasing costs of producing it within the country) in the home market. In this sense quotas are rigid whereas duties permit flexibility in the amount imported.

5. WORLD TRADE DURING RECENT YEARS

We cannot refrain from making a few comments on the course of world trade since the beginning of the depression in 1929. Creditor countries cut down their foreign loans. Hence debtor countries had to develop an export surplus in order to pay interest. But the creditor countries did not welcome a surplus of imports, although that was the only way in which their income from overseas investments could be paid, and they tended to impose duties or quotas to keep down imports. This of course made matters still worse for the debtor countries.

One country after another has tried to defend itself, at the expense of others, from the effects of the depression. One has temporarily stimulated its exports by letting the exchange value of its currency fall, only to have its example followed by others. The consequent uncertainty as to what exchange rates would be, and as to which currency would fall in value next, has gravely hampered world trade and has led to disturbing movements of refugee capital. The fall in the exchange value of sterling, and of currencies linked to sterling, after September, 1931, exerted a downward pressure on the gold prices of commodities and increased the difficulties of those countries which were trying to stay on gold.

Increased Protection in some countries has been followed by increased Protection in others. If some countries become more self-supporting, others are constrained to do likewise. The exports of one country are the imports of another and Protection is a game at which more than one can play. A country which flatters itself that it is keeping out imports soon finds that other countries are keeping out its exports. It is no accident that the heaviest unemployment in Great Britain and other countries has been mainly in the exporting districts.

The growth of exchange restrictions has diverted foreign trade from the directions indicated by comparative costs, forcing it into bilateral channels and reducing its total volume.

According to the 1937 Report of the Bank for International Settlements, world industrial production at the close of 1936 was some 20 per cent above its 1929 level but the volume of world trade was some 10 per cent below its 1929 level. To those who have the intellect to understand the advantages of international division of labour, and the insight to realize what has been happening, the events of the last few years surely provide a striking argument in favour of stable exchange rates and freedom of trade.

WAR

CHAPTER XXXI
WAR ECONOMICS

1. WAR AND ECONOMIC PRINCIPLES

THE world is at war. War brings cruelty and terror, misery and pain. Yet we could not permit oppression and intolerance to rule the world and crush the human spirit for countless years to come. Our only course was to defend freedom and decency with our lives.

The present chapter is partly a postscript, to bring the book up to date, but mainly a discussion of "the economics of war." It refers particularly to Great Britain.

Wars are not won with money. Money may be useful to buy things with from neutral countries. But even in peace-time governments or individuals will seldom accept the paper money of another country in exchange for their products unless they can use it fairly quickly to purchase goods and services from that country. Imports must be paid for with exports. It is true, however, that governments and people may accept gold in final payment for their goods. Great Britain paid for imports worth several hundred million pounds, during the early months of the war, by parting with most of her accumulated gold. Most of this went to the United States. To-day the United States and Great Britain are allies. In order to win the war, all the Allies should virtually "pool" their resources: they should try to make the best use of their combined resources. To send money from one Ally to another will not help their combined war effort. That would be helped only by getting goods from neutrals in exchange for money. But there are very few neutrals left, and it is doubtful whether at present they would supply the Allies with many goods in exchange for gold. The United States now holds some 90 per cent of the monetary gold of the world, but this gold is almost useless for the war effort.

Nor are wars won by productive capacity which is only *potentially* available for war purposes. The steel-making capacity of the Allies is twice as great as that of the Axis powers. The capacity of their metal, engineering, and chemical industries is about 50 per cent greater. But much of this capacity is in the United States and, at the time of writing, has not yet been converted to war purposes. The superior "economic potential" of the Allies is reassuring on a long view, but it must be used, and used efficiently, to make armaments of all kinds before the war can be won.

For wars are won by having enough trained fighting men, adequately armed and equipped, available at the right places and the right times. The sinews of war are guns, tanks, aeroplanes, warships, shells, bombs, torpedoes. The central problem of war economy is to get enough of these things and at the same time to have a large enough army, navy, and air force, whilst supplying the armed forces, the war workers, and the rest of the population with the necessary minimum of consumers' goods.

Apart from supplies imported from other countries, and any stocks existing within the country, the only way to get these sinews of war is to produce them. There are three ways in which the output of them can be expanded. The first way is to set to work people previously doing little or nothing—the unemployed, young people such as students, men who are still fairly fit although retired, and women who are not fully engaged in domestic duties and the care of children, or who can be set free from such tasks. We may include also, under this head, compelling or inducing people to work more hours per week and to have fewer holidays. The second way is to transfer labour and other resources from the production of goods and services which can be dispensed with, wholly or in part, during war-time into the munitions industries or some other kind of essential war work. This implies that there will be fewer consumers' goods available than in peace-time. The third way is to make the most efficient use of labour and other resources. It is obvious that to do this within the war industries will directly increase their output. To do this within other industries and occupations will enable the necessary minimum of consumers' goods to be produced with less labour, thus releasing men and women for the war industries. Finally, it may be possible at times to release temporarily men from the Army to work in the factories, or mines, or fields.

In war-time the fundamental economic principles, those which apply to any society, however organized, are just as valid as in peace-time. Indeed, their validity and importance are more obvious in war than in peace. Take, for example, the principle that some wants can be more fully satisfied only at the cost of satisfying others less fully: to get more guns we must have less butter. In some countries and at some times, notably in the United States in the 'thirties, there were enough unemployed men and resources to make it possible to have more of both. It is to such conditions that the doctrine of Lord Keynes applies. He advocates greater public and private spending. The more we consume of the cake the larger it grows. The good fairy Propensity to Consume, aided by an expansionist monetary policy, waves her magic wand, the Multiplier, and labour and resources previously idle are drawn into employment. But once full employment is attained, and it is attained fairly soon after war breaks out, the Economics of Slump disappear from the picture. There is no longer any controversy among economists about broad practical issues. Consumption must be restricted in order to free labour and resources for the war industries; if more steel is allocated for building destroyers, less than otherwise can be allocated for tanks or aeroplanes. The need to choose in what ways resources capable of alternative uses shall be employed is imperative and plain.

The same applies to the principle that monopolistic restriction of output is wasteful from the standpoint of society as a whole. In peace-time it may be tolerated, perhaps on the pretext that it prevents unemployment. Fish may be thrown back into the sea, cotton ploughed back into the soil, shipyards and ships and spindles scrapped, the more efficient coal-mines prevented from expanding their output, the use of fertilizers forbidden, plant and equipment worked well below capacity. In war-time, once a country has fully realized that the struggle is desperate, such practices will be stopped because they cannot be afforded.

Again, the desirability of taking advantage of division of labour—of putting square pegs into square holes and training others to fit the holes which require filling—and of specialization between areas, and of economies of scale, and of moving resources to where they are more productive[1], is even greater in the urgency of war than in the tranquillity of peace.

[1] To-day, after we have seen millions of persons move from one part of this island to another and whole factories in Russia moved back from the invasion zone, no reader will accuse me of exaggerating, in Chapter XIV, the potential mobility of factors of production.

But although fundamental economic principles apply even more strongly in war-time, the aim of the economy is different. The aim is no longer to satisfy as fully as possible the multitudinous wants of consumers. The aim is to win the war, and, in order to do this, to maximize the war effort even at the cost of greatly restricting freedom of choice. This implies planning and a great extension, in capitalist countries at any rate, of State control.

2. THE NEED FOR PLANNING

If enlistment in the armed forces were voluntary, a country might obtain fewer recruits than it needed. Some would not join because others had not yet joined. Many would say that if more men were needed the Government should apply compulsion. This applies equally to other aspects of the war effort. Many people would prefer restrictions on consumption, and recruitment for the war industries, and for activities such as fire-watching, to be enforced by the Government in order to ensure equality of sacrifice. Otherwise some selfish people might use up labour and materials and other resources to provide themselves with luxuries, when these resources might have been used instead for war purposes; or they might refuse to do their fair share of war work. Hence the people of a country at war, if they are convinced of the justice and importance of their cause and if they realize the need for the greatest possible war effort, will want their Government to exercise very wide powers of compulsion over their persons and their property.

Probably the greatest war effort can be achieved, in such circumstances, by placing everybody, metaphorically, in the Army, and turning the whole country into an armed camp, workshop, and hostel. This would imply the rigorous application of the main principle of a "siege economy": from each according to his ability, to each according to his need. Money would disappear from the picture "for the duration." There would be no money payments of any kind. The Government would provide people, as it provides the army, with the necessary minimum of food, clothing, shelter, and other consumers' goods and services. In return, everybody would have to do what he was told. No property rights, no considerations of social status, no trade-union privileges, no fears of what would happen after the war, would be allowed to stand in the way of the maximum war effort.

In peace-time the arguments against such a system are strong. People value their liberty of action, and their freedom of choice as consumers. They need monetary incentives to work harder or to become more skilled. Private enterprise may be more flexible, and display more initiative, than the Government in recognizing or forecasting changes in demand, and in discovering and applying more efficient methods of satisfying demand. In war-time the whole situation is different. People are prepared to give up their liberty and their freedom of choice in order to promote the war effort, so that output can take the form largely of masses of standardized goods—armaments and equipment of all kinds for the Forces and consumers' goods for all. An urgent desire to win the war, and to win it quickly (perhaps reinforced by the possibility of penalties similar to those to which soldiers are subject) may provide sufficient incentive.

For one reason or another, a complete "siege economy," such as we have outlined, was not adopted by Great Britain. Perhaps it was thought that people would not stand it; perhaps it was feared that it would be too difficult to administer; perhaps it was believed that the war could be won without such very drastic measures. However, as the war went on and the magnitude of the task became more apparent, various measures were taken which did bring the country considerably nearer to an economy of this type. And some of our present difficulties and discontents would have been avoided (although others might have arisen) if we had gone much further in this direction. For then workers would perhaps have been convinced that capitalists were not making large, or indeed any, profits out of their labour; men in the Forces would not have resented the relatively high wages earned by some war workers, enabling them to provide better than they for their wives and families; the desire of firms to be as well prepared as possible for after the war could not have hindered their present war effort; there would have been no "black market."

Even if a government continues to rely, to some extent at least, upon the price-mechanism, it must still make some kind of "war plan." For example, it must decide how large an army, navy, and air force it will need; and how exactly they are going to be armed and equipped. It will have to see that different things are produced in the right proportions and to give "priority," at certain times, to things most urgently needed, for it will not be able to get as much of everything as it wants as quickly as it would like.

One of the first things it will have to decide is how long the war is likely to last. If it expects the war to be short, it can postpone various renewals and replacements until it is over. But if it expects the war to be a long one, it may have to use some resources in ways which will not bear fruit until perhaps two or three years have passed: for example, in renewing rolling-stock on the railways, or in constructing more shipyards and docks, or in putting up new steel plants.

Another thing it will have to decide is how much weight should be given to aims which conflict with the war effort. For example, should war materials be embodied in exports for neutral markets in order to retain trade connections for after the war?

In the following sections we shall give some illustrations of how Great Britain has dealt with the various problems we have mentioned.

3. FOREIGN TRADE

For convenience of exposition, we begin with foreign trade. But this is by no means the most important aspect, as a rule, of a country's war economy. The war effort of Great Britain depends mainly on the size of her armed forces and on her own output of arms. All the same, the part played by foreign trade is quite significant.

Imports help a country to wage war. They may be armaments or war materials, or they may be consumers' goods which set free, for war purposes, resources which would otherwise have been employed in producing similar goods, or substitutes for them, at home. Exports, on the other hand, diminish the war effort in so far as they use up resources which could be employed directly for war purposes.

Hence a country wishing to maximize its fighting strength will import as much as it can from neutral countries provided that it can "pay" by promises—by borrowing from them—or by assets such as gold and securities which are of no use for waging war. But if it has to pay by sending exports in return, the principle of comparative costs applies. It will use labour and other resources in producing exports if it can get in this way imports which it values more highly than anything else which these resources could have produced instead. It will give preference to exports using up labour, materials, land, and plant and equipment, which are fairly "specific" and could otherwise contribute relatively little to the war effort. It will of course take account of costs of transport, including the risk of loss at sea by enemy action.

Great Britain was in this position until the United States entered the war as her ally, or at any rate until the Lend-Lease arrangement came into force. The United States could supply armaments and war materials and other goods that Great Britain needed. But she had to pay for them. She paid partly by sending gold and partly by selling securities (mainly those having a ready market in the United States, such as the stocks of large American and Canadian companies) which her Government had compulsorily bought from her citizens. Over and above this, she had to pay by means of exports. She sent goods such as whisky and textiles, which more or less fulfilled the conditions stated above, and not, for example, steel or machinery. Her export industries were, in effect, munitions industries: their products secured aeroplanes, tanks, and other arms in exchange. The same applied to British trade with other neutral countries, but the United States was by far the most important.

The British Government took over control, which was gradually made complete, of all foreign trade and foreign exchange and shipping.

Control of imports was necessary to prevent "dollars" (foreign exchange available for purchases outside the "sterling area") obtained from the sale of assets or exports from being "wasted" in bringing in imports of luxuries or semi-luxuries which could be done without. It was necessary, also, to divert purchases of goods such as cotton and wheat and tobacco to the sterling area in order to save dollars for the purchase of armaments from the United States. But the main reason for it was the shortage of shipping space. As the war went on, ships were sunk in considerable numbers (although several million tons of shipping were acquired by the British Government from Norway, Greece, and other countries; and the building of new ships formed part of the British war effort); the convoy system gave protection against enemy action but was said to reduce efficiency by some 25 per cent, owing to slower speeds, and delays in assembling ships for convoy; and as time went on Great Britain lost the "short routes" to Europe and through the Mediterranean, so that ships had to make longer voyages. All this was only partly offset by fuller cargoes (in 1938 about a quarter of the shipping tonnage entering British ports came in empty).

We may mention that Germany was worse off than Great Britain in that she could get practically no imports from overseas and had to use a good deal of her labour in producing food and substitutes which were less satisfactory or which used up more resources than the natural products obtained by Great Britain from overseas.

In deciding which things to import in addition to arms and war materials, in order to make the best use of the limited shipping-space available, Great Britain had to consider her own war-time agricultural policy. Her best plan, probably, was gradually to reduce the numbers of her fat stock, which consumed imported feeding-stuffs, and to produce more milk and potatoes, whilst continuing to import most of her grain and sugar, which occupied less shipping space relatively to the nutrition provided than did fresh fruit and vegetables, or meat, or feeding-stuffs for cattle; and in fact something approaching this plan was adopted. Another bulky import which could be and was cut down was wood-pulp and paper. The use of (imported) petrol for private motoring was subjected to increasing restrictions.

The Ministry of Food and the Ministry of Supply took over the purchasing of most goods from abroad: they could buy in bulk and could arrange for shipping. All other imports, after a time, had to be licensed.

We need not detail the various phases of British export policy. After a time, all exports had to be licensed. At first, the volume of exports fell greatly, partly owing to increased risks and partly because the export industries were allowed fewer raw materials needed for war purposes. In February, 1940, an Export Council was formed to promote exports. One of the devices used was that of a general levy on all the firms in an industry in order to form a "pool" out of which the exports were subsidized. Thus all firms in the cotton-spinning industry had to contribute to a pool out of which exports of cotton goods were subsidized.

Exchange control was imposed as soon as war broke out. The main object of the Treasury seems to have been to acquire and conserve dollars in order to pay for arms from the United States. The rate of exchange was fixed, by agreement between the two Governments, at 4.03 dollars to the pound.[1] All dollars, or other foreign exchange, received by British residents had to be surrendered to the Treasury at that rate. The export of capital was prohibited. Otherwise some British exports to the United States would have made no contribution to the war effort; the dollars obtained for them would have been sold by the British exporters to persons anxious to transfer their sterling assets into dollars.

The "sterling area," which we have already mentioned, included the British Empire (except Canada and Newfoundland) and one or two other countries, such as Egypt. Purchases were diverted to this area because they could be paid for in sterling. This meant that, to a considerable extent, they were not paid for by exports. Sterling balances belonging to these countries accumulated in London. Some of these countries, for example India and South Africa, used them to pay off their sterling debts by buying back securities representing loans which they had obtained from Great Britain in the past. Thus the total of British "foreign investments" within the Empire fell.

[1] This gave the pound a rather low value. Before the war, the Exchange Equalization Fund had been keeping it around 4·68. During the week before the war the Fund ceased to intervene and there was some export of capital; even so, the rate fell only to between 4·25 and 4·40. There was no need for a low rate in order to stimulate exports and provide employment; in war-time (and possibly in peace-time too) these objects are best achieved by more direct methods. A high rate might have given Great Britain better terms of trade, yielding more foreign exchange, and the Government would have had to pay less sterling for American armaments. Presumably it was thought that 4·03 was the highest rate that could be maintained. It is certainly true that British prices soon rose considerably whilst American prices remained fairly stable.

On the other hand, she probably would have had to sell more of her other foreign investments (such as her Argentine securities) in order to raise dollars, if she had bought much more from the United States instead of from the sterling area.

At first British exchange control was not complete: foreign-owned sterling balances were not "blocked" (probably because it was thought that this would damage the post-war reputation of London as a financial centre) and some British exports to countries outside the sterling area could be invoiced in "free" sterling. Hence a market for free sterling arose, in New York, in which sterling balances were sold (to American importers of British goods) at rates sometimes well below four dollars to the pound. But by the summer of 1940 all such leaks had been stopped.

Now that the United States is an ally, and few countries remain neutral, the whole situation has changed. There is no longer any desperate need, for example, for Great Britain to acquire or conserve dollars. Questions of payment can be post-poned until after the war. The ideal policy now is to make the best use of the combined resources of the Allies. Their territories should be regarded as a unit, devoted to the war effort, within which specialization takes place. Let us give a few examples. It is wasteful to use labour and materials in mining gold and silver if they could be making some useful contribution to the war effort. It would be wasteful for Great Britain to import goods from a distant Dominion if surplus stocks of similar goods were available in the United States. Protective tariffs between the Allies should be abolished for the duration of the war. For example, there might be a considerable saving of labour if most of the sugar required by the Allies could be obtained from the tropical islands instead of being produced at a high cost, behind tariff barriers, in less suitable regions. Great Britain's most useful exports at the moment of writing are probably arms to Russia.

4. RESTRICTION OF CONSUMPTION

One way to induce civilians to consume less is to leave them less money to spend. In Great Britain, high taxation and propaganda in favour of saving tend to keep down the expenditure of consumers. Incidentally, it is rather a waste of energy to urge people to take money out of their mattresses or out of their banks in order to buy war savings certificates or other Government securities. Provided they do not spend the money, the purpose of restricting consumption is achieved, and the Government has less to pay in interest.

A more direct method, which also was adopted, is to restrict the supply of consumers' goods by cutting out non-essential imports and limiting the supplies of raw materials allotted to industries producing goods such as clothing, pottery, and boots and shoes.

The British Treasury seems to have been acutely aware, from the start, of the danger of inflation. If the total supply of consumers' goods is given, consumers as a whole cannot obtain more than that amount. But if each tries to buy more, the result may be a great rise in prices. This happened in Great Britain with non-rationed goods such as furniture, hardware, and crockery. Before clothing was rationed, the prices of clothing rose about 70 per cent.

Merely to fix maximum prices for goods is not much use. The goods—for example, chickens—tend to disappear from the market and to be sold secretly at higher prices in the "black market" and consumed (possibly in expensive restaurants) by well-to-do people. Alternatively, consumers are made dependent on the favour of tradesmen.

The Treasury apparently wished to prevent the "cost of living"—especially as measured by the official Ministry of Labour index—from rising too much. For this would have made it difficult for employers and Trade Boards, and for the Government itself as an employer, to resist claims for higher wages. And higher wages would have raised the money cost of the war. Further, people with relatively small fixed incomes perhaps could not have afforded to buy enough to keep them alive and healthy if prices had risen very much. Hence the Treasury spent well over £100 million a year in keeping down the prices of certain foodstuffs such as bread, meat, and bacon; and it greatly extended its subsidies on milk for children.

But the obvious solution was to impose equality of sacrifice by rationing, as well as price-fixing, and as the war went on rationing was extended to cover most consumers' goods. The "points" system of rationing, applied to clothing and to some foodstuffs, was particularly flexible. It permitted some freedom of choice to consumers and at the same time enabled supply to be equated with demand: by raising the number of points required for an article the demand for which was outrunning the supply, and lowering the number for articles left unsold. Some writers urged that the total expenditure of a consumer in retail shops should be restricted—for example, to twenty-five shillings per week for an adult and fifteen shillings per week for a child. This would have kept down the prices of non-rationed goods but apart from that it would have done little that could not be achieved equally well by the "points" system. In order to convince people that there was real equality of sacrifice, penalties against the "black market" were made more severe as time went on, although the proportion of goods taken by the black market was probably small. Agitation to fix a maximum price for restaurant meals, and to restrict horse-racing, dog-racing, and private motoring, showed a desire to move still nearer to a siege economy. Possibly consumption would have been reduced further had the Government purchased unused coupons (or held lotteries with the coupons as tickets and Government securities as prizes). The imposition of severe penalties against genuine "swapping" of coupons or bartering of rationed goods probably diminished satisfaction without curtailing total consumption.

Rationing restricts the freedom of choice of consumers and thereby reduces the satisfaction which they get from a given expenditure. Even if the actual prices of rationed commodities are not allowed to rise, a consumer who would like to buy more of them and cannot is thereby forced into a worse economic position as a consumer. Rationing is similar in its effect upon him to a rise in the prices of the rationed commodities. This can readily be shown by means of an "indifference curve" diagram.

In the absence of rationing, a consumer with a spendable income *OA* could apportion this income between a commodity (or a group of commodities), subsequently rationed, and other uses as he chose. He could choose any position on the price-line *AB*. (If he spent his whole income on the commodity he would be able to buy *OB* of it.) In fact, he would choose the position (1), where *AB* is tangential to one of his indifference curves. He would purchase OR_1 of the commodity. Suppose now that rationing is introduced. The price of the rationed commodity (or group of commodities) remains the same, but he can buy only OR_2 of it. His position is now (2). This is

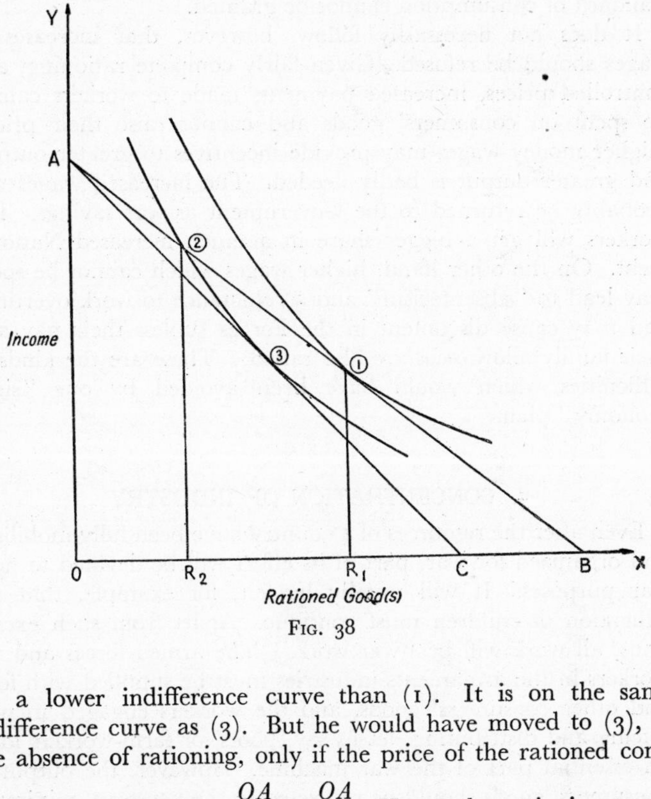

FIG. 38

on a lower indifference curve than (1). It is on the same indifference curve as (3). But he would have moved to (3), in the absence of rationing, only if the price of the rationed commodity had risen from $\frac{OA}{OB}$ to $\frac{OA}{OC}$. Hence the rationing to an amount OR_2 reduces his satisfaction from his income OA, although prices remain the same, as much as the above rise in the price of the rationed commodity would have reduced it in the absence of rationing.

This does not alter the fact that consumption must be reduced, and that rationing is the fairest way to reduce it. In Great

Britain, the bulk of consumption is by the wage-earners and their families, who form the great majority of the population. Hence their consumption must be limited; it will not suffice to cut down only the rich. It follows that demands by workers, other than those who are very badly paid, to retain their pre-war standard of consumption cannot be granted.

It does not necessarily follow, however, that increases in wages should be refused. Given fairly complete rationing, and controlled prices, increased payments made to workers cannot be spent on consumers' goods and cannot raise their prices. Higher money wages may provide incentives to greater output, and greater output is badly needed. The increased wages will probably be returned to the Government as war savings. The workers will get a bigger share in a much increased National Debt. On the other hand, higher wages which cannot be spent may lead to "absenteeism" and a reluctance to work overtime, and may cause discontent in the Forces (unless their pay and their family allowances are also raised). These are the kinds of difficulties which would have been avoided by our "siege economy" plan.

5. CONCENTRATION OF INDUSTRY

Even after the resources of a country have been fully mobilised and organized for war, part of its effort will be devoted to non-war purposes. It will usually be felt, for example, that the education of children must continue. Apart from such exceptions, all work will be "war work." The armed forces and the workers in the armaments industries must be supplied with food and other consumers' goods, and the workers engaged in producing and distributing, let us say, boots for farm-workers form an essential part of the war machine. However, the output of consumers' goods should be restricted to the necessary minimum —which may include such things as cigarettes, if these are deemed necessary to maintain efficiency and morale.

The general principle of comparative opportunity-costs still holds good. Each individual factor of production should be where its marginal productivity is highest. But now its "productivity" must be valued by its net contribution to the war effort. Let us take an illustration. Suppose that the manager of a shoe factory is very efficient at his job. (The best man available to replace him as manager would require considerably more workers to get the same output.) Suppose he would make a good average army officer or munitions worker. Nevertheless it is best to keep him at his job, thus enabling labour to be released from his factory.

In practice, there may be political difficulties in applying this principle. The public may feel that all able-bodied men below a certain age should be conscribed for the Forces. Hence men who would have made a much greater contribution by staying where they were may be called up, their skill being partly or wholly unutilized.

The necessary output of consumers' goods should be produced, and distributed, with as few workers and other resources as possible, provided that the resources released can help the war effort in other spheres. In war-time people are prepared to have less freedom of choice, and to suffer more inconvenience, than in peace-time. This opens the way for mass-production of standardized goods, for cutting down advertising and salesmen, for reducing the number of shops and the extent to which goods are delivered to people's houses. Whether or not the "differentiation" of similar products made by different firms is justified in peace-time, it should not be allowed to waste resources in war-time.

As time went on, the British Government took various steps to prevent resources from being employed in producing goods and rendering services that could be dispensed with during the war. It stopped building and other investment activity in so far as it was not "war work" in the wider sense of the term. It restricted deliveries by shops and transferred some shop assistants to the Forces and the war industries. It greatly restricted supplies of materials to certain industries—including the major textile industries, hosiery, boots and shoes, and pottery—which formed, said Mr. Lyttelton, "the main sources of factory-trained labour for munitions."

The next step was to "concentrate" the output of these industries into fewer factories, all working to full capacity. It was estimated that this step set free some 144 thousand workers and some 45 million square feet of factory space. From 1942 onwards, most of the clothing was to be "utility" clothing—

mass-produced in a number of standard patterns—and cloth was to be saved by suppressing such things as double-breasted coats and trouser turn-ups.

The natural desire of each firm to keep its goodwill for post-war trade, by retaining its own special lines and brands (even if the goods are produced for it by another firm) and its own sales force, and continuing to advertise, conflicts with the aim of releasing resources from the consumption industries and trades.

6. OUTPUT IN THE WAR INDUSTRIES

The present section discusses in general terms some of the factors affecting the output of arms of all kinds, from battleships to bullets. This question is obviously vital.

One important factor is the amount of labour available. The war industries may be able to recruit some additional workers, at first, from the unemployed, and they may draw upon young persons and retired persons. More probably, most workers from these sources will take up other necessary tasks, for which they are better qualified, thus releasing other and more suitable workers for the production of arms. A much larger source of supply will be the industries and occupations engaged in satisfying the peace-time wants of consumers; the purpose of restricting consumption is to release resources from these fields. Are there any other big sources of supply?

There are the many women, not "gainfully employed," who are engaged in looking after their homes. To take a large number of them out of the home and into the factory would create various difficulties, but these might be overcome: in 1941 over nine million women were employed in German industry. They might be overcome mainly by various "economies of scale." Thus the provision of cheap or free meals in factory canteens would help a good deal, although at the sacrifice of some freedom of choice and privacy. Much effort is saved if hundreds of meals are prepared and cooked at once—and if the cook is a good one, they may be more palatable and nourishing than some of the concoctions produced in the home. Similarly, more crèches could be provided; schools could open earlier and close later, to look after older children, who could play during the extra time; schools might also provide meals for the children. Factories might have grocery and general stores attached to them, to relieve the working housewife of some of her shopping worries. Where necessary, special buses might transport workers from their homes to the factory and back again. If they were helped in such ways, many women, even those with children, might be able to work, some full-time and some part-time, in the war industries.

Another possible source of factory-labour is the Army. Skilled workers are needed in the Army, but those whose skill is not being used, and who have had their training as soldiers, might be temporarily released to help on the bench or in the shipyard or the mine. They could be recalled, when needed for fighting, at very short notice. In Great Britain, it has hitherto been decided that the disadvantages of such a plan outweigh the benefits. In Germany, very large numbers of workers were temporarily released from the Army during the first two winters of the war.

Workers going into the factories out of other occupations, or from the home, must be trained. Germany has trained over a million workers a year. There may be obstacles, however, in the way of widespread and efficient training. A firm actively employed in war work may think trainees a nuisance. They slow down its rate of output. But this represents the real cost of an investment—converting "factors" into types more valuable for the war effort—which will bear good fruit later for the country as a whole. Again, who is to do the training? The most suitable trainers may be earning much more on piece-rates at the bench than they would earn as charge-hands instructing trainees. Further, the peace-time attitude of most trade unionists is one of opposition to "dilution" and to the entry of women into their trades; some may find it hard to reverse this attitude suddenly and completely.

The peace-time restrictionist attitude of some industrialists also may not completely disappear. They may be uneasy about greatly increasing "capacity" which will not all be required in peace-time. In general, the desire of each firm to be as ready as it can be for the return to competition after the war may tend to hamper its war effort. For example, in adapting plant and equipment to war production a firm may be tempted to put as few obstacles as possible in the way of switching back to its peace-time products, even if this prevents its war output from reaching its potential maximum.

The task of planning a great expansion of arms output is full of difficulties. Ideally, there should be one supreme planning authority. It would be wasteful to permit different Government departments, and different firms, to compete with one another for labour and materials. These scarce factors should be allotted to those uses where they make the greatest, or the most urgently needed, contribution. In peace-time this problem is solved by the price-system, but in war-time only a supreme authority can adequately balance the claims of different Government departments, and decide the best composition of the total arms output.

For the best composition depends not on consumers' preferences but on technical and strategic considerations. Complementarity is important. Obviously it would be foolish to make thousands of guns without enough shells for them to fire. The same applies to the proportions between different types of arms, such as bombers and fighters or battleships and destroyers. Again, standard designs must be agreed on if full advantage is to be taken of mass-production. But often quality must be balanced against quantity—for example, switching over to an improved type may slow down output or require more scarce materials. In any event, the structure of armaments production is very "capitalistic"—materials must be produced to build new factories, steel to make machinery, and so on. Hence a considerable time must elapse before a large flow of arms is being produced. But the time can be reduced if more labour is used.

The planning authority should ensure that well-equipped engineering works are not left idle, and that some firms do not cling to machine tools or skilled labour which could be employed more fully or to better advantage elsewhere. This probably means that it should have regional committees, with wide powers to carry out its instructions. The easier course of using large firms as its agents, and allowing them to give out sub-contracts, may not always result in the fullest and best use of resources.

Clearly it is no easy task to make and carry out a good plan of arms production, even if there is a supreme planning authority with drastic powers of compulsion. In Great Britain, up to the moment of writing, there has been no such authority. Responsibilities and powers have been divided among different Departments and Controls. Many decisions have been made, in effect, by industrial associations whose peace-time policies were directed towards restricting output and keeping down "capacity." Some deference has been paid to the desires of trade unions. Firms have been allowed a good deal of freedom and so have individual workers. The success achieved measures the extent to which patriotic motives have induced capitalists and workers alike to subordinate considerations of self-interest, and of their post-war prospects, to the urgency of the common cause. Nevertheless the need for still greater output has been steadily pushing the economic system nearer to that of a siege economy.

7. THE MONEY COST OF WAR

In Great Britain the rate of public expenditure kept increasing after the war began. By the spring of 1942 the Government was spending at the rate of well over £5000 million a year, as compared with about £1000 million a year before the war.

The main reason for this was that the greater part of the output of the country (including in this output the services of the men and women in the Forces and in Civil Defence) was being produced for the Government and paid for by the Government. By means of taxation—which covered about 40 per cent of public expenditure—and of borrowing the Government transferred "power to demand" from the public to itself. The Government spent more and the public spent less.

But in part the increase in public expenditure was due to the rise in prices. To that extent, the Government had to pay more money for the same goods and services. By the close of 1941 wholesale prices were about 60 per cent, retail prices (as measured by the Cost of Living index) about 30 per cent, and wage-rates about 26 per cent above the level of August, 1939.

Part of the rise in the prices of goods was because enemy action, such as the sinking of ships and the bombing of factories, and protective measures, such as the convoy system and the black-out, reduced the peace-time yield from a given amount of labour and other resources. But part of the rise was due to inflation.

Inflation is one of those awkward terms for which no brief

definition is satisfactory. We can say, perhaps, that it is an increase in the amount of money which tends to raise prices. But this does not enable us to measure its extent. Prices may rise, as we have just noted, from non-monetary causes. Moreover, certain prices may be controlled: we have already pointed out that the British Government, by means of rationing and price-fixing and subsidies, kept down the rise in retail prices as measured by the official Cost of Living index. Nor does the increase in the amount of money provide a good measure. By the close of 1941 the note circulation of the Bank of England was 40 to 50 per cent above the pre-war level (of about £500 million) and the total deposits of the commercial banks had risen by about the same proportion. But part of this increase was not inflationary. Firms and individuals wanted to hold larger balances in cash or at the bank because the future was more uncertain than usual: for example, a firm or a family might have to move because its property had been destroyed overnight by bombing. Again, the splitting-up of families increased the total demand for money.

Perhaps the best measure of inflation is the rise in the level of money incomes in so far as this does not reflect a corresponding increase in output. By the close of 1941 wage-rates had risen by some 26 per cent on the average, but earnings had risen considerably more—perhaps by 40 per cent—and the total weekly sum paid out to wage-earners and salary-earners was increased by the growing entry of women and others into paid occupations (although, on the other hand, it was diminished by the withdrawal of workers into the Forces).

In so far as workers are paid more money for the same amount of work, costs and prices tend to rise. The Government may succeed in keeping down the retail prices of most goods. But as these goods are produced by firms who must cover their costs in order to keep on producing, the Government will have to pay increasingly large subsidies to keep down retail prices. For example, after the minimum wages of agricultural labourers had been raised to sixty shillings per week, the Government had to fix higher prices for its purchases from farmers. The farmers had to get more for their produce in order to cover their increased labour-costs; if consumers were to be charged the same retail prices, the Government had to make up the difference.

In this way, inflation can increase the cost of the war without a rise in the cost of living.

If factor-prices rise, the Government will have to pay more than otherwise for the arms, equipment and supplies of all kinds which it buys for the Forces. The rise in Government expenditure will be correspondingly greater than the real increase in the war effort. The sums that it receives in taxation will buy less than they would have done when the Budget was drawn up.

In order to cover the excess of its current expenditure over its current receipts from taxation, a Government usually borrows. But what happens if the sums lent to it by the public are not sufficiently large? The Government might print a lot of bank-notes and pay with them. Given a banking system, it would rather increase the cash reserves of the banks, thus enabling them to lend it the money. The banks would buy Government securities, thus increasing their "investments." Their deposits would increase because the money which the Government paid out would reappear in the form of increased deposits by their customers, but their customary ratio of cash to deposits would be maintained. The following figures relate to the London clearing banks. They cover, therefore, perhaps 90 per cent of all commercial banks.

	£ million	
	Monthly Average, 1939	December, 31st, 1941
Deposits	2248	3329
Cash	245 (10·9%)	366 (11·0%)
Call Money	149 (6·6%)	141 (4·3%)
Discounts	255 (11·4%)	171 (5·1%)
Treasury Deposits	—	758 (22·8%)
Investments	607 (27·0%)	999 (30·0%)
Advances	998 (44·4%)	807 (24·2%)

Treasury Deposits are a new item, which first appeared in July, 1940. Nearly all the increase in deposits since that date has been compulsorily borrowed from the banks in that form.

This increase was due mainly to Government expenditure, and the Government has taken it, paying the banks only 1⅛ per cent interest. The banks can withdraw these deposits if they need more cash. Hence the banks are very "liquid." Their ratio of liquid assets (including Treasury Deposits) to deposits is about 40 per cent as against the 30 per cent more or less customary before the war.

We may take this opportunity of pointing out that during this war the Government has kept interest rates low. During the war of 1914–1918 it paid 5 per cent to the banks and the public. During this war it has paid around 3 per cent to the public and the banks on long-term securities and, as we have just seen, has "skimmed off" the increase in bank deposits since June, 1940, at 1⅛ per cent. Since other opportunities for lending are very greatly restricted by control over new investments, and opportunities for spending are also cut down, the Government can borrow at a low rate, thus keeping down the increase in the interest-charge on the rapidly growing National Debt.

We discussed the dangers of inflation, in peace-time, in Chapter XXIV, section 6. But it can reasonably be urged that these dangers may have no relevance for war-time conditions. Suppose that all consumers' goods are rationed and maximum prices fixed. Suppose that all private investment at home, such as building new houses, is prohibited unless deemed essential for the war effort. Suppose that the export of capital is forbidden. Under such conditions, what does it matter how much incomes rise or how much the Government has to pay for arms? After people have spent their fixed sums on consumers' goods, what can they do with the rest of their incomes? If they buy such things as shares or existing real estate or jewellery, the seller is then faced with the same problem. If money is hoarded in the form of bank-notes, the Bank of England prints more notes, and the Government (which gets the net profit from the note issue) in effect receives an interest-free loan. If money is left on deposit with the banks, the Government takes it in the form of Treasury Deposits. The only other possibility is for the money to be lent directly to the Government (or paid in taxation) by the public. In one way or another, all the money paid out by the Government comes back to it again. So why worry?

It is true that the money cost of the war is relatively

unimportant and the methods of public finance a secondary consideration. What does matter is the real magnitude of the war effort. The British Treasury was anxious to keep down the money cost of the war partly because rationing was not complete and some prices (for example, of clothing) were not fixed. Hence a rise in the cost of living would have hit people with relatively small fixed incomes and would have led to general demands for higher wages. But rationing and price-fixing could have been made complete, and did become more complete as time went on. The main reason for the Treasury's attitude was probably the fear of a very large National Debt after the war. Although interest-payments on the internal public debt are merely transfers from some citizens to others, a large annual transfer means high rates of taxation. Much of the increase in the National Debt would be held by wage-earners, who might want to withdraw it and spend it after the war, instead of waiting for the next slump, when increased spending would be desirable.

It follows from all this that, if only people were willing, a government could keep down the money cost of a war by forbidding increases in rates of pay, keeping down the rate of interest, and covering all the cost by taxation. All who would otherwise have lent to the Government, directly or indirectly, because there was nothing else they could do with their money after buying their rations, could have given up the same sum in taxation. But if people had been willing to do this, they would have been willing to do away with money payments and to place themselves and their property unreservedly at the disposal of the Government. In Great Britain, they were not willing to do this, or at any rate the Government thought they were not. The result was a series of compromises and half-and-half measures. The general direction of movement was towards a siege economy but the Government—assuming, of course, that despite appearances to the contrary it did understand the simple principles of war economics—did not move further or faster than it thought public opinion would tolerate.

8. TAXATION AND OUTPUT

We have argued that taxation in war-time should be high. It is the fairest method of imposing equality of sacrifice—as measured by what people have left after paying their taxes rather than by how much they pay; and there is no danger that high taxation will cause unemployment in war-time. There is a danger, however, that it may weaken incentives to work and to make the best possible contribution to the war effort. We shall discuss, from this standpoint, two important British taxes: the income-tax and the excess profits tax.

The Budget of April, 1941, raised the "standard rate" from 8s. 6d. to 10s. in the pound. Large incomes were taxed very heavily. An income of £10,000 was reduced to not much over £3000; an income of £100,000 was reduced to less than £6000. Various allowances were reduced, and most wage-earners came within the scope of the income-tax, many of them for the first time.

These millions of new income-tax payers made necessary much extra administrative work. Moreover, many of them did not properly understand income-tax, especially the time-lag between when they earned and when they paid. A simpler plan would have been a weekly tax on wages as they were earned.[1]

The practice of combining, for tax, the incomes of husband and wife meant that a wife's earnings might be taxed, in effect, at a high rate. Some wives were deterred by this from taking on paid work (and perhaps having to engage a nurse to look after their children). An improvement would have been to give wives the option of being treated, for income-tax purposes, as single women.

In some occupations, where the work is heavy or imposes strain, long hours result in less total output because the workers, after some weeks of this, are too tired. Subject to this proviso, it is clearly desirable in war-time that workers should be willing to accept a rather long working week, and to work overtime when required. How does income-tax affect their willingness to do so?

We have seen (on pages 280–1) that a change in net rates of pay per hour may induce people to work either more or fewer

[1] One suggestion was a "free wage" of £2 a week, or £3 10s. for a married man, plus £1 for each child under sixteen, £1 for a housekeeper, and 10s. for a dependent relative; the first £3 a week of taxable income to be charged at 5s. in the pound, and any balance at 10s. in the pound. This would have greatly simplified administration, and prevented evasion.

hours. But the changes in monetary incentives resulting from the income-tax were more complicated than a change in the rate of pay per hour. A certain minimum income was exempt from taxation. Above that level, the *marginal* rate of tax was above the average rate; and over certain ranges of income very much above it.[1]

Let us take an example. A single man earning £110 a year paid no tax. But if he earned £120 he paid £7 10s. tax (being charged on his income above £80). It is true that the whole of this £7 10s. was credited to him for after the war, but most workers seemed to attach little importance to these "post-war credits." He had to pay in tax 75 per cent of the next £10 he earned above £110 a year—a marginal rate of tax which did not apply again until income reached £5000 a year. Such a man might be tempted to do only enough work to earn £110 a year, and to keep quite free of income-tax. Another point where the deterrent effect might be strong was around £450 a year for the married man with two children. On £450 he paid £76 2s.—an average of about 3s. 4d. in the pound. But he had to pay 10s. in the pound on any extra income.

Moreover, higher wage-rates plus widespread rationing strengthened the desire for more leisure rather than more income. The typical worker earned more than before the war, but there was not much he could buy with extra earnings. Overtime, allowing for tax, might yield him less money per hour than he was earning already. Against this was the strong patriotic incentive to work harder. But "absenteeism" was not unknown, and was made subject to penalties, at least in "essential" industries.

If a man earning £1 a day, who should have worked six days, works only five days and is fined £2 for his absence, his net income for the five days is only £3, or 12s. per day. The income forgone by not working the sixth day is £3. Mr. Paish, who makes this point, suggests that income-tax might be levied on the income *which would have been earned* had the tax-payer worked a standard number of hours, however much or little he actually does choose to work (illness and similar contingencies excepted). He suggests also that privileges—such as cigarettes

[1] This subject is very well treated by F. W. Paish in his article "Economic Incentive in War-Time," in *Economica* for August, 1941.

or extra ration coupons—might be given for overtime. Our own solution, to repeat it once more, would be to put everybody, metaphorically, in the Army.

We turn to the excess profits tax. This was imposed at a rate of 100 per cent. All the profits above those earned in the standard period[1] had to be paid in tax. The main motive for the 100 per cent rate was to convince Labour that capitalists were not making extra profit out of the war. Nor were they. Total profits available for distribution—that is, after paying tax—did not increase much. And then shareholders had to pay income-tax (and sur-tax) at much higher rates than before the war. There is no doubt that, after deducting all tax payments, the share of wage-earners in the national income rose and the share of profit-receivers fell. But whether workers fully realized this is another matter.

Once a firm was earning its standard profits, all extra profits went to the Exchequer.[2] The peace-time monetary incentive to avoid waste, to produce as efficiently as possible, to take risks which offered a good prospect of gain, was removed. It was replaced by the patriotic desire to promote the war effort.

Nevertheless many firms, however patriotic, were reluctant to increase their plant, at their own expense, if the additional plant would be of a type useful only for the production of arms and unlikely to be required after the war. Suppose that a firm borrowed money for such a purpose at 5 per cent. It would be allowed to keep for itself only 8 per cent of the profits from this increase in its capital. Thus it could make only 3 per cent net, and half of this would have to be paid in income-tax. A net return of 1½ per cent was hardly worth the risk. Hence the income-tax authorities permitted firms to include in their costs large depreciation allowances on plant likely to be

[1] Which a firm could select from: 1935 or 1936 or the average of 1935 and 1937 or the average of 1936 and 1937 or any consecutive period of twelve months ending not later than 30th June, 1937. The object was to rule out the high-profit rearmament years of 1938 and 1939 and to give 1937 only half-weight. The "standard" for a company starting after 1st July, 1936, was 8 per cent (in some cases 10 per cent) of the average capital employed; the same applied to any subsequent increases of capital by any firm. "Professions" (e.g. accountants) were exempt from E.P.T.

[2] The 1941 Budget provided that, subject to certain conditions, 20 per cent of the excess profits tax might be returned, less income-tax upon it, some time after the war. This does not seriously affect the argument of the text.

obsolete after the war. Even so, the Government itself had to undertake much direct investment of this kind, which private firms, owing to the excess profits tax, were unwilling to make on their own account.

Expenditure, out of money which would otherwise go to the Exchequer in excess profits tax, on anything which would improve the profit-earning capacity of the firm after the war was quite another matter. Firms must have been strongly tempted to pile up unnecessary stocks or even to acquire equipment of various kinds which they did not really need for their output in the hope that these things would be useful to them later. A conspicuous example was the widespread advertising—at a time when paper was very scarce—of "branded" goods—some of which, such as motor-cars, were not being produced during the war and would become available only when peace had returned.

The excess profits tax strongly discouraged the expansion of output from wasting assets, such as mines. The profits earned from such assets are partly a return of capital. The assets themselves are depleted. For example, if an iron-ore mine expands its output, more ore is taken out of the mine, and the future life of the mine is shortened. Under such conditions, an excess profits tax is a confiscation of capital. However, as time went on this discouragement was largely removed by special tax concessions.

Peace-time incentives are preserved, to a great extent, if a firm has to work hard and efficiently in order to earn its permitted maximum profits. This may depend on the terms of the contracts under which it works for Government departments. For example, a contract to pay "cost plus 10 per cent" offers no inducement to keep costs low. Contracts of this type are sometimes necessary: for instance, when a firm first undertakes work of a kind which is new to it. But peace-time incentives are best preserved by the type of contract which fixes a definite price for a particular job, always provided that the price is a keen one, fixed by Government experts with a good practical knowledge of the work in question and of current prices.

A high yield from an excess profits tax may show that the Government has failed to fix keen prices on its contracts and to prevent inflation.

9. THE REAL COST OF WAR

"But the greatest disaster of all is war." We wrote these words, for the section on "the causes of economic progress," several years ago. To-day their truth is only too plain.

We have already explained[1] that most of the real cost of a war must be borne at the time. Its economic aspects, to which we must restrict ourselves, consist of reduced consumption, longer and harder work, and greater discomfort. But posterity will suffer in various ways, and may be said to bear part of the real cost.

Let us consider how posterity will suffer in Great Britain after the present war. In the first place, repayments to the United States for arms and other goods received under the Lend-Lease agreement may consist of exports for which nothing is obtained in exchange. Posterity will repay our debt. In the second place, before the war the Exchange Equalization Account had bought a considerable amount of gold. The combined holding of the Account and the Bank of England in March, 1938, when it was at its highest, was nearly 120 million ounces. Some of this was exported before the war, and in effect helped to pay for the rearmament programme. When war broke out, the gold in the Bank was handed over to the Account. Most of it has now been exported to pay for goods needed from the United States and elsewhere. Hence posterity, owing to the war, will not inherit this asset. In the third place, some British-owned foreign securities and direct investments abroad have been sold for the same purpose, and parts of the Empire have repaid much of their debt to Great Britain. Hence her total overseas investments, which yielded some £200 million a year before the war, have been considerably reduced, and may be reduced still further as the war goes on. In the fourth place, assets have been destroyed or lost. Ships have been sunk, buildings have been bombed, the earth has been scorched. Malaya, in which British investments were large, is at the moment of writing in the possession of Japan. In the fifth place, the maintenance of various assets, in so far as it was not essential to the war effort, has been neglected. For example, houses have not been kept in perfect repair and worn furniture has not been replaced. In

[1] Page 500.

the sixth place, investments which would have been undertaken in peace-time, such as new and improved housing, have rightly been restricted, and it is doubtful how far the war-time extensions of engineering and similar plant can be said to offset this. Some factories which have been converted to war-time uses may require a considerable amount of resources to transform them back again.

The broad result of all this is that posterity will inherit fewer assets, both at home and abroad, than if there had been no war. A consequence of this is that the "credit" items in the British Balance of Payments will on balance be smaller. Income from overseas investments will have fallen greatly and income from shipping and other services will be less than before. If Great Britain has to pay for much the same volume of imports as before the war she may be forced to expand her exports considerably and may get less favourable terms of trade. In my view, however, it would be deplorable if this prospect led her to raise her tariffs and to adopt a restrictive trade policy, employing for that purpose quotas, bilateral agreements, exchange control, and similar weapons of economic nationalism. We ventured to conclude our last edition with a protest against the growth of economic nationalism; and the 'thirties ended in the smoke of war.

If many men of military age are killed, this also will be a serious economic blow to posterity. Already men of courage and initiative, who might have played a leading part in post-war reconstruction, have lost their lives.

Let us hope that the post-war world will have been worth fighting for. On the economic side, technical progress is a very powerful force. It is capable of greatly raising the standard of living, provided that it is not impeded by restrictionist practices in the supposed interests of various sections of the community. Let us hope that the waste of human resources resulting from inadequate facilities for education, with maintenance, for all children capable of profiting by it, will be avoided. Let us hope that the newer countries will help the older and over-populated countries by permitting some immigration (provided that over-populated countries agree to favour birth-control, their only real remedy in the long run) and by following a generous policy of public foreign investment designed to direct the economic activity of such countries into more labour-intensive channels. Let us hope that, if unemployment cannot be altogether prevented, the fear and worry due to economic insecurity will be abolished, at least in the richer countries, by guaranteeing to all, as a right, a minimum standard of real income.

INDEX